COMPLETE WORKS
OF
PIR-O-MURSHID
HAZRAT INAYAT KHAN

ORIGINAL TEXTS: LECTURES ON SUFISM
1923 I: January-June

New York, February, 1923

PIR-O-MURSHID INAYAT KHAN

1882-1927

COMPLETE WORKS
OF
PIR-O-MURSHID
HAZRAT INAYAT KHAN

ORIGINAL TEXTS: LECTURES ON SUFISM
1923 I: January-June

Source Edition

East-West Publications

London/The Hague

Previous volumes in this series:
Biography of Pir-o-Murshid Inayat Khan (East-West Publications – 1979)
Authentic Versions of the teachings of Pir-o-Murshid Inayat Khan on Sufism – Sayings Part I
Authentic Versions of the teachings of Pir-o-Murshid Inayat Khan on Sufism – Sayings Part II
(East-West Publications – 1982)

Edited by Mrs. Munira van Voorst van Beest. Published by East-West Publications, 78 Anna Paulownastraat, 2518 BJ The Hague in collaboration with the Nekbakht Foundation.

ISBN 90-70104-80-6

"Time! I have never seen thee; but I have heard thy footsteps. Time! in my sorrow thou creepest, in my joy thou runnest, in the hours of my patient waiting thou standest still. Time! thou art the ocean, and every moment of Life is thy wave."

—INAYAT KHAN.

1923.

JANUARY.

S	...	7	14	21	28
M	1	8	15	22	29
Tu	2	9	16	23	30
W	3	10	17	24	31
Th	4	11	18	25	...
F	5	12	19	26	...
S	6	13	20	27	...

FEBRUARY.

S	...	4	11	18	25
M	...	5	12	19	26
Tu	...	6	13	20	27
W	...	7	14	21	28
Th	1	8	15	22	...
F	2	9	16	23	...
S	3	10	17	24	...

MARCH.

S	...	4	11	18	25
M	...	5	12	19	26
Tu	...	6	13	20	27
W	...	7	14	21	28
Th	1	8	15	22	29
F	2	9	16	23	30
S	3	10	17	24	31

APRIL.

S	1	8	15	22	29
M	2	9	16	23	30
Tu	3	10	17	24	...
W	4	11	18	25	...
Th	5	12	19	26	...
F	6	13	20	27	...
S	7	14	21	28	...

MAY.

S	...	6	13	20	27
M	...	7	14	21	28
Tu	1	8	15	22	29
W	2	9	16	23	30
Th	3	10	17	24	31
F	4	11	18	25	...
S	5	12	19	26	...

JUNE.

S	...	3	10	17	24
M	...	4	11	18	25
Tu	...	5	12	19	26
W	...	6	13	20	27
Th	...	7	14	21	28
F	1	8	15	22	29
S	2	9	16	23	30

JULY.

S	1	8	15	22	29
M	2	9	16	23	30
Tu	3	10	17	24	31
W	4	11	18	25	...
Th	5	12	19	26	...
F	6	13	20	27	...
S	7	14	21	28	...

AUGUST.

S	...	5	12	19	26
M	...	6	13	20	27
Tu	...	7	14	21	28
W	1	8	15	22	29
Th	2	9	16	23	30
F	3	10	17	24	31
S	4	11	18	25	...

SEPTEMBER

S	–	2	9	16	23	30
M	–	3	10	17	24	...
Tu	–	4	11	18	25	...
W	–	5	12	19	26	...
Th	–	6	13	20	27	...
F	–	7	14	21	28	...
S	1	8	15	22	29	...

OCTOBER.

S	...	7	14	21	28
M	1	8	15	22	29
Tu	2	9	16	23	30
W	3	10	17	24	31
Th	4	11	18	25	...
F	5	12	19	26	...
S	6	13	20	27	...

NOVEMBER.

S	...	4	11	18	25
M	...	5	12	19	26
Tu	...	6	13	20	27
W	...	7	14	21	28
Th	1	8	15	22	29
F	2	9	16	23	30
S	3	10	17	24	...

DECEMBER.

S	–	2	9	16	23	30
M	–	3	10	17	24	31
Tu	–	4	11	18	25	...
W	–	5	12	19	26	...
Th	–	6	13	20	27	...
F	–	7	14	21	28	...
S	1	8	15	22	29	...

ACKNOWLEDGEMENT

Sharif Graham has become an enthusiastic and most dedicated collaborator in the work of presenting Pir-o-Murshid Inayat Khan's original words, and while lecturing at Pima College in Arizona in the United States, every year he gives up his long summer holidays and spends his time mostly in Suresnes where this work is being done. The presentation of the play "Una" from the old manuscripts is entirely his work. Also, he gave shape to all that had to be said and explained in the preface and in the introductions and gave his attention to many more details.

I feel grateful also to the members of the Editorial Committee, Dr. Rubab Monna and Shaikh-al-Mashaikh Mahmood Maheboob Khan, for the careful attention given to the manuscript before publication and for their very constructive criticism, which has contributed considerably to improving the quality of the book.

CONTENTS

PREFACE

General information on the contents and on the authenticity of the lectures.

This volume includes all the lectures of Pir-o-Murshid Inayat Khan that have been preserved from the first half of 1923, and information connected with them, taken from the source materials available in the archives.

The history of the texts of this period is quite different from that described in the Preface to 1923 II: July-December. Most of the texts published in that volume were based on shorthand records taken down by Sakina Furnée while Pir-o-Murshid Inayat Khan spoke. In this volume, there appear only two lectures taken down in shorthand by Sakina (February 5 and 12), and for the majority of the lectures at our disposal, given in the United States, the earliest and best text is typewritten and already somewhat edited. Therefore, the "original texts" presented in this volume are almost all less close to their source than the texts from the second half of the year. Furthermore, in the second half of 1923 there was only a small number of lectures known to have been given of which we had no records in the archives, whereas for the first half we know about a great many lectures of which no records have yet been discovered (see Appendix C). This is partly due to the fact that the Pir-o-Murshid was travelling very extensively, and partly because he was not being accompanied by one of his secretaries. An American mureed, Khushi (Marya) Cushing, did take down in shorthand many of the lectures in New York and the Eastern United States, but her notebooks, if still in existence, have not been located, and we have her transcriptions of only a few lectures from the latter part of that tour.

Nevertheless, we do possess a large number of lectures given when the Pir-o-Murshid stayed in San Francisco for seven weeks, by far the longest sojourn during his travels. Even though these texts do not fully have the special quality of the precise words as actually spoken by him, they certainly do contain many passages very close to what he said, and in some cases texts which have never before been published or widely distributed. The tone of these lectures indicates that the enthusiastic response which his teachings received in America greatly inspired Pir-o-Murshid as he spoke. Despite the textual problems, this volume presents some of the most important and least-known parts of his teaching.

Background

General background information regarding the texts appeared in the Preface to the volume 1923 II. There was little need for an explanation of the context in which most of those lectures were given, as a great majority was delivered at the Summer School in Suresnes, near Paris, at and around Fazal Manzil, Pir-o-Murshid Inayat Khan's home since 1922. In the first half of 1923, however, the Pir-o-Murshid travelled widely, passing only a short period at his home. In order, therefore, to give the reader a clearer picture of the context in which the lectures in this volume were delivered, in the following paragraphs a brief sketch will be given of the places and personalities visited by him during this period.

Holland, Belgium, England: January

The earliest records presented in this volume come from the Netherlands, around the end of the first week in January. The first material is from a notebook of Baron van Tuyll van Serooskerken, whose Sufi name was Sirdar, who evidently arranged the Pir-o-Murshid's lecture tour in that country with the help of the Theosophical Society, of which he was a member. The texts from Sirdar's notebooks are fragmentary, but during the tour various mureeds took down the lectures in longhand as well as they could. Of course, the lectures were given in English, a foreign language to the writers albeit a familiar one; and even though they were pronounced slowly, it was impossible to catch every word. Nevertheless, we have good and nearly complete texts for the several lectures given in various Dutch towns up to the eighteenth of January. Then the Pir-o-Murshid went on to Belgium, but we have neither title nor text for any of the talks he gave there. From Belgium he proceeded to England; while we have the titles and dates of some of the lectures given there, we do not have the texts themselves. One lecture, however, published as a booklet called *The Sufi Order*, has here been assigned to this period in London.

France: February.

At the end of January Pir-o-Murshid Inayat Khan returned to his home at Suresnes to stay for some time with his wife, the Begum (née Ora Ray Baker, an American), and his four children before leaving for an extended tour of the United States. He gave only two lectures in Paris during this time, one week apart, the second a continuation of the first, on the subject of "Life, a Continual Battle." These were taken down in shorthand by his secretary, Sakina Furnée, who had learned shorthand for this purpose. A running translation into French, sentence by sentence (see Appendix D), was given by a translator as well.

Possibility for a lecture tour through the United States.

The tour of the United States was undertaken at the urgent and repeated request of Murshida Rabia Martin of San Francisco. Mrs. Martin was the Pir-o-Murshid's first mureed (initiate) in the West in 1911, and she had continued Sufi work during his long absence from America (since 1912). Of course, first of all World War I had made travel impossible, and after that the Pir-o-Murshid's residence changed several times, only becoming permanent in 1922 when a Dutch mureed, Mrs. "Fazal Mai" Egeling, put at his disposal a large house, then renamed "Fazal Manzil" (house of blessing), at Val d'Or - St. Cloud, later incorporated in Suresnes. Having at last settled his family suitably, he then felt free to answer the many requests of Murshida Martin and his other American pupils for a return to the United States.

Journey and arrival in New York: February.

Pir-o-Murshid Inayat Khan sailed to America aboard the White Star liner Pittsburgh, which left from Bremen (Germany) via England. Newspaper articles from the time reveal several ethnic incidents during the stormy voyage, but the Pir-o-Murshid in his account only mentions that in the end he had become the friend of almost all the passengers, and that this enhanced his sense of the possibility of brotherhood (*Biography*, p. 168). When a newspaper reporter asked him what he thought of the battling nationalities, "he smiled and was silent." However, Pir-o-Murshid figured in the newspaper accounts mainly because he was detained by the immigration authorities at Ellis Island, the quota of Indians for February having already been filled. This delay, along with the already late arrival of the ship due to the weather, necessitated the cancellation of the first two lectures.

The Pir-o-Murshid's universalistic answers to the questions of the immigration tribunal (From what nation do you come? "All nations." What is your birthplace? "The world." What is your religion? "All religions." and so forth, cf. *Biography*, p. 169) interested them, yet did not answer the requirements of the law. He was ultimately rescued from this situation by Mrs. Marya Cushing, known by her Sufi name, Khushi, a formidable young woman who had already become a mureed in 1922, attended the first Summer School at Suresnes in that year, and assisted in the editing for publication and typing of the manuscript of Pir-o-Murshid's first book of sayings and prayers, the *Gayan*. She was in charge of making the arrangements for Pir-o-Murshid Inayat Khan's time in New York City, where she was living. Whatever she said to the immigration authorities, they seemed "much impressed and embarrassed, and immediately exempted me from the law of geographical expulsion." The last day on board, February 26, Pir-o-Murshid had recited a poem he addressed to America, "Ideal among nations ...", and had given a lecture about the purpose of his trip, "to awaken in souls the consciousness of brotherhood." The irony of his subsequent detention seemed only to amuse him.

Lecturing in New York, Boston, Detroit and Chicago: February/March.

The Pir-o-Murshid remained a few days in New York, giving several lectures, and then went on to Boston, which reminded him of Edinburgh in Scotland, where, in addition to lecturing, he met the eminent art historian Ananda C. Coomaraswami, "the only Hindu ... who occupies a fitting position in the States." He was himself often taken for a Hindu by newspaper reporters, to whom "Sufism" was apparently an entirely unknown word (it appears once a "Sabism"). From Boston he went on to Detroit, where there was a good response to his teaching, and then to Chicago where no arrangements had been made (they were left in the hands of someone who gave little attention to the matter). During this whole part of the journey, Pir-o-Murshid had been accompanied by Khushi Cushing, who later mentions in a letter to him that she had taken down the lectures in shorthand, of which, however, no records have come down to us. Mrs. Cushing remained behind in Chicago to attempt more suitable arrangements for the Pir-o-Murshid's return from California; he proceeded by train from Chicago to Los Angeles.

Short stay in Los Angeles and arrival in San Francisco on 19 or 20 March

The beauty of nature in California again impressed him deeply, as he was driven in a motorcar from Los Angeles to San Francisco along the Pacific coast by his mureeds, Mr. and Mrs. Wolff. On the day of his arrival in San Francisco, Murshida Martin had scheduled private interviews with the mureeds she had initiated in the years of her Murshid's absence. Among those who encountered Pir-o-Murshid Inayat Khan for the first time on that day were: Mrs. Rebecca C. Miller, who became a Khalifa and Cheraga; Mr. George Baum, who was made a Shaikh and Cherag; Mr. Samuel Lewis, later known as Sufi Ahmed Murad Chishti, who remained active in Sufi work throughout his long life (he passed away in 1971); and Mr. Earl Engle, who was initiated that day and given the name Fatha.

Lecturing in San Francisco: 19/20 March to May 8.

The period in San Francisco, about seven weeks, was the most successful of the tour, the arrangements having been made carefully by Murshida Rabia Martin, "whose joy in receiving me in her home was boundless." The Pir-o-Murshid gave several series of well-publicized lectures in the gallery of the Paul Elder bookstore, at the time the leading such establishment in San Francisco. Miss Hayat Stadlinger, who first encountered Pir-o-Murshid there, recalls vividly how he greeted each person who came, serenely sitting in a vestibule. In addition he gave classes for the initiates and many private interviews. There is no certain record of the classes for initiates; however, the series of papers known as "Githa Dhyana" without any doubt dates from this period. The complex history of these papers is given below in a separate introduction (p. 219). A weekly service was inaugurated, and it would appear that San Francisco was the first place where the Pir-o-Murshid's concept of a universal religious service came to be known as the "Universal Worship," which became the accepted name. His lectures were very well attended, and the audience was enthusiastic. He also gave a talk on the radio on April 2, and so positive was the response (numerous "letters of appreciation") that a second one was broadcast the following week. Some arrangements were made to take down the lectures (no details are known), and thus the bulk of the materials presented in this volume derives from this time in San Francisco.

Encounter with Luther Burbank.

While in San Francisco, the Pir-o-Murshid was taken one day north to Santa Rosa, where he met with the famous horticulturist Luther Burbank. They felt an immediate empathy, and when Luther Burbank mentioned that he was working on eliminating the thorns from the cactus, Pir-o-Murshid Inayat Khan replied, "My work is not very different from yours, Sir, for I am occupied taking away thorns from hearts of men" (*Biography*, p. 172).

Mrs. Eggink joins Pir-o-Murshid.

An interesting sidelight to this period is found in the account of a Dutch mureed, Mrs. Eggink-van Stolk, whom Pir-o-Murshid Inayat Khan had asked to accompany him on the trip. Family and health problems had, however, prevented her from accepting that offer at the time of departure. Apparently Pir-o-Murshid thus travelled without secretarial and administrative assistance. However, she was able to join Pir-o-Murshid in San Francisco. When he first saw her there, he said, "So you have come." He instructed her to write several pages each day of an eventual lecture on the Sufi teachings, but she apparently wrote much more than he had asked, and when he saw what she had written, he laughed and was pleased. In her manuscript account of those days she mentions some of the things he said to her on different occasions, such as: "I am a mystery to myself" and "Twelve days in the presence of the master are like twelve years of meditation."

Preparations for a visit to Chicago.

The arrangements which Khushi Cushing had initiated for the Pir-o-Murshid's return to Chicago collapsed in confusion upon her own departure, so he sent Mrs. Eggink ahead to make new arrangements. She was instructed to speak herself to pave the way. When she arrived in Chicago, she found that those who were supposedly making the preparations, a Theosophist professor and a Kabbalistic teacher, had not done anything definite; she then tried to establish contact by attending the Kabbalistic meetings, where some interest was eventually awakened for the Sufi teachings. She was thus able to prepare for a more successful visit.

Lecturing in Santa Barbara and Los Angeles: May.

While Mrs. Eggink was in Chicago, the Pir-o-Murshid concluded his stay in San Francisco and proceeded south to Santa Barbara, where Mr. E.P.A. Connaughton had a rare book-shop. He had gone to England in 1919 to study with Pir-o-Murshid Inayat Khan, having already been initiated by Murshida Martin. The Pir-o-Murshid found him an apt mureed and at the end of his stay in England had initiated him as a khalif. During a four-day stay in Santa Barbara the Pir-o-Murshid delivered one lecture each day, of which only the titles are known. He also apparently was taken up by society, as newspaper clippings from the time announce several teas and a lunch given in his honour. He then made the few hours' journey to Los Angeles, where a program of six lectures had been well organized and publicized by Mr. and Mrs. Wolff. The program for the lectures, some of which were given at the Ambassador Hotel, is in the archives (see Appendix C), but no other records have been found.

Lecturing in Chicago and Detroit, and back to New York: May.

From Los Angeles, Pir-o-Murshid returned to Chicago by train, where Mrs. Eggink had made preparations. Whereas his scheduled talk in March at the Theosophical Society had been virtually unattended, he now had a small but appreciative audience for a few lectures. Accompanied by Mrs. Eggink, he went on to Detroit, where he spoke for three days, in the afternoon and evening, at the Unitarian church. Although the Pir-o-Murshid had had some misgivings about returning to Detroit, everything proved satisfactory. He further found himself again in the social columns, one of which headlines: "Sufi Mystic as Sensation of Society." On May 26, they travelled from Detroit to New York by train. Mrs. Eggink recalled that at one point a serving man entered the compartment and showed a look of resentment at seeing a dark Oriental accompanied by a light-skinned European woman. Noticing this, the Pir-o-Murshid looked at him with such a devastating glance that the man stumbled backwards out of the compartment and Mrs. Eggink felt he must have been cured of his prejudice for ever. Of course, such incidents were common during the Pir-o-Murshid's travels in the West.

Lecturing again in New York and also in Philadelphia: May/June.

In New York they were met by Khushi Cushing, who had been busy organizing the lectures and finding quarters in which to establish a centre. The Pir-o-Murshid had a small room in the apartment Mrs. Cushing had recently rented, but the weather was stifling. Many lectures were given and presumably were taken down in shorthand; we are only able to give texts of two from early in June, one of which probably represents a compilation of several talks. On May 30 and 31 the Pir-o-Murshid made a short trip to Philadelphia, where he gave four lectures, meeting with a good response, and was interviewed by the local newspapers. Having concluded the series in New York, on June 9 he sailed for Europe on board the S.S. Olympic. He was accompanied not only by Mrs. Eggink, but had also been joined by the young initiate from San Francisco, Mr. Fatha Engle, who went to live and work at the Pir-o-Murshid's residence at Suresnes. He was given the task of organizing the Summer School, and during the year and a half he stayed there assumed many other duties, including overseeing the care of the grounds, driving and maintaining the motorcar, and scheduling all personal interviews with the Pir-o-Murshid. In this way he came to know most of the European mureeds, and after returning to New York to lead the centre there, provided a link between Europe and America in the Sufi work.

Return journey: June

In her memories of the voyage, Mrs. Eggink mentions that on board ship Pir-o-Murshid had some leisure for the first time in several months and that one day, to her delight, he sang to her (he had been a celebrated musician in India earlier in his life, but had by this time almost entirely abandoned his music in favour of spiritual teaching). He also gave to her the name of *Bhakti*, meaning "devotion," and began writing a play by the same name about an idealistic young woman devoted to the art of sculpture. He asked Bhakti Eggink to play the lead role, but the character's name and the title of the play were later changed to *Una*.

Return to Suresnes for the Summer School.

By the time the Pir-o-Murshid and Mr. Engle arrived at Suresnes, less than two weeks remained before the opening of the Summer School. The first talks there were given on the second of July, and in this series of books appear in the volume 1923 II: July-December.

Press-articles about Pir-o-Murshid's visits.

Because so many lectures have failed to reach the archives, it would seem appropriate to provide whatever evidence there is as to what Pir-o-Murshid Inayat Khan may have said on those occasions. During this time in America, press coverage was particularly full, and copies of many reports and articles are preserved in a separate collection in the archives. In some cases, the reporters appear to be quoting from lectures they attended; in others, the words or thoughts they attribute to Pir-o-Murshid Inayat Khan appear to have come from interviews. We have extracted from the newspaper articles everything that appears to be a direct or indirect quotation from Pir-o-Murshid, and have inserted the results in the chronological sequence of the lectures. It should clearly be realized, however, that these quotations often represent the reporters' understanding of what the Pir-o-Murshid said rather than his exact words, even when cited as his own in quotation marks. Pir-o-Murshid eventually became quite dissatisfied with the way his words were reported in the American press (cf. *Biography*, p. 176).

Mention of the first publication of a text in the notes.

When a lecture has been published for the first time in the series *The Sufi Message of Hazrat Inayat Khan* (from 1960-1982: 13 volumes), this is mentioned in the notes. In those volumes, however, the texts have been editorially adjusted to such an extent as to render word-by-word comparison infeasible. Publication in these volumes is also mentioned if the only previous publication had been a translation in another language. The publication history of Pir-o-Murshid Inayat Khan's teaching is a complex subject which deserves full treatment, but obviously does not properly belong to this presentation of the original texts from the extant source materials.

Indication of alternative words in the notes.

The language of the lectures, given as *extempore* addresses, clearly is a spoken language, and it sometimes happened that Pir-o-Murshid Inayat Khan repeated a word or used a different word which better expressed his idea. To avoid any confusion, we have indicated in the notes "instead of" or "in place of" whenever there could arise any doubt, to indicate that a later editor replaced the originally spoken word with another.

First and second Headquarters' stencil and the original text.

A close student of the notes to these basic texts will occasionally observe that the second, revised version of a Headquarters' stencil (Hq.st.) comes closer to the shorthand or other earliest version than did the first Headquarters' version of a lecture. Where that occurs, it clearly indicates a revision at Headquarters intending to return to the original text.

Early work on the original texts.

Two documents mentioned in the notes and in the Explanation of Abbreviations require some further description. These are "Sr.Sk." and "Sk.l.t.", both of which came into existence comparatively recently, during the 1950's and 1960's.

"Sk.l.t." (Sakina's later type) is Sakina Furnée's new transcription of a part of her original shorthand reportings. Her original transcriptions were sent by her to International Headquarters in Geneva, from 1922 to 1926. She kept no copy of these in the archives. Over the years, many changes appeared in the texts of the lectures in various versions, which prompted her some thirty years later to undertake the difficult task of making a new transcription so as to restore the text as taken down while Pir-o-Murshid was actually speaking.

"Sr.Sk." (Sirdar/Sakina) is an extensive list of *errata*, in which Sakina Furnée and Sirdar van Tuyll exchanged comments about the revisions which had been made in the texts of the Gathas, Gathekas and many other papers, and especially of those lectures of which Sakina had made no second transcription. The purpose of both--"Sk.l.t." and "Sr.Sk."--was the same: to bring back the texts to the oldest possible version, which was intended as a critical preparation for publication of source materials. The work presented in these *Complete Works, Original Texts* brings out and continues on a larger scale what Sakina and Sirdar had already initiated in the past.

Additional Information.

Appendix A shows a copy of the original program of the lectures given in 1923 at the Paul Elder Gallery in San Francisco.

Appendix B explains some facts about the classification of the lectures in general. Then, as in volume 1923 II, appears a list of the classified lectures in this volume, in the version in which they are known in the Sufi centres, along with these same lectures as in their original form, with indication of the page numbers. A third item with Appendix B is a document in the handwriting of Mahtab van Hogendorp about the classification of papers at the time of Pir-o-Murshid's death.

Appendix C gives the titles, dates and places of delivery of lectures which have not yet reached the archives.

Appendix D shows the original handwritings and shorthand of some of the texts, from which documents the basic texts presented in this volume have been copied.

In addition to a glossary of foreign words, notes on persons, places and works occurring in the texts have been listed separately.

An extensive analytical subject index is added, in most cases identical in its wording to the wording in the texts, in which the different aspects of one subject have been arranged alphabetically.

Conclusion.

The object of this book, as of the whole series of which it is part, may be summed up as threefold:

- To safeguard for posterity the teachings on Sufism of Pir-o-Murshid Inayat Khan as gathered in the Biographical Department;
- To provide as authentic as possible a groundwork for the edition of future publications and translations;
- To make the earliest source materials of Pir-o-Murshid Inayat Khan's words available to scholars, researchers, students and all those interested in finding sources of genuine spirituality.

Munira van Voorst van Beest,
Staff Member of the Foundation "Nekbakht Stichting."

34, rue de la Tuilerie
92150 Suresnes, France.

1985

EXPLANATION OF ABBREVIATIONS

After 1927	-	refers to a communication in the handwriting of Mahtab van Hogendorp in her capacity as secretary of the Sufi Movement at International Headquarters, Geneva. See Appendix B.
Ann.	-	annotation(s)
A.p.	-	preparation of an article (lecture) for publication in a magazine.
Archives	-	archives of the Biographical Department, Suresnes, France.
B.D.	-	Biographical Department, an independent body set up by Pir-o-Murshid Inayat Khan, containing a collection of Sufi documents etc., to which he appointed Sakina Furnée (Nekbakht) as keeper. It has now been incorporated in the Nekbakht Foundation.
Bk.	-	book, first edition.
Bk.p.	-	book preparation by Sherifa Goodenough.
C.	-	copied text.
Ca.	-	circa.
Corr.	-	correction, corrected.
D.tp.	-	draft of a typescript
Gd.	-	Sherifa Goodenough.
Gd.t.	-	a typescript, made on Sherifa Goodenough's typewriter, distinguished by large type.
Gr.	-	Sophia Saintsbury Green.
Hq.	-	International Headquarters, Geneva, Switzerland, which was the administrative and coordinative centre for the different sections of the Sufi Order, which was named Sufi Movement in October, 1923.
Hq.p.	-	preparation by Sherifa Goodenough of the text of a lecture or other teaching to be multiplied at Headquarters, and distributed among mureeds.

Hq.st. - a cyclostyled copy of a Gatha, Gita, Gatheka, Religious Gatheka or Social Gatheka, made at Headquarters, Geneva, of a lecture or other teaching meant for distribution among mureeds, also prepared by Sherifa Goodenough.

Hwr. - handwritten, handwriting.

Ibid. - ibidem, i.e. in the document(s) just cited.

I.K. - Pir-o-Murshid Hazrat Inayat Khan.

Kf. - Kefayat LLoyd, Kefayat LLoyd's copied text.

Km. - Kismet Stam.

Kr. - Miss Kerdijk, an early Dutch mureed.

Lb. - Mrs. E. Leembruggen.

Lf. - Miss H. Lefèbvre, a French mureed from Paris.

Lh. - longhand.

M. - Magazine.

Ms./MS. - manuscript.

Mt. - Mahtab van Hogendorp.

N. - note(s).

Nbk. - Leaves of Pir-o-Murshid Inayat Khan's notebooks.

O.c. - copy of an old typescript, available in the archives only on a microfiche made at Hq.

O.t. - an old typescript, probably made from the original document.

Ox. - *The Shorter Oxford English Dictionary* (Oxford University Press, 1973).

Q.a. - question(s) and answer(s).

R. - reporting, here to mean taken down in shorthand or in longhand while Pir-o-Murshid was giving the lecture.

Sd. - Saida van Tuyll van Serooskerken-Willebeek Le Mair.

Sh.	-	shorthand, shorthand reporting.
Sk.	-	Sakina Furnée, in 1926 renamed "Nekbakht" by Pir-o-Murshid Inayat Khan.
Sk.t.	-	Sakina's typescript.
Sk.l.t.	-	a new transcription of Sakina's shorthand reportings, made by her at a much later date.
S.L.	-	Samuel Lewis, an early American pupil of Murshida Martin's; an old typescript from a collection of Sufi papers used by Samuel Lewis.
S.Q.	-	Magazine *The Sufi Quarterly*.
Sr.	-	Sirdar van Tuyll van Serooskerken; Sirdar's copied text, made from notes taken down by him during the lectures.
Sr.Sk.	-	an extensive errata list (referring to the Gathas, Gathekas and many other lectures), on which Sk. and Sr. exchanged comments on revisions made in the texts. Sometimes a copy of a Hq.st. was used for this purpose.
St.	-	stencilled (cyclostyled), a stencilled copy.
T.	-	= tp. when used with the name of a person (e.g. Sk.t.).
Tp.	-	typewritten, typewritten copy, typescript.
Tr.	-	transcription.
V.	-	*vide*, see.
Zl.	-	Zuleikha van Ingen-Jelgersma, an early Dutch mureed.

Sirdar's longhand reporting in his copybook of January/February 1923, copied by the compiler.

---

1 [2]January 1923.

Divine Grace is a loving impulse of God, which manifests in every form, in the form of mercy, compassion, forgiveness, beneficence and revelation. No action however good can command[3], no meditation however great can attract it. It comes naturally as a wave rising from the heart of God, unrestricted or unlimited by any law. It is a natural impulse of God, when it comes, it comes without reason; neither its coming nor its absence has any particular reason, it comes because it comes. It does not come because it does not come. It is in the[4] grace that God's Highest Majesty is manifested, while pouring[5] his Grace he stands on such a[6] pedestal which[7]

Documents:

Sr.lh.r.
Sd.hwr.c. (a copy in Sd.'s hwr. made from Sr.lh.r. with some additions and alterations by Gd.)
Sk.hwr.c.
Bk.p.
Bk. (*The Unity of Religious Ideals*)

Notes:

1. Sd.hwr.c.: Gd. added "Gatha. Tassawuf" above;
   Bk.p.: "Divine Grace" added above;
   Bk.: Part II The God-Ideal, chapter XVII
2. It is not known on what occasion Pir-o-Murshid said these words about Divine Grace; the sequence in Sr.'s notebook indicates that it was in the first week of January 1923 (in Holland).
3. Sr.lh.r.: "it" added by Sr.;
   All other documents: "it"
4. Bk.p., bk.: "the" omitted
5. Sd.hwr.c.: "out" added by Gd.;
   Bk.p., bk.: "out"
6. Sr.lh.r.: "high" added by Sr.;
   All other documents: "high"
7. Sd.hwr.c.: "which" changed to "that" by Gd.;
   Bk.: "that" instead of "which"

neither law, cause[8], reason can touch[9]. Every blessing has a certain aspect, but grace is a blessing which is not limited to a certain aspect, but it[10] manifests through all aspects.

---

[11]Grace is all-sided ~~it means peace in your heart~~, health[12], providence, love coming from all those around you, inspiration, joy, peace.

---

8. Sr.lh.r.: Sr. crossed out "cause" and wrote "nor a" above;
Sd.hwr.c., Sk.hwr.c.: "nor"
9. Sd.hwr.c.: "it" added by Gd.;
Bk.: "it" added
10. Bk.p., bk.: "it" omitted
11. All other documents have this last sentence immediately following "aspects". The way Sr.lh.r. has it, it could be the answer to a question.
12. Sr.lh.r.: Apparently another word was originally written where the word "health" now appears; the end of this original word still appears, crossed out and illegible.

Dictated by Sirdar to Saida from his longhand reporting, and written down by Saida in Sirdar's blue school-copybook from the beginning of 1923.

---

2 Holland, beginning (7?) January 1923.[1]

Innocence.

The way of attaining spiritual knowledge is quite apart[3] [4]to attain the knowledge of the world. As the sky stands[5] opposite direction to[6] earth, so the source of [7]spiritual knowledge[7] stands[8] opposite[9] knowledge of the world. As man becomes more intel.[10] he knows more[11] of the world, but that[12] does not mean that he [13]grows in spirit[13], [14]he goes further from [15]spiritual knowledge[15] in[16] his thought[17] [18]he understands[18] worldly things, [19]he is able to understand spiritual things[19]. What is the best way of attaining spiritual knowledge? [20]The answer is[20] [21]to first[21] develop at[22] nature

Documents:

Sd.lh. (written down by Sd. in telegraphese, dictated by Sr. from his lh.r.)
Tp. (a version made by Gd. from Sd.lh.)
Hq.t.
Hq.st.

As the texts of Tp., Hq.t., Hq.st. are identical, only the Hq.st. is mentioned in the notes.

Notes:

1. From Sr.'s copybook, in which Sd. wrote down the lecture dictated to her by Sr. from his lh.r., the sequence shows that the date of the lecture is probably 7th January 1923.
2. Hq.t., hq.st.: "Gatheka. Number 28" added
3. Hq.st.: "opposite" instead of "apart"
4. Ibid.: Reordered and completed: "to the way by which one attains worldly knowledge"
5. Ibid.: "is in the" instead of "stands"
6. Ibid.: "the" added
7. Ibid.: "knowledge of spiritual things" instead of "spiritual knowledge"
8. Ibid.: "is" instead of "stands"
9. Ibid.: "to the" added
10. Ibid.: "intellectual" instead of "more intel." [intelligent? intellectual?]
11. Ibid.: "things" instead of "more"
12. Ibid.: "this" instead of "that"
13. Ibid.: "becomes spiritual" instead of "grows in spirit"
14. Ibid.: "on the contrary" added
15. Ibid.: "spirituality" instead of "spiritual knowledge"
16. Ibid.: "by" instead of "in"
17. Ibid.: a colon after "thought"
18. Ibid.: "I understand" instead of "he understands"
19. Ibid.: omitted, "he is able to understand spiritual things"
20. Ibid.: omitted, "The answer is"
21. Ibid.: "First, one must" instead of "to first"
22. Ibid.: "in one's" instead of "at"

that little spark[23] divine and [24]that what[24] shining in[25] infancy, showing something pure, [26]some sign[26] of heaven, [27]something spiritual[27]. [28]What is it in the infant that attracts most? It is its innocence gives impression of pure of heart[28], [29]understands by names and forms called learning[29]. One[30] must not understand this wrongly, the[31] knowledge of the world [32]the knowledge of names and forms[32] is necessary,[33] necessary to live in the world, necessary[34] to make [35]one best in life[35], [36]know to make other happy[36], necessary[34] to serve God and humanity, [37]not necessary to attain spiritual knowledge. Innocence is necessary[38]. [39]Apart from child[39] one sees among one's friends [40]and family[40] something which attracts[41] most [42]the side showing innocence[42]. [43]Often you see[43] people forgive[44], [45]tolerate[46], [47]by seeing, yes,[47] he is wrong, but he [48]has innocence[48]. [49]A purity divine that attracts[49]. [50]Clever person attracted to innocent persons.[50] Innocence is[51] a spring of water[52] in which heart and soul bathe, purifying and making it new[52]. [53]How to attain quality of innocence?[53] ~~The answer is~~

23. Ibid.: "which is" added
24. Ibid.: "which was" instead of "that what"
25. Ibid.: "one's" added
26. Ibid.: "some sign" omitted
27. Ibid.: "something spiritual" omitted
28. Ibid.: "What attracts us most is innocence, it is innocence which gives an impression of purity." instead of "What is it in the infant that attracts most? It is its innocence gives impression of pure heart"
29. Ibid.: omitted "understands by names and forms called learning"
30. Ibid.: "But, we" instead of "One"
31. Ibid.: "the" omitted
32. Ibid.: omitted "the knowledge of names and forms"
33. Ibid.: added "more than necessary, it is"
34. Ibid.: "necessary" omitted
35. Ibid.: "the best of one's life" instead of "one best in life"
36. Ibid.: "know to make others happy"
37. Ibid.: "it is" added
38. Ibid.: "for that" added
39. Ibid.: "Apart from child" omitted
40. Ibid.: "relatives" instead of "family"
41. Ibid.: "one" added
42. Ibid.: ", perhaps this is the side of the nature which is innocence" instead of "the side showing innocence"
43. Ibid.: "Often you see" omitted
44. Ibid.: "those who are dear to them" added
45. Ibid.: "they" added
46. Ibid.: "their faults" added
47. Ibid.: "They say:" instead of "by seeing, yes,"
48. Ibid.: "is innocent" instead of "has innocence"
49. Ibid.: "There is a purity which is divine, and which attracts everyone" instead of "A purity divine that attracts"
50. Ibid.: omitted "Clever person attracted to innocent persons."
51. Ibid.: "like" added
52. Ibid.: "purifying all that is foreign to heart and soul" instead of "in which heart and soul bathe, purifying and making it new"
53. Ibid.: "How can one attain innocence?" instead of "How to attain quality of innocence?"

[54]We all were innocent, it is in us[54]. By being conscious of this[55] we develop it; in admiring that[55] [56]and in taking notice in others[56], appreciating[57]. [58]You will see[58] those who have[59] bad nature, [60]they are observant of bad in others and in time turn their nature[60]. [61]Those who admire innocence get that impression in themselves[61].

During[62] travelling in India [63]on the purpose of paying[63] homage to the sages[64], [65]what appealed[65] was [66]not the power nor the radiance[66], [67]greater was the soul[67], the greater was the innocence. One sees in them innocence [68]but not simpleness[68], [69]that is the difference[69]. The one who is simple does not understand. [70]In everyday life there is one person who notices some way about him and he says, "I understand your way, I catch you." Noblehearted understands but closes eyes.[70] Innocence is to understand and rise above [71]common understanding[71]. [72]Insight that gives man that power to see clearly and rising above.[72] [73]For average person:[73] every person sees another person[74] with[75] own glasses, [76]opinion that he has[76]. [77]Men, they have a colour standing between[77]. [78]Necessary over insight is neutrality[78], [79]comes by innocence[79]. [80]When anyone smiles at a child, it does not know if it is friend or enemy, only smile.[80] [81]When that is developing in man, he

54. Ibid.: "Innocence is not foreign to our nature, we have all been innocent" instead of "We all were innocent, it is in us"
55. Ibid.: "nature" added
56. Ibid.: omitted "and in taking notice in others"
57. Ibid.: added "it, we also develop it. All things which we admire become impressions"
58. Ibid.: omitted "You will see"
59. Ibid.: "a" added
60. Ibid.: omitted "they are observant of bad in others and in time turn their nature"
61. Ibid.: "but who have collected good impressions, will in time turn their nature" instead of "Those who admire innocence get that impression in themselves"
62. Ibid.: "my" added
63. Ibid.: "the purpose of which was to pay" instead of "on the purpose of paying"
64. Ibid.: "of that land" added
65. Ibid.: "the thing which appealed most to me" instead of "what appealed"
66. Ibid.: omitted "not the power nor the radiance"
67. Ibid.: "the greater the soul was" instead of "greater was the soul"
68. Ibid.: "not simplicity" instead of "but not simpleness"
69. Ibid.: "that is the difference" omitted
70. Ibid.: "We see this in everyday life, he closes his eyes." instead of "In everyday life there is one person who notices some way about him and he says, 'I understand your way, I catch you.' Noble hearted understands but closes eyes."
71. Ibid.: "common understanding" omitted
72. Ibid.: omitted, "Insight that gives man that power to see clearly and rising above."
73. Ibid.: "For average person:" omitted
74. Ibid.: "person" omitted
75. Ibid.: "through his" instead of "with"
76. Ibid.: omitted, "opinion that he has"
77. Ibid.: "prejudice stands often between" instead of "Men, they have a colour standing between"
78. Ibid.: "For insight unity is necessary" instead of "Necessary over insight is neutrality"
79. Ibid.: "comes by innocence" omitted
80. Ibid.: omitted "When anyone smiles at a child, it does not know if it is friend or enemy, only smile."
81. Ibid.: "When that attribute is developed one has attained spirituality" instead of "When that is developing in man, he has taken spiritual path"

has taken spiritual path[81]. [82]What is lacking in life is the lack of . People think it is simpleness, but great difference, child innocent,[82] [83]wise innocent of being intell., risen above to state of innocence[83]. [84]The little knowledge so important is nothing.[84] He sees cause behind cause, [85]he judges and tolerates all[85], [86]he understands all[86]. [87]For him is innocence.[87] [88]Is it practical to act[88] according to this principle? [89]No, principle is not to guide, to use, not to .[89] [90]If principle restricts, instead of virtue is sin, it takes freedom.[90] [91]Whenever person makes principle, captives.[91] Life means[92] freedom, [93]developing nobleness[93].[94] [95]When one arrives at stage, may show itself out in action.[95] [96]Sign of sageliness, of piety?[96] [97]No better sign than innocence.[97]

---

82. Ibid.: omitted, "What is lacking in life is the lack of . [probably the word "innocence" was missed] People think it is simpleness, but great difference, child innocent,"
83. Ibid.: "Man becomes wise after having been intellectual, he rises above the intellect" instead of "wise innocent of being intell. [see note nr. 10], risen above to state of innocence"
84. Ibid.: "The little knowledge so important is nothing." omitted.
85. Ibid.: "he judges and tolerates all" omitted
86. Ibid.: "and understands the way of his enemy"
87. Ibid.: omitted "For him is innocence."
88. Ibid.: "Would it be practical to live altogether" instead of "Is it practical to act"
89. Ibid.: "A principle is to be used, not to guide our life", instead of "No, principle is not to guide, to use, not to ."
90. Ibid.: omitted, "If principle restricts, instead of virtue is sin, it takes freedom."
91. Ibid.: "When people make of principle a chain, it becomes captivity" instead of "Whenever person makes principles, captives."
92. Ibid.: "is" instead of "means"
93. Ibid.: "developing nobleness" omitted
94. Ibid.: added, "One cannot force oneself to innocence."
95. Ibid.: omitted, "When one arrives at stage, may show itself out in action."
96. Ibid.: "Can there be any sign of piety or spirituality?" instead of "Sign of sageliness, of piety?"
97. Ibid.: "There is no better sign than innocence with all understanding." instead of "No better sign than innocence."

An old typescript from Sirdar's collection of lectures, of which no original text is available ("O.t.").

1 2

Influence

Perhaps you have read the story of Daniel in the lion's den, therefore you can understand that there is no greater sign of spiritual advancement than man's personal influence; this is an example of advancement in spiritual life. People want to know whether they are progressing or going back. One need not see how much one has read or learned to find out if one has advanced. The principal thing is: if one attracts people or if one repels them, if one is harmonious or inharmonious. This can tell us how far we have advanced. No doubt[3] one day is not the same as the other. One day one may perhaps have more influence than the other. Life is like water, and it will have its waves rising or falling. Sometimes there are conditions or influences which are contrary. By keen observation we can find out if we are advancing. Another sign of advancement is that we must become modest, kind, and respectful to others. Another sign is that we must have wisdom and power; if one has both these things one will create beauty in life.

Now a question is how to attain this advancement. Practices and exercises are the main things. We must have faith and trust in the practices we do. According to our faith we will succeed. Mind and body must be kept in a proper tune. For instance, one moment of excitement takes away the advancement of six [4]months time[4]. It is like a person who is making a necklace of pearls; if the thread breaks, he must do it all over again. If we get excited and our mind and body are out of tune, we spoil the practices of six months[5] time. For those who walk in the spiritual path it is of great value to

Documents:

O.t.
Sk.t. (copied from the "O.t." Sk. added "not in handwriting" over it.)
Hq.st.
Hq.t.

After 1927 the lecture was made into a Gatheka.

Notes:

1. Hq.st., hq.t.: added "Gatheka number 29."
2. Although the lecture bears no date, from a newspaper article it is known that it was given in Holland on 8th January 1923.
3. Hq.st., hq.t.: "Of course" instead of "No doubt"
4. Sk.t., Hq.st.: "time" omitted;
   Hq.t.: "months' time"
5. Hq.t.: "months' time"

keep themselves[6] tuned in[7] the pitch which is necessary. The difficulty is to endure all the time many things which upset one, conditions which excite and exhaust one's patience. We must have the power of endurance in spite of all. Life is a continual battle to fight; and in order to keep fit one must keep one's power reserved and preserved. This is done by keeping tranquil and equable in mind. Practices, concentrations, meditations and prayer will win the battle of your life.

---

6. Hq.st., hq.t.: "oneself" instead of "themselves"
7. Hq.t.: "to" instead of "in"

A typewritten preparation by Murshida Goodenough for the Headquarters' stencil.

1

Sangatha I.

Toward the One, the Perfection of Love
Harmony and Beauty, the Only Being,
united with All the Illuminated Souls,
who form the Embodiment of the Master,
the Spirit of Guidance.

Suluk.

How to Progress in the Spiritual Path in Everyday Life.

[2] In the first place one must keep one's heart tuned. Intuition becomes closed when the heart is out of tune. Every individual is meant to have a certain pitch. One cannot be too good, and one need not be. The question is that one has to be harmonious, friendly and pleasant. You will always find as a sign of evolution that[3] agrees easily; if there is lack of evolution one will agree less. The more one is evolved the more one can agree. This shows that someone who is out of tune cannot agree. To agree one must have happiness[4] within oneself. Depression, ill-luck, bad influences are removed just by keeping oneself in tune. If one is tuned one agrees; disagreement shows a lack of tune. If one is in tune one will have health of mind and body both; it is the greatest healing. There are difficult natures and people of different grades of evolution, but we must try to agree with all. Some say that one cannot remain really honest if one wants to please all. But one need not be dishonest in agreeing[5] with another. The difference is that it is more difficult for a person of a lower state of evolution to understand a

Documents:

Hq.p. (a typewritten preparation by Gd. for the Hq.st. with a few changes in her hwr.)
Hq.st.
Sk.c. (a copy of the Hq.st. made under Sk.'s supervision)

This lecture has been made into Sangatha I, 82.

Notes:

1. It has been discovered from other sources that this lecture was given in Holland on 9th January 1923.
2. Hq.p.: added by Gd.: "In order to progress in the spiritual path in everyday life,";
   Hq.st., Sk.c.: "In order to progress in the spiritual path in everyday life,"
3. Ibid.: "one" added
4. Hq.p.: "happiness" replaced by Gd. with "harmony";
   Hq.st., Sk.c.: "harmony"
5. Sk.c.: "agreement" instead of "agreeing"

person of a higher evolution. By harmony one can hold oneself. The most important thing is to be in tune. When one person is in tune he will tune all others in time. Someone who is advanced and whose opinion is counted, is responsible to keep himself in hand. Then he will rise above all conditions, he will tune the others.

Sometimes it is difficult to get on with people; the best thing is to endure. The endurance of gold, for instance, makes gold precious. Flowers are beautiful for some time, but they soon fade away; they have no endurance. If a person has all good qualities but he has no endurance, then he has no control of himself. A child is helpless, but a[6] sign of being grown-up is that one is independent. An unevolved person is in the hand of conditions. Freedom comes with true evolution. Freedom is an illusion as long as a person is not evolved; it can be attained by evolution. Man begins as a machine, he works by influence. As he evolves there develops in him the faculty of the creator, the faculty of the maker[7], to make his own destiny. The greater master he becomes the greater the faculty will be. First he is the slave of destiny, but in the end man becomes master of his destiny. One has no choice when in being[8] the slave of destiny, but afterwards, when one has become master of destiny, one has choice. Our motive is that the soul may evolve every moment of the day. The stage of the master is the fulfilment of destiny.

---

6. Hq.p.: "a" changed by Gd. to "the"; Hq.st., Sk.c.: "the"
7. Hq.p.: Gd. changed "maker" into "master"; Hq.st., Sk.c.: "master"
8. Hq.p.: "in being" changed to "one is"; Hq.st., Sk.c.: "one is"

In the handwriting of Miss Kerdijk, probably copied from her longhand reporting. This is a copy made by the compiler of the handwritten MS.

Holland, January 1923.

The Coming World Religion.

(Uncorrected Verbatim Report)[1]

Beloved ones of God,

My subject of[2] this evening is the coming religion. There is a great deal spoken in the world about the coming religion or the religion of the future. But it is not only spoken[3] to-day, but[4] it is a very old story. [5]It was spoken in all issues of history and in all issues of the past tradition[5]. It was especially spoken[6] when there was[7] need of a spiritual awakening, when there was a[8] need of a moral reform, when there was a[8] need of a social revival. And whenever there has been a need, the answer has always come, only not always in the same form that[9] man has expected. And that itself shows that the religion is an outward form of the truth which is hidden behind it. There can be many forms, but one spirit; there can be many religions, but one truth. Therefore in whatever age a religion was given, its

Documents:

Kr. (Miss Kerdijk's hwr. version, which seems to be a somewhat revised and completed version of her lh.r. of the lecture).
Kr.Gd. (equals Gd.'s hwr. corr., add. and alterations made on "Kr.").
Tp. (a typewritten copy, made from "Kr.Gd.", over which was added "Verbatim Report, corrected by Murshida Goodenough", and which is nearly identical to the "Kr.Gd."; it has some corr. in Sk.'s hwr.).

From a newspaper article in the *Nieuwe Rotterdamse Courant* of 13 January 1923, it appears that Pir-o-Murshid gave this lecture in Amsterdam on 12 January.

Notes:

1. Kr.Gd.: "(Uncorrected Verbatim Report)" replaced by Gd. with "(Corrected verbatim report)";
   Tp.: "Verbatim report. Corrected by Murshida Goodenough" added in place of "(Uncorrected Verbatim Report)"
2. Kr.Gd.: "of" crossed out;
   Tp.: "of" omitted
3. Tp.: "of" added by Sk.
4. Kr.Gd.: "but" crossed out;
   Tp.: "but" omitted
5. Kr.Gd.: rewritten to read: "It was spoken of at all epochs and in all ~~the traditions~~ ages";
   Tp.: "It was spoken of in all epochs and in all ages"
6. Kr.Gd.: "of" added;
   Tp.: "of"
7. Tp.: "a" added, but crossed out by Sk.
8. Kr.Gd.: "a" crossed out;
   Tp.: "a" omitted
9. Kr.Gd.: "that" changed to "as";
   Tp.: "as"

form was suitable to[10] the people of that particular time, its form was to answer their needs, its form was akin to the development of the people at[11] that time. But the spirit was one and the same. As the truth is unlimited and perfect in itself, with the evolution of humanity the truth cannot evolve, the truth need not evolve. The ways how it is expressed have been different. But what have been the consequences of this difference? Conflicts among the followers of different religions, one considering another pagan or heathen, black[12] or kafir, one considering the faith of another foreign or elementary or strange or something which was not right. The same truth which stood behind every religion as its life, as its spirit, was ignored by[13] the differences of form.

When we come to study the history of the world, [14]all the great wars which have been caused from time to time were most often caused by the so-called differences of religion. The religion in reality, which came as the religious or social or moral reform, the central theme of which has been the brotherhood of humanity, the spirit of which has always been the spirit of uniting mankind, in the understanding of reality, in the realization of that oneness that unites one person to another, that religion was abused and was made a means of hatred to[15] one another, of division between human beings whose happiness only depended upon their unity, upon their sympathy to[16] one another, upon their progress, which could have been united[17]. And the result[18] of this has[19] been the disastrous wars of all ages. And even now when the world seems to have lost the importance of religion, still the shadow of religious differences, still the horrors[20] that have risen remain, and there is[21] all the time the cause for[22] the differences that arise in nations and in the world quarrels. So in education, so in social life, so in the international attitude, there still exists the idea of religious difference, which keeps the nations apart and backwards[23] from that advancement and progress which could be made by unity.

10. Kr.Gd.: "to" changed to "for";
Tp.: "for"
11. Tp.: "of" instead of "at"
12. Kr.Gd.: "black" replaced with "Mlech" which is a Sanscrit word for outcast or barbarian;
Tp.: "Mlech"
13. Kr.Gd.: "by" changed to "because of";
Tp.: "because of"
14. Kr.Gd.: "we find that" added;
Tp.: "we find that"
15. Kr.Gd.: "to" changed to "of";
Tp.: "of"
16. Kr.Gd.: "to" changed to "toward";
Tp.: "toward"
17. Kr.Gd.: "united" changed to "a united progress";
Tp.: "a united progress"
18. Tp.: "results"
19. Tp.: "have"
20. Tp.: "of" added
21. Kr.Gd.: "is" changed to "lies";
Tp.: "lies"
22. Kr.Gd.: "for" changed to "of";
Tp.: "of"
23. Kr.Gd.: "keeps them back" in place of "backwards";
Tp.: "keeps them" instead of "backwards". Sk. added "back" to it.

What has it all come from? It would[24] not have come even if [25]there were a thousand times more religions in number[25]. It has come from the ignorance of the followers of the different religions. When the[26] religion was [27]made as[27] a means of ruling the world, when [28]they became as a means of getting gain[28], then naturally the spirit of the religion was lost and the form remained. There is no magnetism in the dead form; the corpse, however beautiful, is taken[29] to its grave. The whole charm of [30]the individual[30] is in its life. The form [31]of religion[31] is something, but the secret of the beauty of form is hidden in that individuality[32] which is the spirit, which is the life. So is[33] religion. It is form, it is beauty; when [34]lost in[34] the spirit[34], then there was[35] only the [36]form outside[36], its beauty could[37] not remain longer[38], it has lost not only its charm for the[26] others, but [39]the charm[39] for those who follow it. [40]This is not only the state that humanity has expressed[40] for the first time, but[41] age after age, period after period in[42] the

24. Kr.Gd.: "would" changed to "need";
Tp.: "need"
25. Kr.Gd.: rewritten to read: "religions were a thousand times more numerous";
Tp.: "religions were a thousand times more numerous"
26. Kr.Gd.: "the" crossed out;
Tp.: "the" omitted
27. Kr.Gd.: "made as" changed to "~~taken as~~ made";
Tp.: "as" omitted
28. Kr.Gd.: rewritten to read: "it became a means of gain";
Tp.: "it became a means of gain"
29. Kr.Gd.: "taken" changed to "carried";
Tp.: "carried"
30. Kr.Gd.: "the individual" changed to "a being";
Tp.: "a being"
31. Kr.Gd.: "of religion" crossed out;
Tp.: "of religion" omitted
32. Kr.Gd.: "individuality" changed to "being";
Tp.: "being"
33. Kr.Gd.: "is" changed to "it is with";
Tp.: "it is with"
34. Kr.Gd.: "lost in" changed to "is lost" and placed after "spirit";
Tp.: "spirit is lost"
35. Kr.Gd.: "was" changed to "is";
Tp.: "is"
36. Kr.Gd.: "from outside" replaced with "outer form";
Tp.: "outer form"
37. Kr.Gd.: "could" changed to "can";
Tp.: "can"
38. Kr.Gd.: "longer" changed to "very long";
Tp.: "very long"
39. Kr.Gd.: "the charm" changed to "also";
Tp.: "also"
40. Kr.Gd.: rewritten to read: "This state humanity has not experienced";
Tp.: "This state humanity has not experienced"
41. Kr.Gd.: "in" added;
Tp.: "in"
42. Kr.Gd.: "in" changed to "of";
Tp.: "of"

history of the world, one finds there came times when the religions were forgotten, when the spirit was lost, its form only remained, and whatever be[43] the religion, and whoever had given it, when once it[44] lost its spirit, the form was of[45] not much importance to humanity. The consequences were that even in the same religion, Christian or Moslem or any other religion, when that spirit got lost, divisions came. The followers of the same book became divided, those who esteemed the same Teacher, their churches were different, their faith different. Even those who believed in the same book, who had esteem for one Teacher, those [46]divided in[46] thousand churches.

And what does this show? It shows this, that[47] the spirit which is working behind, and which is the life of religion[48], when that spirit[48] becomes lost, then again[49] the need of religion is [49]felt. It is just like the rain. When there is rain and people have sufficient water for their farms, then there is a crop; but when there is the absence of rain, and when the soil is dry, when there is necessity, there comes the need, there comes the anxiety in the heart of the farmer. It is not only the farmer that thinks of rain at that time, but every tree, every plant, every atom of the earth, it[50] seems to be waiting for the call, for the same rain that has gone[51] before, not new, although it is again fresh water, it is the same rain. As Jesus Christ has said: "I have not come to give a new law, I have come to fulfil the law. I have come to give you the same which you had before." Moses had given the law, after that the law must be given again. You may know that it is the same law, it is given differently according to the needs of the day. The way how the message has come from time to time to a section of humanity, to a large section or[52] a small section, [53]has been put in the same way before[53]. If you read the life of Jesus Christ and if you study the life of Krishna in India[54], the[26]

43. Kr.Gd.: "be" changed to "were";
Tp.: "were"
44. Kr.Gd.: "had" added;
Tp.: "had"
45. Kr.Gd.: "of" placed after "not";
Tp.: "of" after "not"
46. Kr.Gd.: "divided in" changed to "were divided into a";
Tp.: "were divided into a"
47. Kr.Gd.: "when" added;
Tp.: "when"
48. Kr.Gd.: ", when that spirit" crossed out;
Tp.: ", when that spirit" omitted
49. Kr.Gd.: "again" placed before "felt";
Tp.: "again" before "felt"
50. Kr.Gd.: "it" crossed out;
Tp.: "it" omitted
51. Kr.Gd.: "gone" changed to "come";
Tp.: "come"
52. Tp.: "to" added
53. Kr.Gd.: rewritten to read: "has sometimes been told in the same manner";
Tp.: "has sometimes told in the same manner" to which Sk. added "been" before "told"
54. Kr.Gd.: added, "you will find this likeness";
Tp.: "you will find this likeness"

Krishna who[55] was given by his parents to a woman who lived in the woods to take care of the child. For at that time there was a king consort[56], who wanted to kill any child born at that time on that day. Then how this child grew in that wilderness, and then He gave the message, the words of which message are still living, so that they could live till now after the constantly blowing wind of destruction, which never allows things to stand in this mortal world. And one sees again the difference, [57]that there have been great poets, there had been great writers in all times of the world[58] history, with great capabilities, with great brains, but these simple words that Jesus Christ has said, ~~when~~- if one does not see them with[59] a scientific point of view, if one does not see them with[59] an artistic point of view, but [60]as one takes[60] them as simple[61] as they are, [62]puts them into practice, one will find that they are living words. And however simple, the more you think of them, the more light will open before you. This is the meaning of living words. They[63] can be [64]beautiful words[64], [65]they can be dead words[65]; they come and fade away. And there can be living words, which come with life, which give life, [66]which live[66], and those who hear them, those who contemplate upon them, those who assimilate them, those who realise their meaning, they become immortal also. And however greatly[67] humanity lives, the beauty of a truth will always be hidden in simplicity. At this time of evolution it seems the multitude is trying[68] after complexities, but after all the search made in complexity one will come to a point where he will be led by a simple truth. If one sees the great scientists of the day, the great scientists of Europe, you will find among them some who have gone into a great many

55. Kr.Gd.: "who" crossed out;
Tp.: "who" omitted
56. Kr.: "consort" was heard instead of the name of the king: "Kansa";
Kr.Gd.: "consort" changed to "Kansa";
Tp.: "Kansa"
57. Kr.Gd.: "in" added;
Tp.: "in"
58. Tp.: "world's"
59. Kr.Gd.: "with" changed to "from";
Tp.: "from"
60. Kr.Gd.: "as one takes" changed to "if taking";
Tp.: "if taking", changed by Sk. to "if one takes"
61. Kr.Gd.: "simple" changed to "simply";
Tp.: "simply" changed back by Sk. to "simple"
62. Kr.Gd.: "one" added;
Tp.: "and" added
63. Kr.Gd.: "They" changed to "There";
Tp.: "There"
64. Kr.Gd.: "words" placed before "beautiful";
Tp.: "words beautiful"
65. Kr.Gd.: "they can be dead words" changed to "but yet dead";
Tp.: "but yet dead"
66. Tp.: "which live" omitted
67. Kr.Gd.: "greatly" replaced with "elaborately";
Tp.: "elaborately"
68. Kr.Gd.: "trying" changed to "seeking";
Tp.: "seeking"

complexities and in the end have come[69] at a simple truth, extremely simple. Sometimes they have taught [70]it as[70] a new thing they have[71] discovered, sometimes it was a thing that is[72] known to everyone. But what has struck them is [73]most times[73] something most simple, and they call[74] wonderful. For an[75] instance, a great scientist, after his whole discovery and talking about his creation, has come to a[76] conviction that life is a[77] movement. He thought that he has[78] discovered something very new, but what does movement mean? It means vibration, and vibration means[79] word. Do you not read in the Bible that "first was the Word and the Word was God"? A man may have read this sentence and passed it over and has never before thought about it. Something simple, not very striking. A person [80]goes over it[80] and thinks nothing about it. For the general tendency of man is to go after complexities, when he cannot understand simplicities. What is not clear before him gives him a desire to understand it. What seems to him simple, he thinks it[81] is something which is nothing. But in reality truth is not something which is foreign to man. The soul of man itself, it[82] is truth. All that he learns is by truth, all that he collects in his mind as a[77] knowledge, as a[77] learning, is a kind of truth. In reality man in himself is truth, for God is Truth. Man is truth, and[83] man realising[84] himself perfectly, at that time

69. Kr.Gd.: "come" changed to "arrived";
Tp.: "arrived"
70. Kr.Gd.: "it as" changed to "that it was";
Tp.: "that it was"
71. Kr.Gd.: "have" changed to "had";
Tp.: "had"
72. Kr.Gd.: "is" changed to "was";
Tp.: "was"
73. Kr.Gd.: "most times" changed to "mostly";
Tp.: "mostly"
74. Kr.Gd.: "it" added;
Tp.: "it"
75. Kr.Gd.: "an" crossed out;
Tp.: "an" omitted
76. Kr.Gd.: "a" changed to "the";
Tp.: "the"
77. Kr.Gd.: "a" crossed out;
Tp.: "a" omitted
78. Kr.Gd.: "has" changed to "had";
Tp.: "had"
79. Kr.Gd.: "the" added;
Tp.: "the"
80. Kr.Gd.: "goes over it" changed to "passes it over";
Tp.: "passes it over"
81. Kr.Gd.: "it" put in parentheses;
Tp.: "it" omitted
82. Kr.Gd.: ", it" crossed out;
Tp.: ", it" omitted
83. Kr.Gd.: "when" added;
Tp.: "when"
84. Kr.Gd.: "realising" changed to "realise";
Tp.: "realises"

truth manifests through man[85] in his[86] fulness. Those who have awakened humanity in its time of need, what were they? God-realised men, in other words, truth-realised people, those who had the knowledge of themselves and out of that knowledge of themselves, they[87] understood and had the knowledge of others. The wrong method that man takes in life, in the search for truth, is that he seeks after truth outside himself. It is just like the[88] seeking for the moon on the earth; the moon is in the sky. Man always seeks for the ultimate truth in things, in the objects that he has before him, but the first way of knowing the truth is to seek that within oneself, to find out the truth of one's own being. Whatever religion, whatever[79] philosophy, whatever [89]cult of mysticism[89], once a person has touched the knowledge of his innermost self, then he has been[90] able to understand the knowledge of life outside, then to him God, so to speak, begins to speak, for God who is hidden in his own heart has then found us[91] a facility, found an opportunity to express Himself.

Friends, is there anyone in this world who is [92]divided of[92] the Word of God? In every heart God speaks, and when one[93] does not hear, it is not because God does not speak to him, it is because he is hearing[94] outside. Self-knowledge is being in[95] oneself. One's meditation, one's concentration, one's manner of silence and prayer and every kind of retirement, it[82] all helps man to find out that which is constantly coming from his heart. There is One far away in the highest heavens, that One, he begins to realise, is nearer to him than even his own body. It is[96] such souls, whatever you call them, prophets or saviours ~~of~~ or Lords of humanity, or great Avatars, who have from time to time come on earth to awaken man[97], who came with the ears of their heart open. The Word of God that from time to time was spoken within their hearts, they interpreted that Word in their

85. Kr.Gd.: "man" changed to "him";
Tp.: "him"
86. Kr.Gd.: "his" changed to "its";
Tp.: "its"
87. Kr.Gd.: "they" crossed out;
Tp.: "they" omitted
88. Kr.Gd.: "the" crossed out;
Tp.: "the" omitted
89. Kr.Gd.: "cult of mysticism" replaced by "the mystical cult";
Tp.: "the mystical cult"
90. Kr.Gd.: "been" changed to "become";
Tp.: "become"
91. Kr.Gd.: "us" crossed out;
Tp.: "us" omitted
92. Kr.Gd.: "divided of "replaced with "separated from";
Tp.: "separated from"
93. Kr.Gd.: "one" changed to "any one";
Tp.: "anyone"
94. Kr.Gd.: "hearing" replaced with "listening";
Tp.: "listening"
95. Kr.Gd.: "in" crossed out;
Tp.: "in" omitted
96. Kr.: "is" changed to "are";
Tp.: "are"
97. Tp.: "men"

language, in their way, to humanity. And when they have spoken, people have considered[74] or taken it as a Scripture, and very often that what they have spoken, people have called this[98] truth. But in reality truth is something ~~that~~ which words cannot speak. How can one fill[99] the whole ocean in a bottle! What can a word express? Can you express in a word your gratefulness if you are really grateful? Can you express in words your devotion if you are really devoted? Can you express your love in words, if you [100]are really in love[100]? Can one express one's disappointment, if one is really heartbroken? What can words say? There is so much behind it. Life is so vast. Its feelings, its sentiments are so fine and so great and so complex, the[88] language is not sufficiently[101] adequate to express all things. We all find [102]our difficulties[102] in expressing our feelings. How then can the truth, the origin and the goal and source of the whole life, which is the light and life and love itself, which is God Himself, be expressed in words? What they have done is that the hidden law, that is useful for man, a[103] man cannot say[104] and cannot understand, they have spoken of it. They have told him how he must live, what will be good for him, how they[105] can live harmoniously, how they[105] can be conscious of some one[105a] about them[106], how they[105] can recognise Him, how they[105] can be conscious of Him, how they[105] must worship Him, how they[105] must learn the law of honesty[107], that will bring [108]in their lives happiness[108], and that the welfare of their[109] life depends upon such morals. It is these things that they have tried to say in their language, and it is out of that that Scriptures have been made and given to humanity from time to time. Man, taking those Scriptures and considering them sacred, said: "Now that such words are[110] spoken to me once, I

98. Kr.Gd.: "this" crossed out;
Tp.: "this" omitted
99. Kr.Gd.: "fill" changed to "pour";
Tp.: "pour"
100. Kr.Gd.: "are really in love" changed to "really love";
Tp.: "really love"
101. Kr.Gd.: "sufficiently" crossed out;
Tp.: "sufficiently" omitted
102. Kr.Gd.: "our difficulties" changed to "difficulty";
Tp.: "difficulty"
103. Kr.Gd.: "a" changed to "that";
Tp.: "that"
104. Tp.: "speak" instead of "say"
105. Kr.Gd.: "they" changed to "he";
Tp.: "he"
105a. Kr.: "one" changed by Kr. to "One";
Tp.: "One"
106. Kr.Gd.: "them" changed to "him";
Tp.: "him"
107. Kr.Gd.: first "honesty" replaced with "reciprocity", then changed back to "honesty";
Tp.: "honesty"
108. Kr.Gd.: "in their lives happiness" changed to "happiness in his life";
Tp.: "happiness in his life"
109. Kr.Gd.: "their" changed to "his";
Tp.: "his"
110. Kr.Gd.: "are" changed to "have been";
Tp.: "have been"

am not going to listen again, because in this Scripture they are given." And as[111] the living Scripture comes, he can and will not listen. The prophets came in the past one after another and brought the life and the message whenever it was necessary, but many have always said: "[112]What can I do with the book[112]? Here it is right[113] in clear words, there is nothing more you can tell me, all that is right[113] here." It is just like the[114] farmer saying: "Last year's rain[115] I have kept in my tanks, if this year's rain comes, I don't want it. [116]It is not my need[116]." But really speaking, last year's rain was for the[88] last year, the rain for this year is for this year. The difficulty is, friends, that people consider their belief as truth, they do not know that the belief is a staircase, the different stairs[117] of a staircase are different beliefs. The wisdom is to climb from one belief to another. In this way from below he goes upstairs. But when a person sticks after taking one step, he might just as well be dead as a living man, for life means progress, and death means the denial of life. When a person stands on a staircase, that is not the place for him to stand, he must go on. So people sticking to their belief instead of getting the spirit of religion to go forward, they[87] take the burden of religion upon their shoulders and stand there. And in this way humanity has kept back from advancing spiritually. The consequence has come[118], that at this moment the[88] materialism has increased to such an extent, that even the form of religion could not resist very much.

From education religion has been absolutely taken away. Man is given an education in order to qualify himself to be[119] able to serve his interests in life best[120], that is all education ~~for~~- does for him. And the ideal that is before him is that his success depends upon what money he makes; whatever his [121]spirit of[121] life, his success depends upon how much he

111. Kr.Gd.: "as" changed to "when";
Tp.: "when"
112. Kr.Gd.: rewritten to read, "I have it in my book";
Tp.: "I have it in my book"
113. Kr.Gd.: "right" changed to "written";
Tp.: "written"
114. Kr.Gd.: "the" changed to "a";
Tp.: "a"
115. Tp.: "rains"
116. Kr.Gd.: "It is not my need" changed to "I don't need it";
Tp.: "I don't need". Sk. added "it" after "need".
117. Kr.Gd.: "stairs" changed to "steps";
Tp.: "steps"
118. Kr.Gd.: "come" changed to "been";
Tp.: "been"
119. Kr.Gd.: "better" added;
Tp.: "better"
120. Kr.Gd.: "best" crossed out;
Tp.: "best" omitted
121. Kr.Gd.: "spirit of" changed to "work in";
Tp.: "work in"

makes. If he is a poet, he must prove that [122]from every work[122] there is a demand for his books, that they are sold. The musician must sell his compositions, he must get money in order to prove that he is a great man. How could[123] music, how could[123] art or literature or anything progress, when it is not for the sake of the ideal, or for the sake of the work itself, but only for what it brings in material gain? And at this time, there is the greatest need for religion, now[124] the eyes of different people are set upon different things, the eyes of some are set on a certain church, or a certain religion, or faith, that some One will come, who will give the Message, who will give a new religion. And every person thinks that perhaps if He comes from a particular society, his society will authorize Him: when my society ~~shall~~- will say: "this is the person," then we will take[125] Him. Others think that[126] perhaps someone will come from the sky, directly descending, of a different nation, of different features, of a different faith, someone who is unlike us, who will work wonders, that we shall listen to him. Now in this conflict has come the question[127]: many persons once wanted that before the time of Moses, and they have wanted it before the time of Jesus, before the time of Mahomed[128], they will want it and still want it for ever. Whenever God has given His Message, He has a thousand forms in which He gives it. He gives His Message through the kind[129] mother to the children, through a kind father to his children, He gives the Message as a brother, as your friend; He gives the Message as your colleague[130], as someone like you, to give His truth to enlighten man in whose heart He himself lives; He does not need to make a special form, He is everywhere in all, and from all sources He manifests and will enlighten His beings. Therefore if the Message was given to one or to ten or to a section of humanity or to a multitude, as[131] long as the Message of truth is given, it is always the Message of God. For God and truth are not two. The hearts that are created to receive His words, to maintain[132] His words, to give His words out, will always give it. And it is not necessary that any claim or any particular show of that be made. We all in our lives,

122. Kr.Gd.: "from every work" crossed out;
Tp.: "from every work" omitted
123. Kr.Gd.: "could" changed to "can";
Tp.: "can"
124. Kr.Gd.: "that" added;
Tp.: "that"
125. Kr.Gd.: "take" changed to "accept";
Tp.: "accept"
126. Kr.Gd.: "that" replaced with a comma and the whole sentence put between quotation marks;
Tp.: ", ..."
127. Kr.Gd.: "question" changed to "message";
Tp.: "Message"
128. Tp.: "Mohammed"
129. Kr.Gd.: "kind" changed to "loving";
Tp.: "loving"
130. Kr.Gd.: "colleague" replaced with "fellowman";
Tp.: "fellowman"
131. Kr.Gd.: "as" changed to "so";
Tp.: "so"
132. Kr.Gd.: "maintain" changed to "retain";
Tp.: "retain"

whatever little thing we do, [133]we carry out[133] His Message. [134]What we do for our brother and sister, for our friend in the way of service, in the way of advice, we all [135]serve, when we serve[135] for Him, either consciously or unconsciously. The principal thing that is needed to-day is not [136]just like[136] many dream, that there will be one church and in that church all will[137] follow their particular church, their particular Scripture, their own prophet, and all will[137] admire that particular prophet. It is just like thinking that all will have the same faith[138]. If all had the same faith[138], it would be very uninteresting. The human being has a great imagination. And very often many go further[139] than what God created. Therefore in the life of all the prophets and servants of humanity, whenever[140] man's ideals always reached further than their limited person; their message is always refused and always opposed. They have stood throughout life as every person who wishes to do some good, who wishes to be in this selfish world a little unselfish[141]. He who does good to his friends, to those around him, gets the worst of it. Still[142] those who consider their reward[143] not in appreciation, nor in thanks, nor in any other form, their reward lies in the work itself. For it does not matter, for an[144] instance, for Jesus, [145]it does not matter[145] whether all appreciated[146] Him or whether they do not appreciate Him. Or[147] those who have come from time to time, [148]their message[148] was not for a person, or for a section of humanity, or[149] for the whole world; they have

133. Kr.Gd.: "we carry out" changed to "carry";
Tp.: "carry"
134. Kr.Gd.: "In" added;
Tp.: "In"
135. Kr.Gd.: "serve, when we serve" replaced with "do";
Tp.: "do"
136. Kr.Gd.: "just like" changed to "as";
Tp.: "as"
137. Kr.Gd.: "will" changed to "shall";
Tp.: "shall"
138. Kr.Gd.: "faith" changed to "face";
Tp.: "face"
139. Tp.: "farther"
140. Kr.Gd.: "whenever" crossed out;
Tp.: "whenever" omitted
141. Kr.Gd.: "must stand" added;
Tp.: "must stand"
142. Kr.Gd.: "for" added;
Tp.: "for"
143. Kr.Gd.: "is" added;
Tp.: "is"
144. Kr.Gd.: "an" crossed out;
Tp.: "an" omitted
145. Kr.Gd.: "it does not matter" crossed out;
Tp.: "it does not matter" omitted
146. Kr.Gd.: "appreciated" changed to "appreciate";
Tp.: "appreciate"
147. Kr.Gd.: "Or" changed into "The message of";
Tp.: "The Message of"
148. Kr.Gd.: "their message" crossed out;
Tp.: "their message" omitted
149. Kr.Gd.: "or" changed to "but";
Tp.: "but"

done it for the sake of the work itself, and not for the sake of any[150] appreciation or gratefulness[151].

But what is the necessity[152] of the world just now? It is not one particular [153]church, religion[153], one does not need one particular Scripture, one does not need to adhere even one particular man. What is necessary in this world just now is the awakening of the spiritual ideal for mankind, the realising of humanity [154]of the Scriptures[154]. The eyes of man today must open to read the Scriptures in the whole life; the whole nature is the Scripture of God, if one only could read it. Look at the sky and see the beauty of the cosmos, the sun and moon and stars. Look at this world and see the beauty of this world; see the[88] human nature, its simplicities and complexities, the various moods of human beings, his[155] love, his[155] hate, his[155] aspirations. If one could only study life, only observe it, its every mood, life would become the reading of the most sacred Scripture. Those who have given to humanity Scriptures, they were reading[156] of this living Scripture, they [157]read from this Scripture[157] their interpretation[158] and gave it in the form of Scripture.

Today what [159]one needs[159] is, of whatever faith they[160] are, just to help them to come out of that narrow [161] to awaken tolerance to one another, a simple attitude to one another, goodwill to one another; that[162] what is needed today is the religion of the heart, to find that[163] our real

150. Tp.: "any" omitted
151. Kr.Gd.: "gratefulness" replaced with "gratitude";
Tp.: "gratitude"
152. Kr.Gd.: "necessity" changed to "need"
153. Kr.: "religion" was written above "church", without "church" being crossed out;
Tp.: "church" omitted
154. Kr.Gd.: "of the Scriptures" changed to "as the Scripture";
Tp.: "as the Scripture"
155. Kr.Gd.: "his" changed to "their";
Tp.: "their"
156. Kr.Gd.: "reading" changed to "readers";
Tp.: "readers"
157. Kr.Gd.: "read from this Scripture" changed to "made";
Tp.: "made"
158. Kr.Gd.: "of this Scripture" added;
Tp.: "of this Scripture"
159. Kr.Gd.: "one needs" replaced by "is needed";
Tp.: "is needed"
160. Kr.Gd.: "they" changed to "people";
Tp.: "people"
161. Kr.: one word undecipherable;
Kr.Gd.: "conception";
Tp.: "conception"
162. Kr.Gd.: "; that" crossed out;
Tp.: "; that" omitted
163. Kr.Gd.: "that" crossed out;
Tp.: "that" omitted

church is[164] in the heart of man, that[165] every person that ~~we touch~~, we meet, in our everyday life, whether friend or foe, whether inferior or superior, that[163] we have a[166] regard for his feelings[167] by our actions, by our movements, by our glances, that[163] we do not hurt his feelings; to consider that the God Whom one worships in a temple, in a church, in a mosque, is in the heart of every man, whatever be his position in life, whatever be his outward appearance, but[168] still there is God in him. A real worshipper of God will respect man. What is [169]today necessary[169] is the overlooking of that which one does not understand in the faith of the[170] other; to understand that we need the forgiveness of the other. How many actions[171] throughout the day [171]one does[171] that[172] one needs [173]ask forgiveness of the other[173]. And it is only forgiving from morning till evening. Everybody cannot think [174]like we[174], not[175] [176]everybody can act[176] as we wish them[177] to act. Those around us, those who come into[178] contact with us, cannot be [179]the same[179] as we wish them to be. Who knows that they are[180] better than we ourselves. Only what we can do, is to keep that spirit of forgiveness alive in us. The only religious moral is to have regard for the heart of man as the real child[181] of God. Once a person has realised this, his church is everywhere, his religion is from morning till evening, his prayer becomes his daily bread.

164. Kr.Gd.: "is" crossed out;
Tp.: "with"
165. Kr.Gd.: "with" added;
Tp.: "with"
166. Kr.Gd.: "a" crossed out;
Tp.: "a" omitted
167. Kr.Gd.: "; that" added;
Tp.: "; that"
168. Kr.Gd.: "but" crossed out;
Tp.: "but" omitted
169. Kr.Gd.: "today" placed after "necessary";
Tp.: "today" after "necessary"
170. Kr.Gd.: "the" changed to "an";
Tp.: "an"
171. Kr.Gd.: "one does" placed after "actions";
Tp.: "actions one does"
172. Kr.Gd.: "that" changed to "for which";
Tp.: "for which"
173. Kr.Gd.: rewritten to read, "to ask the forgiveness of another";
Tp.: "to ask the forgiveness of another"
174. Kr.Gd.: "like we" changed to "as we do";
Tp.: "as we do"
175. Kr.Gd.: "not" changed to "nor";
Tp.: "nor"
176. Kr.Gd.: "can everybody act" instead of "everybody can act";
Tp.: "can everybody act"
177. Kr.Gd.: "them" changed to "him";
Tp.: "him"
178. Kr.Gd.: "into" changed to "in";
Tp.: "in"
179. Kr.Gd.: "the same" crossed out;
Tp.: "the same" omitted
180. Kr.Gd.: "no" added;
Tp.: "no"
181. Kr.Gd.: "child" changed to "church";
Tp.: "church"

If there is any Message that the Sufi Order[182] has to give, if there is any service that the Sufi Order[182] has to render, it is only this: to waken in the hearts of ~~man~~ humanity that consciousness that the divine spirit is in the soul of man. It is [183]out of[183] regard for man and his feelings that is the only religion there is.

184

---

182. Kr.Gd.: "Order" changed to "Movement", which became the official name only in autumn 1923;
Tp.: "Movement"
183. Kr.Gd.: "out of" replaced by "the";
Tp.: "the"
184. The following note was added by Sk. at the bottom of the last page of the lecture in the document "Tp.":
"This lecture has appeared in Dutch translation in *Boodschap en Boodschapper* - Soefi Serie no. 1 [as a booklet]. But the part between p. 5, 2nd par.: From education ... and p. 6: But what is the need ... was omitted."

Only a typewritten copy of this lecture has been found in the archives to date.

Amersfoort, 13th January 1923[1]

Fate and Free Will. **Man, the Master of His Destiny.**[2]

Fate and free will.[3] This subject can be seen from two different points of view: observing the life as one perfect whole, and observing the life of an individual. In order to get a perfect idea of this, you must be considering the one life which has unfolded itself into a limited creation, but at the same time a creation which gives the proof of a perfect wisdom working behind it. One can learn that it is from consciousness to unconsciousness and again that from the unconscious state of being life grows again to consciousness, in other words, the source and the goal is Intelligence itself.

It is Intelligence, called in Vedantic terms [4], in the terms of the Sufis "nur"[5], which has developed out of itself a means in this universe to express itself through it, and to experience its own perfection through this means making the realisation concrete and distinct. Therefore, just like for an engineer his machine is his instrument, it works according to the plan the engineer has made, for the mechanism is planned to fulfil the purpose wherefore the engineer has made it. In this way the engineer experiments, constructs and reconstructs and runs the whole, having his perfect wisdom behind. Therefore if the religions of the past have acknowledged more or less the ideas of fate and destination, [6]have seen[7] by looking at the[8] life as the[9] whole manifested out of God's own Being, being constructed, moulded and being worked by His own wisdom. By the knowledge of this his own

Documents:

Tp. (an early inaccurate typescript, possibly made by Mahtab van Hogendorp))
Corr. (a list of editing-corrections in hwr. Sk.)
C. (a copy of "Tp." in which corrections have been made in Sk.'s hwr. according to Sk.'s list of corrections: "Corr".)

Notes:

1. Tp., C.: Erroneously the year 1922 was written above instead of 1923. Amersfoort is a town in Holland.
2. Ibid.: The title of a second lecture, "Man the Master of his Destiny" (14th January 1923) was added, as both lectures were presented in one document.
3. Tp., C.: In both documents the title was repeated in the text to make it clear that this is the lecture on "Fate and Free Will" and not the one on "Man the Master of his Destiny".
4. C.: "Gnani (?)";
   Corr.: "Jnani" instead of "Gnani" (see Glossary: Jnana)
5. C.: a question mark in pencil after "nur"
6. Corr., C.: "they" added
7. Ibid.: "it" added
8. Ibid.: "the" omitted
9. Ibid.: "a" instead of "the"

wisdom, and by the contemplation of God and His perfection, they have arrived at a state if not more, at[10] some extent[11] they can grasp the reason that is working behind the whole scheme and they attain to that contentment and resignation which brings to the soul that happiness and peace that is the yearning of every soul. [12]All that seems to him good or bad, right or wrong, he has a limited standard with which he wants to grasp the scheme of God that[13] is perfect and unlimited. By[14] trying to[15] this, it[14] is trying to put the sea in a bottle. It cannot be done. And those who by the grace of God begin [16]to look at[16] that wisdom that is working behind this whole scheme of nature, they in time develop that insight into life. They rise to become keen, they begin to notice the justification of all things at[10] a smaller or greater degree. And [17] at life by[18] this realisation and[19] become resigned to the will of God, [20]also seek the pleasure and displeasure of the [21]perfect wisdom[21] behind, in all things they do in life.

There is another point of view, of observing the life of an individual. Often one wonders if man has any free will, or if he is only made to act as a machine to the will that is behind. And man that has not yet grasped the knowledge of the relation between man and God, he is seeing the injustice why God should deprive man of the free will, for there is an inclination, a natural tendency in every soul to seek for freedom. And when one observes the life of individuals, one finds proofs for the[22] belief. The one who believes in fatality, he will find sufficient proofs to make his doctrine true. They are many who are capable in their own direction of work, still[23] always meet with failure. Others with little qualification get their chance and meet with success with less effort. Also those who do not believe in fatality but in the perfect free will, will have many proofs to[24] it.

In order to understand the mystery that lies between these opposite beliefs, and the chain that links these opposite beliefs of free will and

10. Ibid.: "to" instead of "at"
11. Ibid.: ", where" added
12. Ibid.: "For" added
13. Ibid.: "that" changed to "Who", which makes it "God" instead of "the scheme of God" to be perfect and unlimited.
14. C.: "By" and "it" were put in parentheses in pencil
15. Ibid.: "do" added
16. Corr., C.: "to see" instead of "to look at"
17. Tp.: later written in "they look," in unidentified hwr., where first was a blank;
    C.: a blank;
    Corr.: "looking";
    C.: written in by Sk.: "looking"
18. Corr., C.: "with" instead of "by"
19. Ibid.: "they" instead of "and"
20. Ibid.: "and" added
21. C.: "Perfect Wisdom"
22. Corr., C.: "this" instead of "the"
23. Ibid.: "yet" instead of "still"
24. Ibid.: "for" instead of "to"

fatalism[25] can be understood by studying the physiology of human evolution. We cannot imply one rule for all men. There are many more degrees of human evolution than notes on the piano, although at the present time this fact is much overlooked. However it cannot be denied. There is a certain part in man's life through his evolution when man acts as a tool in the hands of the plan which is working behind. There is another part through the[8] life in the evolution of man where man acts as a master of his destiny. One can see the example of this in the life of a helpless infant in his growing to childhood, and in the life of a grown-up person who takes up his life in his own hands.

Now is the question, where can one draw the line? When does the first aspect end and the second begin? I say you cannot even draw the line in a small child; as helpless as it is, it wants to do this or that, has the tendency to act without being interfered with. Often parents let him do and still look after him. They do not always tell it how to act. So it is with every soul. Man has not yet arrived at that grade of evolution when[26] he can do all things at his free will. Still [27]he has the illusion often[27] that he does, though it is often not true, as he perhaps will be acting under the influence of others or circumstances. Still he has the illusion he acts on free will. And under this impression and while he is advancing, there is coming a time that he really does it, just as a child[28] when becoming older he thinks his parents are not guiding and he does it himself still[29] he comes to[30] own responsibility. In this way God Himself has acted with the whole nature: sea, rivers, plants, through all this He Himself experiences life and gets the satisfaction out of life. But the main purpose of all this creation, He best realises in man, so to say the tool. It is this idea which is expressed in a poetic form in the religion of the old, when you read "We have created man in our invention[31]. If you want to see Us you must see Us in the form of man because we recognise Ourselves in man." All the lower creation surrenders to the will of man. It means that God is experiencing life fully in man, all corresponding[32] to His will, fulfilling His wishes. But every man is not necessarily tuned to that plane when[33] God fulfils His purpose. Nevertheless the soul of every man, independent of the state of evolution, is continually longing and working to arrive at that state of evolution when[33] it can fulfil the purpose of God. In order to hasten the evolution of man, the prayer that Christ has given was prescribed to the souls, that "Thy Will be done on earth as it is

25. Corr.: "this" added;
C.: ", this" added
26. Corr., C.: "when" changed to "where"
27. Ibid.: reordered to read: "he often has the illusion"
28. Ibid.: a comma added
29. Ibid.: "till" instead of "still"
30. Ibid.: "his" added
31. Tp.: "invention" changed to "image" in unknown hwr.
32. C.: "corresponding" changed to "responding" in pencil
33. There seems to have been a discussion among some mureeds about whether "when" should be changed to "where", resulting in a letter of 8th November 1964 from Sd. to Sk., in which the conclusion was that "where" would limit the meaning of the fulfilment.

in Heaven." What does it mean? What has to be fulfilled by this [34] ? That by praying man tunes himself to fulfil the purpose of his life. It is the ignorance of man when we say: why Thy Will, why not mine? For he does not know what is His. And the whole process of spiritual evolution is to realise what is man's innermost being, whether he is God's Being Himself or if he has a separate being. If the last, from where does it come? But if he comes from the Self of God, how can he say, I am not of Your Being, or I am not from Your Source?

The difference between the leaf and the tree. The leaf is limited, the tree perfect. Still the leaf is of the tree itself. But when it drops, the tree still exists. This cannot be studied intellectually but it must be lived as an inner realisation, and that becomes the means of that perfection of which stands in the Bible "Be perfect as your Father in Heaven."

---

34. Tp., C.: an empty space

A copy in the handwriting of Mrs. J.H. van Voorst van Beest - van Son probably of a longhand reporting.

Amersfoort, 14th January 1923[1]

Man, the[2] Master of His Destiny.

In this platform[3] of the world where[4] man is made[5] [6]helpless and little[6] amidst influences[7] and conditions that, whatever may[8] be his occupation in life, [9]whatever may be[9] his position in life, he finds himself helpless.

The kings in the history of the world, who have fought and conquered most of the part of the world, have found themselves at[10] the end helpless. We don't need to go far back searching[11] for this in the history of the world, only we need reflect on the life of Napoleon,[12] in what helpfulness[13] this[14] ended. The life of the Tsar,[15] also[16] the life of [17]Emperor Wilhelm[17], where[18] command[19] was taken[20] if it were[21] a command of God,

Documents:

- vV. (a copy in the handwriting of Mrs. J.H. van Voorst van Beest - van Son, probably of a longhand reporting).
- Tp. (an early inaccurate copy in typescript, possibly made by Mahtab van Hogendorp, with many additions and alterations).
- Corr. (a list of editing-corrections in Sakina's handwriting).
- C. (a copy of "tp." in which some corrections have been made in Sakina's handwriting, according to Sakina's list of corrections: "Corr.").

Notes:

1. Tp., C.: date omitted. Amersfoort is a town in Holland.
2. Tp.: "the" omitted
3. Tp., C.: "phase" instead of "platform"
4. Corr., C.: "where" crossed out
5. Tp., corr., C.: "so" added
6. Tp., C.: "limited and helpless" instead of "helpless and little"
7. Ibid.: ", powers" added
8. Ibid.: "may" omitted
9. Ibid.: "whatever may be" omitted
10. Ibid.: "in" instead of "at"
11. Ibid.: "searching" omitted
12. Ibid.: "the victor of the world" added
13. Ibid.: "helplessness" instead of "helpfulness" (possibly a copying error by v.V.)
14. Ibid.: "it" instead of "this"
15. Ibid.: "the most powerful emperor in his time" added
16. Ibid.: "also" omitted
17. Ibid.: "the emperor of Germany" instead of "Emperor Wilhelm"
18. Ibid.: "whose" instead of "where"
19. Ibid.: "there was a time" inserted
20. Ibid.: "as" added
21. Ibid.: "was" instead of "were"

[22]when we see the picture[23] the later part[24] of the[25] lives, [26]which ended in[26] utter helplessness. How[27] in one moment all [28]the power[28] [29]upon which it depended[29] left them in such[30] despair that even [31]in body and mind[31] they found no power of control.

This idea [32]deeply thought out[32], suggests that when man, in[33] seeking for power to master, to govern[34], to rule, he most often seeks it only in a[35] wrong direction. [36]For a while[36] he wishes to hold to control[37] and[38] [39]rule all which is outside of[39] himself, he loses so to speak that power which is hidden in himself, to hold himself, to control[40] and to rule himself. In this way man becomes the possessor[41] of a domain[42] which is not his own and which can easily[43] be snatched [44]away from him[44] when occasion arises. And in the pursuit of the[45] domain which[46] not does really[47] belong to him, he becomes [48]so absorbed[48], that he neglects his first duty, to control, to[49] hold and rule himself.

In reality every man has the possibility of being the master of his destiny. Whatever[50] be [51]his condition, occupation[51] in life, it[52] cannot be

22. Ibid.: "And" added
23. Ibid.: "of" added
24. Ibid.: "parts"
25. Ibid.: "their" instead of "the"
26. Ibid.: "how it all ended in nothing as" instead of "which ended in"
27. Ibid.: "now" instead of "how"
28. Tp.: "the power of them";
    Corr.: "their power";
    C.: "the power of them", changed to "their power"
29. Tp., C.: "upon which it depended" omitted
30. Ibid.: "a" added
31. Ibid.: "on themselves, on their own body and mind", instead of "in body and mind"
32. Ibid.: "when one thinks about it deeply" instead of "deeply thought out"
33. Ibid.: "is" instead of "in"
34. Ibid.: "to go on" instead of "to govern"
35. Ibid.: "the" instead of "a"
36. Ibid.: "While" instead of "For a while"
37. Tp.: "himself" added;
    C.: "himself" added, but crossed out
38. Tp., C.: "to" added
39. Tp.: omitted "rule all which is outside of"
40. Tp., C.: "himself" added
41. Ibid.: "and the controller" added
42. Tp.: "~~that does not clearly belong to him~~"
43. Tp., C.: "easily" placed after "be"
44. Ibid.: "from his hands" instead of "away from him"
45. Ibid.: "that" instead of "the"
46. Ibid.: "that" instead of "which"
47. Ibid.: "clearly" instead of "really"
48. Tp.: "absorbed so";
    Corr.: "so absorbed";
    C.: "absorbed so", changed back by Sk. to "so absorbed"
49. Tp., C.: "to" omitted
50. Ibid.: ", whatever" instead of ". Whatever"
51. Ibid.: "his position, his occupation, his condition" instead of "his condition, occupation"
52. Ibid.: ". It" instead of ", it"

otherwise for the reason that God, the [53]Ruler of the universe[53] is in man. This quotation will help to understand this[54] idea better: "When that[55] glimpse of Our image is caught in man, when heaven and earth are sought in man, then what is there in the world that is not in man, if one only [56]explores them[56], there is a lot in men[57]."

[58]It is not the life of wealth that makes a man[58]. It is the poor opinion of man for manhood, it is this that makes him poor. Man conscious of health has health in store for him. Man who has wealth within the reach of his aspiration has wealth with[59] him. Man who aspires to[60] wisdom, there is wisdom for him; [61]who realizes power, there is power for him. It is the lack of man's belief that brings him the lack of the object he wants. Man sees the lack outside, but the true lack is [62]in himself[62]. [63]Who says that others[64] don't love him, [65]he at the end will find[65] that he himself [66]has lost it from his own heart[66]. He[67] who says there is no beauty, [68]he must know that he has lost beauty from himself.[68] [69] If a man has no mind to work, no success will come by[70] itself at[71] his door. If one has no faith to rise [72]to prosperity[72,73], no one can help him [72]to prosperity[72]. If one feels[74] feeble in his own heart, even the Almighty cannot give him that[75] power, for the source[76] is in himself. Man must[77] see[78] how deep down he has gone. For the true source of all mastery[79] [80]can be[80] found in his own heart.

53. Ibid.: "King-ruler of the whole" instead of "Ruler of the universe"
54. Ibid.: "the" instead of "this"
55. Ibid.: "a" instead of "that"
56. Ibid.: "explored him" instead of "explores them"
57. Ibid.: "man" instead of "men"
58. Ibid.: "It is not the lack of wealth and condition that makes man poor" instead of "It is not the life of wealth that makes a man"
59. Ibid.: "for" instead of "with"
60. Ibid.: "to" omitted
61. Ibid.: "man" added
62. Ibid.: "inside" instead of "in himself"
63. Ibid.: "The man" added
64. Ibid.: "men" instead of "others"
65. Tp.: "will find as end of examination" instead of "he at the end will find";
Corr.: "at the end" instead of "as end";
C.: "will find as end of examination", changed by Sk. to "will find at the end of examination"
66. Tp., C.: "has no love" instead of "has lost it from his own heart"
67. Ibid.: "Man" instead of "He"
68. Ibid.: "in the world he has no beauty in himself; the world is full of beauty." instead of "he must know that he has lost beauty from himself."
69. Ibid.: three sentences which do not appear in vV.: "This all shows that the mastery can be gained from within. The source of all is to be found in oneself. If a patient has no cure in his heart, no doctor will cure him."
70. Ibid.: "of" instead of "by"
71. Ibid.: "to" instead of "at"
72. Ibid.: "to prosper" instead of "to prosperity"
73. Ibid.: "through life" added
74. Ibid.: "weak and" added
75. Ibid.: "that" omitted
76. Ibid.: "of all" added
77. Ibid.: "pick up himself," added
78. Ibid.: "see" omitted
79. Ibid.: "mastership" instead of "mastery"
80. Ibid.: "is to be" instead of "can be"

Friends, we all have our[81] own domain in life. Our family, our work, all that we possess, all that is connected with us, all that we are related with, constitutes one[82] domain. Therefore each person has his domain[83,84]. Even his own world[85], his mind, [86]comes out of[86] his kingdom. When he falls beneath his kingdom, he abdicates himself from kingship. So long[87] he holds the reins of his kingdom in his hands, he rules and governs[88] himself. Every little success in any direction of life, is caused by the mastery of oneself[89], to a smaller or a[90] greater extent.[91] Every loss is mostly caused by the lack of it. Very few in this[54] world know to what extent [92]the influence of one's condition and personality has[92] upon one's affairs in life. [93]Man whose factory is going[94], working on, and who is a hundred miles off[95] [96]and gives the factory[96] in the hands of responsible workers, and then[97] man is resting[98], moving away from his factory, [99]his influence is there, working[100]. If his spirit is not up to the work[101], the factory is either running badly or lacking success[102]. If one only understood the[103] working of the spirit of man in the domain of his life[104], one would[105] certainly come to the conclusion that capability [106]means personality[106], which seems[107] so important in [108]every affair[108,109].

81. Ibid.: "own" omitted
82. Ibid.: "our" instead of "one"
83. Ibid.: "kingdom" instead of "domain"
84. Ibid.: "large or small" added
85. Ibid.: "body" instead of "world"
86. Ibid.: "come under" instead of "comes out of"
87. Corr.: "as" added
88. Tp., C.: "masters" instead of "governs"
89. Ibid.: "one's self"
90. Ibid.: "a" omitted
91. Ibid.: ", and" added, full stop omitted
92. Corr.: "one's condition and personality have influence" instead of "the influence of one's condition and personality has"
93. Ibid.: "A" added
94. Ibid.: "going" omitted
95. Ibid.: "away from it" instead of "off"
96. Ibid.: "a factory that is given" instead of "and gives the factory"
97. Ibid.: "this" instead of "then"
98. Ibid.: "resting" omitted
99. Ibid.: "still" added
100. Ibid.: "in the factory" added
101. Ibid.: "mark" instead of "work"
102. Ibid.: Not found in vV.: "or drifting away from his hands. For it is not outward working that is all, not through mind and body but through the spirit too."
103. Ibid.: "psychical" added
104. Ibid.: "mind" instead of "life"
105. Ibid.: "would" placed before "come"
106. Ibid.: ", means and perseverance" instead of "means personality"
107. Ibid.: "seem"
108. Ibid.: "all affairs" instead of "every affair"
109. Ibid.: added "are but secondary things compared with the power of one's own spirit"

It is a great pity that humanity seems[110] drifting[111] away from the realization of the inner life. Depending only upon[112] the outer[113] things [114]that are[114] liable to destruction, a life which in[115] the end of examination, [116]after he has analyzed it,[116] proves [117]to be nothing than[117] illusion. It is this which[118] has caused the pain[119] and the[120] unrest that one sees today [121]in the world[121]. With all the[122] industrial and commercial[123] progress, has there come any greater happiness? The peace[124] [125]is disturbed[125], [126]misery is greater[126] than at any time in the history of the world. [127]Distrust consideration for the feeling of man, virtues seem to have been lost[127]. People in this world are inclined[128] for a change by a kind of reconstruction of life. There are[129] simple believers who are hoping[130] some blessing [131]one time[131], others [132]who think by political or commercial reconstruction a better doing will come[132]. It is good[133] to be optimistic rather[134] than pessimistic, [135]but the direction that the Sufi[136] has sought to work for God and [137]for life[137] is[138] awakening in man that spirit which[118] brings him the[139] conviction of the divine spark in his soul, [140]the divine in man, which ennobles one's soul and which is the one[141] aim [142]in life[142] and upon which depends the happiness and[143] peace of the world.

110. Ibid.: "to be" added
111. Ibid.: "further and further" added
112. Ibid.: "on" instead of "upon"
113. Ibid.: "outward" instead of "outer"
114. Ibid.: ", things" instead of "that are"
115. Ibid.: "at" instead of "in"
116. Ibid.: "after he has analyzed it," omitted
117. Ibid.: "but to be nothing but" instead of "to be nothing than"
118. Ibid.: "that" instead of "which"
119. Ibid.: "pains"
120. Ibid.: "the" omitted
121. Ibid.: "in the world" omitted
122. Ibid.: "this so-called" instead of "the"
123. Ibid.: "social" instead of "commercial"
124. Ibid.: "of the world" added
125. Ibid.: "is now more disturbed than ever" instead of "is disturbed"
126. Ibid.: "The misery in this world is much greater" instead of "misery is greater"
127. Ibid.: "The coldness that one finds existing between man and man. It is in the pursuit of outer things that man has lost his inner virtue, the real gold, about which depends his happiness" instead of the incomplete passage in vV.: "Distrust [a blank] consideration for the feeling of man, [a blank] virtues seem to have been lost". (The word "about" was changed by Sk. to "upon".)
128. Ibid.: "trying" instead of "inclined"
129. Ibid.: "other" added
130. Ibid.: "and expecting" added
131. Ibid.: "to come sometime" instead of "one time"
132. Ibid.: "think that by the economical or industrial or social reconstruction the betterment will come" instead of "who think by political or commercial reconstruction a better doing will come"
133. Ibid.: "better" instead of "good"
134. Ibid.: "rather" omitted
135. Ibid.: added, "and every thing one tries, is always a success if it is done heartily optimistic"
136. Ibid.: "Movement" added
137. Ibid.: "humanity" instead of "for life"
138. Ibid.: "by" added
139. Ibid.: "to" instead of "the"
140. Ibid.: added, ". It is the realization of"
141. Ibid.: "only" instead of "one"
142. Ibid.: "of man" instead of "in life"
143. Ibid.: "the" added

The matter[144] that one[145] Movement takes[146] to accomplish their[147] object [148]causes that they do not[148] accept one particular scripture, nor by inviting people to unite in particular dogmas[149]. For this we leave [150]the choice to[150] every individual, [151]considering that[151] [152]every individual[152] must be free to follow his life's vocation. Only the Sufi[153] gives [154]the warning of the time that is to come[154]. [155]It reminds the same truth that always has been brought[155]. [156]Sufism does not mean any particular wisdom; any means of unity, understanding of East and West, where the broken trades of nations can be restored.

Man and wife cannot better understand each other than by knowing themselves.

Murshid Inayat Khan.[156]

---

144. vV.: "matter" probably miscopied for "method";
Tp., C.: "method"
145. Tp., C.: "the Sufi" instead of "one" which may have been miscopied for "our"
146. Ibid.: "in order" added
147. Ibid.: "this" instead of "their"
148. Ibid.: "is not by asking humanity to" instead of "causes that they do not"
149. Ibid.: "or creeds" added
150. Ibid.: "to the choice of" instead of "the choice to"
151. Ibid.: "because" instead of "considering that"
152. Ibid.: "everybody" instead of "every individual"
153. Ibid.: "Message" added
154. Ibid.: "a warning for the time to come"
155. Ibid.: "It brings the reminder of the great truths of all religions" instead of "It reminds the same truth that always has been brought"
156. These last sentences are not to be found in the tp. and C.. In vV. they were written on a new page in the copybook, which may have been overlooked in making the type.
The sentence "Man and wife ..." could be an answer to a question after the lecture.

Mrs. E. Leembruggen's longhand reporting, copied by the compiler.

---

15 January 1923, Arnhem. Holland

Beloved ones of God,

My subject this evening is "The word that was lost."

This idea belongs to the inner cult of all ages and to[1] the secret teaching there is this teaching about the word that was lost. Very few [2]know at present[2], [3]at least seem to know the meaning of it. There is[4] difference in belief between the mystic and the materialist; there is not[5] very much difference in the ideal. For instance, the scientist, the materialist, [6]the physical man[6] who seeks for[7] source of the whole creation, comes to the same conclusion, that there is only one source of [8]life in the[8] variety the composing[9] and decomposing[10] of atoms. And [11]these two[11] come on[12] the end of the path to the same thing, Truth. Principally[13] in the ideal both[14] differ. The materialist thinks all this consciousness and intelligence[15] one sees in man is the natural development of life. Whether[16] of[7] rock or[7] stone, of a tree or[17] plant, or[7] consciousness of men[18], all is the same. The mystic says that is

Documents:

Lb. (a lh. reporting by Mrs. E. Leembruggen).
Lb.Gd. (= Lb. with corr., alterations and additions in Gd.'s hwr.).
Tp. (a typescript in which Gd.'s corr. etc. have been included and which shows also a few corr. in Sk.'s hwr.)

As "Lb.Gd." and "Tp." are almost identical, the latter will be mentioned in the notes only where it differs from "Lb.Gd.".

Notes:

1. Lb.Gd.: "to" changed to "in"
2. Ibid.: "at present know"
3. Ibid.: "or" added
4. Ibid.: "not much" added
5. Ibid.: "not" crossed out
6. Ibid.: first "physical" was changed to "material", then the three words were crossed out.
7. Ibid.: "the" added
8. Ibid.: "the life of" instead of "life in the"
9. Ibid.: "composition" instead of "composing"
10. Ibid.: "decomposition" instead of "decomposing"
11. Ibid.: "both the mystic and the materialist" instead of "these two"
12. Ibid.: "at" in place of "on"
13. Ibid.: "Principally" changed to "It is chiefly"; the context indicates that Pir-o-Murshid used the word "Principally" here in the etymological sense of "in the beginning", L.: *in principio*.
14. Ibid.: "both" changed to "that the two"
15. Ibid.: "that" added
16. Ibid.: added, "it is the consciousness"
17. Ibid.: "a" added
18. Tp.: Sk. changed "men" to "man"

not so. The consciousness and intelligence is the same as the illimited[19] consciousness or intelligence, it[20] is only[21] put in different channels, and of[22] that intelligence that existed in the beginning the rest has risen[23]. [24]Picturing the consciousness or intelligence of man to the illimited consciousness or intelligence as of a drop to the ocean[24].

Therefore the materialist sees the intelligence of man[25] as the natural development of humanhood[26] while the mystic sees it as[7] divine Essence, as one, as the Source of all things. In[7] belief of the mystic it is not only man that is seeking for something, it is the plants, the animals, even the rocks and mountains, all look for something. Man who analyses life dividing[27] one object as a thing, another entity as a being, in[28] this way he[29] divides life into[30] many aspects, so many things. But in reality it is one. Therefore he sees intelligence in living beings[31]. But[32] it is especially developed in man;[33] there is [34]also mind in animal[35], in plant[36], in a tree etc.[37] [38]Mind is only[39] a part[40] of the illimited[19] intelligence. Often[41] animal thinks more than man, only one can say that animal is not so[42] developed. According to the mystic [43]it is as well[43] in plants and trees;[44] in rocks and mountains[45] mind is hidden somewhere. ~~This~~ Mind is working in everything[46], [47,48]not

19. Lb.Gd.: "unlimited"
20. Tp.: "it" omitted but reinserted by Sk.
21. Lb.Gd.: "only" placed before "it"
22. Ibid.: "from" instead of "of"
23. Ibid.: "risen" changed to "come"
24. Ibid.: rewritten to read, "Picturing the unlimited consciousness or intelligence as the ocean, the consciousness or intelligence of man is like a drop compared to the ocean"
25. Tp.: "men," changed by Sk. to "man"
26. Lb.Gd.: "humanhood" changed to "humanity"
27. Ibid.: "dividing" changed to "distinguishing"
28. Tp.: "in" omitted
29. Lb.Gd.: "he" omitted
30. Ibid.: "so" added
31. Ibid.: "only" added
32. Ibid.: "though" added;
    Tp.: "thought" instead of "though", changed back by Sk. to "though"
33. Lb.Gd.: the semi-colon changed to a comma
34. Ibid.: "mind also";
    Tp.: "a mind also"
35. Tp.: "animals"
36. Ibid.: "plants"
37. Lb.Gd.: "etc." crossed out
38. Ibid.: "Each" added;
    Tp.: no addition of "Each"
39. Lb.Gd.: "only" crossed out
40. Ibid.: "part" changed to "particle"
41. Ibid.: "an" added
42. Ibid.: "much" added
43. Ibid.: "it is as well" changed to "mind exists also"
44. Ibid.: the semi-colon changed to a comma
45. Ibid.: added a full stop after "mountains", and "mind" written with a capital M;
    Tp.: = Lb.'s version
46. Lb.Gd.: "everything" changed to "all things"
47. Ibid.: "though" added, then again crossed out
48. Ibid.: "not perceptible" changed to "imperceptibly"

perceptible[48,49]. Man only distinguishes his objects[49]. Comparison between two minds [50]gives vast differences[50] but it is difficult to distinguish[51] it. [52]Those that[52] have experienced in life how that[53] often[54] plants respond to influences, especially to[7] human beings around them, how they often [55]dried up[55] in a house[56] where there is distress or disturbance, [3]inharmony, and often keep[57] longer[58] there is harmony, and when their masters[59] can[60] understand plants, they become [61]respondent with[61] love and harmony and sympathy; often plants feel[7] absence of these qualities. The condition of that[62] person's mind, [63]its effect can be found[63] on the plants in his surrounding[64]. [7]Human being is so [65]accustomed to[65] his own affairs that he sees no further than he sees. Generally mankind is too unaware of the condition of others, very often[66] does not know even[7] condition of those[67] near and dear[68]. If it were not so, there could not be some nations being[69] happy and comfortable while other[70] people in other countries were[71] starving and dying by millions, [72]as can be found[72] in[7] ancient fables. [73]There once was [74]a discussion[74] between man and[17] lion, whose fate[75] was more important, man's[76] or[7] lion's. When they voted, [77]opinions proved, all said, that man was more worth than lion[77]. This fable proves that the very[78] reason is[15] man

49. Ibid.: ". Man only distinguishes his objects" changed to "; in all things that man only recognises as objects"
50. Ibid.: "gives vast differences" changed to "shows a vast difference between them"
51. Ibid.: "distinguish" changed to "define"
52. Tp.: "Those that" changed by Sk. to "Some will"
53. Lb.Gd.: "that" crossed out
54. Ibid.: "often" placed after "plants"
55. Ibid.: "dried up" changed to "wither"
56. Ibid.: "house" changed to "home"
57. Ibid.: "keep" changed to "live"
58. Ibid.: "where" added
59. Ibid.: "masters" changed to "owners"
60. Ibid.: "can" crossed out
61. Ibid.: "respondent with" changed to "responsive to"
62. Ibid.: "that" replaced with "a"
63. Ibid.: "its effect can be found" changed to "can be seen in its effect"
64. Ibid.: "surroundings"
65. Ibid.: "accustomed" changed to "much absorbed in"
66. Ibid.: "man" added
67. Ibid.: "who are" added
68. Ibid.: "to him" added
69. Ibid.: "being" crossed out
70. Ibid.: "other" crossed out
71. Ibid.: "were" changed to "are"
72. Ibid.: "as can be found" changed to "This can be seen"
73. Ibid.: "There is a fable which tells that" added
74. Ibid.: "a discussion" changed to "an argument"
75. Ibid.: "fate" changed to "life"
76. Ibid.: "fate" added
77. Ibid.: "opinions proved, all said, that man was more worth than lion" changed to "it proved that each had his own was more important";
Tp.: Sk. added "said" after "had"
78. Lb.Gd.: "very" crossed out

being[79] unaware of[7] secret of his own being, what he wants[80] is to interest himself in the life of the[81][82]other classes of development[82] before he can come to this[83,84] basis, the consciousness of his own being. If you have ever been far away in the woods[85] or the mountains, far away from[86] population, [87]consciously or unconsciously there comes[87] a feeling of romance, the wind that is repeating[88] the sound that is coming[89] from the trees,[90] the rock, the murmur of the water running, all are wanting to get back something that was[91] lost. This particular[92] feeling comes to human beings[93] in the pleasure[94] of everyday life. Then there is a joy that opens something in us; then there comes this yearning, and that feeling one feels on every side in the wilderness [95]of the wood[95]. There comes the feeling of longing, the deep yearning of the heart, the searching for something that has been lost. When we look at the beings living around us we see the same thing. For instance, look at the birds and contemplate on[96] their restless flying[97], the constant[98] roaming of animals in the forest. The first thought that might come, [99]one might think[99] that they were[100] searching for food. But he who has a deeper sight[101] into nature certainly will feel the restlessness sooner or later, the searching of[102] that which is lost. There is the same tendency contains[103] human being[104], although[7] human being has much interest in life by[105] the[106] various occupations, various moods, he finds[17] thousand

79. Ibid.: "being" changed to "is"
80. Ibid.: "wants" changed to "needs"
81. Ibid.: "beings in" added
82. Ibid.: "other classes" changed to "another phase of evolution";
Tp.: "phase of evolution" replaced with "class of development", then again changed back by Sk., as in the "tp." Gd.'s corr. etc. are given. In a separate annotation, however, Sk. indicates that it should read, "beings in another class of development".
83. Lb.Gd.: "this" replaced by "the"
84. Ibid.: "fundamental" added
85. Ibid.: "woods" changed to "forests"
86. Ibid.: "all" added
87. Ibid.: rewritten to read, "you will know that there comes, consciously or unconsciously,"
88. Ibid.: "repeats" instead of "is repeating"
89. Ibid.: "comes" instead of "is coming"
90. Ibid.: "and" instead of a comma
91. Ibid.: "was" changed to "has been"
92. Ibid.: "particular" crossed out
93. Ibid.: "even" added
94. Ibid.: "pleasures"
95. Ibid.: "of the wood" changed to "in the forest"
96. Ibid.: "on" crossed out
97. Ibid.: "flying" changed to "flight"
98. Ibid.: "constant" changed to "ceaseless"
99. Ibid.: "one might think" changed to "is"
100. Ibid.: "were" changed to "are"
101. Ibid.: "sight" changed to "insight"
102. Ibid.: "for" instead of "of"
103. Ibid.: "in" instead of "contains"
104. Ibid.: "beings"
105. Ibid.: "by" changed to "through"
106. Ibid.: "the" changed to "his"

and one excuses for his restlessness, for his depression, [107]for his depressed restlessness[107]. An[108] illusion[109] developed in man is[110], that[17] reason always comes at his demand[111]. There is always someone that will say to a poor man "[112]Sad for you that you are not rich." Someone comes and says "You look depressed, I know there is so much sorrow, that is the reason." But reason is always at[113] command and [114]outside engaged[114] and so[115] can not find the real reason, that is inside[116]. That reason is suppressed behind[117] all the reasoning. Human[118] seeks more than[7] animal kingdom[119], to get back something that was[91] lost. Nowadays life never gives man a moment to be tranquil[120], that he may[121] have a[122] time to breed[123] upon[124] true cause of[113] continual[125] unhappiness, also[126] keeps him in[41] illusion, always looking out[127], and he can never find it[128] outside[129]. It is as if he were looking for the moon on the earth, but[130] moon is in the sky.

But then you[131] ask, "What has man lost?" and the answer is, "[132]God Himself,"[132] that perfect intelligence that is in every being, that intelligence what[133] the Vedantist[134] [135]says is called[135] "light," the verses of Koran say [136]is "light,"[136] "nur," which means[137] light[138] God[139] immanent in

107. Ibid.: "for his depressed restlessness" omitted
108. Ibid.: "An" changed to "and"
109. Ibid.: "is so much" added
110. Tp.: "is" omitted
111. Lb.Gd.: "demand" changed to "command"
112. Ibid.: "It is" added
113. Ibid.: "his" added
114. Ibid.: "outside engaged" changed to "is employed without";
Tp.: "outside" added in parentheses after "without", then crossed out by Sk.
115. Lb.Gd.: "man" added
116. Ibid.: "inside" changed to "within"
117. Ibid.: "behind" changed to "beneath"
118. Ibid.: "And man" was misread for "Human".
119. Ibid.: "does" added
120. Ibid.: "tranquil" changed to "quiet"
121. Ibid.: "may" changed to "might"
122. Ibid.: "a" omitted
123. Ibid.: "breed" changed to "ponder"
124. Tp.: Sk. added "the"
125. Lb.Gd.: "continual" changed to "constant"
126. Ibid.: "it" added
127. Ibid.: "out" changed to "outward"
128. Ibid.: "it" changed to "the cause"
129. Ibid.: "himself" added
130. Ibid.: "though the" instead of "but"
131. Ibid.: "may" added
132. Ibid.: the quotation marks were crossed out.
133. Ibid.: "what" changed to "that"
134. Ibid.: "Vedantist" changed to "Vedanta"
135. Ibid.: "says is called" changed to "calls"
136. Ibid.: "'God is light'" instead of "is 'light,'"
137. Ibid.: "that the"
138. Ibid.: "of" added
139. Ibid.: "is" added

the world of names and forms, in all that consists[140] in this world of variety. Various[141] forms of activity giving[142] various[143] results,[144] men[18] in this[145] illusion keeps[146] the same intelligence, [147]to find[147] its perfection in that state of consciousness where he can feel[148] his own perfection. The religious[149], the mystics, the philosophers of all ages give the key to the secret. That is what Sufism[150] [151]will bring back[151] to humanity. Christ has said it so beautifully, "Be Thou[152] perfect, as Thy[153] Father in Heaven is perfect." [154]and the yearning in[155] every soul is in[156] the realisation of that perfection,[157] of everything,[138] every being in this world, [158]consciously or unconsciously[158]. There [159]has been kept[159] one thing in the whole creation to be[160] like an alarm clock, set on[161] a certain time, [162]that it will[162] make a sound[30] that one may [163]wake up[163]. That clock sounds through all[7] activity [164]in all[164] evolution,[144] when this is touched [165]men wake up[165] by the alarm. That was the word that was lost and it has its echo in the longing.

And now you will ask "How can one listen, how can one find it?" That word rises from one's own heart, re-echoing in [166]all mystics of[166] this universe. If it [167]is not rising[167] from one's own heart it cannot be heard in the outer world. And you[131] ask, "What is the sign? what makes it rise? who can hear it?" And the answer comes "as soon as this word rises in your own heart you touch God, you touch perfection, [168]what is in all beings. In all beings the soul rises to pick it up[168] and[169] begins to understand the divine tongue, the secret that was shut[170] out[171] so long seems to be revealed.

140. Ibid.: "consists" changed to "exists"
141. Ibid.: "Various" changed to "In this world of variety different"
142. Ibid.: "giving" changed to "are producing"
143. Ibid.: "various" changed to "different"
144. Ibid.: "and" added
145. Ibid.: "life of" added
146. Ibid.: "keeps" changed to "has yet"
147. Ibid.: "to find" changed to "which he can realise in"
148. Ibid.: "feel" changed to "be aware of"
149. Ibid.: "religious" changed to "religions"
150. Ibid.: "Sufism" changed to "the Sufi Message"
151. Ibid.: "will bring back" changed to "is ~~bringing back restoring~~, is bringing back"
152. Ibid.: "Thou" changed to "ye"
153. Ibid.: "Thy" changed to "your"
154. Lb.: an empty space, which may show an omission in the r.;
Tp.: instead of the empty space it has a new paragraph beginning with "And"
155. Lb.Gd.: "in" changed to "of"
156. Ibid.: "in" changed to "for"
157. Ibid.: added "that is, the longing consciously or unconsciously"
158. Ibid.: omitted "consciously or unconsciously"
159. Ibid.: "has been kept" changed to "is"
160. Ibid.: "to be" changed to "which is"
161. Ibid.: "on" changed to "for"
162. Ibid.: "that it will" changed to "to"
163. Ibid.: "wake up" changed to "awaken"
164. Ibid.: "in all" changed to "of"
165. Ibid.: "men wake up" changed to "man is wakened"
166. Ibid.: "all mystics of" changed to "everything in"
167. Ibid.: "is not rising" changed to "does not rise"
168. Ibid.: first "what" changed to "that", then the passage "what is in all beings. In all beings the soul rises to pick it up" crossed out
169. Ibid.: a new sentence begins with "And", "then one" added
170. Ibid.: "shut" changed to "closed"
171. Ibid.: "out" changed to "for"

In[172] ancient stories, in[172] the stories of[173] the Bible [174]it is written[174], men speaking with trees, with running water, [175]that repeats[175] sounds coming from the rock. A man without patience will not stop to listen, he hurries on, he is ready to laugh at such a thing. But there is nothing surprising or impossible therein[176]. This world which is [177]going on[177] [178]is the inheritance of man. [179]This word only got true to the picture[179]. It[180] re-echoes in all things. Only man must be aware of this[181] privilege, of this[182] oneness [183]which is hidden[183]. The whole treasure of the universe is[184] the understanding of the mystical idea.

Friends, this lack of religion, this increasing of materiality[185], [186]what is it caused by? It is[187] by the lack of knowledge of religion; it is the spirit of religion that is lost. Humanity[188] cannot be turned all one way. The form does not matter, [189]is nothing without the spirit. What is wanted? What is wanted is [190]understanding of[190] each other's fate[191], to respect each other's ideal, to worship[192] that which is dear to our fellowman[193] and of[194] the other creatures. [195]This effort[195] to make the whole world believers of one faith would be [196]as if the whole humanity[196], as if all [197]the people[197] had the same faces[198], it would become a very uninteresting world.

172. Ibid.: "In" crossed out
173. Ibid.: "of" changed to "in"
174. Ibid.: "it is written" changed to "tell of"
175. Ibid.: "that repeats" crossed out and "of" added
176. Ibid.: "therein" changed to "in this"
177. Ibid.: "going on" changed to "around us"
178. Ibid.: "sounds continually" added;
Tp.: "sounds" changed by Sk. to "resounds"
179. Lb.Gd.: "This word only got true to the picture" changed to "It is a true picture"
180. Ibid.: "It" changed to "The word"
181. Ibid.: "this" changed to "his"
182. Ibid.: "underlying" added
183. Ibid.: "which is hidden" crossed out
184. Ibid.: "in" added
185. Ibid.: "materiality" changed to "materialism"
186. Ibid.: "by" added
187. Ibid.: "caused" inserted
188. Ibid.: "Humanity" changed to "Mankind"
189. Ibid.: "it" added
190. Ibid.: "understanding of" changed to "to understand"
191. Tp.: Sk. changed "fate" to "faith"
192. Lb.Gd.: "worship" changed to "regard"
193. Ibid.: "fellowmen"
194. Ibid.: "of" changed to "to"
195. Ibid.: "This effort" changed to "The attempt"
196. Ibid.: "as if the whole humanity" changed to "if it could succeed"
197. Ibid.: "the people" changed to "men"
198. Ibid.: "face"

The work, therefore, that the Sufi[199] has to accomplish, is to bring that idea of the mystic[200] that it is the spirit, not the form that matters, and to[201] leave the belief of another[202] out of the question, to understand their belief, [203] to come to the realisation of the word that was lost, the seeking of every soul, that men[204] may be enabled to reflect that picture of oneness, and so to hear the word that was lost, to hear it again[205] sounding in one's[206] own heart.

---

199. Ibid.: "Sufi" changed to "Sufi Message"
200. Ibid.: "mystics"
201. Ibid.: "to" changed to "that one should"
202. Ibid.: "another" changed to "others"
203. Lb.: an empty space;
Lb.Gd., tp.: the next sentence follows after "belief", as part of the previous sentence.
204. Ibid.: "man"
205. Ibid.: "again" placed after "sounding"
206. Ibid.: "one's" changed to "his"

A typescript of a lecture of which no original document has been found in the archives to date.

Nijmegen, 16 January, 1923

Mureeds' Class.

On the spiritual path the preparation that is most necessary is to make a location for the knowledge of God, God in one's own heart. If you ask me what I mean by location, the answer is that in the ear for instance there is a location for sound that comes from outside. The reason is, the ear, in it is the space for accommodation, not only for sound, but for every letter and syllable. If it were not for the location that man has in his ear, he could not hear, and so location must be created in one's own heart. This construction of the ear is a perfect picture of the location that is in the heart. Outside, the ear is a hollow, its shape is its receptacle and this is produced by response. The tendency is to take in all that comes; it seems as if some part of the ear has been cut out in order to make a hollow. Some part must be taken out of the heart in order to have capacity. Of course the difficulties of life make all the time this capacity. Then again there is a cover before[1] the ear which helps the sound to be retained in order to become distinguishable. In the heart this is produced by the power of concentration. The thoughts of love, sympathy must become distinguished. It is the concentration which allows it to be distinguished. Intuition is the distinction of all that comes to the heart. The heart must allow it to become clear. An inside organ of the ear is the vibration, this distinguishes every word. In the heart there is an intuitive faculty; every feeling that comes in the heart vibrates. This makes things distinct to one's view. Many consider the heart a picture of the eye, but I consider the heart is more the picture of the ear that hears. The actual sense is located in the centre of the head, that can be pictured like the eye. The work of the intuitive faculty is the perception and conception. There are two ways of knowing, one by the head, the other by the heart. Knowing by the heart is like hearing, and (the)[2] knowing by the head like seeing. Seeing no doubt gives satisfaction, but hearing gives greater satisfaction still. All that is audible touches the depth of one's being and what is visible becomes reflected on the surface of one's heart. The practice of Zikar is meant to make that capacity in the heart in order to turn the heart into the ear. Every repetition of Zikar is like carving with a chisel

Document:

Ann.Sk.: Some annotations in Sk.'s hwr on a separate paper.

Notes:

1. Ann.Sk.: "in front of" instead of "before"
2. Ibid.: "(the)" omitted

something. By carving a part of the heart it may become hollow, and it has the capacity to receive all that comes. The sound has power upon heart and soul. When you are given an exercise, its power is the same as the word or the meaning of the word. Therefore one must cut out the part that hinders the heart to do its proper work. The power of the word is such that all things can be accommodated by it, if one does it rightly. Wonders can be worked by the help of the word. Therefore a mantram is more powerful than a weapon; this is the experience of my whole life.

[3]Of course before one does a deeper practice of Zikar one must control one's thoughts and feelings. If not, one may do a great harm to oneself or others. We must not direct ill-will, anger to anyone, not even to our worst enemy. If one creates compassion, we will tolerate, forgive and take life easy. Then power increases. There are two things, one is to receive inspiration, the other is to gain power, Jemal and Jelal. Jemal is mercy and compassion, Jelal is self-discipline and mastery over one's self.[3]

Another question [4]is for my mureeds[4] that they must know that they are not alone in the spiritual path. They have a guide, not in imagination, but living on the earth, whose happiness and whose sorrow are your happiness and your sorrow. He is someone who is a human being, and has troubles and struggles with himself and others. Therefore we must feel safe in treading the spiritual path. Our guide is in the same world, he has gone through the same life of human being. We must not feel foreign with Murshid, but we must feel nearness and brotherhood. There is someone who understands you and your difficulties. What is necessary are three things:

1) Trust and confidence in Murshid, in his feeling of interest in your happiness and your well-being.

2) To consider the work that may be interesting to you (meditation, etc.) as the kind of the most necessary thing to fulfil your duty. If you did not do it with all your trust he cannot help you in the direction where your effort is necessary. Murshid knows the difficulties of the Western world and therefore he gives you much less work compared with people of the East (none of you has six hours of silence, nor three days' fasting). In the East it is the usual thing. Still we are more privileged than the East. We have not only spiritual teachings that are given, but the Message of God is given <u>here</u> and will re-echo in the East. It begins in the West and goes to the East. We are receiving the Light, which is beyond meditation or studies. The outer meaning is a message of words, the inner meaning is the same as is represented in the Sacrament, as the wine (the blood) and the bread (the flesh). Life itself is Light. A proof is not necessary for sincere mureeds, faithful to Murshid and the Cause; the very fact makes sincere. Our fifteen minutes' meditation is much more than six to ten hours' practice in the East.

3. In and around this paragraph several sentences, spoken by Pir-o-Murshid, seem to have been omitted, as it was expressly asked by him not to take down that part of the lecture. See the note added to the lecture at the end. See also Appendix B.
4. Ann.Sk.: "for my mureeds is"

3) Your part of responsibility in the application of the Message, what you get from the teachings, in everyday life, of which you must give the proof yourself in everyday life. You must be workers of the Cause according to ability and capacity.

---

[5]Parts were not written down, as Murshid specially asked a few times not to write down what he said, especially about what he said about the harm that could be done to others and oneself.

---

5. This annotation was added by the unknown person who took down this lecture; see footnote 3, above.

Mrs. E. Leembruggen's longhand reporting, copied by the compiler.[1]

---

16 January 1923, Nijmegen, Holland.
Pir-o-Murshid Inayat Khan delivered the following subject.

Beloved ones of God My subject of this Evening will be
The Spirit of Guidance.

According to the idea of the mystic this whole creation is a kind of journey of the infinite being from the innermost planes to this[2] earth and in this journey so to speak God Himself travels through different planes of existence and after numberless years arrives in the existence of human beings. God Who is one in his original State of being becomes many manifested in various names and forms. But the nature of creation of this variety is intoxicating. And this intoxication keeps all creatures in a kind of mist where they cannot well see; where they do not know what to do, where they do not know what is their duty, what is their real want, what is their purpose, and so it is not only with the lower creatures, but even mankind has this same feeling of being in the mist. Mostly man is perplexed by that idea why he is here, why he is sent on earth? What is his mission in life? How he can accomplish it? What is his duty. What is nature's secret? What is the best thing in life to do. Besides these perplexities, man has ambitions, he has needs of life, he has needs of his physical existence, his mental existence has needs, his heart feels that it needs something and there is that need in the[3] soul.

Then every man has his[4] occupation in life, from morning till evening differing from[5] another, absorbing from morning till evening. The

Documents:

Lb. (a lh. reporting by Mrs. E. Leembruggen).
Tp. (a typewritten copy of Lb. with a few alterations and corr.).
Lb.c. (a copy in Lb.'s hwr, not an exact copy either of "Lb." or of "Tp.").

Notes:

1. Lb.'s r. was taken down without her being able to grasp the meaning of the sentences concurrently as her knowledge of the English language was limited. Consequently, her r. shows many spelling mistakes and the punctuation is not clear. Besides, as in any lh.r., words and sentences are missing.
Although the present text is a copy of the "Lb.", spelling mistakes have been corrected and the punctuation has been adjusted by the compiler. In this exceptional case, however, a facsimile of the oldest document (Lb.) is added to the copied text.
2. Lb.c.: "the" instead of "this"
3. Ibid.: "his" instead of "the"
4. Ibid.: "some" instead of "his"
5. Ibid.: "one" added

earning of one's life gives absorbing, striving after the things of the world, to think and to understand that he may know how to accomplish the purpose of life; but there come hours or days or moments that some suffering comes. There comes a great trial, a strong blow, at such moments man feels awakened and thinks about those things, then he asks why he is here, what is his duty and about the changeability of life and he realises[6] less importance to that which he has attached such great importance to. Such moments rarely come into life. Often those moments are like passing waves[7]. They throw[7] around life and he forgets soon after. So is man. Having a glass of wine, soon after he is no longer sober; and so it is with all aspects of life. God representing[8] His own being, within a tree, in a plant, within the rock, the mountains[9], the germ, the worm, in all things that have names, they are representing God, Who is perfect in wisdom,[10] ... in this journey finds obscurity. But the plan of the Creator is wonderful.

As[11] a farmer has to journey at night in darkness, he takes a lantern, for he wants light to travel with. He lights his lantern in order to take[12] with him through his journey, knowing that he has to travel there at night. [13]So the Creator is almighty in his journey on[13] this world, in his own immanence so to say. In order that he may see in this obscurity, in order that He may see the road He lights his lantern[13]. And that is called the Spirit of Guidance.

In all ages this lantern which has shown the way clearly to illumine the path of those walking through the darkness of the night. This lantern was carried by someone, whoever happened to be have[14] this lantern, he was the bearer, and whoever was the lantern, his heart has been the server of humanity to show the lost souls their way through the darkness. As you read in the Bible "Knock at the gate then there is an answer."

6. Lb.: part of the sentence is missing;
Lb.c., tp.: the sentence is incomplete.
7. Lb.c.: ", thrown" instead of ". They throw"
8. Tp.: "representing (represents?)". Afterwards Sk. cancelled "representing", replacing it with "represents". The same corr. appears in Sk.'s separate annotations of corrections to be made in the different sets of lectures made by her.
9. Lb.c.: "mountain"
10. Tp.: a full stop after "wisdom" and a dotted line show that here the first part of a new sentence was missed in the "Lb.".
11. Lb.: "As" changed by Gd. to "When";
Tp.: "When"
12. Lb.: "it" added by Gd.
13. Ibid.: The following passage ("So the Creator ... his lantern") was crossed out by Gd., who wrote "incorrect" over it;
Tp.: "(... So the Creator is almighty in his journey in this world, in his own immanence so to say. In order that He may see in this obscurity, in order that He may see the road, He lights his lantern ....)"
14. Lb.: "be", changed to "have", probably in Lb.'s hwr. while Pir-o-Murshid was speaking, or soon afterwards;
Lb.c., tp.: "have"

So this lantern which is the Spirit of Guidance, whoever was the bearer, it has been[15] the answer to individuals and to the multitude[16] in the times of need, to those who[17] were in want of light in the time of darkness.

But then it is not always night. There is a part when it is day, and at that period when it is day, the lantern is not necessary, that period is light. But then there comes the period of darkness and at that time the lantern is looked for.

And the lantern has shown the way, and whether the bearer of the lantern was called Abraham or Solomon or David, whether it was[18] Moses or Jesus or Mohammed, whether it was called Buddha or Krishna or Shiva or Rama. It was the bearer of the lantern in the time of the world's need. The heart of the person that brought it, people did not see. They saw the face and they saw the names and forms. They did not see the flame but the lantern. Consequence was that after he had shown the way, then the lantern disappeared, the people forgot the lantern and its light. But they remembered the name. Sticking to that name, imagining that it was the light, believing in it, being faithful to it, and they fought period after period, for the same reason that some had seen a particular form and heard a particular name and others were sticking to another form and another name for the same lantern they remembered different names and forms.

For an instance after Moses had been the bearer of the lantern which was to guide humanity in times of need, when he had passed away and when then came again night and darkness and there was the need of showing the way again, and to light the lantern again, the lantern was brought by Jesus and when he came people said, this is a different name and a different image. Those among whom he brought the lantern said it is not the same, it is not Moses, it is not the one we look for, it was not the authorised one. "He does not come from our particular Synagogue, he is not the one our people proclaim."

There were some, however, that saw the light. Some only followed it and some among those that followed the light, again followed the name and the form instead of remembering the light, the light which had so many globes of different colour, the outer colour was seen. Some only followed the light. That were the mystics, who through all ages saw it was the same light and called this light the spiritual light. To them this was the thing that mattered and little mattered the personality who brought the light if it was only seen. The light matters, not the lantern, not the person. So it was in the time of Zoroaster, and so it is still.

15. Tp.: "the" stressed by underlining
16. Ibid.: Sk. added an "s" to "multitude"
17. Lb.c.: "that" instead of "who"
18. Ibid.: "called" added, but crossed out by Gd.

The more people can see this Truth, the[19] more force, the more light can be given, which now is lost. But so it has always been, when the light was brought. It was always refused and the divine light was[20] lost to them. Always humanity has shown whatever period of civilisation, however[21], that the workers of[22] the Cause in their faithfulness often work to disadvantage of the divine light. When it was brought, it was refused when the need was felt. Every time that it happened the light was brought, that light was refused and by whom was it refused. Always by those, that were more interested than the multitude through their organisations, institutions social workers that were occupied to welcome it when it was on the earth. They looked for it to come from heaven, perhaps in processions of angels with drums and show. But whenever it came [23]it came[23] just the same as in the time of Moses, it came as every mortal, human mortal[24] comes on earth, not with extra publications or noise or honour. As the one light that is in any mortal man, subject to follies, to mistakes, to learn to understand what earth has to teach, so came the bearer of the lantern. His purpose was to bring the light, of giving light at time of need. Imagine the Jewish people even nowadays, less in the West than in the East, [25]waiting for the Bearer of the light, even now; how many came and went and how many times it will be still[26]. Still they wait fixing their eyes on certain[27] priests that it may be recommended by them in order to be the authentic bearer of the lantern. So it has been many times and will be after that the light was shown in time of need. And when this has been done it has not been of a small effect; millions have been guided. Think of how many souls in Islam were enlightened, how many by Krishna, think of Moses and Jesus, by Zoroaster, still retaining love and esteem for their prophet. And if you ask anyone, "do you accept the one you[28] know?" then there is always the same answer, and the answer is "It is only the one I know. If you do worship another you insult the one we honour." This same way all said the same thing. Consequence has been that there were worse struggles going on time after time between[30] followers of different races, different creeds.

19. Ibid.: "to" instead of "the"; probably a copying error
20. Ibid.: "is" instead of "was"
21. Tp.: afterwards Sk. crossed out "however". The same corr. appears in Sk.'s separate annotations. See note 8.
22. Lb., Lb.c., tp.: "of" may have been omitted
23. Lb.c.: "it came" omitted
24. Lb., tp.: Sk. replaced "mortal" with "being"
25. Tp.: "(are)" added
26. Lb.c.: "still" omitted
27. Ibid.: added, "families, on certain synagogues, others look to certain"
28. Lb.: "(I)" added by Gd.;
    Tp.: "you" changed by Sk. to "I". In Sk.'s separate annotations "you" changed to "I". See note 8.
29. Lb.: "to" crossed out, probably by Gd.;
    Tp.: "(to), later crossed out by Sk.;
    Lb.c.: "to"
30. Lb.c.: "between" omitted

The purpose of bringing the lantern with the light, was therefore not fully accomplished. It was not the purpose that the name was to be followed. So came worse wars and worse sacrileges. Even now that feeling of hatred against one another exists, and does it bring light? It only attracts obscurity and creates ignorance. If a person whatever could fathom the depth of his own religion, if he pondered on it he would find Truth in every existing religion, and he would certainly understand. Does Truth belong to particular creeds or no[31]? God is Himself Truth. God is not one section of humanity. Truth is in all creatures, is created in all. His divine intelligence, His life, where it comes from it does not matter. It is all one source, it is God, it does not matter which name or form. All different Teachings from one time to another time divided in many sects.

But for the bearer of the lantern, it was his duty to give human beings light. Is that light in a particular lantern? No, but in time of darkness the lantern is the Source, the source of light is in the lantern. The light is not only in the lantern for light is everywhere vastly spreading. Therefore the personality is the lantern and the light is in it. Call it Christ, but in it Jesus must be taken as lantern. But the light that appeared was spread, and that He meant when He said, "I am alpha and omega." He would have said otherwise "I have been born in a certain year, not before and not after. The first and the last, that I was not, I was in the middle." He mentioned the light which He brought when He mentioned it in alpha and omega; and it is this light, that in the terminology of the mystic is called the Spirit of Guidance. In reality it is God's own light. Or it may be said that it is the eye of God, the sight of God which sees. Truth though even in perplexity [32] in every soul; no one is without this light smaller or greater[33]. For an instance, as some objects in the room reflect more light other objects less, so it is also with different hearts: according to [34]the one heart[34], there is response.

The most difficult part of humanity has always been man's nature is proud, recognizing God[35] rather in an object than in a person, rather than in his brother. When the[36] light was borne[37] in the bearer, and He studied man, He found that man is too proud to give that sacredness to his brother; therefore He said "Here is a God bow before Him." [38]What is it? It was an idol of stone or rock, "bow before Him!"[38] And don't you think, it was in the

31. Lb.: "no", changed to "not" afterwards;
    Tp.: "not";
    Lb.c.: "no"
32. Lb.: later Lb. added "is";
    Tp.: Sk. added "is"
33. Tp.: "(?)" after "greater" was crossed out by Sk.
34. Lb., Lb.c., tp.: "one's heart" may have been said.
35. Lb.c.: "God" omitted by mistake
36. Ibid.: "the" omitted
37. Lb., Lb.c., tp.: "born"
38. Tp.: this passage was omitted, but added by Sk. in type at the bottom of the page.

ancient days, it was in the past. It was now also still just the same. Some have a particular[39] thing of wood and say this is magnetic, this is something to put in a shrine, something to think about. To listen to his brother? No. Man[40] listens rather to the dead rock than to Him whom he would like; don't you[41] think there is a small number, there are many, [42]there is[42] a large number.

Once I was in a place in England in a village where I was to visit a certain circle for meditation and to speak to[43] some learned people. When I went in that room, they led me to my place and there was someone that came to me and said "I can trust you and now I will show you a secret," and then he brought me to a chimney[44] and said "now look here, now you will understand." But there was nothing extraordinary there. Now I was wondering, you will understand, [45]what was meant[45]. I think I was too material to see the thing. I did not see the Sacredness of a mantelpiece. My advantage depended on that place of the mantelpiece. But now after all, in the end, I found out the Truth of the whole story, what was at the bottom of it. A lady had dreamt a wonderful dream and her dream had had that effect. And it is this effect that worldly life has on men. He cannot find[46] anywhere but in mankind, whose body is the only temple to worship in mind, God. The beauty of God and of His nature if seen anywhere it is to be seen in mankind's beautiful personality, in what they thought what they brought in their personality is so much greater. It is the living God they brought therein. It is far more difficult to imagine the unseen than to imagine what manifests in personality of men.

What is[47] in the Sacrament of wine as blood, and bread as flesh: It is not the Service, it is the feeling of the personality that is a reflecting[48] of God as the perfect mirror and if anything can teach, it is this reflection of God in humankind. If ever seen, it is always seen in personality of men. After thousands of years of[49] Buddha was on earth, it was left here in the personality remembering that perfume which is left in the world. What about Christ, how many hundreds of years' legends that came down by St. Paul form a Book, but what was left? it was the impression of his personality, the atmosphere of what represents light that[50] is left us at present. But what people asked was wonders, and whenever the lantern was brought and

39. Lb.c.: "peculiar" instead of "particular"
40. Ibid.: "he" instead of "man"
41. Tp., Lb.c.: "you" omitted
42. Lb.c.: "there is" omitted
43. Ibid.: "with" instead of "to"
44. Ibid.: "mantel piece" instead of "chimney"
45. Ibid.: "what was meant" omitted
46. Ibid.: "it" added
47. Ibid.: "taught" added
48. Lb.: afterwards "reflecting" was changed to "reflection", probably by Gd.;
Tp.: "reflecting (reflection)". Afterwards Sk. crossed out "reflecting" and replaced it with "reflection".
49. Lb.: "of" changed to "that" by Lb.;
Lb.c.: "of" instead of "that"
50. Lb.c.: "that" omitted

tested it was the asking for wonders, and then the stories were taking the place of the light. Everyone was interested in wonders. But the natural kind of logical wonder was[51] the presence of those that brought the lantern, it was not only belief but it was the living God before those who spoke of God. It was not the literary work. If there was anything, it became living light, life itself. The wonder has always been this, that their presence made things clear even difficult problems. They spoke in their simple words and their presence made people understand Truth. But there is no proof of this Truth,[52] it belongs to every soul. [53]But who cannot see it clearly? They that do not see the lantern, the same light over the whole world.

It is not a new thing that you can get, it is there always. They think they can see it. It is a great wonder. Words are nothing, they are the outward garb of the Spirit that brings the light and life at the moment mankind goes astray. It is the lack of realisation of the light of which, when it is given, suffices the need of its time. [54]The work of the Sufi mainly is to make understand that there may come a better time. They can unite in this common cause.[54]

---

51. Ibid.: "that" added
52. Lb.: one or more words seem to be missing;
    Lb.c.: "Truth is [empty space]" added
53. Lb.c.: added, "How can you give Truth which is property of every soul?"
54. Ibid.: the last two sentences omitted

Ms. Sirdar as found in one of his copybooks of 1923.

1

2 3

[4]... S. represents the form of Islam,

ideal of Chr.[5],
[6]mysticism of Vedanta
[6]philosophy of Buddhism,
[6]tradition of Judaism,
and the sense of Zoroastrianism.

Now as to the question [7]in what way[7], [8]in what manner.[8] The metaphysics [9]in matter of S. cult[9] is in the realm of Islam, since the[10] S.[11] was taught mostly

Documents:

Sr.lh.r. (Sirdar's longhand reporting, of which the first part is missing).
Zl. (a hwr. copy made from Sr.lh.r. by Zuleikha Jelgersma, Sirdar's first wife (1910-1920), who later married Yusuf van Ingen. Possibly she completed the longhand reporting with the help of her own annotations of the lecture.).
Zl.Gd. (= "Zl." with corr. and add. in Gd.'s hwr.).
Zl.Sr. (= "Zl." with corr. and add. in Sr.'s hwr.).
Tp. (a typescript made by Sk. from "Zl.Gd." and "Zl.Sr.").

Notes:

1. The date on which this lecture was given can only have been the 15th or 17th January 1923, the days when Pir-o-Murshid was lecturing at Nijmegen in the Netherlands.
2. Tp.: In Sk.'s hwr. is written above the lecture, "Incomplete report, handwriting unknown". Now it has been found that the handwriting is Zuleikha's, and that an original reporting exists in Sr.'s hwr.
3. Zl., tp.: "Sufism" added
4. Ibid.: the first part of the lecture filled in by Zl. as follows:

"Beloved ones of God,[a]
I would like to speak this evening on the subject of Sufism. At this hour of[b] world's great upheaval the first question that comes from an intellectual mind is that[c] [d]what can be done to bring about a better feeling in humanity[d], and the next question[e] [f]how can it be accomplished[f], and[g] the answer of[h] the first question would be that the principal thing that one can do,[e] to bring the different religions together. For do not think that the day of religion has passed. Even to-day for the order and peace of the world religion is the principal thing. Answering the next question how to accomplish it, I should say not by a new religion but by bringing together different religions. The third question will be in[i] what will these various religions united[j]. The answer will be in[i] Wisdom, the essence of religion[d] Sufism therefore answers the present demand of the world for the very reason that all world's great religions are reflected in Sufism. As to the question how[k] I will say that"

a. Zl.Gd.: these four words were crossed out;
Tp.: omitted
b. Tp.: "the" added
c. Zl.Gd.: "that" crossed out;
Tp.: "that" omitted, and replaced with a comma
d. Zl.Gd., tp.: quotation marks added and a capital W for "what"
e. Zl.Gd.: "is" added;
Tp.: "is"
f. Zl.Gd.: quotation marks and interrogation mark added and capital H for "How";
Tp.: "How ...?"
g. Zl.Gd.: capital A for "And";

in the Moslim world, the[12] terminology of the expression of the S.[13] philosophy [14]and method[14] is borrowed from[15] Islam, therefore in[6] world's history no doubt the authority of Islam opposed S.[11] but in[16] the same time the S.[13] teaching [17]mostly appealed[17] to the world of Islam, for the very reason that the form of I.[18] has been their[19] own form.

[20,21]Why has it Judaistic tradition.[21] [22]The esoteric school of S.[11] is traced back from the time of Abraham, the great patriarch of Judaistic[23] tradition. All the prophets of B.I.[24], whatever religion they[25] taught, [26]were initiated

Tp.: "And"
h. Zl.Gd.: "of" changed to "to";
Tp.: "to"
i. Zl.Gd.: "in" changed to ", in";
Tp.: ", "In"
j. Zl.Gd.: "united" changed to "be united?";
Tp.: "be united?"
k. Zl.Gd.: "how" changed to "How?";
Tp.: "How?"

5. Zl., tp.: "Christ"
6. Ibid.: "the" added
7. Ibid.: omitted
8. Zl.Gd., tp.: "In what manner?"
9. Zl.: "of the matter of Sufi cult";
Zl.Gd.: "of the matter of" crossed out, "the" added;
Tp.: "of the Sufi cult"
10. Tp.: "the" omitted
11. Zl., tp.: "Sufism"
12. Ibid.: "The"
13. Ibid.: "Sufi"
14. Ibid.: "and method" omitted
15. Zl.: "of" instead of "from";
Zl.Gd.: "of" changed back to "from"
16. Zl.Gd.: "in" changed to "at";
Tp.: "at"
17. Zl.Gd.: "mostly appealed" changed to "appealed most";
Tp.: "appealed most"
18. Zl., tp.: "Islam"
19. Zl.Gd.: "their" changed to "its";
Tp.: "its"
20. Zl., tp.: "Now as to the question" added
21. Zl.: "why has Sufism Judaistic tradition";
Zl.Gd., tp.: " ", Why has Sufism the Judaic tradition?" "
22. Zl., tp.: "In answer I will say that" added
23. Zl.Gd.: "Judaistic" changed to "Judaic";
Tp.: "Judaic"
24. Zl., tp.: "Ben-Israel"
25. Zl., tp.: "have" added
26. Zl.: "they" added;
Zl.Gd.: "they" crossed out;
Tp.: "they" omitted

in [27]S. order[27]. [28]The holy Ka'aba, which is placed in the sacred place of Mekka, has been the place of initiation of the S.[13] order[29], until from the time of M.[30] it became the place of pilgrimage for all[31] of Islam. The esoteric schools which existed among Chaldeans, were of [27]the S. order[27]. The sacred names of God which were used as mantras by the mystics of B.I.[32] were the same which have always been used by the S.[33] in their method of inner cult.

[34]Zoroastrian religion[34]: [35]the sense which teaching of Z.[36] represents is the same as[37] understood by the [38]Sufi o.[38] If you read

[39] works of the great Sufi, Shams Tabriz, especially the metaphysics, which he explains in his simple way, how the world was created, how the source of all creation was one and the same, and[40] which was light. [41]Light within and without was the same light, only [42]the difference[42] of aspect. It was not a[43] sun- or fire worship. But it[44] was the worship of light, which S sm[45] understood by the teaching of Zarathustra[46].

Now coming to the idea of Chr.[47], which S.[11] represents, the ideal of S. has always been the life of Christ. His looking up to the source, and calling the source by the name[48] Father, still exist[49] as a custom among Sufis. A Sufi

27. Zl., tp.: "the Sufi Order"
28. Zl.: "And" added;
    Zl.Sr.: "And the" changed to "The"
29. Zl., tp.: "Order"
30. Zl., tp.: "Mohammed"
31. Zl.: "belovers";
    Zl.Gd., tp.: "believers"
32. Zl., tp.: "Israel"
33. Ibid.: "Sufis"
34. Zl.: "Now coming to this most ancient religion of Zoroaster";
    Zl.Gd., tp.: "Now coming to the most ..."
35. Zl., tp.: "there" added
36. Ibid.: "Zoroaster"
37. Zl.Gd.: "is" added;
    Tp.: "is"
38. Zl., tp.: "Sufis"
39. Zl.: "the great" added;
    Zl.Sr.: "great" crossed out;
    Tp.: "great" omitted
40. Zl.Gd.: "and" crossed out;
    Tp.: "and" omitted
41. Zl., tp.: "That" added
42. Ibid.: "different"
43. Zl.Gd.: "a" crossed out;
    Tp.: "a" omitted
44. Zl.Gd.: "it" crossed out
45. Zl., tp.: "Shams Tabriz"
46. Ibid.: "Zoroaster"
47. Ibid.: "Christianity"
48. Ibid.: "of" added
49. Tp.: "exists"

dervish in the East, who walks with a[50] stick, [51]the handle of which is a sign of[52] course[53], and who recognises in all[54] he meets the divine Father, and so[55] calls everybody he comes in contact[56] "bawa[57]" meaning Father. Then renunciation in the path of charity which Christ has taught is the lesson [58] [59]which Sufi thinks this principle for daily life.[59] [60]This principle is for[60] the seeker after truth [61]i.e. moral of Christ:[61]
Beginning[62] lesson in Sufi morals[63] is the same lesson, [64]which [65]J. Christ[65] has taught in his Sermon on the Mountain[66]. Before seeking for any occult powers or for wonderworkings[67] the Sufi seeks first to become humane[68], [69]as to give happiness to the[70] others, with whom he can[71] come in contact, considering every[72] soul is [73]exposed to the constantly pinpricks of human nature[73].

50. Zl., tp.: "his" instead of "a"
51. Ibid.: "in" added
52. Zl.Gd.: "the" added;
Tp.: "the"
53. Zl.: "course" corr. to "cross";
Tp.: "cross"
54. Zl.tp.: "whom" added
55. Ibid.: "so" omitted
56. Zl.Gd.: "with" added;
Tp.: "with"
57. Zl.Sr.: "Baba" instead of "bawa";
Tp.: "Baba"
58. Zl., tp.: "Sufism learns" added
59. Ibid.: This incomplete sentence in Sr.lh.r. was completed by Zl. and reads as follows: "The Sufi thinks that this principle is not a suitable principle for the seeker after the world."
60. Ibid.: "This must be followed by" instead of "This principle is for"
61. Zl.: "As the moral Christ has taught that turned your face to him who beats you, is the";
Zl.Gd.: "The moral Christ has taught: 'If one smite you on one cheek, turn also the other cheek, is the";
Zl.Sr.: "The moral Christ has taught to turn your other cheek to him who beats you, is the"
62. Zl., tp.: "of the" added
63. Ibid.: ". It" added
64. Zl.: "in" added;
Zl.Sr.: "in" crossed out;
Tp.: "in" omitted
65. Zl., tp.: "Jesus" instead of "J. Christ"
66. Zl.Gd.: "Mountain" changed to "Mount";
Tp.: "Mount";
Zl.Sr.: changed back to "mountain"
67. Zl.Gd.: plural "s" crossed out;
Tp.: "wonderworking"
68. Zl., tp.: "human" instead of "humane"
69. Zl.Gd.: "so" added;
Tp.: "so"
70. Zl.tp.: "the" omitted
71. Ibid.: "may" instead of "can"
72. Ibid.: "that" added
73. Zl.: a blank in place of the sentence in Sr.lh.r.;
Zl.Gd., tp.: "an expression of God"

Now coming to the mysticism of Sufism it is[74] no way different of[75] mysticism in[76] Vedanta. There are 6[77] ~~methods~~ courses, which every mystic in[76] Vedanta has to go through: [78]Jap, Tap, Asan [78]
So there are 6[77] courses in S.[11] [79]Namaz, Wazifa, Zikar, Fikar, Kasab, Shackar.[79] There is a little difference in their methods, but their realisation of their whole course of[76] spiritual journey is the same. Yes of course[76] Sufi and[76] Yogi differ in their temperaments[80], but they are never opposed to each other, in[81] the contrary, most attracted. The difference of temperament is such that it might show one, two contrary objects. For the Yogi journeys in his sp.[82] path with indifference, independence, renunciation[83], seeks solitude, practises the[70] princ.[84] of self-denial. The S.[13] on the contrary develops first in him friendliness, giving and taking sympathy, sharing one other's burden through life. Enjoying to its full extent all that is beautiful in form[85], colour, line, movement, in sense and in manner. Instead of going to the cave of the mountain, instead of looking for a desert, he seeks divine beauty even in the[86] crowd. That does not [87]at all[87] mean that[76] S.[13] cannot see from[76] Y.[88] [89]p. of v.[89] and[90] apprec.[91] his life too. [92]So does the Y.[88] Even with their most contrary ways they understand and appreciate[93] another.

[94]Buddhism, the religion of reason, [76]philosophy of wisdom. The S.[13] has the same goal, the s.[95] object which the [96]B. calls[96] Nirwana, and the word Najat in S.[13] terminology is exactly the same as Nirwana. The verbal meaning of Nirwana is colourless, the sense of the meaning of this word is about dif-

74. Zl., tp.: "in" added
75. Ibid.: "of" changed to "from"
76. Zl., tp.: "the" added
77. Zl.Sr.: "6" changed to "7";
Tp.: "7"
78. Zl.: "Jap, Tap, Asan, Dharma, Jasna, Samadhi";
Zl.Sr., tp.: "Jap, Asan, Pramayan, Dhiana, Darna, Mudra, Samadhi"
79. Zl.: this part of the sentence was omitted;
Zl.Sr., tp.: "Nimaz, Wazifa, Zikar, Fikar, Kasab, Shagal, Amal."
80. Zl.Gd.: the plural "s" crossed out;
Tp.: "temperament"
81. Zl.Sr., tp.: "in" corr. to "on"
82. Zl., tp.: "spiritual"
83. Ibid.: "renunciation" omitted
84. Ibid.: "principles"
85. Ibid.: "form" omitted
86. Ibid.: "the" changed to "a"
87. Ibid.: "at all" omitted
88. Ibid.: "Yogi"
89. Ibid.: "point of view"
90. Ibid.: "that he cannot appreciate. He can see from Yogi point of view and" inserted
91. Zl., tp.: "appreciates"
92. Ibid.: "And" added
93. Zl.Gd., tp.: "one" added
94. Zl., tp.: added, "Now coming to"
95. Ibid.: "same"
96. Ibid.: "Buddhists call"

ferences and distinctions. Every wise man at the end of his search of human life must arrive to[97] the same conclusion, [98]there is a plane of consciousness, where[76] soul rises above all distinctions and differences [99]it realises that plane of consciousness[99]. Where the realisation is[100], that all is one, and one is all[101]. There is no difference [102]of a saint and a sinner[102], [103]there is[103] no distinction of a[104] wise and a[104] foolish. [105]Is it a dream?[105] [106]It is above dream[106], for[76] dream is the reproduction of our life on the earth. The life in[107] captivity fixed and divided under[108] different names and forms. Whenever it was necessary that a[109] community should awaken, a reform was given to that community, when nations were to be awakened, in those nations[110] new religion was taught. When world demands a new light the answer is given to that demand.

The S.[13] message is the answer[111] to the world's cry to-day. An answer not only to [112]the cry of[112] a particular sect, race[113] or nation, but an answer to the cry of[76] wh.[114] humanity. It is no[115] new religion, nor[115] system of[116] reform born by[117] human intellect, it is the message of[118] the time. For the wakeful to receive, and for the sleep[119] still asleep [120]it is the to help them in sleep on[120].

---

97. Ibid.: "at" instead of "to"
98. Ibid.: "that" added
99. Ibid.: "it realises that plane of consciousness" omitted
100. Zl.Gd.: "is" crossed out;
Tp.: "is" omitted
101. Zl.Sr., tp.: added "is there, then"
102. Zl.Gd., tp.: "between saint and sinner"
103. Tp.: "there is" omitted
104. Zl.Gd., tp.: "a" omitted
105. Zl.: "It is a dream." instead of "Is it a dream?"
106. Tp.: "Realisation is above the dream of distinctions" instead of "It is above dream"
107. Zl., tp.: "of" instead of "in"
108. Zl.Gd., tp.: "under" changed to "into"
109. Zl.: "the" instead of "a"
110. Zl., tp.: "a" added
111. Ibid.: "answering" instead of "answer"
112. Ibid.: "the cry of" omitted
113. Ibid.: "race" omitted
114. Ibid.: "whole"
115. Ibid.: "not a"
116. Ibid.: "or" instead of "of"
117. Zl.Gd.: "by" changed to "of";
Tp.: "of"
118. Zl., tp.: "for" instead of "of"
119. Ibid.: "soul" instead of "sleep" which may have been written down by mistake
120. Zl.: "to keep him asleep";
Zl.Gd., tp.: "to let him remain asleep"

In the handwriting of Miss Kerdijk, probably copied from her longhand reporting. This is a copy, made by the compiler, of the handwritten MS.

1

The Power of Silence.

(Uncorrected Verbatim Report)[2]

Beloved ones of God,

My subject of[3] this evening is: "The Power of Silence." Silence in the work of a mystic is not necessarily stillness. Silence to a mystic is self-control. The definition of life that a mystic gives is movement, in other words vibration. And control of movement means control of life. In the conception of a mystic silence does not mean only the closing of the lips or the closing of the eyes; silence for a mystic is suspension of every activity, which he gains by different degrees, by controlling the movement, by controlling the words, [4]by controlling the breath[4] and by controlling the thoughts. The mystic attains mastery over himself, which he considers the only mastery worth having, by the practice of silence. Silence does not mean a few hours meditation, sitting quiet, talking to no one, but it means the work of control continued throughout one's daily life from morning till evening. If not, a few moments[5] silence every day do not suffice the purpose. If one was[6] to count[7] how many useless words one speaks throughout the day, words which are unnecessary, and thus spends[8] energy and vigour,

Documents:

Kr. (Miss Kerdijk's hwr. version, which seems to be a somewhat revised and completed version of her lh. r. of the lecture).
Kr.Gd. (= "Kr." with corr., add., alterations, etc. in Gd.'s hwr.).
C.r. (a typescript over which has been added, "(Corrected verbatim report)" and which is nearly identical to the "Kr.Gd.").
Tp. (a typewritten copy of "Kr." partly with Gd.'s corr. as in "Kr.Gd.", partly with other alterations, and a few corr. in Sk.'s hwr.).
Sk. (a separate list with annotations by Sk.).

Notes:

1. Tp.: "Holland, January 1923" added
2. Kr.Gd.: "(Uncorrected Verbatim Report)" replaced by Gd. with "(Corrected Verbatim report)";
   Tp.: no mention is made of an "uncorrected or corrected verbatim report";
   C.r.: added under the title, "(Corrected Verbatim report)"
3. Kr.Gd.: "of" crossed out;
   C.r.: "of" omitted
4. C.r.: "by controlling the breath" omitted
5. Kr.Gd.: "of" added
6. Ibid.: "was" changed to "were";
   C.r., tp.: "were"
7. Kr.Gd.: "one would find" added;
   C.r., tp.: "one would find"
8. Kr.Gd.: "spends" changed to "one expends";
   C.r.: "one expends";
   Tp.: "one spends"

the centre of which is the breath, in this way wasting his[9] breath by speaking the[9a] words that are of no use either to himself[10] or to [11]the other[11]. Many times a man talks because he thinks it is good to be pleasant, and being pleasant means speaking uselessly. If there is nothing to speak about, then he wishes to grumble against[12] the weather. Once a person begins to think that he can amuse others, and he can make the moment pleasant by speaking with others, he then begins to make his conversation as pleasant as possible. And there is no end of lies, and no end of exaggeration. When once a person ~~means~~ wishes to make[13] his conversation as interesting and amusing as possible, he does not consider anything except making it sufficiently amusing. Besides a talkative person loses in time the value of his words. The magnetism, the weight that the word carries, is lost by making use of it all the time for nothing. And the[14] art of understanding the situation and the moment, the art of understanding what to say and what not to say, when to speak and when not to speak, [15]before he has understood this art, which [16]is a[16] lifelong practice, a lifelong study of life and of[17] humanity, before one[18] has studied or known this, when[19] one[20] wants to [21]occupy himself in talking[21] to others, however well-meaning [22]and good-willing[22] he

9. Kr.Gd.: "his" changed to "one's";
C.r., tp.: "one's"
9a. Kr.Gd.: "the" crossed out;
C.r., tp.: "the" omitted
10. Kr.Gd.: "himself" changed to "one's self";
C.r., tp.: "one's self"
11. Kr.Gd.: "the other" changed to "others";
C.r., tp.: "others"
12. Kr.Gd.: "against" changed to "about";
C.r., tp.: "about"
13. Tp.: "to make" omitted
14. Kr.Gd.: "the" changed to "there is an";
C.r., tp.: "there is an";
Sk.: a suggestion to leave this sentence unchanged: "And the art"
15. Kr.Gd.: added, "And when a man";
C.r., tp.: "And when a man";
Sk.: a suggestion to leave this sentence unchanged: "to speak, before"
16. Kr.Gd.: "is a" changed to "needs";
C.r.: "needs" instead of "is a";
Tp.: "needs" instead of "is"
17. Tp.: "of" omitted
18. Kr.Gd.: "one" changed to "he";
C.r., tp.: "he"
19. Kr.Gd.: "when" crossed out;
C.r.: "when" omitted
20. C.r., tp.: "he" instead of "one";
Sk.: "he"
21. Kr.Gd.: "occupy himself in talking" replaced with "busy himself talking";
C.r.: "busy himself talking";
Tp.: "talk", completed and altered in Sk.'s hwr.: "busy himself in talking"
22. Kr.Gd.: "and good-willing" crossed out;
C.r.: "and good-willing" omitted

may be, well[23], he often offends people, well[23], he often says things that he may[24] not have said, and afterwards he repents. Very often he creates disharmony[25], which he could have avoided by not saying[26]. [27]A person who has not yet mastered his mind, his thoughts, opens his lips in a moment of excitement, in a moment of emotion, [28]before anyone, gives out his secret[29] which, perhaps, afterwards he repents[30], he[30] begins to feel[31] that at that moment it was just a conversation to pass[32] time; but after that moment has gone, he would[33] feel that he [34]would have[34] never[35] said it; but ~~it~~ he[36] has given[37] in[38] the hands of that person [37]his head[37] for the[39] whole life. He thinks: "in[40] that person [41]beyond there is[41] my secret." What a terrible situation[42] then. Besides, you will see[43] persons who enjoy talk-

23. Kr.Gd.: "well" crossed out;
C.r., tp.: "well" omitted
24. Kr.Gd.: "~~should~~ might" instead of "may";
C.r., tp.: "might"
25. Kr.Gd.: "disharmony" changed to "inharmony";
C.r.: "inharmony";
Tp.: "disharmony";
Sk.: "disharmony"
26. Kr.Gd.: "saying" changed to "speaking";
C.r., tp.: "speaking"
27. Tp.: "If" added
28. Kr.Gd.: "and" added;
C.r.: "and";
Tp.: "before anyone, and gives"
29. Kr.Gd.: "of" added;
C.r., tp.: "of"
30. Kr.Gd.: ", he" changed to ". He";
C.r.: ". He"
31. Kr.Gd.: "to feel" changed into "by feeling";
C.r.: "by feeling";
Sk.: "to feel"
32. Kr.Gd.: "the" added;
C.r., tp.: "the"
33. Kr.Gd.: "would feel" changed to "feels";
C.r., tp.: "feels"
34. Kr.Gd.: "would have" changed to "had better";
C.r.: "had better";
Tp.: "could better"
35. Kr.Gd.: "have" added;
C.r., tp.: "have"
36. Tp.: "it" instead of "he"
37. Kr.Gd.: "his head" placed after "given";
C.r., tp.: "his head" after "given"
38. Kr.Gd.: "in" changed to "into";
C.r.: "into"
39. Kr.Gd.: "the" changed to "his";
C.r., tp.: "his"
40. Kr.Gd.: "in" crossed out;
C.r., tp.: "in" omitted
41. Kr.Gd.: "beyond there is" changed to "over there has";
C.r., tp.: "over there"
42. Kr.Gd.: "he is in" inserted;
C.r., tp.: "he is in"
43. Kr.Gd.: "that" added;
C.r., tp.: "that"

ing often give a headache to those who hear them, besides making themselves so exhausted in the end, that they cannot understand why. Often they think[44] because the others made them so; they don't know that it is their own talking which has caused it. Many disagreements are caused by excessive talking. And many a misunderstanding can be avoided if only a person had[45] the[46] control over his words. Very often to talk to some people without consideration, without thought, is like giving in[47] their hands a sword or a handling[48], that they may be able to move the one who talks to them in the way they like.

There is an amusing tale[49] in India. It is told that a housewife[50] went to a magnetiser[51] and asked him if he [52]had anything to say[52], or[53] to help her with her trouble at home. The magnetiser[51] asked [54]what was the trouble[54]. The housewife[50] said, "Every day when my husband comes home, he is in a bad mood, and there is every day a quarrel." The magnetiser[51] said: "It is very easy. I will give you some magnetic sweets. What you must do is to keep one in the mouth, especially [55]at the time[55] when he comes home." She was very happy to think that these magnetic sweets may[56] help her in[57] life. And so it happened. The man who used to become nervous and excitable when he came home, and found no answer to his irritation[58], he, after being a little uncomfortable, became quiet, for there was no stimulus to his agitation. When two or three days passed[59] he began to value his wife so much, he thought: "What a great improvement!" He began to see his own

44. Kr.Gd.: "it is" added;
C.r., tp.: "it is"
45. Kr.Gd.: "had" changed to "has";
C.r., tp.: "has"
46. Tp.: "the" omitted
47. Kr.Gd.: "in" changed to "into";
C.r.: "into"
48. Kr.Gd.: "handling" changed to "handle";
C.r., tp.: "handle"
49. Kr.Gd.: "tale" changed to "story told";
C.r., tp.: "story told"
50. Kr.Gd.: "housewife" changed to "woman";
C.r., tp.: "woman"
51. Kr.Gd.: "magnetiser" changed to "healer";
C.r., tp.: "healer"
52. Kr.Gd.: "had anything to say" changed to "could tell her anything";
C.r., tp.: "could tell her anything"
53. Kr.Gd.: "give her anything" added;
C.r., tp.: "give her anything"
54. Kr.Gd.: the indirect speech changed to direct speech: ", What is the trouble?";
C.r., tp.: ""What is the trouble?""
55. Tp.: "at the time" omitted
56. Kr.Gd.: "may" changed to "might";
C.r., tp.: "might"
57. Kr.Gd.: "her" added;
C.r., tp.: "her"
58. C.r.: "invitation" read for "irritation"
59. Kr.Gd.: "passed" changed to "had passed";
C.r., tp.: "had passed"

faults and began to blame himself,[60] how foolish he was himself and how good was [61]this housewife[61]. After a few days the wife had finished the sweets, she went to the magnetiser[51] to thank him and said, "I will give anything if you would[62] give me a lot of that[63] sweet, it is such a wonderful sweet. It has brought harmony in our home, he is so kind and good to me now, all things are changed because of the[64] sweets, I will give[65] anything for it." The wise man said: "My good lady, it is not the sweets, it is the lesson which was behind it. The secret was in keeping the lips closed."

We have all a thousand troubles. Do we not find in our everyday life how many different temperaments we have to meet with, [66]those who are [67]more worldly[67] than we, others who are less worldly[68,66]; those who are tolerant, others who are not; those who easy[69] understand[69] and others who can[70] and will not understand, the more we talk to them the worse they become. How very often very worthy people tell their friends to be very worthy and talk to them of their belief. But just because of their talking the others cannot accept it, otherwise they would have become very worthy themselves. How very often there are people of such temperaments that the very fact of talking to them over[71] anything, causes them to take the opposite view. If you say: "It is very good," they say: "Why is it good, it is bad." If you say: "It is bad," they say: "It is good, why is it bad?" They have always the opposite attitude. There are others who take this attitude: because you say this is right, it is wrong. If you [72]should not have[72] said: it is ~~right~~ ~~wrong~~, then perhaps it could[73] have been right. They themselves could[73] have found it out.

60. Kr.Gd.: "thinking" added;
C.r., tp.: "thinking"
61. Kr.Gd.: "this housewife" changed to "his wife";
C.r., tp.: "his wife"
62. Kr.Gd.: "would" changed to "will only";
C.r., tp.: "will only"
63. Tp.: "those sweets" instead of "that sweet"
64. Kr.Gd.: "the" changed to "those";
C.r., tp.: "those"
65. Tp.: "you" added
66. Tp.: omitted, "those who are more worldly than we, others who are less worldly"
67. Kr.Gd.: "more worldly" changed to "worthier";
C.r.: "worthier"
68. Kr.Gd.: "worldly" changed to "worthy";
C.r.: "worthy"
69. Kr.Gd.: "easy" crossed out and "easily" inserted after "understand";
C.r., tp.: "easy" omitted and "easily" placed after "understand"
70. Kr.Gd.: "not" added;
C.r., tp.: "not"
71. Kr.Gd.: "over" changed to "about";
C.r., tp.: "about"
72. Kr.Gd.: "should not have" changed to "had not";
C.r., tp.: "had not"
73. Kr.Gd.: "could" changed to "might";
C.r., tp.: "might"

If you only study human nature from morning till evening, you will be amused to see the different temperaments, the different attitudes, the different grades of evolution, the different examples of human nature. It would be sufficient to keep one's lips closed and just to look at the world, just to see how it is working, to see how people talk together and how they become friends in[74] any moment, in[75] another moment they become fiends[76] over an unimportant truth[77]. What does it show? It shows that man remains a child in his nature in some part or the[46] other. He is not only[78] child in his infancy, but he is[79] child through his whole life, most[80] in some[81] part of his personality. Some part of a[82] personality remains as[83] a child's. And the better [84]you think[84], the better [85]you feel[85], the more advisable it is to keep[86] lips closed, and to observe life with open heart. Remember that when the lips[87] are opened, the senses[88] become closed. In other words, the sense that sees more than the eyes, is capable of seeing when the eyes are closed. In that way words that come from the soul of man, become audible when the lips are closed. The whole[89] mysticism, the whole[89] esoteric philosophy, is built on this principle, that there is a kind of mechanical closing and disclosing of the different senses, which is related with the closing and disclosing of the centre of different faculties. In short, it is the[90] self-control or self-discipline which is gained by the power of silence, which helps man to the attainment of a higher or a greater life. [91]How our life to ex-

74. Kr.Gd.: "in any" changed to "at one";
C.r., tp.: "one"
75. Kr.Gd.: "in" changed to "at";
C.r., tp.: "at"
76. Kr.Gd.: "fiends" changed to "enemies";
C.r., tp.: "enemies"
77. Kr.Gd.: "truth" changed to "matter";
C.r., tp.: "matter"
78. Kr.Gd.: "a" added;
C.r., tp.: "a"
79. Tp.: "a" added
80. Kr.Gd.: "mostly";
C.r., tp.: "mostly"
81. Kr.Gd.: "some" changed to "one";
C.r., tp.: "one"
82. Kr.Gd.: "a" changed to "the";
C.r., tp.: "the"
83. Kr.Gd.: "as" changed to "like";
C.r., tp.: "like"
84. Kr.Gd.: "you think" changed to "your thought";
C.r.: "your thought"
85. Kr.Gd.: "you feel" changed to "your feeling";
C.r.: "your feeling"
86. Kr.Gd.: "the" added;
C.r., tp.: "the"
87. Kr.Gd.: "lips" changed to "eyes";
C.r., tp.: "eyes"
88. Kr.Gd.: "senses" changed to "inner sight";
C.r., tp.: "inner sight"
89. Kr.Gd.: "of" added;
C.r., tp.: "of"
90. Tp.: "the" omitted
91. Kr.Gd.: "How our life to expand" changed to "How can our life be expanded?";
C.r., tp.: "How can our life be expanded?"

pand[91], how[92] the sages in the East practise silence, in order to attain what is called self-discipline, in other words, in order to gain mastery? In the first place they gain mastery over movement. A person is always liable to make movements when they are not necessary, and he shows nervousness, in other words: lack of control. There is always [93]a tendency in man[93] to be doing something. If there was nothing, he will be playing with a paper or pencil, or drawing, he will be moving something or beating time or doing something. When this tendency grows and [94]no one corrects[94], [95]no one controls[95], in the end he[96] becomes more and more nervous, and it begins to speak[97] upon a person's[98] health, because the energy which should be controlled, is being spent in every movement. And this the sages in the East attain by exercising[99] what they call postures. There are certain ways that[100] the mystic sits, certain ways that[100] the mystic stands, certain ways that[100] the mystic moves, not only the mystics of India or of Persia but also the ancient[101] Egyptians and Greeks. By studying the ancient arts, the different ways in which the ancient kings and monks and sages and ascetics used to sit or stand, we see that every way had a certain meaning, a certain secret, a certain power behind it. That secret, it seems that these ages[102] have lost, but yet it is not lost, it still remains among those who follow the inner cult. Then by taking a vow of silence for certain hours in the day, and by speaking to no one, a[103] mystic develops the power of breath and magnetism. The monk of the[104] ancient times, the Christian monks, they[105]

92. Kr.Gd.: "do" added;
C.r., tp.: "do"
93. Tp.: "in man a tendency"
94. Kr.Gd.: "no one corrects" changed to "one does not correct it";
C.r., tp.: "no one corrects it"
95. Kr.Gd.: "no one controls" changed to "one does not control it";
C.r.: "one does not control it"
96. Tp.: "he", changed by Sk. to "one"
97. Kr.Gd.: "to speak" changed to "to tell";
C.r., tp.: "to tell"
98. Kr.Gd.: "a person's" changed to "his";
C.r.: "his";
Tp.: "his", changed by Sk. to "one's"
99. Kr.Gd.: "exercising" changed to "practising";
C.r., tp.: "practising"
100. Kr.Gd.: "that" changed to "in which";
C.r., tp.: "in which"
101. Tp.: "ancient" omitted
102. Kr.Gd.: "ages" changed to "times";
C.r.: "times"
103. Kr.Gd.: "a" changed to "the";
C.r., tp.: "the"
104. Kr.Gd.: "the" crossed out;
C.r., tp.: "the" omitted
105. Kr.Gd.: "they" crossed out;
C.r., tp.: "they" omitted

[106]used to practise silence also[106]. [107]The Brahmans of ancient India, they[108] used to practise silence.[107] The Moslem saints of[109] the Arabs, they[105] used to keep silence for certain hours of the day. But that is not sufficient. When the[110] movement is suspended and when[111] lips are closed, still the mind may be pondering on different thoughts. For the mind is most difficult to control. Now the control of one's movements and the control of one's speech gives man a greater power in controlling[111] mind. And those who do not gradually develop the power of control by controlling their movement[112] and speech, and who at once wish to control their mind, they[105] find it very difficult. Therefore meditation or concentration is considered in the East a cult which is more important than religion, for this is the essence of religion. Religion is the form but this is the spirit.

One may say, "But what can we do in the West, where the activity is so great, where the life is so heavy and full of occupation and full of responsibilities, that it seems almost impossible to attain to[113] that power of silence." But in answer to this question I will always say that for the very reason that life in the West keeps man more occupied and very active, it is necessary for the Western person to give some of his time to the stilling of the activities of his body and of his mind. He spends his energy more, so he requires energy more. [114]This is part of the energy or [115]of the[115] activity[114] which food [116]nor nourishment can[116] give. The material food which only gives a certain amount of nourishment to[117] flesh and blood is not really sufficient for man, who is not only[118] made of flesh and blood[118]. For in man there are greater possibilities and many different capacities, and therefore he does not only need food or drink or sleep, but he needs something besides it, to make his life normal or full. In what we consider the present progress with all its intellectual progress, industrial and commercial, there seems to be no progress of what may be called individuality, a full expression of personality. And you see that feebleness from time to time, if[119] things went[120]

106. Kr.Gd.: "also" placed before "used" and crossed out at the end of the sentence;
C.r., tp.: "also" before "used"
107. C.r.: this sentence ("The Brahmans ... silence.") was left out.
108. Kr.Gd.: "they" crossed out;
Tp.: "they" omitted
109. Kr.Gd.: "of" changed to "among";
C.r., tp.: "among"
110. Kr.Gd.: "the" crossed out;
C.r., tp.: "the" omitted
111. Kr.Gd.: "the" added;
C.r., tp.: "the"
112. Tp.: "movements"
113. Tp.: "to" omitted
114. Kr.Gd.: "This is part of the energy or of the activity" changed to "It is energy or activity";
C.r.: "It is energy or activity"
115. Tp.: "of the" omitted
116. Kr.Gd.: "nor ... can" changed to "or ... cannot";
C.r.: "or ... cannot"
117. Kr.Gd.: "the" added;
C.r.: "the"
118. Kr.Gd.: "only" crossed out and placed after "blood";
C.r., tp.: "only" after "blood"
119. Kr.Gd.: "if" changed to "when";
C.r., tp.: "when"

as they are going just now; in music, in poetry, in art, in science, in education, a kind of feebleness[121] from time to time arises[121], for the very reason that little attention is being paid to the advancement[122] of personality, to the progress of individuality. Besides there is nothing impossible. Even after[123] the whole day's work a person does in his office or in his factory, or in the midst of the world, when he comes home, if he considered that as he requires food, as he requires sleep, so it is necessary that he must have a certain hour for his silence, for his meditation. If [124]one wished[124] it, it cannot be difficult. It is difficult because one does not count it as a certain important thing in his everyday life, as he counts his dinner. How[125] busy he is, dinner is an important thing for him. If he considered the same thing of silence, that it is an important thing, that it[126] is the dinner of the soul, then he could find some time. There are many people who may be able to find a few minutes even in the midst of the day, in the midst of the hours they give to their business or their work, to go in retirement in a corner where they can get their senses concentrated, their breath being put into rhythm, their nerves stilled, their mind and body gained[127] in hand again after the work of certain[128] hours.

The work of the Sufi Movement in the Western world is to give facility to those seekers after truth, those who wish to learn the cult of life, to give them the opportunity. It is not an activity which answers immediately those who are seeking after wonders or looking for superstitions. For unhappily today there seems to be in the spiritual awakening of the world a kind of wishing for wonderseeking, wonderworking, and a seeking after phenomena. This is not what we bring. We bring [129]simple things[129] as have been said before, simple things of life, how life can be lived fully, and how happiness which is natural, and which is also a part of ~~these beings~~ one's[130] being, can be expressed by a better understanding of life and by its prac-

120. Kr.Gd.: "went" changed to "may be going";
C.r., tp.: "may be going";
Sk.: "go" instead of "may be going"
121. Tp.: "arises" placed after "feebleness"
122. Kr.Gd.: "advancement" changed to "development";
C.r., tp.: "development"
123. Tp.: "after" omitted
124. Tp.: "he wishes" instead of "one wished"
125. Kr.Gd.: "How" changed to "However";
C.r., tp.: "However"
126. C.r.: "it" omitted
127. Kr.Gd.: "gained" changed to "got";
C.r., tp.: "got";
Sk.: "got"
128. Kr.Gd.: "certain" changed to "several";
C.r., tp.: "several"
129. Kr.Gd.: "such" added;
C.r.: "such";
Tp.: "such" placed after "things"
130. Tp.: "man's" instead of "one's"

tice. And really, although people seem to be hankering after complexities, people are looking for something which they cannot understand. If you tell them some stories or certain things, they cannot understand for which reason cannot be given, they think: "there is something, it is really something occult, because we cannot understand, it is too deep to understand." Something which makes a person confused, about that he thinks: "that is really worthwhile." And in this way this re-awakening of the spiritual truth will be blown up[131] by the wind, and no real fruit [132]is to be got[132].

The central theme of the Sufi Movement therefore is to answer the problems of the day, to provide for the simple needs of[133] daily spiritual life. A[134] personal advice on these subjects is given or training is given on such subjects in order to make man practise for himself and see for himself when[135] he himself thinks of life and its mysteries.

---

131. Kr.Gd.: "up" changed to "away";
C.r., tp.: "away"
132. Kr.Gd.: "is to be got" changed to "will be had";
C.r.: "will be had";
Tp.: "will be got"
133. Kr.Gd.: "the" added;
C.r., tp.: "the"
134. Kr.Gd.: "A" crossed out;
C.r., tp.: "A" omitted
135. C.r.: Sk. suggested to change "when" to "what";
Tp.: Sk. changed "when" to "what"

No reporting of this lecture has been found in the archives to date. The present text is from the magazine *Sufism* of March 1923.

1

The Sufi Order.[2]

[3]Report of a Lecture by Inayat Khan.[3]

Beloved ones of God,

I wish to speak a few words this evening on the Sufi Order and its work in the world. In the first place, people often wonder if it is a mission from the East. I answer that neither is it from the East or from the West, it is from Above. It is for the work of God and the service of humanity, in which people of the East and the West, of the North and the South, have all joined together as their sacred task. The word Sufi is eastern as well as western; it comes from the Greek word *Sophia*, and in the Persian language is *Sufia*, so the word should be acceptable both in the East and in the West. It is not the name of a certain sect or religion, but it is the name used for the essence of all religions. No doubt very often people confuse the word wisdom with the word intellect, but in point of fact wisdom is something springing out of the heart of man. The source of wisdom is God Himself, while intellect is knowledge gained in the world, the knowledge of names and forms; worldly cleverness cannot be compared with wisdom. Many are clever, but are they wise? Their wisdom lasts for moments or days and ends in nothingness. All success acquired by worldly cleverness is limited, and when the limited time has passed, it comes to an end. True wisdom is the divine essence hidden deep in the heart of man, and which every man is seeking, some consciously, others unconsciously. *Sophia* or *Sufism* is the name for the real wisdom, springing from the heart of man as a divine stream. In all ages those who have realized this divine spring, which is the heritage of every soul, have called it Sophia or Wisdom. It has been known by other names, [4]such as Vedanta, Bible or Scripture[4], but wisdom in all its forms and at whatever time it has been given to the world is in fact Sufism. No doubt the name was

---

Notes:

1. Although the lecture is undated, it may have been given in the latter part of January 1923, when Pir-o-Murshid was in England.
2. In October 1923 the official name became "Sufi Movement", and only the Esoteric School of the Sufi Movement was from then on called the "Sufi Order."
3. This sentence appears in the Table of Contents on the cover of the magazine.

   A copy of leaflet no. 11, obtained from Sirdar's collection of lectures, and which is a reprint of the article "The Sufi Order" in the magazine Sufism of March 1923, has a few corrections made in the handwriting of Murshida Goodenough. It is not known if these are her own corrections or if they were taken from an older version of this lecture.
4. Added by Gd. on the printed leaflet: "i.e." before "such", and "Bible or Scripture" crossed out.

adopted to distinguish institutions where the students devoted themselves to the study of metaphysics and the inner cult, to the contemplation of God, and to works of charity; and the people who belonged to these institutions were the first whenever a Divine Messenger came, in whatever country, to sympathise and to understand. Their hearts were broad enough to receive the new Message, and they were the great supports of all the Messengers. If we study the traditions of religious wars, we shall find that everywhere and in every period there has always been opposition to the message which has been given as an inspiration to men, people fighting against one another, and saying "Our God is different to your God; our Church is different; the Messenger whom you esteem is different." But to the Sufis in all ages differences do not exist; the one thing they fought against and opposed was that which divided humanity into so many sects and creeds, that the nations should fight one another instead of harmonizing with and understanding one another by the help of religion. No prophet, no Messenger, has ever brought the message to the world with the idea that his followers should be exclusive, that they should look on the followers and disciples of other faiths with hatred and contempt, or that they should say that theirs was the only true message. How many wars and battles in the history of the world have been caused by religious differences? That was not the will of God, nor the motive of the prophets, nor of religion; it was the abuse of religion, made by the authorities of religion for the sake of their own power and control over the followers of that faith. One can trace back through the history of the Hebrew prophets, that Sufism existed in the time of Abraham, who responded to the call of God, and when he came back from Egypt after his initiation it was the Sufis who gathered round him, and an association of the wise was formed. So with Jesus and Mohammed, the Sufis were the first to recognize the Divine Message, and to welcome the Messenger, to sympathise and to understand. The sympathy of the Sufis was great, because they knew how difficult it was for a human being with goodness to live in this false world, and so they realized how much greater the difficulty was for those who bore the Message of Truth. After the passing of the prophet Mohammed, one finds the Sufis existing, and having their institutions in all the civilized parts of the East--in India, China, Persia, Egypt, and Arabia. How could the Hindus and Muslems have ever existed so long side by side with their great difference of religion but for the light of the Sufi wisdom, which taught them to respect one another? Wherever in the East one finds peace among the followers of divers faiths it is by the efforts of the Sufis who lived in contemplation of Truth, and the realization of the source and goal of all beings whom we call *God*. When we consider the condition of the world to-day we find that it is not very different from the days of the past; hatred, prejudice, bitterness still exist between races and nations and the followers of different faiths. All efforts in different directions towards reform, social, commercial or political, have their limitations; they have their selfish side, but no means can be greater than the realization of the Truth, in which all human beings can unite. It is this object which has caused those interested in the service of God and humanity to form a nucleus or Brotherhood which we call the Sufi Order--an Order which consists of members of different creeds and nations. Those who constitute the Sufi Order have their own religion, their own churches, their own Scripture, their own Master whom they esteem, and to whom they offer their devotion. The Sufi Order does not ask them to change their religion, rather it helps them to understand their own religion better. It teaches them that religion cannot be confined to one creed, and that not only in religion but in every aspect of life, tolerance, love and sympathy must be developed. This is the main teaching that the Sufi Order brings to the world; that and the realization of God, not only having belief in God but knowledge; the knowledge of God which is the fulfilment of our life in the world. Belief alone does not give the full satisfaction for which the soul longs. Often great believers in God, after some deep sorrow or disappointment, after some crisis in life when they feel they have been left alone, and no notice has been taken, lose their faith; for instance, how many believers in God have lost their faith after the Great War[5], because belief in God is not sufficient? Knowledge of God is necessary, and that knowledge cannot be acquired by study only, but by a certain method which is called the Inner Cult. The Sufi Order is not a secret society; it has no secrets; if it has any, the secret is God and His realization; only this way of attainment cannot be trusted to everybody, and therefore there is an initiation, and this initiation means a reception, when the member is allowed to enter for the study of the Inner Cult. Initiation into the Sufi Order is not given that it may be talked about and discussed everywhere; it is an entrance to be kept quiet and in humble guise; for the object of the Sufi Cult is to understand, and not to make a show of understanding--to know but not to talk. The Sufi idea is that before the awakened eyes the world is asleep; people moving about and working but at the same time asleep, and according to the teaching of the prophets it is a great crime to awaken a person who has not yet completed his sleep. The work of the Order is to give a helping hand to those who are now beginning to awake; who have been blessed[6] and are changing themselves[7]. By uniting and working together they can be helped, and the entering into this help is called initiation.

Some enter the Order with the idea of the benefit they may gain by its teaching, by meditation and by the blessing that comes from joining with others who are not only interested in the culture of the soul, but work[8] to serve God and humanity by devoting their life, time and thought to the furtherance of the cause.

There are three aspects of work in the Sufi Order. The main aspect is the Esoteric side, which one enters by being received into the Order by an

5. World War I, 1914-1918.
6. "blessed" changed by Gd. on the printed leaflet to "roused"
7. "themselves" changed by Gd. on the printed leaflet to "sides"
8. "work" changed by Gd. on the printed leaflet to "want"

initiation; this is for those who are seeking after the deeper realization of Life. Another aspect is the Exoteric side of our work, which is often called the "Church of All"; it is not only the Church of All, it is in reality All Churches; where the Scriptures of all religions are held in esteem; where the Teachers of all faiths are respected, where we learn not only to offer our prayers to God but to offer our homage to Wisdom in all the aspects in which it has come to the world in all ages, through all the Teachers whether known or unknown to the world, and which has been given in all Scriptures. We observe the form of all the religions of the world which have followers to-day, so that no one attending the service of the Church of All may feel that his religion is not respected in the Church which has no limitations, which acknowledges no differences, the Church which is the Church of the day, and which before long will be the Church of the World.

The third aspect of this movement is the work of promoting the ideal of Brotherhood which is so much needed everywhere to-day. Leaving the East aside, even if we think only of Europe, of the hatred and prejudice existing; so much that if it goes on one cannot think what will be the end, for it is already paralysing social, political and commercial life. Imagine what is the psychic effect of the Great War[5] resulting in millions of deaths, and of the deaths from the famine in Russia, what poisonous vibrations have been set going; for life is creative--if one sows weeds, weeds will grow; if corn, then corn.

The Sufi Message is therefore the answer to the call of humanity; it is service to God and man, with no distinction of caste, creed, race, nation or religion.

Sakina's shorthand reporting, transcribed by the compiler.

Winter 1923[1]

2

3

My subject of discourse this evening will be, "The[4] Life a Continual Battle."

No one in this world, whatever be his position or experience in life, will deny the fact that life means a continual battle. And therefore one's success, failure, happiness or unhappiness mostly depends upon one's knowledge about this battle. Whatever be one's occupation in life, whatever be one's knowledge, if one lacks the knowledge of the battle of life, one lacks the main knowledge which is most important in life.

Now the question arises what that[5] knowledge of[6] life's battle contains. It contains the knowledge of warfare: how to battle and how to make a[7] peace. And as human nature has[8], it is usual, or very often, has one mistake, and that is that it takes one side, either the side of war or[9] the side of peace. And if you will study the history of nations and races, you will find that it is this mistake which has[10] caused the failure of nations and races. For an instance there have been times when nations and races have developed in their character the knowledge of peace. For an instance people such as the Hindus of the most ancient civilization. But it could not bring that satisfaction which was necessary, for the reason that one side of human

Documents:

Sk.sh.
Lf. (an incomplete reporting in the hwr. of M.lle Lefèbvre of a simultaneously given French translation of the lecture).
Sk.l.tp.
Tp. (a typed copy of Sk.l.tp. with a few changes).

This lecture was first published in the magazine *Soufisme* of December 1927 in a French translation. In 1962 it was published in *The Sufi Message of Hazrat Inayat Khan*, Volume VI.

Notes:

1. Lf.: added "16, Av. Victor Emmanuel", the house of Baronne d'Eichthal in Paris where the lecture was given, and the date "5th February";
   Although the lecture appears in Sk.sh. in her copybook "Summer 1922, Winter 1923", in Sk.l.tp. by mistake the year 1922 instead of 1923 was written above.
2. Sk.sh., Sk.l.tp.: added above the lecture "Life a continual Battle"
3. Sk.l.tp.: "Beloved Ones of God,"
4. Tp.: "The" omitted
5. Sk.l.tp.: "this" instead of "that"
6. Ibid.: "in", changed back by Sk. to "of"
7. Ibid.: "a" omitted, but reinserted by Sk.
8. Ibid.: "has" omitted
9. Tp.: "of" mistyped for "or"
10. Ibid.: "has" omitted

nature was neglected and not understood. Now at this present age it seems that the knowledge of battle has developed, but on the other side the knowledge of peace is absent. For the full knowledge of warfare is the knowledge of battle and the knowledge of peace. And this can be learned according to the idea of the mystics by battling one's self and by bringing about peace with one's own soul.[11]

The life of an individual being is not much different from the life of the world. An individual person's home is not different from the world, and individual's body and mind and spirit make[12] the whole universe.

An individual life can fill the gap between the dawn of creation and the last day.

Man does not realize how important is his own life, his self. And it is the study of his own life and his self[13] is the study of the greatest importance. For an instance, a healthy person has waiting at his door several illnesses, several diseases, waiting the opportunity when they can attack him. A person with wealth has many waiting at his door to get the occasion to take away from him what he possesses. A person about whom good is said, how many there are awaiting a chance, a moment that something bad may be said about it. A person who has a power, a position, how many awaiting the opportunity to pull him down and to see him slide down from the place where he stands. And what does it show? Often one may ask the reason, [14]"Why is it so?"[14] You may give a thousand reasons and you cannot give one proper reason. The best explanation[15] is that life is one continual battle. The process of creation has begun like this. According to the science, the light comes from the friction. It is one power against the other power fighting, and by those[16] two different forces striking, there comes out an effect. And that effect really speaking may be called life. And in this lies the secret of love and hate both. One sees therefore in the animal creation that the animals have as their instinct the first tendency to fight one another. And this tendency becomes modified, and it is its modification and its reduced force what[17] produces[18] them what we call virtues.

11. Sk.sh.: Here follows an empty space, nearly half a line. It is uncertain if something has been omitted, or if just a new paragraph begins;
    Sk.l.tp.: The empty space was disregarded and a full stop added after "soul"
12. Sk.sh.: In sh. Sk. uses the same sign for "make" and for "makes";
    Sk.l.tp.: "makes"
13. Sk.sh., Sk.l.tp.: a small empty space, where "that" or "which" may have been said
14. Sk.l.tp.: "Why is it so?" lacks quotation marks
15. Sk.sh.: "that you can give" inserted by Sk. in sh.;
    Sk.l.tp.: "that you can give"
16. Sk.l.tp.: "that" read by Sk. for "those";
    Tp.: "those"
17. Sk.l.tp.: "that" instead of "what"
18. Ibid.: "in" added

As it is said in the[19] Qur'an, the world was created out of darkness. So one can see that wisdom comes out of ignorance. And the best knowledge is not only the knowledge of all that is good and beautiful, all that is harmonious and peaceful, but knowledge of the causes that are behind all conflicts and all the battles that one has to face in life. And the reason why man generally lacks this knowledge is because when he is faced to a battle, he wants to battle instead of wanting to learn it. And the one who without attaining the knowledge of warfare goes in life's battle, ~~both~~ he in the end loses. But the one [20]who all this warfare of life first learns, learns its reason,[20] learns its cause, he becomes more capable of fighting the battle of his life. It is pointing to this secret that Christ has said that, "Resist not evil." This[21] means that if at every time something that appears to you wrong or unjust in another person, you will resist it or you will fight your battle, by that you will always lose your power. For the competent general is not the one who always attacks. The competent general is the one who stands in defence more firm. His success is more secure than the one who continually attacks. Very often one sees in one's everyday life that by losing one's temper with someone who has lost already his temper, one does not gain anything, except striking the path of stupidity. The one who has self-control enough to stand firm at that moment when another person is in temper, he in the end wins the battle. It is not the one who has spoken a hundred words aloud who has won. It is the one perhaps who has spoken one word. ~~Hundred words are nothing-~~

Now for this battle in life the first thing that is necessary is to keep the army in order. And what is this army? This army is one's nervous power. Whatever be one's occupation, one's profession, one's walk in life, if one has not the control of one's own nerves, one will be unable to control one's work[22] in life. Today people are seeking for the study of political economy, and different kinds of ec.[23], but the most essential economy is economising the forces which make one healthy and strong through life. Now this army must be drilled and must be made to work at the command. And one will find its proof that when one can sleep at one's will, when one can rest[24], work at one's will, then really that army is at one's command. Now, then there are the officers of this army, and these officers are the faculties of mind. Now these faculties of mind are five: the f.[25] of retaining thought, the f.[25] of thinking [26], the f.[25] of feeling [26], f.[25] of reasoning [27]and judging[27], and

19. Ibid.: "the" omitted;
Tp.: "the"
20. Sk.l.tp.: Rewritten to read: "who learns this warfare of life, first learns its reasons,"
21. Ibid.: "That" instead of "this"
22. Ibid.: Sk. read "walk" for "work"
23. Ibid.: "economy", abbreviated in Sk.sh. to "ec."
24. Sk.sh.: added "and eat" in lh.;
Sk.l.tp.: "and eat"
25. Sk.l.tp.: "faculty", abbreviated in Sk.sh. to "f."
26. Sk.sh.: an empty space;
Sk.l.tp.: a comma
27. Sk.l.tp.: "and judging" omitted, but reinserted by Sk.

that f.[25] in man which is the principal f.[25], the feeling of "I" or ego. Even with a body with strong nerves, when these five f.[28] which work as the generals of the army, if they[29] are not working in order, if they are not clear, then ~~when~~- one cannot expect a success in life's warfare. And there is a further study, or the practice in the art of training these generals of the army in one's own body.

But now the question comes that even with an army and with competent generals, that one must have the knowledge[30] that against what one is battling. For very often man is battling with his own real interest. During the battle it is an intoxication, he is battling, he does not know where he is going. But at the end of the battle, even if victorious, he finds in his victory his loss.

Now today that[31] there seems to be a great seeking and enthusiasm everywhere to be found. There seems to be a kind of new interest aroused in humanity, to understand life and truth more. There is a very large number in humanity who are looking for the best way of gaining the power in order to battle through life, and there is a small number again who are looking for some way of bringing peace to themselves and to others. But both these in their pursuit lack that balance which can be only brought about by understanding, by studying, and by practising the knowledge of war and peace both together. Without knowing about the war, one cannot know thoroughly about the peace. Without understanding the peace, one cannot know thoroughly about the war. What is necessary at the present is the study of life in general, and in that study the knowledge of such questions as the purpose of life, what is really beneficial in life, what is nature and where is the goal. It is no use trying to practise something before studying it. What does world-wise mean? It means expert in this warfare of life, who knows how to battle, how to make a peace, why to battle, and what aim is accomplished by a peace.

And this must be understood, that the battle with oneself is peace and battle with another is war. And once a person has not practised with oneself, he cannot be [32]very well[32] competent to battle with others. Perhaps all this creation, when one finds out the secret that is hidden, it is only this: that out of one life as the origin and the goal of all, this life of variety has come. Therefore the nature of that life from which this[21] world of variety has come, is peace, and the nature of this life of variety is war. Therefore neither one can be without war, nor one can be without peace. Therefore to say that the war in life must end, one may say it, but yet it

28. Ibid.: "faculties", abbreviated in Sk.sh. to "f."
29. Ibid.: "these" instead of "they"
30. Ibid.: "of" added
31. Sk.sh.: "that" crossed out by Sk.;
    Sk.l.tp.: "that" omitted
32. Sk.sh.: "very well" added in sh.;
    Sk.l.tp.: "very well" omitted

makes no meaning. One might just as well say that the world of variety must not exist. Where there is plurality, there must be a conflict. And although c.[33] seems a tragedy, but the true tr.[34] is the ignorance. And therefore instead of wanting to end the battle of life, or instead of opposing the peace, what one must do is the[35] get the knowledge of life and attain to that wisdom which is the purpose of life.

[36]

---

33. Sk.l.tp.: "conflict", abbreviated in Sk.sh. to "c."
34. Ibid.: "tragedy", abbreviated in Sk.sh. to "tr."
35. Sk.sh.: "the" in sh., apparently a mistake;
    Sk.l.tp.: "to"
36. Sk.l.tp.: "God bless you"

Sakina's shorthand transcribed by the compiler.

Suresnes, Winter 1923[1]

2

3

4

[5]I wish to continue this evening the subject on which I have spoken: "Life a Continual Battle".[5]

In this continual battle of life, the one who stands through it all comes[6] in the end victorious. But with all power and understanding, [7]if one gives oneself[7] up by the lack of hope and courage, [8]has failed.

What brings bad luck in this life, in this battle? [9]Pessimistic attitude. And what helps man to conquer[10] the b.[11] of life, [12]however difficult it is? An optimistic attitude[12].

Documents:

Sk.sh.
Sr. (Sirdar's lh.r. with several omissions, sometimes words taken down from the simultaneous translations into French after each sentence spoken in English).
Lf. (an incomplete r. in the hwr. of Mlle Lefèbvre, of the simultaneously given French translation of the lecture).
Sk.lh. (a hwr. copy of "Sk.sh."; with corr. by Gd.).
Sk.l.tp. (a later typescript, made from "Sk.lh.", without most of the corr. by Gd.).
Tp. (a typewritten c. of "Sk.l.tp." with a few changes).

This lecture was first published in the magazine *Soufisme* of December 1927 in a French translation. In 1962 it was published in *The Sufi Message of Hazrat Inayat Khan*, Vol. VI.

Notes:

1. Lf.: added, "16, Av. Victor Emmanuel", the house of Baronne d'Eichthal in Paris where the lecture was given, and the date "12th February";
Sk.lh.: "? 1922 ? 1923, ? Paris Reported by Sakina Furnée" added above the lecture in Gd.'s hwr.;
Sk.l.tp.: although the lecture appears in Sk.sh. in her copybook "Summer 1922, Winter 1923", by mistake the year 1922 instead of 1923 was written above.
2. Sk.sh.: Sk. added "Life a continual Battle (cont.)" in lh. above;
Sk.lh.: Sk. added "Life a continual Battle II";
Sk.l.tp.: added, "Life a continual Battle. (Cont.)"
3. Sk.lh.: "Beloved Ones of God,", crossed out by Gd.
4. Sk.sh.: Sk. added in the margin "(sent to H.q.)"
5. Ibid.: this sentence was crossed out by Gd.
6. Sr.: "becomes";
Sk.lh.: Gd. put "comes" in parentheses and wrote "is" above
7. Sk.lh.: first changed by Gd. to "if he gives himself", then changed back by her to "if one gives oneself"
8. Ibid.: Sk. added "he";
Sk.l.tp.: "one" added
9. Sk.lh.: Gd. added "The", then crossed it out and wrote "A" instead.
10. Ibid.: Gd. changed "conquer" to "win"
11. All other documents: "battle". Sk. used the abbreviation "b." in her sh.
12. Sk.l.tp.: repunctuated to read, "however difficult, it is an optimistic attitude"

There are some in this world who look at life with pessimistic view, thinking that it is clever to see the dark side of things. [13]So far it is[13] beneficial that one sees also the difficult side, but the psychological law[14] is such that once the spirit[15] impressed with[16] the difficulty of the situation[17] loses its hope and courage. Once a person asked me if I was looking[18] at life with a pessimistic attitude or if I was[19] an optimist. I said, "[20]Optimist with open eyes." Optimism is good as long as the eyes are open. But once[21] eyes are closed, then the[22] optimism can be dangerous.

In this battle a[23] drill is necessary and that[24] drill is the control over[25] one's physical organs, a control upon the faculties of mind. Because if one is not prepared for this battle, however much[26] courageous and optimistic[27], ~~one~~ he cannot succeed. Another thing is to know something about this warfare. It is knowing to [28]make a[28] retreat and to make[29] advance. If one does not know the making of the retreat and one wishes always to advance, he[30] will always be in danger and become[31] victim to[32] life's battle.

There are many people who so to speak in the intoxication in life's battle, go on battling, go on fighting; in the end they will meet with failure. People young and strong and hopeful [33]in life[33], who have had less difficulties, they[34] think[35] nothing but to battle against all that stands before

13. Sk.lh.: reordered by Gd. to read, "It is so far"
14. Ibid.: "thought", changed by Gd. to "condition"
15. Ibid.: "is" added by Gd.;
    Sk.l.tp.: "is"
16. Sk.lh.: "by" instead of "with"
17. Ibid.: "it" added by Gd.;
    Sk.l.tp.: "it" added
18. Sk.lh.: first Gd. changed "was looking" to "look", then put back "was looking"
19. Ibid.: first Gd. changed "was" to "am", then again put "was"
20. Ibid.: Gd. added "An"
21. Ibid.: "the" added
22. Ibid.: "the" crossed out by Gd.
23. Ibid.: "a" crossed out by Gd.
24. Ibid.: "this" instead of "that"
25. Ibid.: Gd. changed "over" to "of"
26. Ibid.: Gd. crossed out "much"
27. Ibid.: Gd. added "one is"
28. Ibid.: Gd. first crossed out "make a", then again put it back
29. Ibid.: Gd. first added "an" after "make", then crossed out "make an", but finally changed it back to "make an"
30. Ibid.: "one" instead of "he"
31. Ibid.: Gd. added "a"
32. Ibid.: Gd. changed "to" to "in"
33. Ibid.: Gd. first crossed out "in life", then put it back
34. Ibid.: "who", changed back by Sk. to "they"
35. Ibid.: Gd. added "of"

them. They do not know that it is not always wise to advance. What is necessary is [36]to make the place first fortified[36], and then[37] advance. The same thing one can see in friendship, in business, in profession. A person who does not understand the secret of the law of warfare cannot succeed. Besides this, to protect one's own from all sides. Very often what one does is in that intoxication of the battle, [38]he goes on,[38] forward and forward and forward, not protecting what belongs to him[39]. How many people in the courts and in the [40]cases at the[40] law[41] for a very little thing perhaps will be spending and spending a lot of money. In the end the loss is greater than the success. Again how many in this world will only because for[42] their fancy or pride, [43]will perhaps[43] lose[44] than[45] gain. There are times when one must give in, there are times that one must let things loose a little bit, and there are times when[46] one must hold fast the rein[47] of[48] life. There are moments when[49] one must be persistent and there are moments when one must be easy.

Friends[50], life is such an intoxication that although everybody thinks that he is working for his interest, but[51] hardly you will find one among thousands who is really working for his interest, and the reason is that they become so absorbed in what they are trying to get, that they become intoxicated by it, and they so to speak lose the track that leads to real success. Very often people, in order to get one particular benefit, sacrifice many other benefits because they do not think of them. The thing is to look all around, not only in one direction. It is easy to be powerful, it is easy to be good, but it is most difficult to be wise. And it is the wise who is truly victorious in life. And the success of those with power and with goodness, perhaps it all has its limitation. If I were to tell you how many people bring about their failures[52] themselves, you will[53] be surprised [54]that there is

36. Ibid.: Gd. first reordered the sentence to read, "first to fortify the place", but changed it back
37. Ibid.: Gd. added "to"
38. Ibid.: Gd. changed "he goes on," to "one goes"
39. Ibid.: Gd. changed "him" to "one"
40. Ibid.: Gd. crossed out "cases at the"
41. Ibid.: Gd. added "suits"
42. Ibid.: Gd. changed "for" to "of"
43. Ibid.: "perhaps" omitted, but reinserted by Sk., and "will" crossed out by Sk.
44. Sk.lh., Sk.l.tp.: "more" added
45. Sk.lh.: Gd. added "they"
46. Ibid.: "that" instead of "when"
47. Sk.l.tp.: "reign" instead of "rein"
48. Sk.lh.: "in," changed back by sk. to "of"
49. Ibid.: "that", changed back by Sk. to "when"
50. Ibid.: "Friends" crossed out by Gd.
51. Ibid.: Gd. changed "but" to "yet"
52. Sk.l.tp.: "failure"
53. Sk.lh.: Gd. changed "will" to "would"
54. Ibid.: Sk. wrote in the margin, "repetition" (see the beginning of this paragraph)

hardly one person among one[55] hundred who really works for his real benefit, although everyone thinks that he is working for his benefit[54]. The difference is that he does not think where is his real interest. The nature of life is illusive[56]. Under a gain, a loss is hidden. Under a loss a gain is hidden. And under this illusion first it is very difficult for man to realize what is really good for him. And even for a wise person much of his wisdom is asked[57] by life and by its battle. You cannot be enough gentle, you cannot be sufficiently kind. The more[58] you give ~~the more~~ to the life[58], the more the[22] life asks of you. There again is a battle. Yes, no doubt the gain of the wise is greater in the end, although he has many apparent losses. When[59] an ordinary person will not give in, the wise will give in a thousand times. This shows that the success of the wise very often is hidden in his[60] apparent failure. But when one compares the success of the wise with that of the ordinary person, the success of the wise is much greater.

[61]In this battle, a battery is needed, and that battery is the power of will. In this[62] battle of life, arms are needed. And these arms are the thoughts and actions which work psychologically towards one's success. For an[63] instance, there is a person who says to himself every morning: "Everybody is against me, nobody likes me, everything is wrong, everywhere is injustice, all is failure, for me there is no hope." When he goes out, he takes that[64] influence with him. Before he arrives at any place, business, profession, or whatever he does, he has sent his influence before him, and he meets with all wrong and all fatal[65], nothing worthwhile, coldness everywhere. There is another one, yes, who knows what human nature is, who knows that one has to meet with all selfishness, all inconsideration all over[66]. But what does he think of all this? He thinks it is a lot of all[67] drunken people. He thinks they are all[68] falling upon each other, fighting each other, offending each other. And naturally a sober person with some thought will not trouble with the drunken. He will help them, he will not

55. Sk.lh., Sk.l.tp.: "one" omitted
56. Sk.lh.: Gd. changed "illusive" to "illuding"
57. Sk.sh.: before writing the sh.-sign for "asked", Sk. seems to have written another word, which could be "demanded". Afterwards Sk. crossed out "asked" and wrote "demanded" instead in lh.;
Sk.lh., Sk.l.tp.: "demanded"
58. Sk.lh.: Gd. changed "The more you give to the life" to "The more to life you give"
59. Ibid.: Sk. wrote the Dutch word "terwijl" meaning "whereas" in parentheses above "When", explaining what the word "when" here means.
60. Ibid.: "an" instead of "his"
61. Ibid.: although in this document no new paragraph follows, Sk. wrote in the margin, "new paragraph"
62. Ibid.: "that", changed back by Sk. to "this"
63. Ibid.: Gd. crossed out "an"
64. Ibid.: "this" instead of "that"
65. Sk.sh.: Sk. wrote "fatal" in lh.;
Sr.: "fatal";
Sk.l.tp.: "failures" instead of "fatal"
66. Sk.lh.: Gd. changed "all over" to "everywhere"
67. Ibid.: "all" crossed out by Gd.
68. Ibid.: "all" omitted

take seriously what they say or do. Therefore naturally in this world of drunkenness a person who is drunken has a greater fight than[69] who is sober, for he will always avoid it, for he will tolerate, he will give in, he will understand, for he knows that they are drunken. You cannot expect [70]from them better[70]. Besides this the wise knows a secret of this nature, and this[71] secret is that the[22] human nature is imitative. For an[63] instance, a proud person will always revive the tendency of pride in his surroundings; before a humble person, even a proud person will become humble, because he vivifies the humbleness in that person. Now, then you can see that in this life's battle you can fight with the proud with pride,[72] and you can fight with[73] the pride with humility, and sometimes gain. Besides this from a wise p.o.v.[74] human nature is childish. If one stands in the crowd and looks at it as a spectator[75], one will see a lot of children playing together. They are playing and they are fighting and they are snatching things from each[76] other's hands, and they are bothering about very unimportant things. One finds their thoughts small and less important, and so their pursuit through life[77] and the reason of the life's battle very often is very small when it is looked at ~~with the~~ in the light of wisdom. And this shows that the knowledge of life does not always come by battling. It comes by throwing light upon it. He is not a warrior who becomes impatient in one moment, who loses his temper in one moment, who has no control on[78] his impulses, who is ready to give up hope and courage. The true warrior is he who can endure, who has a great capacity in him to tolerate, who has depth enough in his heart to assimilate all things, whose mind reaches[79] far enough to understand all things, whose every desire is to understand others and to make them understand. It must be understood that sensitiveness is no doubt a human development, but if it is not used rightly, it has its[80] great many disadvantages. A sensitive person can lose courage and hope much sooner than another person[81]. A sensitive person can be quickly friends, and can run away quickly from his friends. A s.[82] person is ready to take offences[83][84]and ready to take[84] all things that come to him, and the[22] life can become unbearable for him. And if a person is not sensitive, then he is not fully living. Therefore the idea is to be sensitive and not to abuse it. Abusing sensitive-

69. Ibid.: Gd. added "one"
70. Ibid.: reordered by Gd. to read, "better from them"
71. Sk.l.tp.: "that" instead of "this"
72. Sr.: "and you can lose;"
73. Tp.: "with" omitted
74. All other documents: "point of view"
75. Tp.: "speculator" instead of "spectator"
76. Sk.lh.: "the" changed by Sk. to "each"
77. Sk.l.tp.: "life. And"
78. Sk.lh.: Gd. changed "on" to "over"
79. Ibid.: "seeks" instead of "reaches", but changed back by Gd. to "reaches"
80. Ibid.: Gd. crossed out "its"
81. Ibid.: Gd. crossed out "person"
82. All other documents: "sensitive". Sk. used the abbreviation "s." in her sh.
83. Sk.lh.: Gd. crossed out the "s" of the plural.
84. Ibid.: Gd. crossed out "and ready to take" and added "in".

ness is yielding to every impression and every impulse that attacks one. There must be a balance between sensitiveness and between[85] the[22] willpower. By willpower one must be able to endure all influences, all conditions, all attacks that ~~come-to~~ one meets with[86] from morning to evening. And by sensitiveness one must be able to feel life, to appreciate and to live in the beauty of life.

In conclusion to what I have said just now, I would like to tell you that the most advisable thing in life is to be sensitive enough to feel life and its beauty, and to appreciate it, but at the same time to consider that your soul is divine, [87]and all else is a foreign thing for it[87], and that all that belongs to the earth is a foreign thing for your soul. It must not touch your soul. All things come before the eyes. When the [88]objects come[88] before the eyes, [89]they come[89] in the eyes. When they are gone, the eyes are clear, and therefore your mind must retain nothing but all beauty, all that is beautiful. For one can search God in His beauty. All else must be forgotten. And by making that practice every day, forgetting all that is disagreeable, [90]which is[91] ugly[90] [92] and to remember [93]only all[93] that is beautiful, which gives happiness [94] one will attract to oneself all happiness that is in store.

Question: *By the cultivation of willpower does one not sometimes wrongly[95] persuade[96] oneself? One is not infallible.*

Answer: Yes, there is that danger, but there is danger in everything. There is a danger in being healthy even. But that does not mean that one must be ill. But what I have said is that we must acquire balance between power and wisdom. If the power is working without the light of wisdom behind[97], the power always will fail, because the power will prove to be blind in the end. But now, you will tell me, what is the use of the wise person without the use of his hands and feet, one who has no power

85. Ibid.: Gd. crossed out "between".
86. Tp.: "with" omitted
87. Sk.lh.: Gd. crossed out "and all else is a foreign thing for it".
88. Ibid.: "object comes" changed back by Sk. to "objects come"; Sk.l.tp.: "object comes"
89. Sk.lh.: "it comes", changed back by Sk. to "they come"
90. Sk.l.tp.: "which is ugly" omitted
91. Tp.: "is" omitted
92. Sk.sh. and Sk.l.tp.: an empty space; Sr.: "in the past and present"; Sk.lh.: a comma instead of the empty space
93. Sk.lh.: "all only", changed back by Gd. to "only all"; Sk.l.tp.: "only" omitted, but reinserted by Sk. before "all"
94. Sk.sh.: an empty space; Sk.lh., Sk.l.tp.: a comma in place of the empty space
95. Sk.lh.: "wrongly" omitted
96. Ibid.: Gd. wrote "mislead" above "persuade".
97. Ibid.: Gd. crossed out "behind".

of action, no power of thought? This shows that the[22] wisdom directs, but by power one accomplishes. Therefore for the battle of life both are necessary.

Question: *In what measure can free will counteract a condition of karma such as ill health?*

Answer: [98]This I must tell you, that a[99] difference between human and divine is the difference of[100] two ends of the same line. Now one point represents limitation, the other point represents the unlimited. One point represents imperfection, the other perfection. But if we take all human beings of this world, they all[101] do not stand near the same point. They fill the gap between the one extreme and the other. Although [102]just now the world[102] is going through such a phase of the idea of what they call equality, that the nobility of the soul even to[103] its divinity is ignored. The whole arrangement of life is just now like this. When there is one vote for everybody in the state, then the same thing in the home, the same thing everywhere. But when we come to understand the spiritual life of things, we shall always realize that just like[104] in the piano all[105] notes are not the same, so all the souls are not the same souls. Man starts his life as a mechanism, a machine, and can develop to[106] the state where he is the engineer. Therefore the restriction of a[107] karma is for the machine. No doubt every soul has to be a machine once, in order to be an engineer later, and that[108] one does not turn out[109] at once into an e.[110] But one gradually changes out of a m.[111] into an e.[110] Therefore the influence of the[22] k.[112] on every soul is not the same. And at the same time one must realize that it is after all the ignorance of the divine part of one's soul that keeps one away from God, not only from

98. Ibid.: Gd. added "For" before "This".
99. Sk.lh., Sk.l.tp.: "the" in place of "a"
100. Sk.lh.: Gd. changed "of" into "between the"
101. Ibid.: Gd. placed "all" before "stand"
102. Ibid.: "the world just now", changed back by Sk. to "just now the world"
103. Ibid.: Gd. crossed out "to".
104. Ibid.: Gd. changed "like" to "as".
105. Ibid.: Gd. added "the".
106. Tp.: "to" omitted
107. Sk.lh.: Gd. crossed out "a".
108. Ibid.: Gd. crossed out "that".
109. Ibid.: Gd. crossed out "out".
110. All other documents: "engineer". Sk. used the abbreviation "e." in her sh.
111. Ibid.: "machine". Sk. used the abbreviation "m." in her sh.
112. Ibid.: "karma". Sk. used the abbreviation "k." in her sh.

God, but from the birthright of his[113] power. But [114]when one[114] becomes conscious of the divine power, then one rises above being the m.[111], then one becomes the e.[110]

Question: *Does not sensitiveness bring surprises for us, which come upon us too quickly for us to avoid the evil they cause?*

Answer: What is s.[115]? S.[115] is life itself. And as life has its good and evil, so s.[115] has its good and evil. And if one expects all its experience[116], so from s.[115] all experience[116] must come. However, as I have said that[108] s.[115] must be kept in order to know and understand, and know and appreciate all that is beautiful. And not to attract all depressions and all sorrows and all sadness and all the woes of the earth[117]. Once a person has become so s.[118] as to become offended with everybody, and to feel that everybody is against him, trying to wrong him, then he is abusing[119] his sensitiveness. He must be wise together with being s.[118] He must realize before being s.[118] that he is in this world among children, among drunken men. And as one would take the actions of the children and the drunken ones, in that[120] way all that comes[121] must be taken. Then s.ness[122] can be beneficial. If with s.ness[122] one has not developed one's willpower, it is certainly dangerous. No doubt, spirituality is seen in a person who is s.[118] to feel others. No one can [123]spiritually develop[123] without being s.[118]

Question: *How can one distinguish between the difference of the wisdom of the warrior and his want[124] of courage in the battle of life?*

Answer: Everything is distinguished by its result. There is a very well-known saying in English: "All is well that ends well." If in the end of the battle the one who was apparently defeated has really conquered, of course that was his wisdom, that was not

113. Sk.lh.: Gd. changed "his" to "His";
Sk.l.tp.: "one's" instead of "his"
114. Sk.lh.: "one when", changed back by Sk. to "when one"
115. All other documents: "sensitiveness". Sk. used the abbreviation "s." in her sh.
116. Sk.l.tp.: "experiences"
117. Sk.lh.: "world", changed back by Sk. to "earth"
118. All other documents: "sensitive". Sk. used the abbreviation "s." in her sh.
119. Sk.lh.: Gd. changed "abusing" to "misusing".
120. Ibid.: "this" instead of "that"
121. Sk.sh.: afterwards Sk. added "from all sides" in sh.;
Sk.lh., Sk.l.tp.: "from all sides" added
122. All other documents: "sensitiveness". Sk. used the abbreviation "s.ness" in her sh.
123. Sk.lh.: "spiritually develop" changed to "develop spiritually" by Gd.;
Sk.l.tp.: "be spiritually developed"
124. Sk.l.tp.: "lack" instead of "want"

his lack of courage. Very often that apparent courage leads to nothing but disappointment in the end. Bravery is one thing, the knowledge of warfare is another. Brave is brave, but not victorious always. The one who is victorious knows, understands; he knows the law of life.

From one of Pir-o-Murshid Inayat Khan's notebooks of 1923. The poem was also found in an old typescript in a somewhat different version, as an introduction to a lecture known to have been given on board the ship "Pittsburgh" of the White Star Line, in the Bay of New York, on 26th February 1923.

[1]

[2]Ideal among nations[2], [3]in principle free,
[4]Child but wide awake
[5]America blessed be[5].
Thy heart is open to all, [6]old and young[6] alike
[4]High note of brotherhood,
indeed thou dost strike.
Thou hast inherited
the [7]knowledge from all[7]
And thou givest[8] the[9] same
to those[10] on thee call.
[11]O desire[11] of nations, in thee we all meet.
Blessed America, thee I humbly greet.

Beloved ones of God:

My coming to the United States at this time when the world has not yet arrived at its normal state, after the great strain of war, is to awaken in souls the consciousness of brotherhood, on the principle of which this great nation was founded. The central theme of the formation of the Constitution of the United States of America, and the undertone of Abraham Lincoln's noble reform, was brotherhood.

Documents:

Nbk. (leaves of Pir-o-Murshid's notebooks of 1923, given here as the original version).
O.t. (old typescript with a later version of the poem than the one found in the "Nbk.").
Hq.t.

After 1927 this lecture was made a Gatheka (no. 40).

Notes:

1. O.t., hq.t.: added "My greetings to America!" above the poem
2. Ibid.: "The desire of all nations" instead of "Ideal among nations"
3. Ibid.: "and" added
4. Ibid.: "a" added
5. Ibid.: "blessed America be" instead of "America blessed be"
6. Ibid.: "to friend and foe" instead of "old and young"
7. Ibid.: "sense of nations all" instead of "knowledge from all"
8. Ibid.: "bestowest" instead of "givest"
9. O.t.: "the" omitted
10. O.t., hq.t.: "who" added
11. O.t.: "Oh! Ideal" instead of "O desire";
    Hq.t.: "Ideal"

The nation which was nursed with the milk of the ideal of brotherhood from its infancy, is the one to be attuned to its predisposition at this time of the world's greatest need.

In spite of the wonderful phenomena that science has produced through the modern civilization, if a sober minded person reflects on the question if we are really progressing, an answer will come to him, not altogether. If we ask ourselves what is missing, we shall realize without difficulty that it is the ideal which expands the limited soul to perfection, which raises the mortal to God.

It is the all-prevailing[12] materialism and the flood of overwhelming commercialism which has drowned the ideal. The nations of today stand in the quest of their own material benefit regardless of other nations, in the same way as an individual today who is called a practical man, proves to be best qualified in guarding his interests in life. This has made the world a battlefield of continual struggles where life is nothing but a chaos; the world which was purposed to be the place of aspiration, rest and peace.

The education today tends to teach the youth the best way to acquire, own and possess all the goods of this earth, and naturally the more souls become qualified by this education, the greater the struggle of life becomes. The competition which exists today in trade and profession seems to lead man to the tendencies of the primitive man. As relations between nations are only based upon their material interests, so in the same way relations between individuals exist. It has blunted all the fineness and beauty of unselfish, friendly devotion.

In order to bring humanity to the realization of the law of beneficence, it is not necessary that a new religion be taught. It is the light of truth thrown upon every religion that will bring to human perception wisdom, which is the underlying stream behind all the great religions of the world.

The good tidings that the Sufi Message brings to the world, is the recognition of the Divine in the soul of man. The knowledge of living right is the only religion which will answer the need of the world. The efforts of the Sufi Movement are directed to bring mankind to understand that the real well-being of each depends on the well-being of all. The whole humanity is as one body, all nations its different members, and the pain and injury caused to one nation, in time develops into the disorder of the whole.

12. Hq.t.: "all pervading" instead of "all-prevailing"

The Sufi Message is the answer to the cry of humanity for it warns souls to unite beyond all differences and distinctions between caste, creed, nation and religion.

May your ideal of liberty expand to the liberty of nations. May your principle of freedom rise to the height of freedom of souls. May the message of God reach far and wide, illuminating and making the whole humanity one brotherhood, in the Fatherhood of God.

From a New York newspaper, *The Evening Telegram*, 13 March 1923

New York, February[1]

"The great need of America, and of humanity, is that men understand one another. Humanity is prone to forget reality, because the life of the world is so absorbing. It is a lack of the knowledge of reality that leads to misunderstanding.

"I do not say it is America's duty to lead the world. That is not a duty, but conditions in the world today have placed America where she can lead, and if she leads others will follow."

When asked if he thought America was living up to the things she should be doing ... "I would have to study America before I could feel qualified to answer that question. But I can say that America has always meant to do her best.

"I am not concerned with politics at all. I am interested in the humanitarian side of the world. If the general attitude develops, humanity will think and act better and the effect will be seen in politics as well as in education, social relations and religion.

"The day humanity awakens to the need of brotherhood, conditions will be better in all the affairs of the world. It matters not what religion a man professes. This is not the time to advance any particular sect, church, or belief. We have too many sects. They are only the outer forms. The things that really matter are deeper.

"I have always hope. Hope is my greatest strength. I do not require that my hopes be fulfilled as fuel to keep the fire burning. My hopes are kept alive in my faith."

Note:

1. Although this article was not published until March 13, Pir-o-Murshid Inayat Khan was in New York only from February 26 through March 5, when he went on to Boston and then Detroit. As his lectures are indicated as in the future in this article, it is assumed to be from early in his stay, perhaps February 27.

From a New York newspaper, *The World*, March 18, 1923

New York, March[1]

"When I was here in 1911 and 1912 America was not ready for my religious message. I returned to India to wait for conditions to change. They have now changed. The World War was responsible for that. Not only is America now hungry for religion, the entire world is seeking the truth and the peace of God.

"If I plant only a little seed it will grow; it will spread like the waves from the dropping of a pebble into the sea."

Asked to tell something about his religion, he said:

"The doctrine of the Sufis has been set forth in a great number of treatises. God alone exists. He is in everything and everything is in Him. All beings emanate from Him, without being really distinct from Him. The world exists for eternity; the material is only an illusion of the senses. Sufism is the true philosophy of Islamism [*sic*], but religions have only a relative importance and serve but to guide us toward the reality.

"God is the author of the acts of the human race; it is He who controls the will of man, which is not free in its action. Like all animals man possesses an original mind, an animal or living mind, a mind instinctive: but he has also a human mind, breathed into him by God, and of the same character as the original and constructive element itself.

"The soul, which existed before the body, is confined in the body as in a cage; death, then, is the object of the Sufi's desires, since it returns him to the bosom of the Divinity. This metempsychosis permits the soul, which has not fulfilled its destiny here below, to be purified and worthy of a reunion with God.

"The Sufi, during his sojourn in the body, is uniquely occupied in meditating upon his unity with God, and the progressive advancement in the journey of life up to his unification with God. Human life has been likened to a voyage, where the traveller is seeking after God. The aim of

---

Note:

1. Although this article was not published until March 18, this article is based on Pir-o-Murshid Inayat Khan's stay in New York from February 26 through March 5, and, as the article mentions the large audiences at the lectures, seems to come from late in that visit. The material quoted in the latter part of the article does not seem characteristic of Pir-o-Murshid Inayat Khan's teaching, and may have been partly derived from more traditional sources. The reporter has apparently misunderstood what Pir-o-Murshid said about returning to India also, although there are other indications that he desired and planned to do so.

the voyage is to attain to a knowledge of God, for human existence is a period of banishment for the soul, which cannot return to God until it has passed through many successive stages."

From a New York newspaper, the *Detroit Free Press*,
10 March, 1923

Detroit, March[1]

"I believe that the whole of humanity is as one body, and that if a part of that body is hurt, the pain will have its effect, sooner or later, on the whole body. Therefore, man must awaken his sympathy for his fellow man beyond the boundaries of caste, creed or nation, and recognize the fact that the happiness and well being of all depends upon the happiness and well being of every one. Sufuism [*sic*] sees in truth, the underlying stream of all religions, and the mission of the Sufi is to awake in the consciousness of humanity, the divine, which is in every man.

"Caste is forgotten among those who are in the order. I recognize no caste, no nationality, no creed. We are all brothers, and in every man is a spark of the divine. Perfect international unity and harmony is our aim.

"So far, in my 10 years of lecturing, I have found none who disagree with our belief. Our troubles in this world will remain with us, however, until the human conscience is raised above hates and discords. Our mission is to warn all men and to bring them to sane consideration of their duty one to another.

"Through all channels, wisdom must flow."

Note:

1. Pir-o-Murshid Inayat Khan arrived in Detroit from Boston on March 9. Because this article was published on March 10, it was probably based on an interview of March 9. The first sentence is similar to one in the lecture "Universal Brotherhood of Humanity," believed to be of March 11, below.

From a New York newspaper, the *Detroit News*, (11 March 1923?)[1]

Detroit, March[1]

"I am not coming with anything new. The Sufi philosophy is almost as old as consciousness, and it is based on tolerance, natural life, simplicity, self-realization, friendship, benevolence, forgiveness, and God. No reason exists for a follower of any faith to change--all that is required of him is that he search his own heart for the truth, his own religion for its truths, practice tolerance and demonstrate his faith in humankind.

"I was born at Baroda, India, and received a thorough training under my grandfather, Moula Bux, who conducted a musical academy there. I became somewhat of a master of the 'vina,' an ancient Indian instrument of the guitar type. In addition to my musical studies and activities I took up that of religion, going deeply, even as a child, into leading systems, and under noted Oriental scholars. I studied deeply, a characteristic of my race. In the Sufi school of philosophy I eventually found what my soul craved--perfect wisdom combined with freedom. The faith is that which inspired the ancient Persian poets Rumi and Hafiz, and influenced Omar Khayyam.

"The Sufi philosophy aims to express life in terms of love, harmony, and beauty. So thoroughly has this ancient mystic faith taken possession of me that I find every moment of my time taken up in spreading it. My first visit to the United States was with my two brothers and a cousin in 1910. I sought to harmonize the East and West through music. It did appeal to those with imaginations, but I felt the need of the spoken word to reach the multitude. I had to give up my beloved 'vina.' And now I find my time so taken with more important matters that I rarely even put on my turban, which cannot be arranged quickly. Nor do I find time to continue my writings with the assiduity some of my friends believe they merit.

"My purpose in making this visit to America is to deliver a few lectures on my way to and from San Francisco where I shall visit the Sufi temple, and then I shall return to Europe and in Paris conduct summer classes in Sufi philosophy. On the continent I speak in English, employing a translator when necessary. I am not an Indian, nor do I recognize such a thing as caste. I am a cosmopolite, and a brother to all man-kind. Had there been a

---

Note:

1. Although the existing copy of the newspaper article has written on it (not printed) "March 11-1923", Pir-o-Murshid Inayat Khan gave his first lectures in Detroit on that day, and the article seems to indicate those lectures as in the future. Therefore the article may have appeared earlier, and in any case seems to be based on an interview of March 9 or 10.

clearer and better understanding of the Sufi doctrine and its mystic, but thoroughly understandable and simple, philosophy, there would not have been any world war, nor even another similar conflict between peoples. There would be the peace of understanding growing out of tolerance and forgiving.

"Is it possible for the world to be brought under one great religion, and made to accept one all embracing thought? No, not one dogmatic religion; yes, one all-embracing thought. Sufism offers a message of spiritual liberty which possesses a universal appeal.

"The situation in India as it concerns the natives and Great Britain? I have nothing to do with that. I am not a disciple of strife, or a disseminator of violent propaganda, but a humble philosopher from a land that was old while the remainder of the world was in its swaddling clothes, who seeks to establish in the western world the Sufi truths, and to lead, or direct, humanity through an ancient door way to where the One Light, shining in all directions, may be seen illuminating many roads that lead to the one Goal."

From a New York newspaper, the *Detroit Free Press*, March 12, 1923

Detroit, March[1]

Man's trust in preacher, in riches and in dogma and his little trust in self makes him more or less a machine most of his days, with few exceptions, *said Inayat Khan....*

Yet at birth, *he said,* no soul is without the spark of mastery, "an heir of the divine substance."

"The object of the Christian, the Buddhist, the Moslem and the Confucian is one and the same--the freedom of the soul. Yet each in turn misses his objective. The work of living is so great that man can think only of how he can live and he takes small time to ponder the prospect of his soul.

"If he gets sufficient to live, he is content. If he has a roof, he is satisfied, yet he holds within him the spark of expansion which flames only when death tears away the false self that he has built in life about his soul, a false self which in life has kept him from realizing the Kingdom.

"Man pursues the material ends and ultimately they are to him the same prison as the web to the spider. He becomes a machine. If God lives anywhere in man it is in his heart, and it is only by man reaching into his own heart that he will ever enjoy the oneness of life."

Note:

1. This article seems to be reporting on the lecture, "Man, the Master of His Destiny?" given on March 11 at 3 pm at the Unitarian Church in Detroit. No other reporting of this lecture is known.

From a San Francisco newspaper, the *Journal*,
26 March, 1923

San Francisco, March[1]

Sufism has no creed or even special doctrine, *said Murshid* ... It is a desire and a striving for spiritual advancement and its name is derived from the Greek word meaning wisdom. It teaches that spiritual progress and material progress are concomitant, and that there can be no genuine or lasting material progress without the spiritual quality.

Questioned as to spiritual advancement in Europe ... he declared that the world is "hungry for a spiritual awakening."

Note:

1. This article seems to be based on a personal interview, perhaps on March 25.

From a San Francisco newspaper, the *San Francisco Chronicle*, 27 March 1923

San Francisco, March[1]

The intelligence of American women whose hearts always are open to truth and the spiritual qualities they are bringing into business and world affairs, *according to Pir-o-Murshid Inayat Khan*...constitute the only hope of successfully combating the wave of materialism that is sweeping over the world. *He asserts that* avarice and greed are the cause of world unrest today, and that the hope of the future rests with the women.

Note:

1. This indirect quotation appears in an editorial, and must have become known from some talk of Pir-o-Murshid the preceding week, perhaps the otherwise unreported lecture on "The Coming World Religion" of March 25.

From a San Francisco newspaper, the *Call-Post*,
27 March 1923

San Francisco, March[1]

"True spirituality is not necessarily a fixed faith or belief--it is the ennobling of the soul by rising above barriers of material life."

He speaks...of Indian literature, and music, with its base in the ancient days when Sanskrit was the medium for expressing the thoughts of the Indian poets in their lovely, haunting beauty.

Now, *he says*, art, with the subtle coloring that the Moguls brought to it, is more complete. It is mystical still, but it touches all sides of life. *He credits* Tagore with the achievement of bringing before the world the loveliness that is hidden in literature of the Orient, but *he calls* Ameer, Dagh and Hali the foremost writers.

"We distrust those who talk, talk, talk. We do not say what we feel deeply, we Sufists [*sic*]. Our love is something to understand, to feel; something that is too beautiful to discuss."

Note:

1. This article may reflect material from Pir-o-Murshid Inayat Khan's lectures during his first week in San Francisco, from March 21.

A typescript of a lecture handed down by Mrs. Prebble (a pupil of Murshida Martin's) to Martha Burk, and inherited from the latter by Miss Hayat Stadlinger, an American mureed, initiated in Suresnes in 1926, who passed it on to the Biographical Department in Suresnes.

The Science and Art of Hindu Music. 1

Music, literature and philosophy are akin to our souls, whatever be our faith or belief or our way of looking at life.

This morning our subject is "The Science and Art of Hindu Music." India, in the history of the world, represents a country and a people who engaged themselves in the search for truth through the realm of music, philosophy and poetry, at a time when the rest of the world had not yet begun its search for truth. Therefore it is necessary to study Indian music, philosophy and poetry in order to see the foundation of words. The linguists of the day state that the Sanscrit language was the origin or mother of all language. The origin of the science of music is to be found in Sanscrit. It is an undeniable fact that not only art, but even science, has its origin in intuition. This seems to have been forgotten lately, when man is so busy with his search through matter. Undoubtedly even the scientist is helped by intuition, although he may not recognize the fact. Scientists who have touched the depths will admit that science has its source in intuition.

Intuition working to answer the need of mind and of body and inventing through matter things of use, and gaining a knowledge of the nature and character of things, is called "science." And intuition working

Documents: (No original MS has been found in the archives to date.)

Tp. (received from Miss Hayat Stadlinger in 1983).
O.t. (very similar to the tp., from papers in Gd.'s possession. Both these documents, "tp." and "o.t." seem to have been copied from the same document. But then, handed down over the years by different lines of mureeds, they underwent some separate changes. Probably the "tp." kept nearest to the original text.).
Gd.'s corr. (corrections made by Gd., in the "o.t." copy, of which a microfiche was made).
Sk.tp. (a typescript made by Sk. from the "o.t."; the "tp." at that time had not yet been added to the archives.)

This lecture was published in *The Sufi Message of Hazrat Inayat Khan*, Volume II (1960), Music, chapter V.

From an article in the *San Francisco Call and Post* of 31st March 1923, it appears that this lecture was given on 28th March 1923 in the Paul Elder Gallery, San Francisco, U.S.A.

From a program issued by Paul Elder (see Appendix A) of three series of lectures, which Pir-o-Murshid Inayat Khan gave in San Francisco at that time, it can be seen that this lecture was the first one in the series on Music.

Notes:

1. Sk.tp.: added by Sk.: "America, Spring 1923"

through the beauty that is produced in the form of line and color and the form of rhythm, is called "art." Therefore the source of science and art is intuition. Realizing this source, the Hindu music was based on intuition, and the practice of Indian music has been a culture in stimulating intuition and awakening the faculty which appreciates beauty and afterwards expresses itself in beautiful form.

The science of Indian music has come from three sources: astrology, psychology and mathematics. We find this in Western music also, that the whole science of harmony and counterpoint is derived from the science of mathematics. And so the science of Hindu music is called by a Sanscrit word (Prestara) meaning "mathematical arrangement of rhythm and modes."

In the Indian system of music there are about 500 modes, and 300 different rhythms, which are used in their everyday music. The modes of Indian music are called "Ragas." There are four classes of ragas; one class has seven notes, such as you have in the music of the West in the natural scale. Then there are the modes of six notes (omitting one note from the seven note raga) that gives[2] quite another effect to the octave and has a different influence on the human mind.

Then there are the ragas of five notes, omitting two notes from the scale (any two notes). In China they also use the scale of four notes, but not in India.

Some say that the origin of the scale of four notes or five notes, is in the natural instinct that man shows in his discovery of instruments. The first instrument was the flute, symbolical of the human voice. It seems natural that after taking a piece of reed from the forest, and making in the heart of that reed four holes in the places where he could naturally place the tips of his fingers, ~~there~~ their[3] distance apart corresponding to the distance apart of the finger tips, and then making one hole below, that made the raga of five notes.

It was afterward[4] that scientists came with knowledge of different vibrations. But this scale comes naturally when one places the[5] hand on the reed, and a great psychological power seems attached to it. It has a great influence on human nature. And this shows that all things that have been directly derived from nature, their power is much greater than when man has changed and turned and altered them to make a new form of art.

2. Tp.: "gives" changed to "give"
3. O.t., Sk.tp.: "there" instead of "their"
4. O.t.: "afterward" changed to "afterwards"; Sk.tp.: "afterwards"
5. O.t., Sk.tp.: "his" instead of "the"

Now, from the astrological point of view. The science of astrology was based on the science of Cosmic vibration. All depends on vibratory conditions; also the position of the stars, the planets, of individuals, nations, races and all objects. A great deal of the secret power which the Hindus have found in the science of music has been derived by[6] the science of astrology. Every note of Indian music has a certain planet; every note has a certain color; every note denotes a certain pitch of nature; a certain pitch of the animal world.

The science that[7] existed in the ancient Vedas was the science of elements: fire, water, air, ether; but these words should not be taken as one takes them in everyday language. Element of water signifies liquid state; fire signifies heat or warmth. Through this science the Hindus have been able to fix ragas or modes to be sung or played at a certain time of day or night, or a certain season. After these songs have been sung for thousands of years, the race has developed such a sense of appreciation of these ragas, that even an ordinary man of the street cannot bear to hear a raga of the morning sung in the evening. He may not know the form or the notes, but to his ears it sounds disagreeable, he cannot stand it. We may say it is a matter of habit, and that is true, but at the same time I have made experiments with different ragas; and a mode that should be sung in the midst of night, if we sing it at noon, it loses its beautiful influence.

Every planet has a certain influence and there must be a certain mode to answer it. If it is not that, then the music becomes perhaps a matter of pastime, but it does not do the work for which music is designed.

To an Indian, music is not an amusement or something for entertainment. It is something more than that. Music for the Indian is the food of his soul. It answers the deepest demand of his soul. Man is not only a physical body. Man has mind, and back of the mind there is the soul. And it is not only that the body hungers for food. The mind hungers for food, and the soul hungers for food. And what generally happens is that man only ministers to his bodily needs and gives no attention to his inner existence and its demands. He experiences momentary satisfaction, then hungers again, not knowing that the soul is the fineness of man's being, and so that unconscious craving of the soul remains.

In the undeveloped, that silent craving of the soul causes one to be disagreeable, restless, irritated. He does not feel contented with anything in life. He feels like quarreling and fighting. In the person of fine feeling, this hunger of the soul expresses itself in depression, despair. He finds some satisfaction in love of reading, love of art.

6. Tp.: a suggestion by Miss Stadlinger to change "by" to "from"
7. O.t., Sk.tp.: "which" instead of "that"

The soul feels buried in the outer, material world, and the soul feels satisfied and living when it is touched with fine vibrations. The finest matter is spirit, and the grossest spirit is matter.

Music being the finest of the arts, it helps the soul to rise above differences. It unites souls because even words are not necessary. Music stands beyond words.

The art of Hindu music is very unique in its character, for every player and singer is given perfect freedom of expressing his soul through his art. The character of the Indian nation can be understood through their spirit of individualism. The whole education tends to individualism; to express oneself, in whatever form one is capable of. Therefore, in some ways to their disadvantage, in many ways to their advantage, they have expressed this freedom. Uniformity has its advantages, but uniformity very often paralyses progress in art. There are two ways of life, uniformity and individualism. Uniformity has its strength, but individualism has its beauty.

When one hears an artist, a singer, of Hindu music, the first thing he will do is to tune his tambura to give one chord and while he tunes his tambura he tunes his own soul, and this has such an influence on his hearers that they can patiently wait for fifteen minutes. Once he finds he is in tune with his instrument, with that note, his soul and mind and body all seem to be one with the instrument. A person with a sensitive heart listening to his song, even a foreigner, will perceive the way he sings into that chord, the way he tunes his spirit to that chord.

And by that time he has concentrated; by that time he has attuned himself to all who are there. Not only has he tuned the instrument, but he has felt the need of every soul in the audience and the demand of their souls, what they want at that time. Perhaps not every musician can do this, but the best. And then he synthesizes and it all comes automatically, and as he begins his song, it seems that it touches every person in the audience, for it is all an answer to the demands of the souls who are sitting there. He has not made the program for the music beforehand. He does not know what next he will sing, but every moment he is inspired to sing a certain song, or play a certain mode. He becomes an instrument of the whole cosmic system, open to all the inspiration that comes; at one with his audience; in tune with the chord of the tambura; and it is not music only, but phenomenon itself that he gives to the people.

The songs of India consist of folk songs, and those composed by great people and handed down for ages from father to son.

The way music is taught is different. It is not always written; it is taught by imitation; the teacher sings and the pupil imitates, therefore all the intricacies and subtleties are learned by imitation.

It is the mystical part which has been the secret of all religions. The great ones of this world, such as Christ, Buddha and others, have come from time to time to be examples for the people and to express that perfection which is the object of every soul. The secret which was hidden behind all these great religions and in the work of these teachers, was for man to reach to that utmost height which is called perfection, and it is that principle which is taught from the first lesson the musician gives his pupil. The pupil not only imitates the teacher but he focuses his spirit to the spirit of the teacher, and he not only learns, he inherits from his spirit.

The lack we find today, with all this spiritual awakening, the reason so many seekers after truth do not come to a satisfactory result, is this, that always they pursue outwardly; they take it from a book or learn it from a teacher. There was a time in the East (and even it exists now), when a little boy went to learn from a teacher, his regard for the teacher was great; his respect, his attitude towards his teacher was something like one has towards his priest, therefore in this manner he learned to value and appreciate and respect knowledge, and he not only learned but he inherited knowledge from a[8] teacher. If one would read the lives of the great singers of India, how they imitated their teachers, and how they became even greater sometimes than their teachers. It is most wonderful.

The object of Indian music is the training of mind and soul, for music is the best way of concentration. When you tell a person to concentrate on a certain object, the very act of trying to concentrate makes his mind more disturbed. But music which attracts the soul, keeps the mind concentrated. If one only knows how to appreciate it, to give one's mind to it, keeping all other things away, one naturally becomes developed in the power of concentration.

Besides the beauty of music, there is that tenderness that brings life to the heart. For the fine, life in the world is very trying. For a person of fine feelings, for a person of kindly thought, the life of the world is trying. It is jarring, and it sometimes has a freezing effect. It makes the heart, so to speak, frozen. In that condition one experiences depression and the whole life becomes distasteful. And the very life which is meant to be Heaven, becomes a place of suffering.

8. Ibid.: "the" instead of "a"

If one can focus one's heart to music, it is just like heating something which was frozen. The heart comes to its natural condition. And the rhythm regulates the beating of the heart, which helps to restore health of body, mind and soul, and to bring it to its proper tune.

The joy of life depends upon the perfect tune of mind and soul.

A typescript of a lecture from the legacy of Murshida Martin, handed down by Mrs. Duce to Sirdar, and copied by Sk. In a separate annotation Sk. writes: "doubtful whether authentic." Parts of the text do not seem to be Pir-o-Murshid's own words. The text of the lecture has remained incomplete.

The Universe in Man.

Beloved Ones of God,

(It is to Mr. Paul Elder by whose interest in furthering the spiritual culture that we have united here to day, and we are grateful to the efforts of Murshida Rabia Ada Martin, by whose enthusiasm we meet today at this gathering.)

My subject this evening is: "The Universe in Man." Man's limitation belongs to the absence of the knowledge of this fact. The whole tragedy of life in whatever form it may appear outwardly in the point of fact is the limitation of man. But if asked of one's deepest self, if it is really true that man is limited, after some patience, he will hear the answer from within that the limitation of man is mostly caused by the ignorance of himself. And therefore great souls and prophets and the wise men of the world who have knowledge of life and have helped man in his journey toward perfection have taught as Ali, the great Sufi has said: "If you wish to know God, know yourself." If self knowledge was not in view, worship of God, or belief in God would surely not profit man.

In this world there are many who believe in God and (are) yet far from Him, God in heaven, and they on the earth, (with) no communication between them except their belief. There are others who go worshipping in the same way, perhaps, as their forefathers have for ages, but after a continual worship of many generations, they do not seem to arrive at the stage where they can obtain from Him their peace, their happiness, their strength which is the continual yearning of the soul.

Document: (No original MS has been found in the archives to date.)

Tp. (a typewritten copy made by Sk. of a typescript which was sent by Murshida Duce to Sr.).

It is not known who put words in parentheses in the "tp.".

This is the first in a series of six lectures on Spiritual Philosophy, and was given by Pir-o-Murshid Inayat Khan on 29th March, 1923, in the Paul Elder Gallery, San Francisco, U.S.A. (For the program, issued by Paul Elder, see Appendix A.)

An annotation made by Sk. with a view to the authenticity of the text of this lecture, reads [translated from Dutch by the compiler]: "We [Sirdar and Sakina] have been able to compare some fragments received from Mrs. Duce with parts of lectures of which the original text is in our possession. It appeared that the version sent by Mrs. Duce to Sr. is a very poor rendering of the original text of the lecture, in many places garbled and distorted."

In the heading of this lecture, the "Universe in Man," can be seen from two points of view. The universe in man can be pictured in the same way as the seed in the flower and the flower coming out of the seed. That in the seed there is everything which you see in the flower, in its colour, in its fineness, in its beauty, in its delicacy. Yet in the seed you do not see it, but it is there already. So under this human garb which outwardly is limited, there is the universe to be seen if one only looked at it with (the) keen sight.

With the analysis that the wise of all ages have made of the facts of the world, they have found that not only all the elements which compose and make all objects in this world are there, but everything made, every jewel, every plant, every atom of whatever kind represents itself distinctly or indistinctly in the formation of the human world. If you look at the human body as an instrument, you will see that all instruments have been made after it. Call it a flute, call it a lute, it is a lute. There is the mineral kingdom; the bones represent it; the vegetable kingdom is seen in the natural growing of the hair; the animal kingdom expressed by the flesh, and the human or angelic kingdom in the organs of the senses.

The physicians and alchemists of ancient times, their research of the physical body brought them to the realization of the truth behind it and therefore they expressed the philosophy they have gained by the study of the human body by the name, the science, which is called: Alchemy, or from which the word alchemy comes. The great Sufi of Persia, Abi Sima (Avicenna?)[1], whose works have inspired the medical men of medieval times--and there is much to be explored in his works still--has looked at medical science as the philosophy of the soul, of life. To him spiritual philosophy and material philosophy were not two things, they were one thing. It is a scientific point of view from which he saw the spiritual philosophy because he had not followed out the other.

UNFINISHED.

Note:

1. The correct form of the name, known in the West as Avicenna, is Ibn Sina.

A typewritten lecture handed down by the American mureed Hayat Stadlinger, initiated during the Summer School Suresnes in 1926. She inherited it from Martha Burk, who got it from Mrs. Prebble, a pupil of Murshida Martin.

1

Poet and Prophet.[2]

Beloved ones of God,[3]

[4]My subject for this afternoon is "The Poet and the Prophet."[4] In the English language there is a saying in which always the name of "prophet" is connected with that of "poet," although "prophet" denotes much more than the meaning sometimes attributed to this word in the West. The reason is that very often the word "prophet" is used for someone who tells the future, who makes prophecy, but in point of fact the field of the prophet is much larger than making prophecies only. The word "Prophet" includes Master, Saint, Seer, Mystic and Teacher.[4]

The source of poetry and of the prophetic gift is no doubt one and the same. Poetry receives its inspiration from the same source as prophecy only if the poet is a real poet. Nevertheless, a poet is not necessarily a prophet, but a Prophet is certainly a poet.

The reason for this you see illustrated in the mythology of the Hindus by Sarasvati, the Goddess of music and Literature[5]. Her ornaments, her sitting with the peacock, with the vina, holding in one hand the cards, in

Documents: No original MS has been found in the archives to date.

Tp. (a typescript, sent to the B.D. by Miss Stadlinger in 1983, which probably is nearest to the oldest version).
O.t. (very similar to the "tp.").
T.B. (a typewritten version, slightly different from the "tp.", from the legacy of Shahbaz Best).
Gd.a.p. (the version of the "o.t.", used by Gd. as a first preparation of this lecture for an article to be published in the magazine *The Sufi* of September 1935, combined with the lecture "The Poet and the Prophet" of 17th December 1922).
M. (magazine *The Sufi* of September 1935).

Notes:

1. This is the first lecture in a series of six lectures on Sufi Poets, given by Pir-o-Murshid Inayat Khan on 3rd April 1923 in the Paul Elder Gallery, San Francisco, U.S.A. (For the program issued by Paul Elder, see Appendix A.)
2. M.: "The Poet and the Prophet by Inayat Khan" instead of "Poet and Prophet"
3. Ibid.: "Beloved ones of God," omitted
4. Gd.a.p.: the first sentence was crossed out and later the entire first paragraph was crossed out; M.: the first paragraph omitted
5. Gd.a.p.: "L" changed to "l"; M.: "literature"

the other a lotus flower; all this means that a true knowledge of divine wisdom expresses itself in the realm of beauty[6]. The beauty of tone and rhythm in music.[6] And what in[7] poetry? It is half music. It is the music of ideas. It has sharp and flat notes as in [8]music. It has different modes. Its[8] rhythm represents music. Divine inspiration always expresses itself in[9] beautiful form; it is never without beauty. This explains to us that all that is beautiful is a divine expression;[10] the more beautiful it is, the greater it is in divine essence.

No doubt in receiving the inspiration of poetry, action is necessary from both sides; from the side of the poet and from the [11]divine spirit[11]. A poet who brings his heart to a condition which allows him to[12], so to speak, [12]swim in the ocean of divine wisdom will naturally move his arms in rhythm. It is not that he expresses poetry in rhythm, but he receives knowledge in rhythm[13]; the rhythm he receives is the only rhythm.[13] The music he hears in life,[14] he expresses in words, according to the knowledge of language he possesses.

There is a wonderful example of this in a Hindu poet of long ago. He was a man of very humble origin, the son of a cotton weaver; a man who in childhood received no education;[15] All the education he had was from life;[16] what life taught him; and his life became his rhythm, and was so harmonious that the Brahmans of that day, who never allowed the other castes to come near, invited him to a dinner party. A feast of the Brahmans has a peculiar way in which it is arranged. Every one has his own board on which he sits, and the dinner is served on leaves. The poet was no doubt honored by their invitation, but his board was not placed in the same row with the Brahmans[17]. He noticed this, but his rhythm was not changed; he accepted.

6. Gd.a.p.: ", in the beauty of tone and rhythm in music.";
M.: ", in the beauty of tone and rhythm, in music."
7. All other documents: "is" instead of "in"
8. Gd.a.p.: "music. It has different modes. Its" changed to "music, it has different modes; its";
M.: "music, it has different modes; its"
9. Gd.a.p.: "a" added;
M.: "a"
10. Gd.a.p.: the semi-colon changed to a comma;
M.: "expression. The"
11. Gd.a.p.: "d" and "s" changed to capital letters;
M.: "Divine Spirit"
12. Gd.a.p.: "to" crossed out and placed before "swim";
M.: "to swim"
13. Gd.a.p.: the semi-colon replaced with a full stop, and "the rhythm he receives is the only rhythm." crossed out;
M.: a full stop after "rhythm", and omitted "the rhythm he receives is the only rhythm."
14. Gd.a.p.: the comma crossed out;
M.: the comma omitted
15. Gd.a.p.: the semi-colon changed to a full stop;
M.: a full stop
16. Gd.a.p.: the semi-colon replaced by a comma;
M.: a comma
17. Gd.a.p.: added an apostrophe after "Brahmans";
M.: "Brahmans'"

And there comes a kind of entertainment during the dinner, when each one has a chance of expressing himself by reciting or singing. This shows what they like, what they fancy, what they are, to what key their soul is tuned. And when it came[18] the turn of the poet to say something, he said a verse which he had made then and there. It is a beautiful verse, but its meaning is that[19], "thanks[20] be to the Creator who has brought me into an insignificant family, that has made me greet all, high or[21] low, whatever they may be. If I were[22] born in a high caste, probably I would have been dead, as many proud ones have died, of conceit."

The Brahmans were embarrassed, and they saw the truth of the philosophy. It was beautiful, and no thoughtful person could deny the beauty that lies in recognizing the divine in man, regardless of his rank or birth. And it was said on the occasion when the feast was given, "The one who knows Brahma, he is[23] Brahman." In other words, the one who sees God, the one who recognizes God in all, is a Brahman.

The wonderful book of verses that this Indian poet wrote was held for centuries as a scripture[24]; it[24] is still regarded as a scripture, and there is a great following of this particular creed or philosophy. And the language of this man is very ordinary[25]; so[25] you may wonder that his poetry would be accepted in a country rich in languages, as India is with its Sanscrit, Hindustani and sixty different dialects. There must be some reason for it. The reason is that inside it was all literature[26]. Within[26] the outer cover was the true inner form. It was a living beauty.

Writing poetry by making an effort is like doing any other labor. It is a mental labor. The true poet, or the poet who is linked with the Prophet[27], does not make any effort. It comes to him like the falling of the rain. Yes, he must express it in words, but that also becomes easy for him. It is not true that words come from the divine source, for words do not belong there, words belong here. But the words come so easily, one cannot help but think that they come from the divine source.

18. Gd.a.p.: "to" added;
M.: "to"
19. Gd.a.p.: "that" crossed out;
M.: "that" omitted
20. Gd.a.p.: "t" changed to capital "T";
M.: "Thanks"
21. All other documents: "and" instead of "or"
22. M.: "had been" instead of "were"
23. Gd.a.p.: "a" added;
M.: "a Brahman"
24. Gd.a.p.: "; it" changed to ". It";
M.: ". It"
25. Gd.a.p.: "; so" changed to ". So";
M.: "So"
26. M.: "; within" instead of ". Within"
27. Gd.a.p.: capital "P" changed to a small "p";
M.: "prophet"

But what in reality comes from the divine source is that light in which nothing is closed to the eyes of the mind. The mind begins to see. The mind of the inspired soul differs in this way from the ordinary mind. The ordinary mind is in a room where there is everything, but no light. He cannot find the things that are there; he cannot touch anything or see anything. The inspired mind is able to touch everything that is there. Therefore as ideas become revealed to the heart of the inspired[28], so words and verses come to him[29]; the[29] language stands out as if it were revealed, but it is only the light. When the light has fallen, all is clear and he has only to select for himself.

So for the inspired poet,[30] it is not at all difficult to express. It is all there. You may ask, "Where does the light fall? What becomes clear?" It is his own world. All that he has learned. All that he has heard and acquired[31]. That[31] is his world. And when that light has fallen, the dark room is light. All that he could not see before has become plain to him. It is wonderful.

In the life of many inspired people we read that the door of their inspiration was opened from the moment that they loved someone in this world[32]. Poetry[32] began in their life from the time that love sprang out of the heart. What a beautiful and wonderful conception.[33] But if there is any divine element, it is in the heart of man. And when the heart of man has opened,[34] the divine element rises and manifests to the world. How true it is[35]. The rhythm[35] of life dies when love is done. It seems as if the rhythm of life is gone when the heart has become cold.

There are other instances[36]; when[36] a person has gone through a great deal of pain, then poetry springs up[37], but[37] only if pain has melted the heart[38]. Not[38] if the heart is frozen. But if the heart is melted, then the

28. Gd.a.p.: "one" added;
M.: "one"
29. Gd.a.p.: "; the" changed to ". The";
M.: ". The"
30. Gd.a.p.: the comma crossed out;
M.: the comma omitted
31. Gd.a.p.: ". That" changed to ", that";
M.: ", that"
32. Gd.a.p.: ". Poetry" changed to ", poetry";
M.: "; poetry"
33. Gd.a.p.: the full stop changed to an exclamation mark;
M.: "!"
34. Gd.a.p.: the comma crossed out;
M.: the comma omitted
35. Gd.a.p.: ". The rhythm" changed to "that the light";
M.: "that the light"
36. Gd.a.p.: "; when" changed to ". When";
M.: ". When"
37. Gd.a.p.: ", but" changed to ". But";
M.: ". But"
38. Gd.a.p.: ". Not" changed to ", not";
M.: ", not"

nature responds. Poetry is the innate nature of man, and it comes out as the soul develops. You do not need to be a poet in order to express it. You can express it in all things[39]. In[39] painting or writing, in action, in the everyday life[40]; one's[40] thoughtfulness;[41] one's consideration in dealing with others;[41] one's courtesy[42]. It[42] all comes as poetry in the form of manner. It is all poetry[43]. When[43] one remembers to say nothing that will make a dissonant chord;[41] when one thinks to speak the word that will bring harmony and sweetness. You do not need to write, you can express your heart in a different way. The poetic spirit, the poetic gift, can be expressed in your life.

The poet who cannot express his poetry in his life,[44] is not complete. He has not reached that stage where his poetry can be called a ripened poetry. It is not what we say, it is what we are. We each express our heart, soul[45] and condition in all we do. But[46] the tendency of receiving all the beauty we can receive and giving it to others, that is the poetic tendency, and this grows into the Prophetic[46] tendency. The great soul must express himself. Why does he do it? He does it because it is a natural human inclination that all the beautiful thoughts, [48]wonderful things,[49] that man sees, his first thought is to show them to one who is standing near,[50] "Look, how wonderful[51]." He cannot be satisfied without. When we see in the history of the world, Solomon, David, Abraham, Moses, Zarathustra, Jesus, Mohammed, Rama, Krishna, Shiva, Buddha, all of them, they have given truth[52] in poetry, in verse. The reason is that it makes their souls dance when they feel this, when they are conscious of being in God. It is said, "We live, move and have our being in God." If the soul became conscious of this,

39. Gd.a.p.: ". In" changed to ", in";
M.: ", in"
40. Gd.a.p.: "; one's" changed to ". One's";
M.: ". One's"
41. Gd.a.p.: the semi-colon changed to a comma;
M.: a comma
42. Gd.a.p.: ". It" changed to ", it";
M.: ", it"
43. Gd.a.p.: ". When" changed to "when";
M.: "when"
44. Gd.a.p.: the comma crossed out;
M.: comma omitted
45. Gd.a.p.: a comma added;
M.: a comma
46. Gd.a.p.: "But" crossed out, "the" with capital "T";
M.: "The"
47. Gd.a.p.: capital "P" changed to "p";
M.: "prophetic"
48. Gd.a.p.: "the" added;
M.: "the"
49. Gd.a.p.: the comma crossed out;
M.: the comma omitted
50. Gd.a.p.: "to say:" added;
M.: "to say:"
51. All other documents: "beautiful" instead of "wonderful"
52. Gd.a.p.: "truth" changed to "Truth";
M.: "Truth"

it would dance, it could not stand still. The dancing soul cannot express itself except in rhythm and in poetry. It cannot refrain from expressing itself in a music which appeals to other souls.

The poetry of Hafiz, of Rumi, is still,[53] in the East,[53] something living. After them many poets came;[54] took up the same way of expressing themselves;[41] but no one could strike the same note. In spiritual things there is no competition. Competition is in material things. So there have been many poets since Hafiz, but no one could strike the same note. No[55] one could equal him.

The inspiration of Rumi was different. It was more mystical. The feeling that one has in the poetry of Rumi is different than[56] in Hafiz. In the poetry of Hafiz there is rhythm, beauty, love. In the poetry of Rumi there is deep insight and love[57] and recognition of the divine in all beings[58]. Many souls in the East have arrived to[59] the stage of saintliness by reading the inspired writings of Rumi. And even now, after many centuries since he passed, no one with tender and fine feelings can read his poems without shedding tears. It seems it has life. Behind the words there is divine light. It has an influence which can pierce through the heart, which can remind man of the true character of life. It is truth[52]; it is nature. Rumi presents to humanity an unveiled secret of the word[60] of life in the form of poetry.

The presentation of Hafiz is different, although Hafiz has a great respect for the writings of Rumi. He says in his remarks regarding the writings of Rumi[61] which he has written in Persian verse, "When I think of the great work of Rumi, though I will not call him a prophet, yet he has brought to the world a scripture."

53. Gd.a.p.: the comma(s) crossed out;
M.: the comma(s) omitted
54. Gd.a.p.: the semi-colon changed to "and";
M.: a comma instead of the semi-colon
55. Gd.a.p.: ". No" changed to ", no";
M.: ", no"
56. Gd.a.p.: "than" changed to "from that";
M.: "from that"
57. Gd.a.p.: a comma added;
M.: a comma
58. T.B.: "things" instead of "beings"
59. Gd.a.p.: "arrived to" which is an obsolete usage of "arrive at" (see Ox.)
60. Ibid.: "word of life" changed to "world, of life";
M.: "world, of life,"
61. M.: a comma added

Now the question is, "Are poets [62]born?" "Are[62] prophets born?" The answer is that we are all born;[63] born for all that we do and have and accomplish in life. No soul in the[64] world is without a particular mission to perform and accomplish, and the misery of every soul is in not having come to the understanding of the purpose for which he is born. The lifetime of confusion is always caused by souls wandering all the time away from the purpose for which they were born. There is a great mistake man often makes. He is so ready to take a fancy to things,[53] and to go after his momentary fancies, going from one thing to another[65], so[65] in time he loses the thread which makes him feel his way, [66]his work in life, his place,[66] and what he was to accomplish. And once this thread is lost, then man is away from home. He does not find himself at home[61] in his own country, in his own home[67]; take[67] him to Paradise and he will not feel at home because he has lost that thread. [68]There is a song called "Home, Sweet Home," but our true home and the sweetest home is the place which is our place in life.[68]

In the heart[69] there is a place for every wire, and when that wire is not placed right,[53] it will not serve the purpose[70]. It[70] will not give the sweet sound that is expected of it. All human beings in this world are as different strings of one instrument, the universe, on which the Divine Being plays His music, and the power of feeling that is given to man,[53] is for him to seek through life his place, his purpose. And the closer he comes to his purpose, the better he feels,[71] for his only happiness is in his purpose through life.

It is no use asking of people who tell fortunes, or of clairvoyants or spirit mediums, what one's purpose is. What right or what power has another,[53] to know one's place.[72] It is one's own responsibility to find out.

Poetry and prophecy [73]has its[73] roots in every soul. There is a faculty of intuition from which poetry and prophecy both are born. Although there

62. Gd.a.p.: "born?" "Are" changed to "born, are";
M.: "born, are"
63. Gd.a.p.: the semi-colon changed to a hyphen;
M.: a comma
64. All other documents: "this" instead of "the"
65. M.: ". So" instead of ", so"
66. All other documents: "his place, his work in life,"
67. Gd.a.p.: "; take" changed to ". Take";
M.: ". Take"
68. Gd.a.p.: this whole sentence was crossed out first, then reinserted.
69. Gd.a.p.: "heart" changed to "harp";
M.: "harp"
70. Gd.a.p.: ". It" changed to ", it";
M.: ", it"
71. M.: a semi-colon instead of a comma
72. Gd.a.p.: the full stop changed to a question mark;
M.: a question mark
73. Gd.a.p.: "has its" changed to "have their";
M.: "have their"

are differences, and great differences, between individuals, at the same time there is no individual who has not in his heart that spark which may be called divine[74], and[74] if one realizes this, one will see that nothing is impossible to man[75]. There[75] is no attainment which is not possible for a human being[76]. Or,[76] if there is, the lack is on his part, not on the part of God. It is by our lack of patience, thought, stillness, power of will, action that produces harmony and peace, that we become confused through life and wander away from that cord that connects us with our purpose, with divine life, with all inspiration and knowledge, which[61] if one sought thoughtfully and earnestly, one could certainly find.

Yes, there are two distinct[77] works that are the works of the poet and the prophet. The distinct work of the poet is to prepare the heart to receive that light which comes; and the work of the prophet is to bring that light and pour it into the hearts of men. This work is done by each individual in a small way. Mothers can do this for their children[78]. Kind[78] friends can do this for their fellowmen. They can prepare their hearts with gentleness, with living love, and they can sow in their hearts all that is necessary there to be produced.

But not everyone can do this, and when one who is not ripe for the work attempts it, he does more harm than good. Very often people are only anxious to make sister, brother or friend,[53] see from their own point of view, or act as they wish them to do, and they arouse antagonism. They only produce a kind of irritation, and the more they touch this irritation, the more it becomes sore,[79] and the outcome is fatal. Therefore,[80] it is not the work of everyone to do this. Before one[81] tries, one[82] must see if he can stand on his own feet;[83] and then one[84] must see how thought and influence work upon another. And the best way of teaching is by example. Words only annoy. And words without life have no power. What brings the best results is in[85]

74. Gd.a.p.: ", and" changed to ". And";
M.: ". And"
75. Gd.a.p.: ". There" changed to ", there"
76. Ibid.: ". Or," changed to ", or";
M.: "; or"
77. T.B.: "different" instead of "distinct"
78. Gd.a.p.: ". Kind" changed to ", kind";
M.: ", kind"
79. Gd.a.p.: the comma changed to a semi-colon;
M.: a semi-colon
80. Gd.a.p.: the comma crossed out
81. Ibid.: "one" changed to "a person";
M.: "a person"
82. Gd.a.p.: "one" changed to "he";
M.: "he"
83. Gd.a.p.: the semi-colon changed to a comma;
M.: a comma
84. M.: "he" instead of "one"
85. Ibid.: "in" omitted

acting one's own theory;[83] living one's belief[86]. Practising[86] one's idea[87]. This makes one[81] the example of his idea, and then he does not need to say[88]. He is.

Those whose hearts are awakened cannot help but accept the teaching, the thought, the help that is given. But in point of fact[89] what the great teachers have done, is that they have brought to the world a living God.

In the world there is a belief in God, but where does one find the living God? What one wants is the living God.

For those who turn their backs on God, [90]it is[90] not for the reason that they are against God, but for the reason that they cannot find the living God.

What was brought by the prophets of all times was the living God, to enlighten, [91]to help, to strengthen[91] humanity towards perfection.

92

---

86. Gd.a.p.: ". Practising" instead of ", practising";
    M.: ", practising"
87. T.B.: "ideas"
88. Gd.a.p.: ". He" changed to ", he";
    M.: "to say he is."
89. Gd.a.p.: a comma added
90. M.: "do it" instead of "it is"
91. Gd.a.p.: "to help, to strengthen" changed to "to strengthen, to help";
    M.: "to strengthen, to help"
92. T.B.: "Thank you all for your sympathetic response.
    God bless you."

A typewritten lecture handed down by Mrs. Prebble (a pupil of Murshida Martin's) to Martha Burk, and inherited from the latter by Miss Hayat Stadlinger, an American mureed, initiated in Suresnes in 1926, who passed it on to the Biographical Department in Suresnes.

The Psychic Influence of Music.

In the field of music there is much to be explored, and this subject of the psychological influence of music seems to have been little known to modern science. According to modern science we are taught that the influence of music, or of sound and vibration, comes to us and touches the senses from without, but there is one question which remains. What is the source of the influence that comes out from within? The real secret of the psychological influence of music is hidden in the source; the source where sound comes from.

No doubt it is more plain and easy to understand that the voice has a certain psychological value, and one voice differs from another, and every voice expresses its psychological value and has its psychological power. Very often one feels the personality of one who is talking at a distance on the telephone. A sensitive person can feel the effect of the voice alone without seeing the speaker. And many do not depend so much upon words, but more upon the voice that is speaking the words. This shows that one's psychological development is expressed in speaking, and more especially in singing.

In the Sanscrit language, breath is called prana. The very life. And what is voice? Voice is breath. If there is anything in life, in man's constitution, which may be called life, it is the breath. And breath manifested outwardly is called prana; the sound of the voice. Therefore a person can express himself most in song, or in what he says. If there is anything in the world that can give expression to the mind and the feelings, it is the voice. Very often it happens that a person talks on a subject in a thousand words, and it has no influence. There is another person who expresses a thought in three words, and makes a deep impression. This shows that the power is not

Documents: (No original MSS have been received by the archives to date.)

Tp. (a typescript sent by Miss Hayat Stadlinger to the B.D. in 1983. This version probably is nearest to the oldest one.).
O.t. (a nearly identical copy of the "tp.").
Sk.tp. (an exact copy of the "o.t.", dated "America, 1923").

This lecture was published in *The Sufi Message of Hazrat Inayat Khan*, Volume II (1960), Music, chapter XII.

From a program of three series of lectures which Pir-o-Murshid Inayat Khan gave in San Francisco, issued by the Paul Elder Gallery (see Appendix A), it appears that this lecture was given on 4th April 1923 as the second one in the series on "Music."

in the words, but in the voice which comes from prana. According to the strength it has, it impresses the listener. The same thing is found in the finger tips of the violinist, and coming from the lips of the flute player. That, according to the influence coming from his thought, he produces through his instrument that influence. A person may be very skilful, but if his finger tips do not produce a feeling of life, he cannot make a success. Apart from the music one plays there is the value of the prana or psychological power that he gives to what he plays.

In India there are vina players who do not need to play a symphony in order to have an influence, in order to produce a phenomenon. They only have to take the vina in hand and strike one note. As soon as they strike one note it goes through and through and through. In striking one or two notes they have tuned the audience. It works on all the nerves. It is like playing the lute that is in every heart. Their instrument becomes only a source, the response to which is found in the heart of every person, friend and foe alike. Let the most antagonistic person come before a real vina player, and he cannot keep his antagonism. As soon as the notes have touched that person, he cannot prevent the vibrations which are created in him. He cannot help turning into a friend. Therefore, in India they are often called, instead of musicians, "vina magician." It is magic.

No doubt the power of music depends upon the grade of spiritual evolution that a person has touched. There is the story of a Hindu who was a musician at the Court of a great Emperor. The Emperor asked him, "Tell me, O great musician, who was your teacher?" He replied, "King, my teacher is a very great musician, but more than that. I cannot call him musician, I must call him Music." Said the Emperor, "Can I hear him sing?" The musician answered, "Perhaps, I may try. But you cannot think of calling him here to the Court." The Emperor said, "Shall I go where he is?" The musician said, "His pride may be revolted even there, thinking that he is to sing before a king." The Emperor said, "Shall I go as your servant?" The musician said, "Yes, there is hope then." So both of them went up into the Himalayas; into the high mountains, where the sage had his temple of music in a cave; living with nature; in tune with the Infinite. When they arrived, the musician was on horseback, the Emperor walking. The sage saw that the Emperor had humbled himself to come to hear the music, and he was willing to sing for him, and when he felt in the mood of singing, he sang. But his singing was so great, it was a psychic phenomenon and nothing else. It seemed as if all the trees and plants of the forest were vibrating; it was a song of the universe. The deep impression made upon the Emperor and the musician was more than they could stand; they went into a state of trance, of rest, of peace. And while they were in that state, the Master left the cave. When they opened their eyes he was not there. The Emperor said, "O, what phenomenon! But where has the Master gone?" The musician said, "You will never see him in this cave again, for once mankind has got a taste of this, he will pursue it, though it cost life itself. It is greater than anything in life." When they were home again, the Emperor asked the musician one day, "Tell me what raga, what mode did your Master sing?" The musician told him the name of the raga, and sang it for him, but the Emperor was not content, saying, "Yes, it is the same music, but it has not the same life. Why is this?" The musician replied, "The reason is this, that while I sing before you, the King of this country, my Master sings before God. That is the difference."

Friends, if we study life today, in spite of the great progress of science, the radio, telephone, phonograph, and all the wonders of this age; yet we find that the psychological aspect of music, poetry, and art does not seem to develop as it should. On the contrary it is going backward. And if we ask what is the reason, the answer will be that in the first place the whole progress of humanity today is a mechanical progress, and this hinders, in a way, the progress of individualism.

A musician has to submit to the law of harmony and counterpoint; if he takes one step different from the others, his music is questioned. When in Russia I asked Tanieff, a very great musician who was the teacher of Scriabine, what he thought of Debussy's music, he said, "I cannot understand it." It seems we are restricted by uniformity; that there is no scope; and you will find the same thing in the medical and scientific worlds. But in art especially, where the greatest freedom is necessary, one is restricted by uniformity. Painters and musicians cannot get their work recognized. They must follow the mob, instead of following the great souls. All that is general is ordinary, because the great mass of the people are not highly cultured. Things of beauty and good taste are understood, enjoyed and appreciated by few, and there is no way for the artist to reach these few. In this way what is called uniformity has become a hindrance to the individual development.

What is necessary today is that in the education given to the children, the psychological value of music must be taught. That is the only hope, the only way by which we can expect, after some time, better results. That the children learning music must not only know the music, but they must know what is behind it; how it is presented.

Of course, there are two sides; outward conditions, and the presentation of the art. Outward conditions may be more or less helpful. I myself have seen in my musical life that music or a song, performed before two or three people, congenial, sympathetic, harmonious, understanding and responsive, brought quite a different vibration, created a different effect than the same thing given before five hundred people. What does this mean? It means that some people are like instruments; when good music is presented before them, they respond, they become attuned to it, they are all music. They take a share in the music, and therefore a phenomenon is created. And this phenomenon can reach even that highest ideal that is to be expected of music, and that is the realization of the soul's freedom. What is called Nirvana or Mukti in the East, and Salvation in the Christian world.

For there is nothing in this world that can help one spiritually more than music. Meditation prepares, but music is the highest for touching perfection. I have seen wonders by the psychological power of music, but only when there were congenial surroundings. Five or six people, not more. A moonlight night, or dawn, or sunset. It seems that nature gives its help to make the music complete, and music and nature both work, for they are one.

Now, if a great opera singer, or violin soloist, has to play before ten thousand people, with all his ability, he cannot touch every soul there. It depends upon the greatness of the artist, of course. The greater the artist, the more he will reach. But he has to consider what will please his audience, not what will be pleasing to God. When music has to become commercial, its beauty is lost. It has lost much of its value.

There was a time in the East when every effort was made by the aristocracy of India to keep the art of music from being commercialized, and they were successful for some time in doing so. Musicians were not paid a certain sum of money; their needs were supplied, even though they were extravagant. But they felt that they must have surroundings of harmony and beauty; they were generous; their doors were always open to others, and they were always in debt; but their debts were paid by the kings.

Besides that, the musician was not restricted by his programme. He was left to see from his intuition what the people wanted. He must decide at the same time when he sees them. And as he goes on playing or singing, he knows more. The chemical effect of the minds[1] of the listeners[2] tells him what they want; and so at the end it was a spiritual treat.

The secret of all magnetism, whether expressed through personality, or through music, is life. It is life which is charming, which is attractive. What we are always seeking for is life, and it is the lack of life which may be called lack of magnetism. And if musical teaching is given on this principle, it will be most successful in bringing about psychological results. It is on the health of the physical body, on thought, on imagination and on the heart (which is very often cold and frozen) that the psychological power of music depends. And it is this life which one puts through his finger tips on the violin; through his voice when singing.

Notes:

1. O.t., Sk.tp.: "mind"
2. Ibid.: "listener"

What the world is seeking; what human souls yearn for, is that life, whether it comes through music, color and line, or words. It is the life which every one desires. It is life which is the real source of healing. Music can heal if life is put into it. There is no great secret about it, if a person is able to understand the truth in its simplicity.

When a person plays mechanically, the fingers running about the piano or violin almost automatically, it may create a temporary effect, but it soon passes.

Very often one hears disagreeable music. At the time it does not seem so disagreeable, but afterward one realizes the bad effect. It is exciting; it is harsh.

But music that heals the soul, is music with a soothing effect. One can have the soothing effect, or one can have the harsh effect. And this depends not only upon the musician, but upon the composer also; the mood that has inspired him. A person awake to the psychological effect of music will find it easy to understand what mood the composer was in when he wrote. Every page shows his mood and his development at the time when he was writing. He can put life and beauty into his music, and after a thousand years it will still prove to be beautiful and life giving. No doubt, study and qualification help him to express himself better; but what is really needed is life behind it, which comes of the expanded consciousness, which comes of the realization of the divine light which is the secret of all true art, and which is the soul of all mysticism.

A typescript of a lecture from the legacy of Murshida Martin, handed down by Mrs. Duce to Sirdar, and copied by Sk. In a separate annotation Sk. writes: "doubtful whether authentic." Parts of the text do not seem to be Pir-o-Murshid's own words.

The Spirit of Guidance.

Beloved Ones of God:

My subject of this evening is "The Spirit of Guidance." There is a spark of divine intelligence in every soul which may be called a spark of the spirit of guidance, that, in spite of all the errors and faults, and in spite of all the ignorance through which man treads his path in his life, there is always something telling him, ... to some audible, to some inaudible, but in the heart of everyone, in the heart of the saint, in the heart of the devil, there is something speaking continually. And it is a sign of that spirit, the existence of which makes man responsible for his actions, the spirit of guidance.

There would not have been a sin, there would not have been right and wrong, if there was not that sense which is at the bottom of the heart of every man. One may prove one's actions, one's point of view, one's attitude and outlook on life, one's opinion with a thousand different reasons and proofs, but still there is a light which tells him what is right and what is wrong, what is really good and what is bad. Therefore the most wicked person in the world, he does not want others to treat him accordingly; he may do it, being absorbed in selfishness, but that spirit of guidance tells him that that is wicked, that it is not right. He accuses the other for treating him badly. He does not judge himself, but at the same time the spirit of guidance is even there guiding him.

Documents: (No original MSS have been received by the archives to date.)

Tp. (a typescript, received by Sirdar from Mrs. Duce, and copied by Sk.).
Sk.ann. (a few annotations in Sk.'s hwr. on separate papers.).

It is not known who put words in parentheses in the "tp.".

This is the second lecture in a series of six lectures on "Spiritual Philosophy" given by Pir-o-Murshid Inayat Khan on 5th April 1923 in the Paul Elder Gallery in San Francisco, U.S.A. (For the program, issued by Paul Elder, see Appendix A.)

An annotation made by Sk. with a view to the authenticity of the texts of a series of lectures, including this one, reads [translated from Dutch by the compiler]: "We [Sirdar and Sakina] have been able to compare some fragments received from Mrs. Duce, with parts of lectures of which the original text is in our possession. It appeared that the version of the lecture sent by Mrs. Duce is a very poor rendering of the original text, in many places garbled and distorted."

The tendency which one sees in the higher mountains to accommodate the rocks and plants and trees and water, and the tendency that we see in the animal kingdom of warning their fellow creatures, of taking care of them, the source of the splendour and the wonderful working behind the scheme of nature, that spirit of guidance even there shows its guidance, being even perfect there.

Those who have studied the lives of the elephants when they are in the forests, in that wild state, they have found a wonderful natural inclination among them, that there is always a leader in the herd of elephants. Behind that elephant, many elephants who walk, and the leader elephant is the experienced one, the elder brother who takes a stem of a tree in his trunk, and as it goes on it examines the ground. If there is a pit, that elephant gives a signal with a kind of cry of warning. As soon as the elephants hear that warning they run away, because the way they catch elephants is that they put some worn out straw in the pit, and as the elephants coming, being heavy animals, fall in the pit (they) can be starved. Then they approach and catch them. Also, of this danger the leader elephant always warns the herd.

There are monkeys in the forest and there is always a leader. At the time of danger and trouble, he gives them a warning, a kind of cry by which they know if there is a danger awaiting them.

Among the birds, the flocks of birds which travel from land to land, there is always one who is foremost, and that one can (act as) a compass which (braves) storm and wind and land and weather and knows which way it must take, and all others are guided by it.

What do we see in this? We see in this sympathy, love, insight into nature. And what comes out of it? The consideration for the well-being of one's fellow creatures. Of all the wisdom or spirituality that one gains through life, it is born in man to be useful, to be serviceable, an inclination to protect and support the feeble, the weak, and to give one's knowledge and thought and strength to those who need to learn.

Then the same spirit one finds developed in the human race. We see it in a kind and loving mother for her child, or devotion and sympathy or selfsacrifice. As in the East they say the mother is the first road through life, and what the mother has taught, no one can teach, their sympathy, goodwill and unselfishness. One sees that in a kind father, one sees it even in an innocent child, the same tendency. One sees that tendency in an inspiring teacher, in a kind and sympathetic friend, one sees it from all around.

Friends, it is a spirit which is so alive not only from within, but from without, it always guides, and when man makes a mistake, an error, it is at times when he does not listen to that spirit. The more one is conscious of this spirit, the spirit of guidance, the more one is ~~conscious~~ open to its guidance, the more one listens to the lesson it gives, the more the spirit is guiding him.

But one does not listen to it. Very often it so happens to be a stranger to those[1] whom it might tell something which is important for us to think and learn. A servant may tell us something who perhaps may never have read, he might tell one about something or tell something which may perhaps be of use to a learned man. Sometimes elderly people can tell something which a person with his experience does not know.

The more we seek that guidance, the more that guidance comes to teach from all sides. When we open our eyes, when we open our ears to the voice of that spirit of guidance, from all sides we get the answer to our questions. We see ourselves there is a spirit of guidance, a spirit which may be called a divine spirit.

Many men take this guidance by calling (on someone from the) other side, a spirit called fairy, master ... many recognize it outwardly as advice from a teacher, father, mother or child. Call it (what you may), it is all from the same source and the same one coming from one source, it is only a difference of recognition. As we recognize, so the voice comes, call it the voice of this[2] father, friend, servant, loved-one. Call it what you will, it is the voice of one being, the spirit of guidance, the same being who spoke through Jesus Christ, the outer person of the master or the spirit behind it. The outer person of the master is historical. We find a certain time of his birth and a certain time when he was more (advanced).

... It is the spirit, call it the Christ spirit, but it is always there. Close your eyes, it is there; open your eyes, it is before you. The more you take notice of it, the more it appears to you. The more one's eyes are closed, the further it goes. But the fault is on the part of man who does not listen.

The custom of the great prophets and seers has been their belief. It does not mean that they alone had belief in God. No, there is (rarely an un-) believer. If one becomes a believer, there is very little more to obtain in this world, because the stage of the believer is the stepping stone to perfection which is divine perfection. Many people believe, but if they believe, there is very little more to find in life.

Notes:

1. Tp.: "those" crossed out by Sk.
2. Ibid.: "this" crossed out by Sk.

Man is fond of complaining. He loves to be fooled. Give him something to fool him, he is glad of it. Fool him more and more, he is pleased. If we look at the face of life, what is it? The life of the intellect, what is it? It is a puzzle, a puzzle which has two doors, one to enter and one you take out. The door of complexity is the entrance to this door. The door of simplicity is the exit.

But man loves puzzles. The puzzles in the cartoon are made for the enjoyment of man. Think how many people go to the moving pictures and what do they see there? The same as every day. The moving picture that is going on every day, they read in the newspapers. They want to see something unreal, one which takes them from the simple and true life, that divine life which is the full one. They go to the theatre and cinema and think they are enjoying life, but life is full of enjoyment if one opened his heart to every experience. The friendship of friends and the enmity of enemies, all is interesting and reveals the truth, and in all parts we see the beauty if only our eyes will open to see the beautiful.

In the language of the Buddhists, it is the spirit of guidance which is called "Bodhisattva" and it is most wonderful to think that every word of Sanskrit, of the ancient language is not only a name of a certain person or thing or condition, it is expressive of its secret nature and character. "Buddha" means reason. "Sattva" means the essence of reason. We see in the water that the surface of the water has a different temperature, different colour and is different altogether from the[3] deeper. The water in the depths of the sea and lake is quite different from what is on the surface. So it is with reason. Reason on the surface is a different reason from that in the depth. In the depths is the cream of the reason. The picture is made by the people who dive deep and bring pearls from the depths of the sea. So the souls who learn to dive to this depth, the Bodhisattva, and what they bring from there is nothing but pearls.

It is not a different form of thinking, it is only deep thinking. It is not a different form of feeling, it is only a deep feeling. There is very little difference between understanding and comprehending. You can understand, but in order to comprehend, you must go a little further.

In the history of the world we find that this Bodhisattva, this spirit of guidance in whatever personality it expressed itself for us, has never failed to make its impression directly or indirectly, for truth is living and life alone can make impressions. In whatever part of the world anyone expressed this essence of intelligence purely for the well-being of his fellows, for the good of his people or the peace of the world, it has always appealed to the innocence of people. And yet there has always been something standing between the Message of truth and the people, and what stands[4] is what man calls his mind.

3. Ibid. "the" changed to "that" by Sk.
4. Sk.ann.: "between" added

A mind full of one's beliefs, one's own opinion and the knowledge one thinks "This is my opinion, my belief." He does not know it has never been his belief. If one has believed or heard a thing, he begins to think it is his opinion. But it is part of his nature, it is a fault on the part of man. Very often he confuses himself with the body instead of identifying himself with the soul. That is why it has always been taught by the seers and the great souls that the only solution and way out of this puzzle was self-knowledge, self-realization.

Those who have come from time to time, what were they? They were nothing but the expressions of that Bodhisattva, that Christ spirit, that spirit of Alpha and Omega in whatever name or form they came or come, whatever be their personality or condition in life, whatever nation or race, that does not count. They came with that knowledge, that inspiration and life which is the need of souls.

When we read about the prophets of the past, the wisdom of Solomon is not yet forgotten. Though thousands of years have passed it is there. The message that Moses gave his life for, stands, though generations have passed, many centuries have past, but it is living.

Jesus Christ spoke to so few. Who could have ever thought the whole world could be blessed by that teacher! No one can ever imagine how few he spoke to when he talked and gave the message.

But the living word can never die. If the hearts of men are not accommodating, the sages of the world will conceal them safe, will (guard them) and make another effort to teach in time. For God is Truth and truth is God. All that is success only belongs to truth. Truth alone is successful. This success which we see in our everyday life of rank, position, power, how long does it last? It is here for a day and (passes like a dream) and becomes nothing but a source of (hardship) that man finds in the end dust, from which he obtains nothing. As in Sanscrit it is said that success only belongs to the truth.

You will see in the history of those who have given their lives in the service of truth, to the refinement of humanity, to elevate mankind, they have had great trouble, many miseries, their lives passed through burdens, but at the same time success belonged to them. How many years since Buddha has passed? Can anyone erase Buddha from the hearts of those impressed with his teaching, and can the ~~call of truth~~ sea rise over the influence of Buddhistic teaching? Can it? Man cannot resist the call of truth. He must sooner or later benefit by it.

A typescript, of which no original document has been found in the archives to date.

--~~America 1923.~~--[1]

The Healing Power of Music.

The idea of healing through music is really speaking the beginning by development by the art of music, the end of which is attaining by music what is called in the words [2]as in vedanta Samadi[2].

In the first place all[3] medicines which are used for healing purposes, if we saw what is at the back of them, if we asked[4] what it is in them that heals, we shall find that it is the different elements which constitute our physical existence. The same elements are there, and that which is lacking in us is taken from them for[5] that effect which should be produced in our body, is produced by those medicines. That vibration which is to be

Documents: (No original MSS have been received by the archives to date.)

Tp. (a typescript with "America 1923" in the upper right hand corner. This version, before the corrections by Sk., seems to be the oldest one.).
O.t. (a typescript which may have been copied from the same old document as the "tp.", but has reached the archives in Suresnes through a different line of mureeds, and underwent more changes than the "tp.").
Sk. considered the "o.t."s to be the oldest available documents for several other lectures in the same series given in San Francisco, U.S.A., in 1923. She was right at that time, as the "tp."s of those lectures, which reached the archives only in 1983, were unknown to her.
With this lecture, even though another typescript ("tp.") was added to the archives in her time, she took the "o.t." as the one giving the oldest version.
Sk.corr. (corrections in Sk.'s hwr. in the "tp.", making thereby the "tp." identical to the "o.t.". These corrections, therefore, are not mentioned as such in the notes.).
Sk.tp. (a typewritten copy of the lecture, with "Sk. corr." included, identical to the "o.t.". Therefore "Sk.tp." is not mentioned in the notes as a separate document, except in note 1).
T.c. (another typewritten copy, very inaccurate, showing omissions and changes).
Sk.ann. (Sk.'s separate paper with annotations).

This lecture was published in *The Sufi Message of Hazrat Inayat Khan*, Volume II (1960), Music, chapter XIII.

This is the third lecture in a series of six lectures on "Music," and was given by Pir-o-Murshid Inayat Khan on 11th April 1923 in the Paul Elder Gallery, San Francisco, U.S.A. (For the program, issued by Paul Elder, see Appendix A.)

Notes:

1. O.t.: "America 1923" omitted;
   Sk.tp.: "America 1923" added
2. O.t.: "of the Vedanta `Samadhi'";
   T.c.: "of Vedanta `Samadhi'", "the" added by Sk.
3. O.t., t.c.: "the" added
4. Ibid.: "ask"
5. Ibid.: "or" instead of "for"

created in the body, is created by their power; and that rhythm which is necessary for our cure is brought about by putting the circulation of the blood into a certain rhythm and speed. And the intensity of vibration, which may be necessary for our health is brought about by the medicines.

In this we learn that health is a perfect condition of rhythm and tone. And what is music? Music is rhythm and tone. When the health is out of order, it means the music is out of order. The music is not right in ourselves, and therefore to put ourselves into a state of harmony and rhythm, what is most necessary is the help of harmony and rhythm. This way of healing can be studied and understood by studying the music of one's own life; by studying the rhythm of the pulse; the rhythm of the beating of the heart, and of the head. Physicians who are sensitive to rhythm, determine the condition of the patient by examining the rhythm of the pulse, the beating of the heart, the rhythm of the circulation of the blood. And a physician, with all his material knowledge, to find the real complaint, must depend upon his intuition and the use of his musical qualities.

In ancient times, and even now, in the East we have two principal schools of medicine. One which comes from the ancient Greek school, through Persia; the other which comes from the Vedas and is founded on mysticism. And what is mysticism? It is the law of vibration.

Understanding the nature of complaint by the rhythm and tone that can be perceived in the human body, and by regulating through rhythm and tone, according to one's understanding of the proportions of rhythm and tone that make a proper health.

Besides this, there is an other way of looking at it. Every illness apparently has its peculiar reason, but in reality all illnesses come from one reason. One reason, or cause, or condition, and that is the absence of life, the lack of life. Life is health. Its absence is illness, which culminates in what we call death. Life in its physical form, as perceived through the physical spheres, is called "Prana" in Sanscrit.

Now, this life is given by food or medicine; or the body is prepared by a certain food or medicine to be able to breathe in this life itself, in order that the body may become in better health, may experience perfect health. But this Prana [6]that comes[6], which means a[7] breath, the central breath, this attracts from space all different elements which are there. As the herbs and plants and flowers and fruits all attract the same element in them from space, which they represent, but all these elements are attracted by the breath. Therefore the great mystics, whether from Greece, Persia or India, have always had as their bases of spiritual evolution, the culture of

6. Ibid.: "that comes" omitted
7. Ibid.: "the" instead of "a"

breath, the science of breath. [8]And the source of all feeling[9] has been the science of breath.[8] Even until now, you will see in the East, the healers, who magnetize water, or food or the atmosphere. Where lies the secret of this magnetism? It is their breath. It is the influence of their breath in the water or food.

The religious people of India have a ceremony, something like a sacrament, given by the holy person to another who is suffering, and it helps them. It is the power of breath, which is so balanced, so purified and developed, that it attracts all elements. All that you can get from a herb, flower or fruit, and[10] even more. Therefore, what medicine can do, a thousand times more than that their breath can do. There are healers in the East, who whisper some spiritual words, but what is whispering? It is breath again; breath with words directed through it.

There was a physician in Delhi who mostly used his[11] healing power with his patients, and one day a sceptical friend came to consult him. The physician whispered a few sacred words before the patient, and said, "Now you may go." This sceptical man said he could not understand how such a method could have any effect on his health, and the physician did something quite unusual in his life, that is, he offended the man by speaking very harshly to him. The man became very angry, and said, "How can you, a physician, say such words to me!" The physician said, "Usually I never do such a thing, and I only did it to prove something to you. If my words can make you angry and ill, they can also make someone well. If words can make one ill and upset, they have the power[12] back of them to harmonize the patient and put him in good condition."

Now, what is music? According to the Sanscrit thinkers, there are three aspects of music, singing, playing and dancing. All three represent rhythm[13] and all three represent tone in some form or other. And what is the effect of music? The effect of music is to regularize[14] the rhythm of another person and[15] tune another person to the music that is being performed. What secret is there in music which attracts all those who listen to it? It is the rhythm which is[16] created. It is the tone of that music which tunes a[17] soul and raises a soul above the depression and despair of everyday life in this world. And if one ~~new-~~ knew what rhythm is needed for a particular indi-

8. T.c.: this sentence was omitted
9. O.t., t.c.: "healing" instead of "feeling"
10. T.c.: "or" instead of "and"
11. Ibid.: "this" instead of "his"
12. Sk.ann.: "at the" added
13. T.c.: "music" instead of "rhythm"
14. Ibid.: "to regulate" instead of "to regularize"
15. O.t., t.c.: "to" added
16. T.c.: "being" added
17. O.t., t.c.: "the" instead of "a"

vidual in his trouble and despair, and what tone is needed, and to what tune that person's soul should be raised, then he could[18] heal a person with music.

There was a time in India when music was used for healing. It was healing for the mind, for the character; healing for the soul. Because it is health of the soul which[19] brings health of the physical body, but healing of the physical body does not always help the soul. That is why the material science of medicine can do good for some time, but does not entirely suffice the need of the patient. I do not mean by this that outward treatment is absolutely useless. There is nothing in this world that is useless, if we only know how to make use of it. All things in this[20] world are needed, all things have their benefit and use, if we only know how to use them properly. The only thing is, if a cure is brought about outwardly, while inwardly the illness remains, sooner or later the[21] illness which is buried in the body must come out and show itself.

Once I met with a person, who said she had been to many physicians for the complaint of neuritis, and was for the moment cured, but it always comes[22] back, and she said, "will you tell me something that will help me?" I asked her a question. I said, "Is there any person in the world whom you dislike, whom you hate, or whose action is troubling your mind?" She said, "Yes, there are many people whom I dislike, and especially there is one person whom I cannot forgive." "Well," I said, "That is neuritis, that is the root of the disease. Outwardly it is a pain of[23] the body; inwardly it is rooted in the heart."

Often the cause of illness is within, though no doubt many things are caused outwardly. No one rule will cover everything. No doubt, as things have changed in the world and materialism has spread throughout the world, it has influenced things, not only in the West, but in the East also. The use of music for spiritual attainment and healing of the soul, which was prevalent in ancient times, is not found to the same extent now. Music has been made a pastime; the means of forgetting God, instead of realising God. And it is the use of[24] things which constitute their fault or their virtue.

Still the remembrance of the ancient use of music remains among the poor. Among the poor in India there are healers who have their particular instrument of healing, the instrument they play, and the people go to them for healing. And by playing that instrument they arouse that certain feeling which has become cold, and that deep feeling which was buried begins to come out. It is really the old way of psycho-analysis. Music helps

18. T.c.: "would", but Sk. wrote "(could)" above
19. O.t., t.c.: "that" instead of "which"
20. T.c.: "the", but Sk. wrote "(this)" above
21. Ibid.: "that" instead of "the"
22. O.t., t.c.: "came" instead of "comes"
23. T.c.: "in" instead of "of"
24. Ibid.: "as" instead of "of". Sk. added "that" in parentheses before "as".

that person to express[25] the hidden influence which was there. And in this way many people are helped without going to a physician. But that [26]is no doubt[26] a crude and ordinary form[27] of healing. A nobleman, knowing that healing can be accomplished through music, introduced concerts in certain hospitals, and the amusing[28] result was that all those who were suffering began to cry out, "For God's sake, keep quiet. Go away." That was not the music to soothe them. It only made them suffer more. It was like giving a stone for bread. In order to give healing through music, one must study what is needed, what is wanted. In the first place, one must study what the complaint is; [29]what elements are lacking[29]; [30]what is its symbolical meaning,[30] what mental attitude is behind[3] illness; and by a close study, one can do[31] great good to the patient, by the help of music.

Even if music was[32] not used as a prescription particularly intended for a certain illness, still the power of illness, which has as a burden[33] in the heart of man, that power can be reduced by lifting his heart, by changing his thought. What brings illness is the thought of illness, rather than illness itself. The existence of illness in the body no doubt may be called a shadow of the true illness, which is held by man in his mind. By the power of music, mind may become so exalted, that it rises above the thought of illness, then[3] illness is forgotten.

And you will ask, "What music can heal man, [34]what sort of music[34]? Is it singing or playing, or in the way of dance?" Singing is[3] most powerful, for singing is living. It is Prana. It is life itself. It is voice. No doubt it is life, which is working through an instrument also, by the touch[35]. But in singing it is the direct life; the breath touching the heart of the listener. But now the idea is, what must be behind this voice? There must be a heart prepared with the battery that is needed. And what is that battery? That battery is what we call love and sympathy, the greatest power there is.

A person who is material, who is fighting for his own from morning to evening, who is looking for his own benefit, who is in trouble and bitter,

25. O.t., t.c.: "in full" inserted
26. T.c.: "no doubt is", changed back by Sk. to "is no doubt"
27. Ibid.: "way" instead of "form"
28. Ibid.: "amazing" instead of "amusing"
29. Ibid.: this phrase was omitted, but reinserted by Sk.
30. Ibid.: this phrase was omitted
31. O.t., t.c.: "a" added
32. T.c.: "were" instead of "was"
33. In the "tp." Sk., following the text of the "o.t.", changed "as a burden" into "its abode", probably because of the word "has", which precedes it. "Has" could well have been heard, however, while "lies" was said;
    O.t., t.c.: "has its abode"
34. T.c.: this part of the question was omitted, but reinserted by Sk.
35. Ibid.: "voice" instead of "touch"

who is in the midst of fighting and[36] he is fighting too, he cannot heal. The healer must be free; free to sympathize; free to love his fellowman even more than himself.

What teaches this love? Where can one learn it? Where can one get it? The key to this love-element is God. As we look upon life today with all its progress, what is lacking? It is God. God is the key to that unlimited store of love which is in the heart of man.

I was once very amused and surprised at an answer. A very godly and goodnatured maid working in the house, could not answer a knock at the door as[37] quickly as it should[38] have been answered, and the lady-visitor who was waiting at the door became very impatient and spoke crossly to the maid. I asked the maid what had happened. She was not cross at all; she smiled and said, "yes, yes, that lady was very cross with me." I said, "Well, what was the matter with her; what made her cross; what was the reason?" And this[39] maid with innocence in her face replied, "the reason? there is no God." A beautiful answer. Where God is lacking there is no love. Wherever there is love, there is God. [40]Wherever there is God, there is love.[40] If we interpret it rightly, what causes pain and suffering? It is the lack of life. What is life? It is love. And what is love? It is God. What every individual wants, what the world wants, is God. By music, by harmony, by tone, by the science of right attuning[41], by the life of good, all we have to attain, all we have to gain to bless our lives is God. This is the central theme of all good.

---

36. Ibid.: "and" put in parentheses
37. Ibid.: "so" instead of "as", changed back by Sk. to "as"
38. Ibid.: "could" instead of "should"
39. Ibid.: "the" instead of "this"
40. Ibid.: this sentence was omitted, but was reinserted by Sk.
41. O.t., t.c.: "tuning"

A typescript of a lecture from the legacy of Murshida Martin, handed down by Mrs. Duce to Sirdar, and copied by Sk. In a separate annotation Sk. writes: "doubtful whether authentic." Parts of the text do not seem to be Pir-o-Murshid's own words.

Revelation When Awake and When Asleep.

If there is a divine essence that is to be found in man, it is intelligence, and when the intelligence learns from the names and forms of the objective world and collects knowledge in this way, it is the collection of this knowledge which may be called intellect. But when the same intelligence finds another source of knowledge, that source which is within oneself, not without, it is that source of knowledge which may be called wisdom.

We in our daily use of the words intellect and wisdom very often confuse these two words; very often we [1]say to[1] a wise man, [2]'clever man' and very often we call a clever person wise. Anyone who is intelligent enough to guard his interest in his everyday life may be called a clever man; he cannot be called a wise man at the same time. A wise man is he who sees further than every person. And how can we recognize that wisdom in man? It is not difficult to recognize it. It is natural. The first sign of wisdom is gentleness; it makes a person gentle and gentle means everything. Gentle means considerate, gentle means forgiving, gentle means understanding, gentle means sympathetic. Gentle shows all different qualities which show in man as humane qualities.

When a person makes use of his intelligence for the[3] life, the objective life, the outside life, he no doubt profits by it, but does not fully profit

Documents: No original MSS have been received by the archives to date.

Tp. (a typescript, sent by Mrs. Duce to Sirdar, and copied by Sk.).
Sk.corr. (Sakina's corrections made in the "tp.").
Sk.ann. (a few annotations made by Sk. on a separate list).

It is the third lecture in a series of six lectures on "Spiritual Philosophy" given by Pir-o-Murshid Inayat Khan on 12th April 1923, in the Paul Elder Gallery in San Francisco, U.S.A. (For the program, issued by Paul Elder, see Appendix A.)

An annotation made by Sk. with a view to the authenticity of the texts of a series of lectures, including this one, reads [translated from Dutch by the compiler]: "We [Sirdar and Sakina] have been able to compare some fragments received from Mrs. Duce, with parts of lectures of which the original text is in our possession. It appeared that the version of the lecture sent by Mrs. Duce is a very poor rendering of the original text, in many places garbled and distorted."

Notes:

1. Sk.corr: "say to" replaced with "call"
2. Ibid.: "a" added
3. Ibid.: "the" crossed out

by something which is the most valuable thing in his life. He can only profit fully if he uses the same intelligence[4] for the life without[5] for the life within. It does not mean in the least that the intelligence must not be used outside, but must be used only to gain knowledge from within. It would make a person unbalanced even if a person became a saint or a mystic. He would only be a dream. That is not the ideal situation to be in.

The ideal is that the intelligence is the light of the eyes and intelligence is the eye of the heart and intelligence is the soul itself. Intelligence is something which expresses and represents the divine in man. Therefore it must be used to gain knowledge not only from without but also from within. The fulfilment of the purpose of our life and the satisfaction of this ever yearning soul is in the attainment of that knowledge which can be gained not only from that part of this life which is without, but also from the great phenomena of life which can be seen by turning the soul within.

We see [6]the difference in an ordinary person,[6] the difference between an ordinary person and a thoughtful person, that a thoughtful person sees a little further. He takes ~~a~~ precautions; before he utters a word, he thinks; before he acts, he feels. The ordinary man, with every impulse he has to say or to act, acts regardless of what results it will produce. Very few in this world we find who have, so to speak, control over thought, word or action. It seems so simple and yet it is so difficult, it seems the whole life is not sufficient to gain that control over one's words and acts.

And how absurd, when people spend their lives and trust in wonder-workings, after investigating phenomena, discussing about the laws that are hidden, discuss about revelations and sacred prayers, analyse them and scatter them to pieces, to overlook a simple thing like this--to have control over words and acts. And this mastery would produce a living phenomenon.

One does not need to study it in books; one does not need to gain this by any wonder-working or by anything mysterious. A simple wonder, most useful and precious in everyday life! How few think about it! Many are ready to claim their desire to know the truth, to know the mystery of life, to be able to work wonders, wishing to see phenomena. Life itself is phenomenal. Its every moment is full of miracle if one only knew what is life.

If I were to say what is life: life is revealing and life is a veiling; and it is the condition that unveils. And at the same time the veil is not over this life which is the objective life. The veil is over the heart of man. It is the life that is open, it is the eyes that are closed. Life is revealing, if one only knew what it is.

4. Ibid.: "not only" added
5. Ibid.: "but also" added
6. Ibid.: "the difference in an ordinary person," crossed out

Not only do living beings express their feelings, their thoughts, their secrets, their past, present and future in everything they do, but in their expressions, in their eyes, in their movement, in their voice, in their looks, nothing there is in this world which is hidden, and yet everything is hidden. If you can see, nothing is hidden; if you cannot see, all is hidden. Not only the life is hidden, but your own self is hidden. When we cannot see, we see nothing, and when we can, we can see ourselves and the whole life. It all becomes a scripture, an open page in ourselves, explaining in detail all we see, speaking out aloud in every form.

People wanting to have telepathic communications, communications perhaps with those who have passed, communications with the sages or with masters, if they only knew that every aspect of life, every form of life is open for communication. Even the rocks, as dead as they appear, you can communicate with them; the plants, trees, flowers, planets and living beings who pass before us, those who have passed and those who are living, all are open to communication if one knew and realized the nature and character of the secret of life which is ever revealing. What man lacks is the preparation for the attunement which enables him to communicate with the[3] life, life in all its aspects.

One experience which perhaps everybody has to a smaller or greater extent in his everyday life is what may be called 'impression.' Woman is more open to this impression than man for the reason of her responsive character by nature. Among men, the man of gentle and refined nature is more impressed and is more capable of having impressions. And what is this impression? Everything that reveals, everything that is reflected on the heart of man begins to reveal its nature, its character, its secret, and that is what is called impression.

When a person says that he saw a friend and that friend was very kind in his words and manner, but he does not think that person is straight--that is an impression. Now every word the person said, perhaps, and every action seemed all right and yet there was a reason for this person who had this impression to say this person was not straight, it was a feeling, a feeling without any reason. That is an impression. And for this a person need not be especially advanced spiritually or mystically. A person with a candid heart, kind intentions, a straightforward person is always open to impression. It is the reward of his goodness.

Then there is another manner in which one perceives a kind of warning, a feeling intensely rises from the heart, pertaining to his business, his domestic affairs, his friendship, his affairs of heart, a feeling that something will become right or something will go wrong. If you ask that person, "what reason can you give?", he has no reason, only he knows something is going wrong or coming right. When something is coming right, there is a hope, a consolation, a kind of ease. When something is going wrong, one feels despair, depression in some form or other, that something is going wrong. He may not get a clear idea, but a feeling comes, and it is this which is called "intuition."

Man has a greater share in intuition than the animals. But as man is so absorbed in the small things of life, his occupation and activities which divide his mind, thought and energies, it makes him less capable of receiving and understanding that message which comes as an intuition, than even the horses and dogs and cats. The domestic animals such as horses and dogs and cats and the birds which are accustomed to live in the human surroundings, they very often perceive conditions. When there is grave news to come, they begin to give signs and those who know something of their language have perceived it, and people of all ages called this superstition.

All is superstition when one does not know it, and it is all science when one understands it. Friends, the[3] life is music, and when there is a false note every keen heart begins to feel there is a false note, there is a wrong harmony, there is a rhythm lacking. The lack speaks and that language even the animals and birds understand. When man does not understand, what does that mean? Man is made to understand much more than the animals and birds, only man has become so one-sided. Day and right he gives all his intelligence to the outer things and has very little time for the inner. Therefore his intelligence is formed for the outer things and it is kept back from knowing and attaining the knowledge which comes from within.

During the wartime many who had thought the intuition a kind of superstition had begun to see that though it is a superstition, it is true. How many mothers and how many wives have known the illness or the death of their beloved son or husband? How they have felt from a distance their pain, their suffering, their torment and longing, their love! No person with the slightest feeling in his heart and fineness in his thought can doubt the fact that there is a faculty of intuition in man, more or less, which brings to him a knowledge for which he can give no reason, or if asked, he has none.

And there is another channel of knowledge which is called "inspiration." There are many who wish to write a poem or a play or something. They will go on desiring for months and months but it never comes to them satisfactory, and as it does not satisfy them, it does not satisfy us. It is a labour which is lost, wasted. And there is another person[7]who may[7], perhaps, in writing a poem or music, that[8] there might come a moment when he feels like writing, and if he has a pencil and writes it down, it comes as an answer to a satisfaction, and there is an air of ease, and when that is shown to the people it cannot but attract their appreciation and love for it, for it is something living, something harmonious.

7. Ibid.: "who may" crossed out
8. Ibid.: "that" crossed out

What is inspiration? Inspiration is a knowledge which is born from harmony. It is the harmony of the soul which gives birth to inspiration. Does not[9] it take time for a perfect theme of music when inspiration comes? No, it is a flow of water, it is like a spring, spontaneous. Its coming brings harmony. When you record it, it becomes as a picture of harmony. Whoever sees it will read it at once as harmony. [10]He does it[10] in architecture, in sculpture, painting, singing or dancing. Whatever comes of an inspiring character, it quickly pleases the heart, it is a magnet in whatever form it comes.

What is the meaning of art? Art is beauty, the beauty which is received from the divine source, the offspring of harmony. When that beauty is placed before us, it will make its impression, and there is no need to be a poet, a musician or painter in order to receive inspiration. Whatever the occupation of your life, if you receive inspiration at all you will show the harmony and beauty in whatever you do. The whole life is before us to express our soul, if our soul only speaks that harmony which is the inner essence of the whole creation.

It is a great pity, friends, that the art, poetry and music should so decline as we see to-day in the whole world. Why do we not find many Wagners, Beethovens, many Mozarts? Why do we not find the blessed poets who existed for us in the past, [11]every century back?[11] It shows that it is the fault of the musician, poet or writer; it is the condition against which he has to fight. The life's condition has become so difficult to struggle with that his whole effort goes in struggling. Therefore someone capable of receiving inspiration very often struggles for years and years.

And it becomes very hard and rarely one comes, perhaps, who is able to do something. But many of the artists are real seekers after truth and beauty and genuineness in their art and science, and they are deprived of inspiration in their expressions in poetry and music by the condition of life which is too hard to get through.

There is another way of revelation which is generally seen in the dream and especially in such dreams that are called "visions." A vision does not necessarily come when a person is fast asleep, but mostly comes when a person is half asleep. The subject of the dream is the most interesting subject especially for a man of a scientific bent of mind, how every dream, if one studies it, is an expression of a certain sense. It conveys to us something of the past or of the present or of the future. If one does not understand it, it is the lack of one's understanding. And the most interesting part about it is that the symbolical dream of every person is peculiar to his particular temperament and his particular stage of development.

9. Sk.ann.: "not" crossed out
10. Ibid.: Sk. suggests to change "He does it" to "It may come"
11. Ibid.: after "every century back" Sk. put a question mark.

It is therefore that no one in the world has ever been able to gather a kind of language of dreams because the language of every person's dream is peculiar to himself, and the best reader of such language is that person for himself. If he were not advanced he would never know the meaning, but if he is advanced spiritually and if he knows and understands, there is no one who will understand better than himself.

It is the same with one's illness, that science will not be able to tell you fully, if you yourself cannot understand it. No one can be a better doctor than yourself. The physician knows what you tell him and what little he sees from outward signs, but you can do it for yourself. So it is with dreams; when a heart can see through life, when his mind is able to focus its opinion from impression, then certainly a new world is before him. [12]Through that if one looks[12] or in the night when asleep, he only sees it.

Of course visions are of many different kinds. Vision can communicate more with all things and with all worlds, with the seen and the unseen. There are some people who may see in a condition called trance, when half asleep and when they just nod for a moment in a comfortable and easy condition they feel it. But besides all these different ways by which one perceives the knowledge of life, it all sums up in one word and one thing, and that is revelation.

Once the heart is open to the life which is within, to the subjective world and the objective world, when one is able to turn the heart from the objective to the subjective world and from the subjective to the objective world, one has given a new life to oneself. Thus Sa'di has said, "Every tree can become as a page of the Bible if the heart is open and the inner eye is able to see their thought."

There is not one thing in life [13]that its whole being[13] is not revealing. If there is a veil, it is the veil of man's ignorance. If there is a veil that hides from our eyes, it is the veil we carry in our hands. We cover things instead of unveiling life. We cover life by our ignorance of life. And if you will say, "How can one attune to these revelations? How can one rise to that plane that reveals?" I will say a study, a study is necessary to some extent, meditation is necessary; yes, concentration is also necessary. But what is there besides? There is knowledge too that concentration helps, that meditation helps, that study of mystical philosophy helps. But what is most helpful? It is simple and yet so little known and so little thought about.

12. Ibid.: after "Through that if one looks", Sk. put a question mark.
13. Ibid.: after "that its whole being", Sk. put a question mark.

The most essential thing in the pursuit of truth is true living. How very simple it seems and how very difficult it is to live in the world of falsehood, morning and evening things of false nature and false character tempting and distracting us from our life's hope, pulling us from that path which is the real and right path. It is a test every moment of our life, whatever be the grade of our evolution. Therefore the most essential thing is to be able to be strong enough to fight and stand against and strive for the right path. And besides study, meditation and concentration one thing is needed, and that is to love truth and to resist the bent[14] of thoughts and everything that comes to us, not to forget truth as the ideal, as the source, the path, and the goal.

---

14. Sk.corr.: "(trend)?"

From a San Francisco newspaper, the *San Francisco Examiner*, 16 April 1923

San Francisco, April[1]

"Day by day I am growing better and better, as a creed, has but one fault. That fault is found in all parts of the world today. In place of the pronoun I, Coué should have said we."

Americans are children by comparison with us of the Orient. They are constantly yearning for the truth, and this frame of mind makes them open to right and wrong both. Americans do not discriminate in their search for religion.

You say religion and science fight each other? In the beginning they were the same thing. But like spiritual impulse they grew at a different rate. Now science is ahead of spirit and man says, "Lo! see what I have done."

Love is like water. It expands everywhere, it may be a drop or an ocean; it helps the earth or it destroys the earth.

According to Inayat Khan, everyone tries to express himself in some way--it may be by writing, or singing or by dealing in business. *The Sufists* [sic] *believe* music to be the most satisfactory means for self-expression, and sing or play for many hours at their ceremonies.

Note:

1. This article contains material which apparently comes from a personal interview, perhaps on April 13.

A typewritten lecture handed down by Mrs. Prebble (a pupil of Murshida Martin's) to Martha Burk, and inherited from the latter by Miss Hayat Stadlinger, an American mureed, initiated in Suresnes in 1926, who passed it on to the Biographical Department in Suresnes.

Jallal-u-din Rumi.[2] 1

Beloved ones of God,

My subject this afternoon is Jallal-u-din Rumi, the greatest poet the world has ever known. A poet whose message, in his life and work both, marks a distinct line as a new era, a new step in Sufism, which was the most ancient school of Mystics and Philosophers, and which originated from the ancient mystic school of Egypt. The first and best known initiate of that particular school was Abraham, the father of the three great religions of the world, Judaism, the Christian religion and the Islamic religion.

Jallal-u-din Rumi gave a new life and a new form to the mystical current, and it is from his time that the Sufi Mystic culture spread throughout the world. The reason was that he was not only a mystic and dreamer, but he was the most learned man of his time. A great statesman and politician, at the head of the law of his country (like a chief judge) and he had a great reputation among the people as a most learned man. A man of reason, most practical and wide awake; a master of theology. In point of fact, he was the man of the day in his country. He had read poetry, and some of the poems of Attar, but his learning was based upon theological training.

Documents: No original MSS have been received by the archives to date.

Tp. (a typescript received from Miss Hayat Stadlinger in 1983).
O.c. (a copy of an old typescript, only available in the archives on a microfiche made by Hq.).
Sk.tp. (a separate annotation in Sk.'s hwr., dated "September 1954", says that the document from which Sk. copied the lecture is missing in the B.D. This missing document probably is the "o.t." The "tp." had not yet been added to the archives at that time.)

The "tp." and "o.t." in these series of lectures given in America in 1923 seem to have been copied from the same old document. But then, while handed down over the years by different lines of mureeds, they underwent some separate changes. Probably the "tp." kept nearest to the original text.

Sk.corr. (corrections made by Sk. on a separate paper).

This is the third lecture in a series of six lectures on "Sufi Poets," given by Pir-o-Murshid Inayat Khan on April 17th, 1923, in the Paul Elder Gallery, San Francisco, U.S.A. (For the program issued by Paul Elder, see Appendix A.)

Notes:

1. O.c.: added "San Francisco, U.S.A., Spring 1923";
   Sk.tp.: "America 1923" added.
2. See, for the accepted spelling of the name: "List of persons, Places and Events" on p. 415

The story of his life is most wonderful, especially his awakening to the Sufi ideal. Once he was sitting at leisure with his manuscripts. At that time there was no printing, no books, so manuscripts were treasures. And there entered a man in rags. From the appearance of that man any one would have thought that he was a beggar, a pauper; at the same time he walked[3] like a king. And instead of a salutation of any sort, the first thing he did was to remove all the manuscripts that were there.

Rumi could not understand a man in rags coming into the house of a leading citizen and throwing away all the manuscripts he had so valued. But he was a great man; he did not allow himself to express his annoyance with this conduct. He was perfectly self-disciplined; only he asked him, "What do you wish to do?" And this man said, "What are you reading? Is it not finished yet? You have been reading all your life and still it is not finished. You are reading in small pages which cannot contain what the book of life is continually revealing, and this has absorbed all your life. What little is left, is that also to be absorbed in this?" Rumi said, "What is there to think about? What do you wish to point out?" "I wish to ask you if you have considered what is the purpose of your life. Is this position you occupy just now, this rank and position and fame, is this the purpose? What are you growing to, what are you looking forward to? What aim and object do you have before you? Is your life so momentary as one sees it from birth to death which is not more than four days, or is it a continual life? If it is continued, where is it continued? If this exalted position belongs to you now, it once belonged to somebody else, and it will again belong to somebody else. Even if it is something important, it really does not belong to you. And these helpless manuscripts, they are subject to destruction one day. If that is your wisdom, how long will it last? Have you looked into the manuscript of your heart? Have you looked into life, to see what life is continually teaching everyone? You have worshipped God, have you talked with Him? Have you seen Him? Have you really known Him? What is the use of your worship? A religion that all your life you have followed, do you know where it came from? What is the source of it? Do you wish to live as everybody in this world is living, not knowing for what they are living? The horses and camels also live and they are busy, but there is no credit in their being busy. The credit of one's occupation, is in the virtue of the occupation. Have you thought of the virtue of your occupation, is it reliable? If it is a passing virtue, it is not a reliable virtue."

This made Rumi think, and this moved Rumi to tears. And the personality of that ragged man, what it poured out to Rumi! It was like unlimited wealth. Rumi had nothing to say. He was overwhelmed with all that this

3. O.c., Sk.tp.: "in" added

chance stranger had told him, and as certainly[4] as this chance stranger had come, [5]so certainly[5] he had gone. When he had gone, Rumi said, "That God Whom I have worshipped all my life, today I saw him[6] in human form."

The man in rags was Shams-i-Tabriz[7], and Rumi was so impressed by what he had said to him, that he followed him. The first thing Rumi had to meet with was bitter criticism on all sides. No one could understand how a man so learned, a man of such ability and education, could spend his time always walking with this ragged stranger. But wherever he walked or stood, there Rumi walked and stood, and if a hundred people stood around, or a thousand people stood around, he did not care. And this seeming misfortune ended in the resignation of Rumi from his position. He could no longer hold his position with the increasing criticism, and he had no time to explain to everyone. He was too much absorbed in listening to Shams-i-Tabriz[7]. He had no time to argue. All his time was taken to understand what Shams-i-Tabriz[7] said. And this apparent misfortune ended in a sudden shock. One day, in the same way as he had come, so suddenly Shams-i-Tabriz[7] disappeared.

Then Rumi found himself alone, and yet not alone in the world of thought that was surrounding him. Rumi could see nothing but the deep ideas that Shams-i-Tabriz[7] had given him. He had opened his outlook on life. It was more than he said, it was something awakened and opened in the heart of Rumi. It was a kind of expansion of Rumi's consciousness. It was not a learning or a teaching, more than that, it was a phenomenon. Yet Rumi, like a child, had absorbed every word that fell from the lips of Shams-i-Tabriz[7], and treasured them in his heart. He could not dry his tears for days and days, and for weeks and weeks. He thought if it was goodness, it was not goodness as we conceive ~~it~~ of it; it was the greatest goodness that could exist. It was a divine mercy and compassion. If it was education, it was not as man knows education. It was a shower of knowledge. It was like a key to Heaven and earth. It was something which words could not explain.

Now, on the one side Rumi had lost his position and to some extent his reputation in the eyes of the world, and even in the eyes of those near and dear to him, because they could not understand. And on the other hand the only one he had to lean upon was Shams-i-Tabriz[7], and he was gone too. Therefore, naturally the life of Rumi became a life of contemplation; a life of studying nature, and a life of devotion to a divine personality that had once appeared before him. So, all that is necessary for the spiritual life, came into the life of Rumi, all that was needed to tread the spiritual path.

4. Sk.corr.: "suddenly" instead of "certainly"
5. O.c., Sk.tp.: "as certainly";
Sk.corr.: "as suddenly" instead of "so certainly". See the sentence in the next paragraph: "so suddenly".
6. O.c.: "Him" instead of "him"
7. Sk.corr.: "Shams Tabriz" or "Shams-i-Tabrizi". See, for spelling: "List of Persons, Places and Events", p. 415

Therefore, the life of Rumi became the kind of life that Sufis for many centuries have followed.

At times when his thoughts and feelings made him think there was a kind of congestion on his heart, he would ask the musicians to come and sing, in the meditative way of singing. They sang mostly the words of Shams-i-Tabriz[7] and Rumi. Words of the heart of man waking to higher devotion; words pointing out the divine ways of life and the secret of concentration. That custom exists even now in India and Persia. There are times when the beautiful words of such great poets as Rumi and Shams-i-Tabriz[7] are sung with music, and the people sit there and listen and enjoy and are benefitted by it, and they are tuned to that pitch where they can get the real benefit out of that music, and this assembly is considered the most sacred assembly, when the sacred music is played. And from this a new way was found which was different from the existing Yogism[8] in the East, and where this way was different was that a tendency to look at the whole life as an illusion, which is true, and to try to get detached from it, that one may not be caught by this life, which keeps man back; this tendency made a sort of wall between the Yogi and the world. Rumi's way of contemplation was, after the contemplation of his teacher and what he[9] said, and the truth that was given to him; after looking at life in that way, then to melt it all with the vibrations of music.

It is all attachment and yet above attachment, which means on the sea, and yet not in the sea. It is the same symbology as that used in the Bible, the walking of Christ on the water. There are three ways of living life: walking upon the water, swimming in the water, and the third way is to be drowned. Those who are drowned are those attached to the material world, and this attachment in the end sinks them. Then there is a way of going through life which is like swimming. And the third way is walking on the water, that is going through all things and yet not touching them, standing above them, to be in the world but not of it.

And this has[10] won the greatest reward for the Sufis of the East, and that reward was the charm of their personalities. The feeling developed by divine contemplation enabled them to spread the waves of love and affection, and to look at life with optimism and hope, and with hope to make the best of it; and if it is hard and disappointing, still to make the best of it. To bend all material towards its best purpose and to make every aspect of life turn into the means of the fulfilment of the whole creation, that no material be lost.

To the Sufi, saint and sinner both come close to him. Friend or enemy, he is the well-wisher and lover of both, for behind the friend and the

8. Ibid.: "Yoga" instead of "Yogism"
9. O.c., Sk.tp.: "had" added
10. O.c.: "has" omitted, but reinserted in Sk. hwr.

enemy he sees his Beloved. His power over his enemy is great, because his enemy cannot longer hold him so when he sees in him a friend. It is the contemplation of the Beloved that the Sufi carries ever with him. It is the one being[11] he knows, and he is always in His presence. He cannot keep enmity; the fire of his love burns up the sting of enmity.

The greatest pity of the day is how little we understand the word "love." Very often man understands by love no more than a bargain; if you give me sixpence, I will give you a shilling. That is not love, it is too small when one expects a return. The first lesson man should learn from love, there is no "I." "I" is the very enemy of love. People think there cannot be a greater loss than losing "I." If they only knew, there cannot be a greater gain. Because when the "I" is lost, then all is gained. The whole process of esoteric or spiritual attainment is this, to give up "I" and gain all. This is the only secret which is at the back of all religions, philosophies and mysticism, if one can understand it. Little can be said about it, but it is [12]to practise[12]. In every little thing one does, this small "I" comes up, and to keep it subdued takes time and practice. The Sufi teachings have all been given for this. How can this little "I" be kept down, that it may not spring up and stand in the way of one's growth? Friends, we may have many enemies and many who oppose us, but if we looked at life closely and understood it, we should find that we have no greater enemy than ourselves. All that we wish is pushed away by this "I."

And Rumi has made a most beautiful picture of this philosophy. He begins his most wonderful work "The Masnavi" by saying: "Listen to the flute and hear what it says. What is it that comes from the flute that wins your soul, that pierces through your heart?" Then he gives us an example. The flute, a piece of reed that was cut from its stem and was brought away from its origin, has its story to tell. It is hollow; its heart is empty; but besides that emptiness, several holes were made to its heart, that it may give all the notes that it is asked to give out, from the lowest to the highest note. And then he goes on to say, "But what is this flute and where is its voice?" The one is under the lips of the Beloved, and the other is singing to the world outside.

There he leaves it for man to solve the riddle. There he has given a picture of man. Man is a piece of bamboo cut away from its stem; that stem is whole, is perfect; the piece is imperfect; life has cut holes to its heart that it may sound all the notes. Once the holes are made, it begins to give the music that wins the souls of men.

Besides this example of the flute, there is one verse of Rumi's which is most beautiful: "Many became my friends through love, who have not understood what it is in me that brings me closer. If they only knew this,

11. Sk.corr.: "Being"
12. O.c.: "to be practised" instead of "to practise"

they would solve the whole problem of life." What does he mean by this? He means that it is the hollowness and emptiness of the reed that brings it nearer to the lips of the divine love, and so it is with the heart of man. The heart of man is the flute of God, and it touches the lips of God when it is empty. As long as it is not empty, it does not touch the lips of God.

All revelation, the whole secret, can be found in the heart of man; there is nowhere else man can find the secret of life except within himself. No doubt Rumi has shown in one of his verses the way to the goal, in which he says, "If you wish to attain God, and at the same time to attain to all things of this world, you should not strive for it, for it is not possible." This does not mean that all things in this world must be renounced. But if the position in life presents a condition where there are two things to do, either to renounce the very object that we have within us, or to renounce something on the outside, it is better to renounce that something on the outside, and keep that object within. This is the study of everybody in this world. Everyone has good intentions; everyone wishes to get the best there is in life. But the first place where man finds difficulty is in something that he values the most, and yet he does not know if it exists; and there is something else that he values less, but at the same time he knows it _is_.

And the value of all religion, philosophy and mysticism is to help man to perceive that object within. It is something your ideal only can touch; something only known to your consciousness and even your consciousness cannot make it intelligible enough for your mind to grasp. And to hold to this in the midst of so many things which are intelligible, this is the test. Man thinks, "Shall I take this that I know, or shall I go in pursuit of something of whose existence I am not certain; shall I not be at a loss?" For modern life teaches commercialism. Man hesitates to do something in which there is no gain; it does not appeal to him. Virtue is not precious to him, but in reality it is the greatest gain, because nothing else in the world can satisfy.

Therefore, in the end one comes to the conviction that there is only one thing in the world worthwhile, and that is spiritual attainment, or the attainment of God. Only what one needs is to strengthen the faculty of faith, which stands by its own strength even when you touch an ideal which has nothing else to hold it.

Friends, the difference between the world and God can be seen by understanding the difference between the sun and the things of the earth. All things of the earth must have something to hold them, if not they[13] fall down. But the sun, nothing is holding it; it stands[14] itself, supported by nothing. And so with God. All things of this world are supported by reasoning. If there is anything that stands without reasoning, it is God. And why is

13. O.c., Sk.tp.: "will" added
14. O.c.: "by" added, then crossed out

it so? Because His true being[15] is yourself. It is only seeing yourself in its perfection which is the vision of God. But at the same time it must be understood that there are two ways of looking at it. God, the inner and true God, we cannot even call "God." It would be an error if we tried to give Him a name; it would be limited. If we call Him "One," it is addition and division, which God has not. Words cannot explain. If one is to explain the real God, his explanation is "silence."

There is another way of looking at it. In order to attain to that God, we must make a God within ourselves. Therefore, the God of each one is different. By giving God a personality and by thinking of that personality, we lose our own personality. By raising Him to a height, we are raised to a height. Until it so happens that the man-made God carries one along until he touches the real God. The man-made God protects, and the real God lives.

And[16] this is the fulfilment of all religion, all philosophy, all mysticism. And it is this realization of truth which closes the lips of those who have realized it. This is the great secret of life.

Thank you all for your sympathetic response. God bless you.

---

15. O.c.: "Being"
16. O.c.: "And" omitted

A typewritten lecture handed down by Mrs. Prebble (a pupil of Murshida Martin's) to Martha Burk, and inherited from the latter by Miss Hayat Stadlinger, an American mureed, initiated in Suresnes in 1926, who passed it on to the Biographical Department in Suresnes.

Spiritual Development[1] by the Aid of Music.

Beloved ones of God:

My subject this morning is [1]"Spiritual Attainment by the Aid of Music."[1]

Before commencing the subject I should like first to explain what the word spiritual means. [2]Is it[2] goodness which may be called spiritual, or is it a great wonder-working, or a power of miracle, or great intellectual power? The answer is, no. Life when put together in all its aspects is one music, and to tune [3]one's self[3] to the harmony of this perfect music, is the real spiritual attainment.

You may ask me, "What is it that keeps man back from spiritual attainment?" The answer will be, that it is the denseness of this material existence, and that he is unconscious of his spiritual being. Divided into limitations, this prevents that free flow and free movement which is the nature and character of life. For instance, what do I mean by this denseness? There is a rock and you want to produce sound from it; it does not give resonance; it does not give an answer to your desire of producing sound. But the string

Documents: No original MSS have been received by the archives to date.

Tp. (a typescript, received from Miss Hayat Stadlinger in 1983).
O.t. (very similar to the "tp.", from Gd.'s legacy.

These two documents, "tp." and "o.t.", seem to have been copied from the same old document. But then, handed down over the years by different lines of mureeds, they underwent some separate changes. Probably the "tp." kept nearest to the original text.).

Sk.tp. (a typewritten copy made by Sk. from the "o.t."; the "tp." at that time had not yet been added to the archives).
Gd.corr. (corrections made by Gd. in the "o.t."-copy of which a microfiche was made).

This lecture was published in *The Sufi Message of Hazrat Inayat Khan*, Volume II (1960), Music, chapter XIV.

This is the fourth in a series of six lectures on "Music", given by Pir-o-Murshid Inayat Khan on April 18th, 1923, in the Paul Elder Gallery, San Francisco, U.S.A.

Notes:

1. In the program issued by Paul Elder (see Appendix A), the title of this lecture is "Spiritual Development by the Aid of Music," and as such it was passed on. The subject, mentioned by Pir-o-Murshid in the first sentence, however, is "Spiritual Attainment by the Aid of Music."
2. Sk.tp.: "It is", followed by a question mark, so it probably is a mistake.
3. Gd.corr.: "oneself"

or wire, that will give an answer to the tone you want. You strike it and it answers. There are objects which give resonance to sound. You wish to produce in them a sound, and they sound it; they make your music complete. And so with human nature. One person is heavy and dull; you tell him, he cannot understand; you speak to him, he will not hear. He will not respond to music, to beauty or to art. What is it? It is denseness. There is another person who is ready to appreciate and understand music and poetry, or beauty in any form; in character, in manner, in every form beauty is appreciated by such a one. And it is that which is the awakening of the soul, which is the living condition of the heart. And it is this which is the real spiritual attainment. Spiritual attainment is to make the spirit live; to become conscious. When man is not conscious of soul and spirit, only conscious of material being, he is dense; he is away from spirit.

You may say, "What is spirit, and what is matter?" The difference between spirit and matter is as the difference between water and snow; frozen water is snow, and melted snow is water. It is spirit in its denseness which we call matter; it is matter in its fineness which may be called spirit. Once a materialist said to me, "I do not believe in any spirit or soul or hereafter. I believe in eternal matter." I said to him, "Your belief is not very different from mine, only that which you call eternal matter, I call spirit; it is a difference in terms; that is not a thing to dispute about, because we both believe in eternity; so long as we meet in eternity, what difference if one call it matter, and the other spirit. It is one life from beginning to end."

Beauty is born of harmony. What is harmony? Harmony is right proportion; in other words, right rhythm. And what is life? Life is the outcome of harmony. The whole creation has at the back of it, and the whole secret of creation is harmony. Intelligence longs to attain to the perfection of harmony. What man calls happiness, comfort, or profit and gain, all that he longs for and wishes to attain, is harmony in smaller or greater proportion; is longing for harmony. Even in attaining the most mundane things, he always wishes harmony. But very often he does not adopt right methods. Very often his methods are wrong. The object attained by both good and bad methods is the same, but the way they try to attain them, that turns them into right or wrong. It is not the object which is wrong, it is the way one adopts for attaining it.

[4]No one, whatever his station in life, wishes for inharmony, for all suffering, pain, trouble, are inharmony.[4]

To attain spirituality is to realize that the whole universe is one symphony; in this, every individual is one note, and his happiness is in becoming perfectly harmonious to the harmony of the universe. It is not following a certain religion that makes one spiritual, or having a certain belief, or being a fanatic in regard to one idea, or by becoming too good to live in this world. Many good people there are who do not even understand

4. Ibid.: this paragraph was added to the previous one.

what spirituality means. They are very good, but they do not know yet what ultimate good is. Ultimate good is harmony itself. For instance, all the different principles and beliefs of the religions of this world, taught and proclaimed by priests and teachers, but which men are not always able to follow and express, come naturally from the heart of a man who attunes himself to the rhythm of the universe. His every action, every word he speaks, every feeling he has, every sentiment he expresses, is all harmonious; it is all virtues, it is all religion. It is not following a religion, it is living a religion, making one's life a religion, which is necessary.

Music is the miniature of the whole harmony of the universe, for the harmony of the universe is music itself. And man being the miniature of the universe, must show the same harmony, in his pulsation, the beat of his heart, and in his vibration he shows rhythm and tone, harmonious or inharmonious chords. His health or illness, joy or discomfort, all show the music or lack of music in his life.

And what does music teach us? Music helps us to train ourselves in some way or other to harmony, and it is that which is the magic or secret behind music. When you hear music that you enjoy, it tunes you and puts you in harmony with life. Therefore man needs music; he longs for music. Many say that they do not care for music, but they have not heard music. If they really hear music, it will teach[5] their souls, and certainly they cannot help but love it. If not, it only means that they have not heard music sufficiently, and they have not made their heart calm and quiet in order to listen, and enjoy and appreciate it. Besides, music develops that faculty of appreciation, by which you learn to appreciate all that is good and beautiful, in the form of art and science; in the form of music and poetry. Every aspect of beauty you can appreciate.

What deprives man of all the beauty around him, is his heaviness of body or heaviness of heart. He is pulled down to the earth, and by that all has become limited, and when he shakes off that heaviness and feels joyous, he feels light; and all good tendencies, such as gentleness and tolerance, forgiveness, love and appreciation, all these beautiful qualities come, by being light; light in the mind and soul and body.

Where does music come from? Where does the dance come from? It all comes from that natural spiritual life which is within. When that spiritual life springs forth, it lightens all the burdens[6] that man has. It makes his life smooth; floating on the ocean of life. The faculty of appreciation makes one light. Life is just like the ocean. When there is no appreciation, when there is no receptivity, one sinks like a piece of iron or stone, to the bottom of the sea. He cannot float like the boat, which is hollow, which is receptive.

5. Ibid.: "touch" instead of "teach"
6. Ibid.: "burden"

The difficulty in the spiritual path is always what comes from ourselves. Man does not like to be a pupil, he likes to be a teacher. If man only knew, of the great ones who have come from time to time to this world, their greatness and perfection was in their pupilship, and not in teaching. The greater the teacher, the better pupil he was. He learned from every one, the great and the lowly, wise and foolish, old and young. He learned from their lives, and studied human nature in all its aspects.

One learning to tread the spiritual path must become as an empty cup in order that the wine of music and harmony may be poured[7] down in[7] one's heart. You may say, "How can one become an empty cup?" I will tell you how the cups show filled instead of empty. Very often a person comes to me and says, "Here I am, can you help me spiritually?" "Yes," I say. But he says, "I want to know first of all, what do you think about life or death, or the beginning or the end?" Well, now, I wonder what his attitude will be if his previously conceived opinion does not agree with mine. He wants to learn, and yet he does not want to be empty. That means to go to the stream of water, and close the glass, and want[8] water, and yet the glass is closed; the glass is closed with preconceived ideas. But where have the preconceived ideas come from? No idea can be called one's own. All ideas have been learned from one source or another, but in time one comes to think they are one's own. For these ideas one will argue and dispute, although they do not satisfy fully, at the same time they are his battle ground, and all the time will keep his cup closed.

Mystics therefore have adopted a different way. They have learned a different course, and that course is self-effacement, or in other words, unlearning what one has learned.

Therefore in the East they say, the first thing that is learned, is to understand how to become a pupil. They do not learn first what God is, or what life is. The first thing to learn is how to become a pupil. But one thinks that in this way one loses his individuality. But what is individuality? Is it not what is collected? One's ideas and opinions, what are they? They are just collected knowledge. This should be unlearned. How can one unlearn? You will say that the character of the mind is such that what one learns is engraved upon it, and how then can one unlearn it?

Unlearning is to complete the knowledge. To see a person and say, "That person is wicked." That is learning. To see further, and recognize something good in that person, that is unlearning. When you see the goodness in some one whom you have called wicked, you have unlearned. You have unraveled that knot. First you learn by seeing with one eye, then you learn to see with two eyes, and that makes complete sight. You have once

7. Ibid.: "into" instead of "down in"
8. O.t., Sk.tp.: "the" added

said, "I hate him." That is learning. And then you say, "Oh, no, I can like him, or I can pity him." And when you say that, you have seen him with two eyes.

All that we have learned in this world is a partial knowledge, and when this is uprooted by another point of view, then we have knowledge in its completed form. That is called mysticism. Why is it called mysticism? Because it cannot be put into words. Words will show us one side of it, but the other side is beyond words.

The whole manifestation is duality, the duality which makes us intelligent, and behind the duality is unity. If we do not rise beyond duality and go towards unity, we do not attain perfection, which is called spirituality.

This does not mean that our learning is of no use. It is of great use. It gives us[9] the power of discrimination and of discerning differences. This makes the intelligence sharp and the sight keen, so that we understand the value of things and their use. It is all a part of human evolution, and all useful. So we must learn first, and unlearn afterwards. You do not look at the sky first when you are standing on the earth. First look at the earth and see what it offers you, to learn and observe, but at the same time do not think that your life's purpose is fulfilled by only looking at the earth. The fulfilment of life's purpose is in looking at the sky.

The wonderful thing that one finds in music is that it helps man to concentrate, or meditate, independent of thought, and therefore music seems to be the bridge over the gulf between the form and the formless. If there is anything intelligent, effective, and at the same time formless, it is music. Poetry suggests form; line and color suggest form; but music suggests no form. And besides there is that resonance which vibrates through the whole being, lifts the thought above the denseness of matter, almost turns matter into spirit, into its original condition, through the harmony of vibrations touching every atom of one's whole being.

The beauty of line and color can go so far and no further; the joy of fragrance can go a little further; music touches our innermost being and in that way produces new life; a life that gives exaltation to the whole being, raising it thereby to that perfection in which lies the fulfilment of man's life.

Thank you all for your sympathetic response.

God bless you.

---

9. Sk.tp.: "us" omitted, but reinserted by Sk.

A typescript of a lecture from the legacy of Murshida Martin, handed down by Mrs. Duce to Sirdar, and copied by Sk. In a separate annotation Sk. writes: "doubtful whether authentic." Parts of the text do not seem to be Pir-o-Murshid's own words.

The Word that Was Lost.[1]

This idea of a lost word is a most ancient idea. In the traditions of all religions, of all mystical and sacred cults, in all different philosophies, it is found somewhere or other. You will find this belief existing in all ages, and this idea has occupied the mind of man in various ways in his looking for the truth.

Man is a lover of curiosity, he is curious from the moment of his birth, and he continuously treads the path of curiosity. All the knowledge of heaven and earth that man attains is due to his curiosity, and there is no idea in religion or in tradition which takes prevalence over this idea, the idea of the Word having been lost. It has given a facility to those great teachers of truth, of the inner life, of symbolism, of mysticism. To give the truth that was written in their hearts as an answer to this problem.

At the same time it has given an opportunity to those who wish to mystify things more and more before the world in order to confuse those who are already confused, to keep them bound in their confusion. Verily, truth is simple. The difficulty is with us, we are not content with simplicity. We look for complexity, and simplicity does not satisfy us. Therefore we overlook something which is in hand and go in pursuit of something which is all the time in our pocket.

Documents: No original MS has been received by the archives to date.

Tp. (a typewritten copy made by Sk. from a typescript which was sent by Murshida Duce to Sr.).

It is not known who put words in parentheses in the "tp.".

This is the fourth in a series of six lectures on "Spiritual Philosophy," which was given by Pir-o-Murshid Inayat Khan on 19th April, 1923, in the Paul Elder Gallery, San Francisco, U.S.A. (For the program issued by Paul Elder, see Appendix A.)

An annotation made by Sk. with a view to the authenticity of the texts of several lectures, including this one, reads [translated from Dutch by the compiler]: "We [Sirdar and Sakina] have been able to compare some fragments received from Mrs. Duce, with parts of lectures of which the original text is in our possession. It appeared that the version of the lecture sent by Mrs. Duce to Sirdar is a very poor rendering of the original text, in many places garbled and distorted."

Notes:

1. In the program issued by Paul Elder (see Appendix A), the title of this lecture is "The Lost Word."

The key to this question that the word was lost can be found in the simple words of the Bible where you read that "First was the Word, and the Word was God." Who was lost? God was lost. To whom was it lost? To mankind who has closed its heart to Him Who is the yearning, Who is the seeking of the soul, and opened its heart in some other direction which can provide everything but God. And when one says, "I pursue what was lost," where is the key to the idea, the mantra or syllable which was lost? That word was lost which is mentioned as "First was the Word, and the Word was God." That was the Lost Word.

And now to explain, how can it be lost? Friends, nothing can be lost and nothing is lost. It is the illusion of a moment which gives one the idea that it was lost. It was not lost. What was lost is returned to you the moment your faith is able to penetrate through life, as soon as your heart is able to expand through life, and the moment your egoism gives you the power to change and seek after that which was lost, so long as it is lost. The moment you have God, it is there, and then you realize it was not lost. The loss is for the moment.

When we consider the process of the whole manifestation, of the whole creation, the whole process is summed up in this little idea that the Word was lost. The difference between the spiritual outlook on life and the material outlook on life is this, that the material man says that everything has evolved, evolved from something which was non-intelligent, everything has evolved through something which was unconscious, and through the evolution it has come that with effort it has awakened to a certain consciousness, and in man it shows more fully awakened.

If there is any difference between the spiritual outlook on life and the material outlook on life, it is only this, but at the same time the spiritual person also has the same outlook. For instance, what Darwin has perhaps in detail given, that behind all creation is this evolution, you can find in the words of a Persian poet of a thousand years ago[2] who said that in the mineral kingdom God slept, in the vegetable kingdom He dreamed, in the animal kingdom He woke, and in the human evolution He realized His own Self. This gives a proof of that saying of Solomon, that there is nothing new under the sun.

Man makes some little discoveries in his own consciousness or in his ideas and says: "I have brought something new, something which no man has ever thought about." If one only knew the phenomena[3] which is working inwardly and outwardly, one would find that it is the same thing which is outward, [4]matches his inward word, and what is working inwardly, is reflected outwardly. Therefore in the inner and outer planes and between these two planes his own work is going on.

2. The poet is Jalal ud Din Rumi.
3. Pir-o-Murshid often used "phenomena" for "phenomenon".
4. There are several other instances where in similar cases Pir-o-Murshid omitted "that"; so this sentence could well be as spoken by him.

What is absent in the outer planes is present in the inner plane. There is an action and reaction of the inward and outward continually going on. It is the whole scheme of nature. Therefore the only difference between the outlook of the material person and the spiritual person is that the spiritual person says that intelligence which fully manifests in man is not an outcome of this manifestation, it is the origin and source of this manifestation. And the hint that is given in the Bible in such simple words that no one could ever think science or metaphysics could be attached to it, seems to have the greatest secret of science and metaphysics, which explains that first was the Word, and the Word was with God and the Word was God.

In other words, that first was the Intelligence, the Word that afterwards manifested through man, by which man is called a person or an individual or a living entity or a knowing being; well, the very same thing, the very same life and spirit existed before. To a simple reader of the Bible it is a simple phrase. To the mystic it is the key, the key to the whole manifestation, that it did not start blindly; it started in intelligence. Blindness came afterwards, intelligence was before.

In this I shall make a difference between what I call Intelligence and what is called Intellect. Intelligence is that faculty, that knowing faculty which is capable of knowing all that is to be known. Intellect is that faculty of knowing, saturated with the impressions of names and forms which it has collected. Therefore Intellect is a knowledge, Intelligence is the faculty of knowing. Knowledge is different from knowing; knowing is the faculty, knowledge is what it attracts, conceives, apprehends and possesses.

But the wonderful phenomena[3] in the study of the process of manifestation is that as that original intelligence went further toward manifestation, all that it manifests, that very manifestation became the name. The picture will be like this--that an artist who was so keen about every corner of his studio, who wanted to keep everything in this studio so well and dusted and clean--he made a little statue and the interest in making that statue and studying that statue and what that statue revealed to him made him so absorbed in that statue that very soon all his vision which enabled him at one time to see every speck of dust in his studio, he could no longer observe. For his glance, his sight became concentrated on that little object.

This shows the picture of that original Intelligence, the Creator behind all, the Author, or the Perfection, or the Perfect God, or the Architect of the Universe, whatever you call him. Every step forward in creation or manifestation became less perceptive until that perception was so veiled, when it came to the material world, or dense manifestation, that Intelligence became, so to speak, buried in its own creation.

A person full of feelings, a person who has intuition, whose heart can feel life deeply, gets an impression from the rocks and stones and from the hills and mountains when he is among them, that there is something beneath them, that there is something behind them, a longing, a yearning, an aspiration continually striving to rise upward, to break the bonds of its condition. It is the same tendency which breaks out as an eruption of volcanoes, and it is the same tendency of intelligence which breaks out as streams of water from the mountains. That intelligence, that life which is buried under it, wishes to break out and makes it way outward in order to express itself.

A poet, an artist, an idealist, a dreamer, a thinker, a lover, a man of meditation or contemplation, for him the hills and the mountains are the greatest inspiration. They speak to him his yearning for that self-expression, his spirit longing to rise above the limitations which bind him. They all feel sympathy with him and that same feeling he finds in the rocks and mountains. For the rocks and the mountains cannot express, but there is something that is lost. What is lost? The same word is now buried under the dust of its creation and wants to make its way out, and that feeling is felt by those who can feel it.

They say the saints and sages of ancient times used to speak with trees and plants. It is not only the people of the past who were able to speak, every day man can speak if his heart be open. Those who do not know are the ones whose hearts are not open, yet no person in this world can fail to find the feeling of sympathy and the attraction that he feels in the woods, in the forests, near the trees and plants. Sometimes they attract and hold him more than human beings, more than his own friends and relations.

The more he is with them, the more he stays quiet. One can read behind them, one will be able to see there is a deep longing, a perfect silence, a silence with bared head and with arms raised up in prayer, continually longing and yearning for that moment to come when that Intelligence of the Word which was lost, the word which is in the heart of every object in this world, and which it wants to express and which wants to manifest, will come after that silent longing. And that longing you can feel in the presence of the trees as you sit in a meditative mood, in a meditative attitude.

You may ask why everybody does not see it. My answer would be, is it the same journey if one is walking through the forest and looks at the sights, and another is going on horseback or driving an automobile, and another is in an aeroplane, is their vision the same? No, the one who is walking on foot, he has time, he has time to look, he seems to be at one with nature. The one who is speeding past has not time to look.

Friends, this very life which is open to him, is in itself the true, it is one with his life, his heart-beat is in communion with this Word. There is another who has not made his communion; there are many things in this world which he has covered with his own heart. If there is any beauty, if there is any perfection, if there is any goodness, it is all there. If there are any impressions or awakening thoughts, it is all here and all this can be known and understood by your communion with life around.

The same trees and plants can speak so much to a person, they can inspire a person to hear and make him hear. To a poet, a thinker, they convey a feeling, they seem to be talking. To another they mean nothing, he cannot converse with them. To the one whose ears are open they speak. And we also feel in our contact with domestic animals, with birds, a tendency for expression. How they respond to one's love, one's sympathy, one's affection. How they look to you. That shows they are seeking after something. They strive for some conclusion, they wish to find something, to know and learn something.

If there was not this desire, then people would not be able to teach. They are able to teach because there is a desire to learn. No one can teach someone who does not wish to learn. But the desire of intelligence through rock, animal or plant is to know and to understand, and the same desire continues to manifest in man. Man's tendency for knowledge shows something is behind it.

A little child, with everything he first sees, he seeks to know what it is called, what is its name, what it is. He wants to know. And this shows that there is something in his spirit, in his soul, which is yearning to arrive at certain knowledge. In other words, his soul has lost something, and it wants to find it. In that even a child shows the search for the Lost Word. But the influence of life is such that the life gives him quite a different answer from what he wants. If a child is crying for the Lost Word and he is given his food, his sustenance for his body, his soul is still starving though his body is satisfied for the moment.

What has happened? He is deluded; he thinks it is the sustenance called food that he wanted. He has forgotten what he wanted. So through our whole life we always think that if there is any need which is pressing, we think that it is what we are missing, and if we had that in our life, we would be happy. If some one should make an experiment and give a man all the earth, the man would not long for the earth but for something else. Give him all he wants and every day would see new desires still.

Why? Because he does not know his desire. He knows what he is lacking outwardly but he does not know his innate desire. As many souls as there are, still so many different desires. At the same time the right desire is one and the same for every soul. And what is that desire? The Lost Word. Every soul is seeking after that Word which is lost; that Intelligence which was freedom, that Intelligence which was peace, that Intelligence which was above all limitation, that Intelligence which is perfect desire. Man cannot find it, he has lost it.

But who has taken it away from him? Where has it been stolen? It is he himself, his ego, his illusion, his delusion, they have taken it, covering that wealth, that search of his soul, that yearning of his soul. And therefore instead of seeing it under the cover of his own self which is most difficult to see, after looking for it outside, he wants to find it in pleasure. But pleasure is not necessarily happiness. He wants to find it in gold, but gold is in the earth. He wants to find it in a friend, but he has not found a friend. The friend he is looking for is different. He does not know. He wants to find it in worldly knowledge, but the worldly knowledge is not that goal that his soul is seeking. The knowledge his soul is seeking after or the friend he is looking for, or that peace he wants or that happiness he wants to experience, it is all one and the same thing, it is that Lost Word, and it is found in himself.

The Lost Word has made him and he has become the cover over it, and that Lost Word is lost in him, in his own being. And now the question is how to find it. And for that also you will find the key in the Bible, lost for the man overlooking a simple thing. It is a phrase which says "Seek ye the Kingdom of God and all things will be added."

How often man overlooks that simple thing. He wants everything but God. Tell him he will be taught how to work wonders and now ten thousand people will come. He is going to work some magic that will attract and they will come. Tell him his memory will be good, say some kind of trick that will make the memory good, he will take it. But a simple phrase like this one passes over. It is good, it is in the Bible, it is not new. The thoughts of such people are gross, mere child's pursuit of truth in the contrary direction. That which is to be found within, he is looking for without, by raising one's head, one is looking on the wrong side. That is the condition.

Now coming to this word, this phrase, "Seek ye the Kingdom of God." Where could this kingdom be found? Is it to be found in Heaven, in the skies? No, it is to be found within oneself. And what is the first step toward it? The first step is to recognize what this body is, this material body which has so far served to cover that word which was lost, for what is it really meant? Is it meant to cover that which is lost in it? Or is it meant for some other purpose?

The answer will be that the body is the sacred temple, the sacred shrine of God, and if one considered it as His sacred shrine, His temple, he would keep it as His sacred shrine, His temple where he could give praise, give his home to the One who owns it, to whom it belongs. As soon as you think on that phrase, you begin to think that first you must make a home for Him you are looking for, and that home is your body. And it is by preparing that home you will fulfil your first duty.

And how to prepare this home to be a home of happiness, a home of peace and rest for Him to whom it belongs? And you may ask a question, how can we know that this body is a home for happiness and peace, and how can we make it ready for that One to whom it belongs? The answer is that if this can give you the happiness, the comfort you want, if you wish to find harmony, if this is that peace your soul longs for, that perfection which your soul longs for, you certainly have prepared your body to be the temple for the right Master, the God who _is_ your innermost being, He is not apart from you.

It is you who have taken[5] his identity, his Ego; you have taken from yourself, the Lost Word; you have covered by your individuality that perfection which is in Him within, and by so preparing your body, your mind, your personality for your spiritual ideal, for your innermost being, for your friend, for that peace and harmony for which the soul continually yearns, you will fulfil your life's purpose.

The whole process of spiritual attainment is the unveiling of that truth which is covered, but what is covering it is nothing but ignorance. The Word is lost because we ourselves have covered it.

The whole process of meditation, or concentration, or prayer, or contemplation or whatever the manner by which we seek after Truth, after God, or the higher ideal, that whole process is an uncovering process of the truth, the truth which words can never explain.

The prophets and teachers who have come from time to time in order to give a part of it to humanity, in order to get him through his trouble and difficulty, have been able to guide him in a certain way, but no one has ever been able to tell him what Truth is. For Truth cannot be put into words. Truth is (realization). Truth is the attainment of that Word which was lost, and when that lost Word is gained, when it is attained, what happens? All that is within and without becomes revealed.

In the Persian language God is called Khuda[6], Khuda means self-revealing. Someone who does not want to be taught or told or explained; someone about whom nothing can be explained, something that is self-unveiling, in other words, the Word ~~was~~ that was lost is attained.

Now the question: in order to find the Word, which was lost, what is to be found? The Self is to be found. By finding the Self, the Word which was

5. In the "tp." "away" was added in Sk.'s hwr.
6. For spelling and pronunciation of *Khuda*, see Glossary.

lost is to be found. And the question is, "don't we know the self? We all know to some extent ourselves!" This can be answered, how little we know! Knowing another person (apart), we do not even know ourselves, we do not know what we say, very often we do not know what we feel, we do not know what we are looking for, what we are seeking, for very often we do not know if we have done it or if we have said it.

If one studied oneself, one's own self, one will find it is going on like a machine working, [7] converging around him; and to find oneself is to know oneself, to know what I am, what I am doing, to know what I perceive, who is my friend and who is my enemy.

---

7. A blank in the "tp."

From a newspaper, the *San Francisco Journal*,
23 April 1923

San Francisco, 22 April 1923[1]

"My coming to the United States at this time, when the world has not yet arrived at its normal state after the great strain of the war, is to awaken in souls the consciousness of brotherhood, on the principle of which this great nation was founded. The central theme of the formation of the Constitution of the United States of America and the undertone of Abraham Lincoln's noble reform was brotherhood.

"The nation which was nursed with the milk of the ideal brotherhood from its infancy is the one to be attuned to its predisposition at this time of the world's great need.

"It is the all-pervading materialism and the flood of overwhelming commercialism which has drowned the ideal. The nations of today stand in the quest of their own material benefit regardless of other nations, in the same way as an individual today who is called a practical man, proves to be the best qualified in guarding his interests in life. This has made the world a battlefield of continual struggles, where life is nothing but a chaos; the world which was purposed to be the place of aspiration, rest and peace.

"Education today tends to teach the youth the best way to acquire, own and possess all the goods of this earth, and, naturally, the more souls become qualified by this education, the greater the struggle of life becomes. The competition which exists today in trade and profession seems to lead man to the tendencies of the primitive man. As relations between nations are only based upon their material interest, so relations between individuals exist. It has blunted all the fineness and beauty of unselfish friendly devotion."

Note:

1. This article reports an otherwise unknown talk given at the Native Sons' Hall "last night".

A typescript of a lecture handed down by Mrs. Prebble (a pupil of Murshida Martin's) to Martha Burk, and inherited from the latter by Miss Hayat Stadlinger, an American mureed, initiated in Suresnes in 1926, who passed it on to the Biographical Department in Suresnes.

1

Shaikh Muslih-ud-din Saadi.

[2]Beloved ones of God:[2]

My subject this afternoon is Saadi, the great Sufi poet of Persia. In point of fact all the poets of Persia were Sufi poets. Their point of view is recognized as the Sufi point of view. And not only the poets of Persia, but also the poets of India.

The works of Saadi have been considered in the East simple, and [3]at the same time[3] educational, and at the same time uplifting.

[4]The beauty of the works of Saadi is that they begin with the education of children[4]. His "Carima" is taught to children of nine, [5]ten or eleven[5], and at the same time it is not just a legend or[6] amusing story; it is like a seed sown in the heart of the[7] child of that age, that in time it may flourish and bring forth fruits of good thought and imagination. "Carima" is [8]a thanksgiving poem[8]; in it the first lesson Saadi gives is to learn how to be grateful; how to express gratitude; how to appreciate; and so he teaches the lesson of

Documents: No original MS has been received by the archives to date.

Tp.: (a typescript received from Miss Hayat Stadlinger in 1983).
Hq.st.: (a revised version of the "tp." made at Headquarters, Geneva, where the lecture was made into two Social Gathekas).
Hq.t.: (a typewritten copy of the "Hq.st." showing very few minor differences).
Tp.c.: (a typewritten copy of the "Hq.st.", very similar to both the "Hq.st." and the "Hq.t.").

An Italian translation of the first part of this lecture was published in *The Sufi Quarterly* of June 1925, and in 1965 it was published in *The Sufi Message of Hazrat Inayat Khan*, Volume X.

It is the fourth lecture in a series of six lectures of "Sufi Poets," given by Pir-o-Murshid Inayat Khan on April 24th, 1923, in the Paul Elder Gallery, San Francisco, U.S.A. (For the program issued by Paul Elder, see Appendix A.)

Notes:

1. Hq.st., hq.t., tp.c.: added "Social Gatheka Number 18" and the invocation: "Toward the One, ..."
2. Ibid.: "Beloved ones of God:" omitted
3. Ibid.: "at the same time" omitted
4. Ibid.: rewritten to read, "And in India they begin the education of children with the works of Saadi"
5. Ibid.: "or ten" instead of "ten or eleven"
6. Ibid.: "an" added
7. Ibid.: "the" changed to "a"
8. Ibid.: "a poem of thanksgiving"

gratefulness and appreciation for all in the world; for the kindness and love of mother and father, and of[9] friend and companion, by teaching first the[10] gratefulness to God for all the blessings and benefits man receives. Saadi begins in "Carima" by saying: "O Lord, most merciful, I ask Thy forgiveness, for I am limited and in this life of limitation I am always apt [11]to make errors[11]."

He teaches in the first lesson [12]for mankind to recognize[12] his limited condition, and that this[13] limitedness makes him subject to error, and at the same time he suggests the innermost desire of every soul to rise above the[10] limitations and keep from error, to seek divine love and ask pardon, and to appreciate all the blessings he receives in life, in order to rise towards that ideal stage of the humane man. And as we see life today it seems this is the very thing which is lacking.

When children grow up without that tendency of appreciation, they often cannot understand what their mother has done for them, what their father has done for them, what their duty is to their kind friends, to elderly[14] people, to their teacher. And when they grow without developing that gratefulness in their nature, the egoistic nature which naturally develops becomes terrible. A boy who does not appreciate in his childhood all that his mother has done for him, cannot then learn to be tender and gentle to his wife, for his first lesson he has learned from[15] his mother.

Everything that by nature springs up, has to be refined, and in its fulfillment it has to become perfect. In human nature there is a self-asserting tendency from childhood. Most pronounced in the nature of the child is "I," and[16] everything that he possesses he says "my." And if that is not changed, if the same attitude remains, when that child grows older, he becomes hard on[17] those around him, for his "I" and what he calls "my," becomes difficult for all those around him.

The whole religious, spiritual and philosophical teaching leads us towards the development of the personality. There is something that is made by nature in man, but there is something that the man himself has to make. Man is born as man, but man develops to become humane. And if man remains only man as he is born, and the other[18] qualities with which he is born remain undeveloped, and without being made[19] refined, then he does

9. Tp.c.: "a" added
10. Hq.st., hq.t., tp.c.: "the" omitted
11. Ibid.: "to err" instead of "to make errors"
12. Ibid.: "that man should recognize"
13. Hq.t.: "his" instead of "this"
14. Hq.st., hq.t., tp.c.: "older" instead of "elderly"
15. Ibid.: "from" replaced by "with"
16. Ibid.: "of" added
17. Ibid.: "to" instead of "on"
18. Ibid.: "same" instead of "other"
19. Ibid.: "made" omitted

not fulfil the object of life. [20]All the great Teachers and Masters of this world who have come from time to time, and whom we recognize as Saints and Sages, Masters, Teachers and inspired helpers, it is not always the philosophy they taught man, it is not always the dogmas or the form of religion they gave[21]; what has been of the greatest importance is their personality, is[22] their person.

The teachings of Buddha are held by many millions, but more than his teachings, in[23] the life he lived and the wisdom he expressed in his life, for there is the fulfillment. Man is born with a purpose, and that purpose is fulfilled in the refinement of his personality. This unrefined nature of the ego, when developed through life, has an effect like the sting of a thorn. Wherever, whoever, whatever it touches, it causes some harm or disturbance, some destruction. And so personalities in human beings, when they are not refined, and they have before them all temptations, all things that attract them, things they like and admire and wish to have, then they go against the conflicting activities of life, they rub up against everything like a thorn tearing it in[24] pieces. And what happens? No doubt when thorns rub against thorns they crush one another and they feel it less. But when thorns rub against flowers, they tear them to pieces.

If you will ask individuals in this world, in all walks of life, "Tell me, what is your difficulty in life?", perhaps they will tell you that they lack wealth or power or position, but mostly the complaint will be that they are in some way or other hurt by others; by friend or parent or child; life-mate or neighbor or co-worker; they are disturbed or troubled and in difficulty by[25] this thorn-like[26] influence from morning to evening touching them and scratching them. And yet man does not seem to think deeply on this subject. Life is blinding, and it keeps man busy and engaged finding fault with others. He does not find the thorn in himself, he always sees the thorn[27] in others.

Saadi in[28] simple language has tried to give man a helping hand towards the development in his personality of that flowerlike quality; to train this personality which was made to be a flower and to help. His whole life's work has been to explain to man how life can turn into a flower. He has called his books "Gulistan," which means a flower-bed or rose-garden, and "Bustan," a place of all sorts of fragrances, a place of fragrance. In this

20. Ibid.: "With" added
21. Ibid.: "that was of the greatest importance" added
22. Ibid.: "is" omitted
23. Ibid.: "is" instead of "in"
24. Ibid.: "to" instead of "in"
25. Ibid.: "from" instead of "by"
26. Ibid.: "thorn-life" instead of "thorn-like"
27. Tp.c.: "thorns"
28. Hq.st., hq.t., tp.c.: "a" added

he has tried to explain to man how the heart can be turned into a flower; in reality it is a flower; it is made to be a flower; it is made to spread its perfume; if only you trained it and tended it; it would show the delicacy and beauty and fragrance of a flower; and that is the purpose of your life.

There is no mystification in Saadi's poetry. It is full of wit and intelligence, and at the same time original. And the most wonderful thing that one sees in the poetry of Saadi is his humorous trend of mind. He is ready to look at the funny side of things and to amuse himself and enjoy. And how few of us in this world know what real, true mirth means; humor that is not vulgarized, not abused. It shows the rhythm and tune of the soul. Without humor life is dull and depressing. Humor is the reflection of that divine life and sun which makes life like the day. And a person who reflects divine wisdom and divine joy, adds to the expression of his thought when he expresses his ideas with mirth.

One day Saadi was sitting in a book-seller's shop, where his books were sold; the book-seller was absent, and some one came in and asked for one of Saadi's books, not knowing that he was speaking to Saadi himself. Saadi asked[29], "What do you like about Saadi's books?" He replied, "O, he is a funny fellow." Whereupon Saadi made him a present of the book, and when he wished to pay for it, said, "No, I am Saadi, and when you called me a funny fellow, you gave me all the reward I wish."

He wanted life to be joyous. Spirituality is not in a long face and deep sigh. No doubt there are moments when you will sympathize with the troubles of others; there are moments that move you to tears, and there are times when you must just close your lips. But there are other moments when you can see the joyous side of life and enjoy its beauties. Man is not born into this world for depression and unhappiness. His very being is happiness. Depression is something unnatural. By this I do not mean to say that sorrow is a sin or suffering always avoidable.

We all have to experience both in life, to accomplish the purpose of life. We cannot always be smiling. There is no spiritual evolution in ignoring either side of life. Spirituality is in every side of life. As long as one is not bound, it is no sin to stand in the midst of life. Man need not go into the forest, away from all people, to show his goodness and virtue. Of what use is his goodness and virtue if he buries himself in the forest? It is [30]right in the midst[30] of life that we have to develop and express all that is beautiful and perfect and divine in our souls.[31]

29. Ibid.: "said" instead of "asked"
30. Ibid.: "in the very midst" instead of "right in the midst"
31. Ibid.: Here ends Social Gatheka no. 18.

[32]Saadi has expressed a wonderful thought in his work called the "Gulistan," and in simple words. He says, "Every soul was meant for a certain purpose and the light of that purpose was kindled in that soul." It is one little verse, but it is a book[33] in itself. What does this suggest to us? That this whole universe is like one symphony, and all souls are as different notes. There activities are according to the rhythm of this symphony, and their life is purposed to perfect this symphony.

People are anxious to do something, and wait for years and years, unhappy, in despair, waiting for that moment to come. It shows that the soul knows in its subconsciousness that there is a note to strike, and the moment when it shall[34] strike that note, that soul shall[34] be satisfied, and yet does not know what note it is nor when it shall[34] be struck.

What is life, and what keeps us living in this world of limitation, [35]world of continual changes, world[36] full of falsehood and world full of suffering and trouble? If there is anything in this world that keeps us alive, it is hope[37]. Hope,[37] the honey of life.

There is not one soul in this world who says, "Now, I am satisfied; I have no further desire." In everyone, whatever be the position in life, someone very rich or one very poor, one full of life and the other ill, in all conditions, man is continually yearning and waiting for something to come, he does not know what, but he is waiting. The real explanation of life is waiting; waiting for something. And what is it that man awaits? It is the fulfilment of the purpose of life, which comes when the soul strikes that note; that note which is meant to be his note; and this he seeks, whether in the outer plane or the inner plane.

And man has not fulfilled his life's purpose until he has struck that note which is his note. And the greatest tragedy in life is the obscurity of purpose. When purpose is not clear, man suffers, he cannot breathe. He knows not what is the purpose, what he must do.

This life will present to him things that will interest him for the moment, but the moment he possesses that thing he will say, "No this is not it, it is something else." So man goes on, in an illusion, constantly seeking, and yet not knowing what he seeks. Blessed is he who knows his life's purpose, for that is the first step to fulfilment.

32. Ibid.: added "Social Gatheka number 19" and the invocation: "Toward the One, ..." and "Shaikh Muslih-ud-Din Saadi (cont.)"
33. Ibid.: "book" changed to "volume"
34. Ibid.: "will" instead of "shall"
35. Ibid.: "this" added
36. Ibid.: "world" omitted
37. Ibid.: ". Hope," omitted

And how are we to know our life's purpose? Can anybody tell us? No. No one can tell us. For life in its very nature is self-revealing, and it is our own fault if we are not open to that revelation which life offers to us. It is not the fault of life, because the very nature of life is revealing.

Man is the offspring of nature, therefore his purpose is nature. But the artificiality of life brings obscurity, which prevents him from arriving at that knowledge which may be called the revelation of one's own soul.

And if you ask me how one should proceed, I would advise you to study every object, whether false or true, which holds and attracts you, to which you are outwardly attracted and also inwardly attracted. And do not be doubting and suspicious. What Christ taught from morning until night was faith, but the interpretation of this word is not made clear. People have said faith in priest, in church, or in sect. That is not the meaning.

The true meaning of faith is trust in one's self. A person came to me and said, "I wish to follow your ideas; will you receive me? Will you have[38] me follow you?" I said, "Yes, but will you tell me if you have faith?" This person looked perplexed for a moment, then he said, "Well, I have faith in you." I asked, "Have you faith in yourself?" He said, "Well, I am not sure." I said, "Your faith in me would be of no use to me; what I need is your faith in you."

Friends, what we must learn in life, is first to trust ourselves. This wobbling tendency of mind: shall I, or shall I not; [39]whether it is[39] good or [40]it is[40] bad; this[41] keeps man in confusion. And for years he may have the best intentions, but he will linger in the same place. He will not advance, for his own confusion will paralyze his legs[42]. He will think he is going on, but he will be stepping[43] in the same place where he is standing.

Man must have initiative. And this is the word from which comes initiation. Who is the initiate? The brave, the courageous. Who is brave and courageous? The one who trusts himself. Only his trust in himself will be of any use to himself or others.

People say, "Those of simple faith and trust suffer much and come to failure." I will say no, because what is gained is so much more than what is lost. In order to strengthen the trust, one has to meet with some failures. I would rather trust and be badly treated, than to[44] distrust. The strength that

38. Ibid.: "let" instead of "have"
39. Ibid.: "whether it is" changed to "is it"
40. Ibid.: "is it"
41. Ibid.: "this" omitted
42. Ibid.: "legs" changed "limbs"
43. Ibid.: "stopping" instead of "stepping"
44. Ibid.: "to" omitted

faith and trust gives, is the divine strength. The man who trusts his fellow creatures, inspires trust in others. He can so develop that he will turn the untrustworthy into the trustworthy, with sufficient trust in his heart, he can develop the power to do this.

I always remember the blessing I received from my holy Master, my Teacher. It was, "May your faith be strengthened." Being young, I wondered that he said nothing about happiness, long life or prosperity. I have now learned to understand the meaning of that blessing, and understand it better every day. All the blessings that man attains in life, all that is in Heaven and earth, become the possession of man when his faith is strengthened.

We read every day in the scriptures of "faith," but how little we think of it, and how many people at the present moment are beginning to laugh at it. Faith they give no attention to. It is something that conveys nothing to them. It is so simple and yet so complex. It is a miracle. It is a wonder. All our weakness, all our failure, all our limitation[45], all our suffering, comes from lack of that substance which is faith. All success, happiness, and advance, all that is achieved, the credit is due to faith.

The works of Saadi from the beginning teach the first lesson of faith, of understanding; that we are not here in this world in vain, to waste our lives. We are here for a purpose, and each one of us for a particular purpose. And each one of us makes[46] an atom of this universe, and completes[47] the symphony, and when we do not strike our note, it means that note lacking in the symphony of the whole; and when we do not fulfil our life's purpose in this way, for which we are created, we are not living right, and therefore we are not happy.

Our happiness depends on living right, and right living depends on striking that note; and the realization of that purpose is in the book of our heart. Open that book and look at it. All meditation, all concentration and contemplation is only to open this book, to focus our mind, and to see what purpose there is in our life. And no sooner do we see that our ultimate goal and our life's object and happiness, our true health and well-being and our real wealth and welfare, are in the fulfilment of our purpose, then the whole trend of life will change.

---

45. Tp.c.: "limitations"
46. Hq.st., hq.t., tp.c.: "make";
Hq.t.: changed back by Sk. to "makes"
47. Hq.st., hq.t., tp.c.: "complete";
Hq.t.: changed back by Sk. to "completes"

A typescript of a lecture handed down by Mrs. Prebble (a pupil of Murshida Martin's) to Martha Burk, and inherited from the latter by Miss Hayat Stadlinger, an American mureed, initiated in Suresnes in 1926, who passed it on to the Biographical Department in Suresnes.

The Mystery of Sound and Color. [1]

Beloved ones of God:

My subject this morning is, "The Mystery of Color and Sound." The attraction that one finds in color and in sound, makes one wonder if there is a mystery hidden behind it; if there is a language of color and sound that could be learned, and the answer is that the language of color and sound is the language of the soul, but it is our outward language which makes us confused as to the meaning of that inner language. Color and sound are the language of life. Life expresses itself in all different planes of existence in the form of color and sound. Although the outward manifestations of life are so rigid and so dense that the secret of their nature and character becomes buried underneath.

Why is the world called an illusion by the Mystics? For the very reason that the nature of manifestation is such that it envelops its own secret in itself, and stands out in such a rigid form that the fineness and the beauty and the mystery of its character are hidden within itself, and therefore the seeker[2] after the truth of life, the student[2] of life, strikes[3] two

Documents: No original MS has been received by the archives to date.

Tp. (a typescript received from Miss Hayat Stadlinger in 1983).
O.t. (very similar to the "tp.", coming from Gd.'s legacy).

Both documents, the "tp." and the "o.t.", seem to have been copied from the same old document. But then, handed down over the years by different lines of mureeds, they underwent a few separate changes. Probably the "tp." kept nearest to the original text.

Sk.tp. (a typewritten copy made by Sk. from the "o.t." with some grammatical corrections following the suggestions of a teacher of the English language). The "o.t." was the only document at Sk.'s disposal. The "tp." at that time had not yet been added to the archives.
Sk.ann. (an annotation written by Sk. on a separate paper).

This lecture was published in *The Sufi Message of Hazrat Inayat Khan*, Volume II (1960), Music, chapter X.

This is the fifth lecture in a series of six lectures on "Music," given by Pir-o-Murshid Inayat Khan on April 25th, 1923, in the Paul Elder Gallery, San Francisco, U.S.A. (For the program, issued by Paul Elder, see Appendix A.)

Notes:

1. Sk.tp.: "America" added
2. Ibid.: plural "s" added
3. Ibid.: "strike"

opposite paths. One wishes to learn from its external appearance; the other wishes to find out the secret which is hidden behind it. The one who learns from the external, gets the knowledge of the external, which we call science. The one who finds out from the[4] within, that which is hidden within this manifestation, he is the Mystic. The knowledge he gains is Mysticism.

The first question that comes to the mind of the intelligent person is, "What is it in color and in sound that appeals to man?" I will answer, "It is the tone and rhythm of color, as well as of sound, which has[5] an influence on the tone and rhythm of our being." Our being is our capacity for the resonance of tone and rhythm that comes from sound and color. This capacity enables us to be influenced by sound and color. Thus, some have a liking for a certain color, others have a liking for another color. In the way of sound, some are attracted to a certain kind of sound. In the form of voice, some are attracted to the baritone or bass voice, others are attracted to the tenor and soprano. There are some to whom the deep sound of the cello appeals; there are others who are interested in the sound of the violin; some can enjoy even the thick sound of the horn and trombone; others can enjoy the flute. What does this show? It shows that there is a certain capacity in our hearts, in our beings, and it depends upon that particular capacity, what kind of sound appeals to us.

At the same time, it depends upon man's grade of evolution, his character, his nature; whether he is gross or fine; also his temperament; if he is of a practical nature or if he is dreamy; if he loves the drama of life; if he is absorbed in the ordinary things of life. According to man's condition, his temperament and his evolution, color and sound [6]has its[6] effect on him. And the proof of this fact is that so often man changes his fancy in color; there is a time when he is so fond of red; there are times when he longs to see purple; there are times when he dreams of mauve. And then there comes a time when he takes a fancy to blue; he craves for yellow, for orange. There are some who like deep colors, others light colors. It all depends upon their temperament and their grade of evolution.

Music of every kind appeals to some one. The best or the worst, somebody likes it. Have you not seen how children can enjoy themselves with a little tin can and a stick? The rhythm comes within their capacity of enjoyment. Human nature is such, when you put it all together, it takes in everything, from the highest to the lowest. It has such a wide capacity that there is nothing left out. All has its place and all is assimilated by human nature. But at the same time there is action and reaction. It is not[7] only the

4. Ibid.: "the" crossed out
5. Ibid.: "has" changed to "have"
6. Ibid.: "has its" changed to "have their"
7. Ibid.: "not" omitted, then reinserted by Sk.

grade of evolution that makes man change his fancy to different colors and tones, but it is different colors and tones that help him also in his evolution, and they change the speed of one's evolution.

Very often man gives a great importance to color and tone, so much so, that he forgets something which is behind it, and that leads man to many superstitions, fancies and imaginations. Many people have fooled the simple ones by telling them what color belonged to their souls, or what note belonged to their lives. And man is so ready to respond to anything that can puzzle him and confuse his mind; he is so willing to be fooled. He enjoys it so much if somebody tells him that his color is yellow or green; or his note is C, D or F on the piano. He does not care to find out why. It is like telling somebody that Wednesday is your day and Tuesday is some other person's.

In point of fact all days are ours; all colors are ours. It is man who is the master of all manifestation. It is for man to use all colors and tones; they are at his disposal, for him to use and make the best of. It would be a great pity if we were subject to one color or tone. There would be no life in it; it would be a form of death. The staircase is made for us to ascend, not for us to continue stepping in one place. Every step is our step, if only we take it.

Now coming to the mystical point of view. The first aspect that makes intelligence conscious of the manifestation is sound; the next aspect is light (or color). The proof of this can be found in the Bible as well as in Vedanta. The Bible says, "In the beginning was the Word and the Word was God." And in another place it says, "First was word, and then came light."

What is color? It is an aspect of light. And when we come to read the Vedanta, there it says: "The first aspect of the Creator, the Source from which the whole Creation was made, was sound." In the Koran it is said, "The first command was, give us a sound, and all became manifest."

All the mystics and prophets and great thinkers of the world in all periods of history, in expressing the history of creation, have given the first place to sound. And the scientist of today says the same thing. He will call it radium, atom, electron; and after going through all the different atoms of substance [8]he gets into[8] the substance he calls movement. Movement is vibration. It is only the effect of motion which we call sound. Motion speaks, and speech we call sound, because it is audible. When it is not audible, it is because there is not sufficient capacity. But the cause of sound is movement, and movement is always there; which means that the existence of the movement does not depend upon capacity.

8. Sk.ann.: "he comes to" instead of "he gets into"

And what is color? Color also is movement. And its[9] capacity makes color concrete to our vision. At the same time, although we may say that this is green or red or yellow, every color is different to each person; in fine shades of color, people do not see alike, because the capacity is different in each. The tone is according to the capacity. In other words, it is not the tone or color which in its value is different; it becomes different when we sense it, when we feel it. In its relation to us it is different.

The conception of the five elements, which the mystics have held in all times, cannot be explained in scientific terms, because the mystics have their peculiar meaning. Although it may be called water, fire, air, earth, it must not be taken as such; its nature and character, according to the mystics, is different, but as words are few, one cannot give different names to these elements, although in Sanscrit we have different words for these elements. And so "ether" is not ether as the scientists mean it. It is capacity. Water is not water as we understand it in everyday language; it is liquidity. Fire is understood differently; it means glow or heat or dryness or radiance, all that is living. All of these words suggest something more than we mean by earth, fire, water, etc.

Now, the working of these five elements is distinguished by different color and sound. The five elements are represented by sound. In the musical scales which are called "ragas" in India and China, the raga of five notes is considered the most appealing, and I myself have experienced that the scale of five notes is much more appealing than the scale of seven notes. The scale of seven notes lacks some vital influence that the scale of five notes possesses. In ancient times, the scales by which miracles were performed, were mostly the scales of five notes.

And now one sees that there is a relation between sound and color. The first tendency a man has, is to open his eyes when he hears something, to see if he can see the color of it. That is not the way to see it. Color is a language. The very life which is audible, is visible also; but where? It is visible in the inner plane. The mistake is that man looks in the outer for it. When he hears music, he wants to see the color before him. Every activity of the outer world is a kind of reaction, in other words a shadow, of the activity which is behind it, which we do not see. And there is a difference in time. There is an activity which has passed twelve hours before and it is now in color in the outer plane, and the same is the reason for the question of the effect of dreams on life. Something that one has seen in the dream perhaps at night, its effect he will see in the morning, or next week, and therefore this shows that there is some activity which takes place behind the scenes and it is reflected on the outer life, according as the activities of the outer life are directed.

9. Tp.: "its" changed to "our" by Hayat Stadlinger

This is the reason why a seer or mystic is able very often to know beforehand his own condition, and the condition of others; what is coming, or what has passed, or what is going on at a distance. For he knows the language of sound and color. And now the question is, on which plane does he know the language of sound and color? In what way does it manifest to him? One cannot restrict it under a certain law, and at the same time it has a certain law. And where does he see it? He sees it in his breath.

Therefore, the whole culture of spiritual development is based upon the science of breath. The Yogis, the Mystics, what made them see happenings of the past, present and future? Some law behind creation. A certain working of the mechanism which is a finer mechanism. And how can it be seen? By opening one's vision to one's self.

According to the Mystics, there are five capacities of one's being, which may be called five akashas. The one capacity which everybody knows and is conscious of, is what may be called the receptacle of food, which is this body. And the other which is more or less recognized, is the receptacle of sense, which is in the senses. And the third capacity the receptacle of life, and this capacity is a world in itself, where one is conscious of the finer forces of life which are working within himself. They can convey to him a sense of the past, present or future, for the reason that they are clear to his vision. He sees them.

But you may ask, "How can he find out the condition of another." It is not because he knows[10] more about others, for one is made to know most about himself, but many are unconscious of the third receptacle, that of life. The one who is conscious of his receptacle of life, he is able to empty the capacity he has and give a chance for the life or another person to reflect upon it. He does it by focusing upon the life of another, and by that he covers the past, present and future. Only he has to make the camera stand in the right place. It is exactly like photography. The plate is there; it is clear because he is able to empty his own capacity; and the black cloth which the photographer puts over the camera and over his own head, is concentration. When man has mastered concentration, he becomes the photographer. He can focus all the light upon one spot. It is all scientific when we understand it in that way. It becomes a puzzle when it is put before us as a mystery. All is mystery when we do not know it; when we know it, all is simple. The true seekers after truth are lovers of simplicity. The right road is simple, clear, distinct. There is nothing vague about it.

And the more one follows this path of the mystery of life, the more life becomes revealed to him. Life begins to express its secret, its nature. What is required of man is an honest following of life's law, and nothing in

10. O.t., Sk.tp.: "can know" instead of "knows"

this world is more important than knowing[11] human nature and the study of human life, and that study lies in the study of self, and it is the study of self which is really the study of God.

---

11. Ibid.: "the knowing of" instead of "knowing"

A typescript of a lecture from the legacy of Murshida Martin, handed down by Mrs. Duce to Sirdar, and copied by Sk. In a separate annotation Sk. writes: "doubtful whether authentic." Parts of the text do not seem to be Pir-o-Murshid's own words.

The Solution of the Problems of Today.[1]

2

Seeing the condition of the world as it is today, a question arises from the heart of every person [3]about what may be[3],[4] what would be the solution of this problem [5]of the day[5]. One asks oneself, if we are really progressing and the answer comes, "Yes, in certain directions we are progressing." But there are many things in this world to prove the fact that there are certain directions in which we are not progressing, and this partial progress has brought about a condition, the like of which cannot be found in the history of the world.

If we can think of the precious lives of young men who had [6]for generations[6] inherited the culture[7] and had taken, so to speak, a part in the evolution of the whole humanity, [8]have become the victims of [9]the war which has passed[9], not one person who thinks deeply and who can feel, will deny the fact that if we are missing something, it is something which is most

Documents: No original MS has been received by the archives to date.

Tp. (a typescript, handed down by Mrs. Duce to Sirdar and copied by Sakina).
Sk.ann. (some corrections made by Sk. on a separate paper).
S.Q. (magazine *The Sufi Quarterly*, Vol. II nr. 1 of June 1926, edited by Ronald L. Mumtaz Armstrong, in which this lecture was published).

This is the fifth lecture in a series of six lectures on "Spiritual Philosophy", given by Pir-o-Murshid Inayat Khan on April 26th 1923 in the Paul Elder Gallery in San Francisco, U.S.A. (For the program of these lectures, issued by Paul Elder, see Appendix A.)

A lecture with the same title was given on 28th May 1923 at New York during Pir-o-Murshid's same lecture tour through the United States. This lecture could have been taken down by Mrs. Marya Cushing, who organized a series of lectures given at that time in New York, but it has not reached these archives as yet.

Notes:

1. The title in the Paul Elder program reads, "The Solution to the Problems of Today"; S.Q.: "The Solution of the Problem of the Day"
2. S.Q.: added, "By Inayat Khan, the well-known musician of India and Sufi Mystic."
3. Ibid.: "about what may be" omitted
4. Ibid.: the comma replaced with a colon, and a quotation mark added
5. Ibid.: "of the day" omitted. In its place a question mark and quotation mark.
6. Ibid.: "for generations" omitted
7. Ibid.: "of generations" added
8. Ibid.: "who" added
9. Ibid.: rewritten to read "the past war"

important to us. We see in the tradition[10] [11]there have been battles[12], the battle[13] of the Mahabharata, and the battle[13] of Kerbela, and the battle[13] of Jerusalem, and the battle[13] of Palestine, but no battle[13] has been equal to the battle[13] that has just been fought.[14]

The numberless precious lives that it has swallowed, and the pain it has given besides, and the amount of grain[15] that has been destroyed and burned and sunk in the sea, and then the famines which[16] took place after the war and have continued in different countries, swallowing [17]the remaining part of humanity[17]. [18]The contribution that they advanced for politics or science has given to this great wave of destruction, that shows[18] that progress has been made in one direction, and the other direction which was most necessary has been neglected, has been forgotten.

But if we ask ourselves if the end of war has ended strife, it is not so. The strife has been continued, the strife has become worse. The unrest that exists in different nations, and the prejudice of nations and the prejudice between races which exists today, and which is working directly or indirectly, knowingly or unknowingly, shows that it might lead into a still worse catastrophe.

The outlook of a[19] mystic tells him that every disease, every pain, every disorder in the body has something behind it. There is some inner source there. In the same way, if there exists a prejudice in a nation, in a race, against another nation or race, it is like reserving a poison and keeping a poison of a certain disease in oneself. In time it must burst out, and in time it must show its worst results. And therefore whatever little civilization that seems to be remaining, even that is in danger, in a[20] great danger, although one does not see just now in what form that danger may manifest. But if the heart had eyes to see, if the soul could penetrate through life and see it with a keen sight, even now the beginning of the coming disaster would become manifest.

The number of nervous cases that today we see; the loss of memory in people that we see today; and that spirit of inharmony and disagreement

10. Ibid.: "traditions"
11. Ibid.: "that" added
12. Ibid.: "battles" changed to "wars"
13. Ibid.: "battle" changed to "war", the last instance referring to the First World War (1914-1918).
14. Ibid.: "with" instead of full stop, and the following paragraph added to this one
15. Ibid.: "grain" changed to "food"
16. Ibid.: "that" instead of "which"
17. Ibid.: rewritten to read: "a part of humanity that remained"
18. Sk.ann.: "this sentence needs revision";
S.Q.: rewritten to read: "The contribution that the advance of politics and science has given to this great wave of destruction shows"
19. S.Q.: "a" changed to "the"
20. Ibid.: "a" omitted

that we see among individuals; that lack of happiness we see in homes, it seems it is paralyzing the whole life. You can go in any country and ask, they will have more or less the same thing to tell you, that the trade is paralyzed. If you will find[21] some countries not yet, [22]they must wait a little while and you will see the same thing.

Why is it paralyzing[23]? Because the[24] trade has become something mechanical, it has lost the spirit at the back of it. If you ask about art, that also seems to be disappearing for the[24] want of appreciation, for the[24] want of an ideal, for the[24] want of that condition which inspires the artist. The[24] art in the form of music or poetry or painting or whatever form it be, by being commercialized, it[25] is losing its beauty. And the artist does not get that rest and peace which might help his inspiration.

With[26] education no doubt it was right that God-ideal[27] and religion, which at that time seemed [28]destructive in some forms[28], were[29] taken away, and education was[30] made free of religion. But nothing was given as a substitute. Therefore education remained something dry, and something without a spirit, mechanical. The ideal of education today is to qualify oneself to guard one's own interests best. The best qualified man is called a practical man, a man of common sense. Is it the[24] common sense with which we can bring peace to ourselves? Is it the[24] common sense with which we can bring happiness to our neighbor? No! [31]Those who have reached that stage where they felt for their neighbour, it was not common sense, it was supersense. When that supersense is buried under materialism, and common sense is used, the sense which suggests nothing but to get for oneself all that is best, and[32] although in appearance it might seem for some time a successful achievement, in the end it will not prove successful. For it is this tendency which has increased enormously the spirit of competition.

You will find the spirit of competition in every progression[33]. [34]And, friends,[34] man's life is purposed to teach[35] the perfection which is hidden in his heart. And if man is not fulfilling that purpose, his tendency will be

21. Ibid.: "it in" added
22. Ibid.: "so" added
23. Ibid.: "being paralysed" instead of "paralyzing"
24. Ibid.: "the" omitted
25. Ibid.: "it" omitted
26. Ibid.: "With" replaced by "In"
27. Ibid.: "God-ideals"
28. Ibid.: "destructive in some forms" changed to "a dead form"
29. Ibid.: "were" replaced by "should be"
30. Ibid.: "was" omitted
31. Ibid.: "In" added
32. Ibid.: "and" omitted
33. Ibid.: "progression" changed to "profession"
34. Ibid.: "And, friends," omitted
35. Ibid.: "to reach" instead of "to teach"

something like[36] the lower creation, gratifying his needs. And in competition he expresses [37]that tendency of[37] deceit which hides from the soul that light which is hidden in him as divine light. Remember,[38] there was a time when the word of[39] man was greater than a crown[40]. Today we have to take twenty signatures[41] and perhaps[42] thirty stamps put on it, and still it is not legal. Man cannot trust his fellowman. With all these stamps that one has to put on his agreements, the courts are full, the lawyers are busy, and it has all become so mechanical that it all seems to move onwards[43] towards some mechanical end, very often without the smallest virtue of[44] truth in it.

When we think of this, a question arises, [45]what may be done in order to better things? It is the economic condition [46]and situation[46] which is making us [47]in this way[47,45]. But [48]I should say[48] money is blinding. Even if the economic condition of the world was different still selfishness, that desire to have more than one's full[49] amount, remains just the same. That does[50] not fully suffice the purpose, although it would help to a very great extent.

Today the struggle between capital and labour is something which exists in all parts of the world. And a time has come when the capitalist as well as the one who labours, both are in trouble. [51]None gains better than the others[51]. One has one kind of trouble, the other has another kind of trouble, and [52]times have[52] come when both rich and poor have their complaints, both are not at ease, and both do not experience peace.

With all our political methods so developed and refined, the smallest problems that rise among nations are not solved to their satisfaction. Conference after conference takes place, from country to country. They meet and discuss the smallest thing and argue and dispute it, and in the end do not come to a satisfactory decision.

36. Ibid.: "that of" added
37. Ibid.: "the tendency to" instead of "that tendency of"
38. Ibid.: "Remember," omitted
39. Ibid.: "a" added
40. Ibid.: "crown" changed to "bond"
41. Ibid.: "for a bond" added
42. Ibid.: "have" added
43. Ibid.: "on" instead of "onwards"
44. Ibid.: "of" changed to "or"
45. Ibid.: the questions put between quotation marks
46. Ibid.: "and situation" omitted
47. Ibid.: "in this way" changed to "be so?"
48. Ibid.: "I should say" omitted
49. Ibid.: "full" changed to "fair"
50. Ibid.: "would" instead of "does"
51. Ibid.: rewritten to read, "Neither is better off than the other"
52. Ibid.: "the time has" instead of "times have"

If one asked, "How can this all be helped? Is there anything which can be called as[53] a main cause of the whole trouble which exists in different forms?" I will[54] say in short, that it is the lack of what may be called an ideal. Friends,[55] a living God, if belief in Him does not help you to progress and[56] go forward, is of no help to you, but if an idol of rock can help you to go forward, it is more helpful.

[57]What has happened today? Is it that the ideal has turned into an idol? Man goes so far and does not go further.[57] Today we laugh at the family feuds which existed in the East and in the West. [58]For instance, in Scotland one clan fought with the other clan. For years and years and years there was a fight between clans because each clan had its own flag, its own plaid, its own family, and they only had the interest of that particular clan, and were all the time fighting. And the rest and peace came in their country as that clan spirit diminished, and they became all Scotch.

And the same thing was in Arabia where every family had its genealogy of which they were very proud, and they discussed and argued for generations about that genealogy. And there were family feuds. Revenge was taken for some insult which was done to somebody's grandfather, the revenge was taken by the grandchild, and when he had taken that revenge by causing harm or pain or hurt to the other, he felt he had accomplished his duty.

Now we laugh at it.[58] We look at it as so small and so narrow, and so foolish. And what do you suppose[59] after four or five generations, our children will think? [60]After a hundred years from now,[60] what will they think when they read of the nations going against nations, fighting against one another, many among them not knowing with whom they were fighting, for what reason they were fighting, many going there only because the conditions made them go. Even on the battlefield they felt[61] nothing but love, not only for their fellowmen, but[62] for the men they were shooting. Many have hid[63] that feeling while shooting their fellowmen[64], or even, as it turned out, while shooting their own father.[64]

53. Ibid.: "as" omitted
54. Ibid.: "would" instead of "will"
55. Ibid.: "Friends," omitted
56. Ibid.: "to" added
57. Ibid.: these sentences continue the previous paragraph.
58. Ibid.: this whole passage has been omitted.
59. Ibid.: "think" instead of "suppose"
60. Ibid.: rewritten to read, "A hundred years hence,"
61. Ibid.: "often" added
62. Ibid.: "even" added
63. Sk.ann.: "had" instead of "hid";
S.Q.: "hid"
64. S.Q.: a full stop after "fellowmen", and the remaining part of the sentence omitted

What then will the children of the future think of us when they will grow[65] and read the accounts of what the world has gone through? The differences[66] between the time of these[67] family feuds and now is that they had[68] built walls around their families.[69] We build walls around our nations. They called it a family patriotism; we call it national patriotism. We take pride upon[70] it, we consider it a virtue, and [71]it has reached now to a point when[71] religion has lost its power and importance, [72]that it[72] has almost taken the place of religion.

Friends[55], there is no doubt[73] a person who braves[74] his life for his duty to his fellowman, to his nation, [75]no doubt[75] shows virtue, he is brave, it must be appreciated. But [76]what I say is that[76] the fault lies in standing on an ideal and not passing through it. For all ideals, such as love for one's family, the duty of citizenship, or the patriotism of nations, or the pride of race, or the service of humanity, all these are steps toward perfection. As long as man is going toward perfection, every step is a virtue; it is his merit. But the same ideal becomes an idol when man stands there and does not move.

Humanity was progressing as long as it went further. But[77] destruction came when it stuck up[78] to an ideal and did[79] not now move further. It is still standing there. Many say[80] an economic revival, if[81] on some fair basis if the economic condition of the world could be improved, the conditions would become different. But how very[82] impossible with the outlook man has today from the place[83] he is standing! How difficult it is for him to make a just and fair arrangement, to bring[84] the solution to the world's economic problem! People say politically[85], if the world will solve its problem[85], there will come some ease. But how? Man will think or say[86] or act according to his outlook on life, according to the pitch his spirit is

65. Ibid.: "up" added
66. Ibid.: "difference"
67. Ibid.: "those" instead of "these"
68. Ibid.: "had" omitted
69. Ibid.: "while" instead of the full stop
70. Ibid.: "in" instead of "upon"
71. Ibid.: rewritten to read, "things have reached a point now, that"
72. Ibid.: "that it" replaced with "when that"
73. Ibid.: "that" added
74. Ibid.: "braves" changed to "risks"
75. Ibid.: "no doubt" omitted
76. Ibid.: "what I say is that" omitted
77. Ibid.: "the" added
78. Ibid.: "up" omitted
79. Ibid.: "does" instead of "did"
80. Ibid.: "by" added
81. Ibid.: "it were" added
82. Ibid.: "very" omitted
83. Ibid.: "where" added
84. Ibid.: "about" added
85. Ibid.: "politically" moved to after "problem"
86. Ibid.: "say" changed to "speak"

tuned[87]. You cannot expect him to do something heavenly when he is standing on the earth; you can only expect what an earthly man can do.

[88]A great poet[88] has taught a simple moral, "A person says or does according to his particular evolution, and it is a great mistake if you get offended, for he cannot do better." That is the condition of humanity today. To expect better is a mistake. You cannot expect better. You can expect what man can give you today.

And what may be done? There is only one way, and that is to change the outlook of man. And how can it be done? It can be done by changing the spirit of individuals, changing the mind of individuals, awakening humanity to the spirit of brotherhood, to the[89] same truth which Christ has taught, "Love your neighbour." Today there seems to be a great awakening everywhere for spirituality, and it is true that the souls are longing for spirituality. And there is a reason that[90] the souls have gone through such a[20] suffering for all these years that naturally saint and sinner both are longing for a little relief from this disturbed state and condition.

But at the same time everybody does not seem to know how to proceed in his pursuit. Some are looking for phenomena in the form of spirituality; some want to work wonders; some want to get magnetic powers; some want to meet with ghosts and spirits and fairies and all things that are unseen; some want to float in the air and some want to see the different colours and different lights.

Many seekers after truth are eager to be fooled. The more they are fooled, the more they are pleased with it, and therefore their activity in that direction [91]is made[91] from every kind of source. Simple, optimistic and good people dabble into[92] things which they think spiritual, whereas the pessimistic and intellectual ones, they[93] are so afraid of the name "spiritual" that they do not wish to go near such a thing. They want to avoid every church, every religion, everything of a spiritual or occult nature.

This shows that it is worse than dead[94]. It would have been better they had not such longing[95]. It is like hungering for food and getting stones.

87. Ibid.: "to" added
88. Ibid.: "Our great poet, Saadi," instead of "A great poet"
89. Ibid.: "that" instead of "the"
90. Ibid.: "that" replaced by "for"
91. Ibid.: "is made" changed to "comes"
92. Ibid.: "in" instead of "into"
93. Ibid.: "they" omitted
94. Ibid.: "dead" changed to "a dead thing"
95. Ibid.: "longings"

And how has it come[84]? It has come[84] because of the commercial nature of the time[96] they want everything brought into the world in a commercial form.

But is it the fault of those who present it in a commercial form? Not altogether. It is the fault of the age. The time has changed conditions so that there is some commercial form necessary. [97]If I were not speaking to you in this house, if you had not read the advertisements in the papers, you would not have come here. If I were speaking in the street you would not have stood there.[97] The condition of the times before was different. The commercial age demands[73] everything to[98] be put in commercial form, and that is the great lack, and[99] a great pity that it should be so. Because now man has begun to think that everything[100] he can buy or sell[100], even spirituality.

[101]There are some who come, thinking they can buy like something at a drug store, ten lessons on Yoga, or a course, it is like buying a certain medicine and curing themselves. And people have become so accustomed to buy and sell, there are people waiting with their money, thinking they could buy some truth, and after having been disappointed all their life, having money to buy and not having gotten, they think, this is like everything else, always disappointed.

A wonderful thing I remember now. An American had been to India. He had heard in India there are great saints and sages and thinkers and people of great powers and inspiration, and he hoped he would find someone. The poor man was disappointed, after all his trip through India from North to South. When he came back he met me and once he told me that people talk so much about India and its meditative people and their great powers. He said, "I went all through India from North to South and did not find one." I said, "Did you look for a signboard? Did you expect to find him under a signboard? Did you expect to see his advertisement in a paper?" No.[101]

A Persian Sufi has said, "Be [102]friend to[102] God inwardly, and outwardly be indifferent." There are many on the path of God, but the one who follows this path is rare. [103]And what has it made?[103] It has made us think so little of religion, little of God, little of the sacred path. It has, in a way, taken away all the value and sacredness of spiritual attainment, the attainment which is the only worth while attainment in life. And at this time

96. Sk.ann.: a comma added after "time";
S.Q.: a full stop after "time"
97. S.Q.: this passage was omitted.
98. Ibid.: "to" omitted
99. Ibid.: "It is" instead of "and"
100. Ibid.: "everything" omitted and placed after "sell" instead
101. Ibid.: both these paragraphs were omitted.
102. Ibid.: "a lover of" instead of "friend to"
103. Ibid.: rewritten to read, "And what is the result of this commercialising?"

when religions have no greater[104] power and hold upon man, most of humanity seems to be hungering after some truth, after some peace and rest, hungering after some enlightenment on the path that can bring some rest, peace and consolation in the midst of this great strife and great disappointment that humanity[105] is[106] going through. And then they are all[107] disappointed.

And now the question is, what is the right path? I[108] cannot point out that a particular church is the right path. I[108] cannot point that a particular sect is the right path, I[108] cannot point that a particular religion is the right path. Nor can I[108] point[109] that this particular doctrine or this particular law is the right path. The message that Sufism has to give to the world is the message of wisdom, Sophia. The only path there is, is the path of wisdom, the path of understanding one another, the path of learning the point of view of another. What will bring about a better understanding between races, between nations, between the peoples of the East and West? It is the understanding of one another.

And now there is a question, "How can one help it? What can help to bring about this understanding between one another better?" Man is born with a living faculty of understanding, and what covers this faculty is his absorption in his selfish affairs in life. The less selfish he becomes, the more capable of understanding he becomes. The faculty of understanding becomes open in a certain way with man's development toward unselfishness. But now the question is, [110]what gives man unselfishness? Forgetting of himself[110]. When he forgets himself, then he is less selfish. The more he forgets himself, the more unselfish he becomes. And then there is a question, how can one forget oneself when oneself is next to one every moment of the day?

Friends[55], [111]this is[111] the process which is called spiritual attainment, the process of the mystic, [112]this is the process[112]. If there is anything to be learned or if anything is to be practised or studied as the essence of religion, it is this process of forgetting oneself. And what helps this? It is God Who helps this. That is where[113] the value of the God ideal comes[114]; that is where[115] the use of the God ideal comes[114]. If the God ideal has not helped in forgetting oneself, then there is something missing in one's reli-

104. Ibid.: "more" instead of "greater"
105. Ibid.: "humanity" changed to "men"
106. Ibid.: "are" instead of "is"
107. Ibid.: "all" omitted
108. Ibid.: "I" changed to "One"
109. Ibid.: "out" added
110. Ibid.: "what produces in man unselfishness, the forgetting of himself?" instead of "what gives man unselfishness?" as a question, and "Forgetting of himself" as the answer.
111. Ibid.: "this is" replaced with "By"
112. Ibid.: this phrase was omitted.
113. Ibid.: "comes in" added
114. Ibid.: "comes" omitted
115. Ibid.: "comes" added

gious belief, and it is therefore that every believer in God is not necessarily an unselfish person. Every believer is not necessarily a spiritual person. If he has not made use of his belief, if his belief has not sufficed the purpose, then his belief has not done anything for him.

There is a little story. It happened in India. A girl was passing through a farm, going from her village to another village and there a religious man was offering his prayers in the open. The religious law forbids anybody to pass that place where somebody is offering his prayers. They must wait[116]. When the prayer is finished, they may pass.

This girl, not noticing the man, passed over there. After some time, when she was hurrying back, this man who had offered his prayers stopped her and said, "How terrible of you, O girl, you passed over this place when I was offering prayer." She said, "Did I? I am sorry. What did you say?" [117]He said, "You foolish girl, you do not know what prayer means? Prayer means thinking of God." "Oh," she said, "I am so sorry. I was going to see my young man in the other village, and I was thinking so much about him, therefore I did not see you. And I am surprised that when you were thinking of God you could see me."

The religious man became so[118] embarrassed and from that day he learned that it is not the offering, the[119] prayer, it is the forgetting of self, that is the real and true prayer, that principle[120] motive for which God is the key.

---

116. Ibid.: "a while" added
117. Ibid.: added, "He said: "I was offering prayer." She said: "Prayer? What do you mean by it?""
118. Ibid.: "much" instead of "so"
119. Ibid.: ", the" omitted
120. Tp., S.Q.: "principle", but probably "principal" was meant.

From a newspaper, the *San Francisco Chronicle*, 27 April 1923

San Francisco, April[1]

"What is Sufi? Is it an offshoot of Brahmanism or Buddhism?"

"It came from Egypt, and it is the basis of four great religions, Christianity, Judaism, Mohammedanism and Zoroastrianism. It is not a church, but religion. It seeks to teach people to seek the real."

"By the real you mean God?"

"Exactly."

"How long have you been lecturing?"

"Many years. When I felt the call to go out and try to help spiritualize the world I went. I have traveled all over the world. I feel that everyone, German, Englishman, American, Hindu--all of mankind--is my brother. The world has grown very material and needs all the spirituality that can be put into it. The people do not take time for meditation; they rush about and lack repose."

"Where did you study?"

"In the Academy of Baroda. Indian music is an art, and expresses itself in improvisation. The scale is one of quarter tones, in which it differs from music of the West. The musician may have a set melody of three or four lines, but he improvises on this theme and shows his skill in that way. I learned four Indian languages so that my songs might be heard in all parts of my country."

Note:

1. From an interview, possibly on April 26

A typescript of a lecture handed down by Mrs. Prebble (a pupil of Murshida Martin's) to Martha Burk, and inherited from the latter by Miss Hayat Stadlinger, an American mureed, initiated in Suresnes in 1926, who passed it on to the Biographical Department in Suresnes.

1

Khwajah Shamsu-d-din Mahomed Hafiz.[2]

[3]Beloved ones of God:[3]

[4]My address this afternoon is on the subject of Hafiz, whose name[4] is well known to everyone interested in the poetry of Persia, because among the Persian poets Hafiz stands unique in his expression, in his depth of thought, in the excellence of his symbolical expression of certain thoughts and philosophy.

There was a time when a deep thinker and a free thinker had great difficulty in expressing his thoughts, and that time has not altogether ceased, but at the same time, in some ways, there seems to be much more freedom of expression in this age than in ancient times. At this time, anyone who expressed his thought freely about life and its hidden law, about soul, God, creation and manifestation, met with great difficulty. The difficulty was that the religious authorities of all kinds governed, and under the religious reign, the principles of the exoteric religion reigned, and therefore

Documents: No original MS has been received by the archives to date.

Tp.: (a typescript received from Miss Hayat Stadlinger in 1983).
Hq.st.: (a somewhat revised version of the "tp.", made at Headquarters, Geneva, where the lecture was made into two Social Gathekas).
Hq.t.: (a typewritten copy of the "Hq.st.", nearly identical in wording).
Tp.c.: (a typewritten copy of the "Hq.st.", with a few minor differences).

The obviously unedited division into paragraphs and sometimes the separate sentences, as well as the phonetic spelling of "force" for "false" (see note 16), shows the "tp." to be nearer to the originally spoken words than the other documents.

A translation in French has been published in the magazine *Soufisme* of April 1928, and a Dutch translation can be found in *De Soefi Gedachte* of 1951, numbers 3 and 4.

This lecture was published in *The Sufi Message of Hazrat Inayat Khan*, Volume X (1964), Sufi Poetry, chapter VII.

It is the fifth lecture in a series of six lectures on "Sufi Poets" given by Pir-o-Murshid Inayat Khan on May 1st, 1923, in the Paul Elder Gallery, San Francisco, U.S.A. (For the program issued by Paul Elder, see Appendix A.)

Notes:

1. Hq.st., hq.t., tp.c.: added, "Social Gatheka number 26", and the invocation: "Toward the One, ..."
2. See "List of Persons, Places and Events"
3. Hq.st., hq.t., tp.c.: "Beloved ones of God:" omitted
4. Ibid.: the first part of the sentence was reduced to "The name of Hafiz"

those who attained by the esoteric side of philosophy, always had difficulty in telling it to the people. Many were persecuted; they were stoned, they were flayed, they were put to death. All sorts of punishment were inflicted upon them, and in this way the progress of humanity was retarded. Today we do not see this. At the same time, the limited attitude of the human mind on religious and philosophical questions is to be found in all ages.

The Sufis, who found by the help of meditation the source of knowledge in their own hearts, for them it was very difficult to give to the world in plain words what little they could explain of the truth. It is true that the truth cannot be spoken in words, but at the same time, those gifted with poetic and prophetic expression, have always had that inclination and tendency of expressing what their souls experienced.

Hafiz found a way of expressing[5] the experience[6] of his soul and his philosophies[7] in verse. For the soul enjoys expressing itself in verse. Because soul itself is music and when it is experiencing the realization of divine truth, the tendency of the soul is to express itself in poetry. Hafiz therefore expressed his soul in poetry. And what poetry! Poetry full of light and shade, line and color, and poetry full of feeling. No poetry in the world can be compared to that of Hafiz in its delicacy. Therefore, only the fine soul, who has the finest perception of light and shade expressed in words, can grasp the meaning of the illumination of the soul.

At the same time, the words of Hafiz have won every heart that listens. Even if they do not wholly understand it, the phrase, rhythm, charm and beauty of expression win[8] them. It is the same style that Solomon adopted. But it was spoken in the language of the time. Hafiz spoke in the language which was most appropriate and most suitable to poetry. The Persian language is considered in the East, the most delicious language; a language which stands supreme to[9] all Eastern languages in poetry. It is soft and its expression is tender. It is expressive. Every object has perhaps ten names for the poet to choose from. Every little thought can be expressed in perhaps twenty different ways, and the poet has that freedom of choice. And therefore the Persian language and Persian poetry both are rich in expression.

The mission of Hafiz was to express to a fanatically inclined religious world, the presence of God, which is not to be found only in Heaven, but to be found here on earth.

5. Hq.st.: "expression";
   Hq.t., tp.c.: "expressing"
6. Hq.st., hq.t., tp.c.: "experiences"
7. Ibid.: "philosophy"
8. Ibid.: "wins"
9. Ibid.: "among" instead of "to"

Very often religious belief in God and in the hereafter has kept man sleeping, waiting for that hour and that day to come when he will be face to face with his Lord, and he is certain that that day will not come before he is dead, and therefore he awaits his death in the hope that in the hereafter he will see God, for Heaven alone is the place where God is to be found, there is no other place where God will be found. And[10] that there is only a certain place which is a sacred place of worship, that is, the church, and that anywhere else God was[11] not to be found. The mission of Hafiz was to take away this idea and to make man conscious of the Heaven by his side, and to tell man that all he expects in the hereafter as a reward, could be had here, if he lived a fuller life.

The same ideal which one sees in all religions, which Jesus Christ taught, saying, "God is love," that was the main idea of Hafiz, the idea that he has expressed from morning to night in the Diwan. If there is anything divine in man, it is love. If God is to be found anywhere, it is in man's heart, which is love, and if[12] love element is awakened in the heart then God is made alive, so to speak, and is born in one's self. But at the same time Hafiz has shown in his poetry the key to this, and that key is appreciation of beauty in all forms.

Beauty is not always in an object or in a person; beauty depends upon one's attitude towards life; how one looks at it; and its effect depends upon our power of appreciation. The very same music or poetry or painting will touch one person so that he feels its beauty to the very depth of his being, and perhaps there is another person who looks at it, but he does not see it. The whole manifestation has its beauty; sometimes the beauty is manifest to you; sometimes you have to look for it. There comes a good person; we are always charmed by the beauty of goodness. There comes another person who looks bad. But at the same time good is somewhere hidden in him, if we would look for it, if we have the desire to draw it out. The look of bad is not always in objects and persons, but in our looking.

The whole trend of the poetry of Hafiz is to awaken that appreciation of beauty and love of beauty, which is the only condition through which to experience that bliss for which our life is purposed.

Someone asked a Sufi the reason for this whole creation, and he answered, "God, Whose being is love itself, had desire[13] to experience the nature of His own being, and in order to experience it, He had to manifest Himself."

10. Ibid.: "he thinks" added
11. Ibid.: "is" instead of "was"
12. Ibid.: "the" added
13. Ibid.: "desired" instead of "desire"

God Himself, and His manifestation, the soul and God. This dual aspect can be seen in all forms of nature, in the sun and the moon; in night and day; in male and female; in positive and negative; and in all things of opposite characters.

[14]In order that this love principle, itself the original and the only principle at the back of the whole manifestation, may have the scope of its full play[14] and[15] therefore the fulfilment of the purpose of life, was[11] in the full expression of the love principle.

Very often people by learning philosophy and by looking at this world with a pessimistic thought, have renounced the world and have called it material and force[16]; and have left this world and have gone to the forest or desert or cave and have taught the principle of self-denial and self-abnegation and renunciation.

That was not the way of Hafiz. He said it is like journeying over the sea and coming to a new port and before landing one becomes frightened, saying, "But I shall perhaps be attacked by the people; or the place will attract me so much that I will not be able to go back where I have come from." But he does not know why he has taken that journey. He has not taken the journey to go back without landing. The attitude of Hafiz is to land there. Risk it. If it is an attractive place, he is ready to be won. If it will crush him, he is ready to be crushed. This is a daring attitude. Not running away from this false world, but in this false world to discover glimpses of the true. And in this maze to find God's purpose.[17]

[18]Besides this, there is another great revelation which Hafiz has brought before humanity in a most beautiful form. Now, there are many people in this world who have once believed in God, in His mercy and compassion, in His love and His forgiveness, but after having suffered, after seeing catastrophies[19] and injustice, have given up belief. Many people after great sorrow and suffering have given up religion. The reason is that the religion they have followed has taught them God as goodness, God as judge. Well then, they ask from a judge justice. Justice to satisfy their own ideas. They think their standard of justice is God's. They look for goodness as they understand it. And therefore there comes a time of struggle in their hearts. They do not see justice, because[20] looking from their own point of view. They are looking for goodness, kindness and mercy from their own

14. Ibid.: this part of the new paragraph continues the previous paragraph.
15. Ibid.: beginning of a new sentence: "And ..."
16. Ibid.: "false" instead of "force" which is the same in sound.
17. Ibid.: Here ends "Social Gatheka nr. 26."
18. Ibid.: added "Social Gatheka Number 27" and the invocation: "Toward the One, ..." and the title, "Khwaja Shams-ud-Din Muhammed Hafiz (continuation)."
19. Ibid.: "catastrophes"
20. Ibid.: "they are" added

point of view. And there are many conditions which make them think there is no justice, that there is no such thing as a forgiving element.

But the way of Hafiz is different. There is hardly the name of God to be found in the Diwan. He does not give that belief of God the just and good. His God is his Beloved, to whom he has surrendered in perfect love and devotion, and everything coming from the Beloved is taken by him with love and devotion as the reward. He prefers poison coming from the hand of the Beloved to nectar from another. He prefers death to life if it is the wish of the Beloved.

But you may say, "Is it fair?" There is no question of fairness where there[21] is love. Love stands above law. Law is beneath love. Law is born of love. The mistake in this day is that we keep law higher than love. We do not see that the divine principle which is love stands above law. Man makes God a judge who is bound by law; who cannot do His will, but has to do according to what is written in His book.

God is not justice. Justice is His nature, but love is predominant. People give such importance to one's actions and their results. They do not know that above action and result is a law which can consume the fire of Hell; which can dominate if the whole world were[22] being drowned in the flood of destruction. That the love power is greater than any other.

Think of the hen when she takes care of her little ones. If they were threatened with danger, though it were a horse or an elephant, she would fight, because the love principle is predominant. A kind mother is ready to forgive when her son comes with his head bowed and says, "Mother, I have been foolish, I have not listened to you, I have been insolent, I am sorry." She is ready to understand. She is ready to forgive. So we see mercy and compassion going out as love. A stream of love which can purify all the evil actions of years. Then, if a human being can actually forgive, can [23]not God[23] forgive? Many of the dogmatic religions have taken away the love element which is predominant, which makes God sovereign. And they make a God who is limited, who is bound by the book, and who cannot show his compassion. If God were so limited He could not be just. An individual would be better, because an individual can forgive.

Hafiz gives a picture of human nature: hate, jealousy, love, kindness, vanity; the play of friendly impulse, the play of pride. All aspects of life. Hafiz is not a poet, he is a painter. He has made a picture of the different aspects of life. Every verse is a picture. And in every picture, whatever

21. Tp.c.: "there" omitted
22. Hq.st., hq.t., tp.c.: "was"
23. Ibid.: "not" placed after "God"

be its color; vanity, pride or[24] conceit; love, mercy or compassion, in all its garbs, he sees only one spirit, the spirit of the Beloved. And he shows his devotion, appreciation and love to all the manifestations of that one and the same Beloved.

There are many religions and beliefs where it is said that there will come a day when man will be able to communicate with God. But when will that day come? Life is so short and our hearts so hungry. And if it does not come today perhaps it will not come at all. Therefore the only thing that Hafiz has pointed out from beginning to end is this, "Do not wait for that day to come tomorrow. Communicate with the Beloved just now." He is before you here in the form of your friend and in the form of your enemy; with a bowl of poison or with a rose. Recognize it and know it, for this is the purpose of life. Religions have made this like a journey of millions of miles. Hafiz has made it right[25] at hand.

Man likes complexity. He does not want to take one step. It is more interesting to look forward to millions of steps. The man who is seeking the truth gets into a puzzle, and that puzzle interests him. He wants to go through that puzzle a thousand times more. Just like children; their whole interest is in running around[26]. They do not want to see the door and go out, until they are very tired, and so with the grown-up people. They all say they are seeking truth, but they like the puzzle. That is why the Mystics made the greatest truths a mystery, to be given to the few who were ready for it, and to let the others play, because it is the time for them to play.

As the love principle, according to the idea of the Sufis and according to the idea of all the Prophets and Knowers who have ever come to this world, is the first principle, so it is the last principle.

There are different Yogas practised by the people of India, which are the Intellectual, Scientific, Philosophical and Moral paths to God, but the most desirable path to God that the Hindus have ever found, and which makes the whole life beautiful, is Bhakta Yoga, the path of devotion, because it is the natural path. Man's inclination is love. If he is cold, it is because he is longing for love; if he is warm, it is because love is alive. If one is suffering from depression, is yearning or sorrowing, it is because the love principle is not alive. The only life, the very source of inspiration, salvation and liberation, is love.

And among[27] those great souls who have brought the message of God to humanity from time to time; Buddha, Krishna, Jesus Christ, Moses, Abraham, Zarathustra; they were well known as most learned men, and what they learned, they learned from the love principle. What they knew was

24. Tp.c.: a comma instead of "or"
25. Hq.st., hq.t., tp.c.: "right" changed to "close"
26. Ibid.: "about" instead of "around"
27. Ibid.: "among" omitted

compassion, forgiveness, sympathy, and tolerance; that attitude of appreciation; that opening of the heart to humanity. What they taught was love, a simple truth. If religions seem complex, they have been added to. In every case what was brought by the Prophet was simple, and it was expressed in his personality and his life, and it is that influence that has remained for centuries after they have passed away. It is not the literature they have left. Most of the literature is from their pupils. It is the simple truth shown in their personalities and their lives.

The error of this day and age is that we cannot understand the simple truth; the truth as manifested everywhere; instead of trying to find truth covered in a shell.

Hafiz at the same time teaches one to see the ultimate truth and the ultimate justice in one and the same thing and it is God; that justice is not in related things; perfect justice is in totality. And he shows that the power behind manifestation is the love power, and it is by this power that this whole world was created. It is the love principle whether it works through God or man. And if that principle is at the back of the whole creation, then it is the same principle which helps man to fulfil the purpose of his life.

A typescript handed down by Mrs. Prebble (a pupil of Murshida Martin's) to Martha Burk, and inherited from the latter by Miss Hayat Stadlinger, an American mureed, initiated in Suresnes in 1926, who passed it on to the Biographical Department in Suresnes.

The Music of the Spheres.

Beloved ones of God:

My subject this morning is "The Music of the Spheres." By this title I do not wish to encourage any superstition, or any ideas that might attract people into the fields of curiosity, but in this subject I wish to direct the attention of those who search for truth, towards the law of music which is working throughout the whole universe, and which in other words may be called the law of life, the sense of proportion, the law of harmony, the law which brings about balance, the law which is hidden behind all aspects of life, and which is holding this universe intact; and working out through the whole universe its destiny; fulfilling its purpose.

Music as we know it in our everyday language is only a miniature which our intelligence has grasped from that music or harmony of the whole universe which is working behind us. The music of the universe is the background of the little picture which we call music.

Our sense of music, our attraction to music, shows that music is in the depth of our being. Music is behind the working of the whole universe. Music is not only life's greatest object, but music is life itself.

Documents: No original MS has been received by the archives to date.

Tp. (a typescript, received from Miss Hayat Stadlinger in 1983).
O.t. (very similar to the "tp.").

Both these documents, the "tp." and th "o.t.", seem to have been copied from the same old document. But then, handed down over the years by different lines of mureeds, they underwent some separate changes. Probably the "tp." kept nearest to the original text.

Sk.tp. (a typewritten copy made by Sk. from the "o.t."; the "tp." at that time had not yet been added to the archives).

This lecture was published in a revised form in *The Sufi Message of Hazrat Inayat Khan*, Volume II (1960), Music, chapter II, together with some parts of another lecture on the same subject, given in December 1922.

It is the last lecture in a series of six lectures on "Music," given by Pir-o-Murshid Inayat Khan on May 2nd, 1923, in the Paul Elder Gallery, San Francisco, U.S.A. (For the program issued by Paul Elder, see Appendix A.)

Hafiz, our great and most wonderful poet of Persia, says, "Many say that life entered the human body by the help of music, but the truth is that life itself is music." And I would like to tell you what made him say this. There exists in the East a mythological legend that God made a statue of clay in His own image and asked the soul to enter into it, but the soul refused to enter into this prison, for its nature is to fly about freely and not to be limited and bound to any sort of captivity. The soul did not wish in the least to enter this prison. Then God asked the angels to play their music, and as the angels played, the soul was moved to ecstasy, and through that ecstasy, in order to make this music more clear to itself, it entered this body.

It is a beautiful legend, and much more beautiful is its mystery. The interpretation of this legend explains to us two great laws. One is, that freedom is the nature of the soul. And for the soul the whole tragedy of life is the absence of that freedom which belongs to its original nature. And the next mystery that this legend reveals to us, is that the only reason why the soul has entered this body of clay, or matter, is to experience this music of life, and to make this music clear to itself.

And when we sum up these two great mysteries, the third mystery, which is the mystery of all mysteries, comes to our mind, which is that the unlimited part of ourselves becomes limited and earth-bound for the purpose of making this life, which is the outward life, more intelligible. Therefore, there is one loss and one gain. The loss is the loss of freedom, and the gain is the experience of life which is fully gained by coming to this limitation of life which we call the life of an individual.

What makes us feel drawn to music, is that our whole being is music; our mind, our body, the nature in which we live, the nature which has made us, all that is beneath and around us, it is all music. And as we are close to all this music, and live and move and have our being in music, therefore it interests us, and attracts our attention and gives us pleasure; because it corresponds with the rhythm and tone which is keeping the mechanism of our whole being intact. What pleases us in any of our arts, whether drawing, painting, carving, architecture or sculpture, and what interests us in poetry, is all the harmony behind it, which is music. It is music which[1] poetry suggests to us, the rhythm in the poetry, or the harmony of ideas and of phrases.

Besides this, in painting and in drawing, it is our sense of proportion and our sense of harmony which gives us all the pleasure we gain in admiring art, and at the same time, what appeals to us in being near to nature, is

---

Notes:

1. O.t.: "that" instead of "which"

nature's music, and nature's music is more perfect than that of art. It gives us a sense of exaltation to be moving about in the woods and to be looking at the green, and be standing near the running water, which has its rhythm and which has its tone, and it is harmony. And the singing[2] of the branches in the forest, and the rising and falling of the waves, it all has its music. And once we contemplate and become one with nature, our hearts open to its music. We say, "I enjoy nature." But what is it in nature that we enjoy? It is its music. Something in us[3] has been touched by the rhythmic movement, by the perfect harmony which is so little to be found in this artificial life of ours, which lifts one up and makes one feel that that is the real temple, the true religion. One moment standing in the midst of nature with open heart, is a whole lifetime, if one is in tune with nature.

When one looks at the Cosmos, the movements of the stars and planets, the laws of vibration and rhythm, all perfect and unchanging, it shows the Cosmic System is working by the law of music, the law of harmony. And when[4] that harmony in the Cosmic System is in any way lacking in proportion, then disasters in the world come, and its influence is seen in many destructive forces which manifest in the world. The whole astrological law, the science of magic and mysticism, behind it, if there is any principle upon which it is based, it is music. Therefore the most illuminated souls who have lived in this world, like the greatest of all the prophets of India, his whole life was music. From the miniature music which we understand, he expanded to the whole universe of music, and in that way he was able to inspire. And the one who gets the key to the music of the whole working of life, it is he who becomes intuitive, it is he who has inspiration. It is he to whom revelations manifest, for then his language becomes music. Every person who comes to us, every object we see, is revealing, but in what form? It tells us its character, nature and secret. Every person tells us his past, present and future, but in what way? Every presence explains to us all that it contains, in what manner? In the form of music, if only one can hear it.

There is no other language. It is rhythm; it is tone. We hear it, but we do not hear it with our ears. A friendly person shows harmony in his voice, in his words, his movements and manner. An unfriendly person, in his every movement, his glance and expression and his walk, in everything he will show inharmony, if one can only see it. I used to amuse myself in India with a friend who was very easy to be cross. When he came before me, I would say, "Are you cross today?" He would say, "Now, how did you know that I was cross today?" I said, "Your turban tells me. The way you tie your turban does not show harmony."

One's every action shows an harmonious or inharmonious attitude. There are many things one can perceive in handwriting. But the principal thing in reading handwriting is the harmonious or inharmonious curve. It

2. In the "Sufi Message" Volume II (see above): "swinging" instead of "singing"
3. O.t.: "you" instead of another word, perhaps "man" which was wiped out
4. Ibid.: "whenever". In the "tp." Hayat Stadlinger added "ever".

almost speaks to you, and tells you the mood in which that person wrote. Handwriting tells you many things; the grade of evolution of the writer, his attitude towards life, his character, and his mood in[5] writing. You do not need to read the letter; you only have to see his handwriting. For line and curve will show either harmonious or inharmonious, if one can only see it.

Friends, in every living being you can see this, and if one sees with an open insight into the nature of things, he will read this even in the tree. The tree that bears fruit or flower, what music it expresses.

You can see from the attitude of a person, whether that person will prove to be your friend, or will end in being your enemy. You do not have to wait until the end, you can see at the first glance whether he is friendly inclined or not. Because every person is music, perpetual music, continually going on, [6]night and day[6], and that music your intuitive faculty can hear, and that is the reason why one person is repellent, and the other attracts you so much. It is the music he expresses. His whole atmosphere is charged with it. There is a story of Omar, the well known Khalif of Arabia. Some one who wanted to harm Omar was looking for him, and he heard that Omar did not live in palaces although he was the king. He spent most of the time with nature. This man was very glad to think that now he would have every opportunity to accomplish his object. As this man approached the place where Omar was sitting, the nearer he came, the more his attitude became changed, until in the end he dropped the dagger which was in his hand, and said, "I cannot harm you. Tell me, what is that power in you that keeps me from accomplishing the object which I had come to accomplish?" Omar said, "My atonement with God."

No doubt it is a religious term, but what is that atonement with God? It is being in tune with the infinite, in harmony with the whole universe. In plain words, Omar was the receptacle of the music of the whole universe. The great charm that the personalities of the holy ones have shown in all ages has been their respondence to the music of the whole being. That has been the secret why they have become the friends of their worst enemies. But it is not only the power of the holy ones. This manifests in every person to a greater or smaller degree. Every one shows harmony or inharmony, according as he is open to the music of the universe. The more he is open to all that is beautiful and harmonious, the more his life is tuned to that universal harmony, the more he will show a friendly attitude to every one he meets. His very atmosphere will create music round about him.

The difference between the material and the spiritual point of view is that the material point of view sees matter as the first thing, and from this intelligence and beauty and all evolving afterwards. From the spiritual point of view, we see the intelligence and beauty first, and from it comes

5. Ibid.: "when" instead of "in"
6. Ibid.: "day and night"

all that exists. From a spiritual point of view, we see what one considers last the same as first. And therefore in the essence of this whole being there is music as its basis, as one can see that in the essence of the seed of the rose there is the rose itself; its fragrance, form and beauty, although in the seed it is not manifest, but at the same time in essence it is there. And the one who tunes himself, not only to the external, but to the inner being and to the essence of all things, he gets an insight into the essence of the whole being, and therefore that fragrance and flower which he sees in the rose, to the same extent he can find and enjoy, even in the seed.

The great error of this age is that activity has increased so much that there is very little margin left in one's everyday life for repose. And repose is the secret of all contemplation and meditation; the secret of getting in tune with that aspect of life which is the essence of all things. When one is not accustomed to take repose, one does not know what is behind his being.

This condition is experienced by first preparing the body by purification, and the mind also by means of purification; and by making the senses finer, one is able to tune one's soul with the whole being. It seems complex, and yet it is so simple. When one is open to one's tried friend in life, one knows so much about him; it is only the opening of the heart; it is only atonement with one's friend. We know his faults and his merits. We know how to experience and enjoy friendship. Where there is hatred and prejudice and bitterness, there is loss of understanding. The deeper the person, the more friends he has. It is smallness, narrowness, lack of spiritual development which makes a person exclusive, distant and different from others. He feels superior, greater and better than others. His friendly attitude seems to have been lost. In that way he cuts himself apart from others and in this lies his tragedy. That person is never happy.

The one who is happy, is he who is ready to be friends with all. His outlook on life is friendly. He is not only friendly to persons, but also to objects and conditions. It is by this attitude of friendship that man expands and breaks those walls which keep him in prison, and by breaking these walls, he experiences atonement with the absolute.

And this atonement with the absolute manifests as the Music of the Spheres, and this he experiences on all sides. Beauties of nature; color of flowers; everything he sees; everyone he meets. In the hours of contemplation and solitude, and in the hours when he is in the midst of the world; always the music is there; always he is enjoying its harmony.

A typescript of a lecture from the legacy of Murshida Martin, handed down by Mrs. Duce to Sirdar, and copied by Sakina. In a separate annotation Sk. writes: "doubtful whether authentic." Parts of the text do not seem to be Pir-o-Murshid's own words.

May 3rd, 1923.

The Coming World Religion.

Beloved ones of God,

My subject for this evening is: The Coming World Religion. In this I do not wish to make a prophecy about what is coming, but I would like to explain what is passing, how we stand in our religious quest today. This shows four different definitions of the word: religion, and most of them call their creed a religion. Many have considered their community a religion; many consider their view a religion; many consider a certain organisation, a religious organisation, to be their religion. But in the point of fact, religion in the true sense of the word is the right living, or in other words, the natural life. Therefore in the ancient scriptures of the Hindus, Dharma means "duty"; religion is considered duty. Plainly speaking, the way of living, the manner of living rightly is considered religion.

The Prophet of Islam has said that every soul has his own religion peculiar to himself, and how true it is. People living in the same family, or following the same church, believing in the same scripture, adhering to, perhaps, the same teacher, and at the same time, in their sacred ideals, in their way of looking at things, in their way of living, they are not the same, they are different. There has never been any period when there existed in

Documents: No original MS has been received by the archives to date.

Tp. (a typescript, apparently made from an incomplete reporting, handed down by Mrs. Duce to Sirdar, and copied by Sakina. Sk. made a few corrections in the "tp.).
Sk.ann. (some corrections in Sk.'s hwr. on a separate paper).

It is not known if the words in parentheses were added by the person who transcribed the longhand or shorthand reporting, or if Sk. added them.

This is the sixth and last lecture an "Spiritual Philosophy" given by Pir-o-Murshid Inayat Khan on May 3rd 1923 in the Paul Elder Gallery in San Francisco, U.S.A. (For the program, issued by Paul Elder, see Appendix A.)

An annotation made by Sk. with a view to the authenticity of the text of this lecture, reads [translated from Dutch by the compiler]: "We [Sirdar and Sakina] have been able to compare some fragments received from Mrs. Duce, with parts of lectures of which the original text is in our possession. It appeared that the version of the lecture sent by Mrs. Duce is a very poor rendering of the original text, in many places garbled and distorted."

reality two religions, and there will never be, in the true sense of the word "religion." There has always been one religion and there will always be the same. Those who know many religions, they do not know the meaning of religion. The one who realizes that one religion, he knows what religion means, for he sees behind all different religions one religion. For instance, those who say there are many gods, they do not know God. There cannot be many gods, there can only be one God! The Only God! So there cannot be many religions in spite of so many churches and scriptures, and the ideals that the followers of different religions adhere to. To the wise one who sees, there is one and the same. It is the lack of keen sight which has made man fight over the question of the differences of religion, and called such fighting religious wars, and considered it a great virtue to give his life in such wars as religious wars.

Religion contains five different aspects when you look at it with an analytical view. [1]At one[1] aspect is the God ideal. Another aspect is the teacher they adhere to. The third aspect is the scripture they consider the Holy Scripture. The fourth aspect is the law that is taught by a certain religion. And the fifth aspect is the exaltation which the followers of the different religions experience in their own way considered a spiritual (?ecstasy)[2].

Now coming to the question of law. There was a time when religion alone was education, and the law that governed the state among the Hindus, among Arabs, among ancient Egyptians, and in all parts of the world, it was a religious law that governed. And people followed that law, not only because[3] the fear of the police court and the court of Justice, but besides that, with the fear of God and His Justice. But times changed and conditions have made life different now. Now, in every nation, in every country, there is a law of the state, founded to a great extent on those ancient principles, because the fundamental principles will be the same. They may be differently interpreted, or differently put, but no nation or state will be able to change entirely the fundamental principles which are the religious principles. Only that the law which today governs different nations is not a religious law, it is called a law of the state.

Therefore there remain four more aspects of religion. The form of exaltation for an instance. The people of different countries had a form most suited to their life. There was a custom among the Moslems in Arabia to make five times ablutions in the running water before they performed their prayers. If the same thing was followed in Russia where it is cold, they

---

Notes:

1. Tp.: Sk. put "At" in parentheses and took "one" as the first word of the sentence.
2. The word "(?ecstasy)" may have been added by Sk., as she put a question mark before it and put it in parentheses.
3. Sk.ann.: "of" added

would give up such a religion in two days. The form is most suited to the people, to the country, to the need of the country. There is a certain form in India which is suited to the Indians (Hindus) mostly. According to their custom of ancient times a form has been taught. People have given such a great importance to different forms of worship that they have very often lost from their view the important factor of worship which is behind worship, and have usually held on the external form of the spirit and considered themselves separate from the words because of the external form.

It is not the form of worship, it is the attitude in worship which is counted. There is a story of an Arab during the time of the Prophet. He was running to join the congregation when the Prophet was leading the prayer. But he could not reach there in time, and on his way he met with people coming back from the Mosque. He asked one of them if the prayer be over. The man said "Yes, the Prophet was leading the prayer." This man heaved a deep sigh. Seeing this, the man whom he asked the question said: "Would you like to exchange with me the worshipping of prayer for your sigh?" He innocently, for the moment, said "Yes!" and after he went home he heard a voice that night where the Prophet appeared. The Prophet appeared to him in a vision. "What a wrong thing you have done in exchanging your sigh with one prayer with that man. Do you know what your sigh was worth? It was worth the whole of life."

This shows that what one gets from worship, from prayer, it does not depend upon the form, it depends upon the motive behind it. It depends upon one's attitude. It depends upon the depth of feeling, the devotion the man has. Adhering to such outward forms, very often people make their prayers quite formal. It becomes a social affair. They go for a change, perhaps, join together and wait there, and go through the whole form. And when they go away, it is nothing; it was just a pastime. And in spite of that all the differences that arise and the arguments which separate humanity, people belonging to one religion different from the others have mostly differences coming from the difference of the form of worship.

Kabir, the great poet of India has said that the Lord does not look at (where?)[4] you worship; if He looks at anything it is with what heart you worship. It is the depth of feeling, it is the right attitude in prayer that is counted and not the external appearance of it. All different concentrations and contemplations, different ways of meditations or prayers, they are all practised with one principal motive. That principal motive is to dive deep into the ocean of life, even for a few moments during the day after having lived every moment of one's day in the external affairs of life. And how true it is that the activity of today, if people are busy, each man in business or in some work or something, it becomes such a strain on them, and if they have a change in the way of a little play, or a game, or a little recreation of any

4. Ibid.: "(where or the way?)"

kind, that does not suffice the purpose of their life. As for a clock winding is necessary after some hours, so it is necessary for mankind to have a moment of that concentration, a moment of deep meditation when he may be able to touch the depths of life and be touched by that depth, where there is divine perfection that might help him in every way, physically, morally, mentally and spiritually. The restlessness and impairment and the agitation we see today in life, it all comes from the absence of that winding which is necessary for that mechanism we call the body, heart and soul.

At the present moment the lack of this is working in some certain way, bringing about a kind of restlessness in the multitude. But it will not be very long when the effect of this will be felt in the physical constitution of mankind, and then man will see that it is most necessary that there should be some form, some way by which one could charge the depths of one's life which is the real divine being.

And now coming to the question of the Scriptures. Most of the dispute that exists even today is over the scriptures, the scriptures which have been handed down for generations, and very often have been translated and changed about in many ways. And from different teachers they have come at such times when there was no press, nor any way of keeping them in type. There are some who make interpretation in one way and there are others who interpret in another. But when you look at it, what is the Scriptures? You will see the scripture is an interpretation of that reading, which the seers and holy ones of all ages have been able to read in life, the page of the whole life around them, whether their own nature, human nature and human race besides. This has been their scripture. From this we know they have read and learned, and what they have read and learned they have tried their best to put into words in order to make it intelligible to man. Man has not always been able to get it and keep it intact. Much has been lost. A little has been retained, and the people have changed that besides. And the difficulty has been that whenever a seer came, a great soul who was able to read in this living scripture of life, if he were to tell the people the interpretation, they always say "No, this does not agree with what is written in our books which we know are sacred scriptures."

They have kept the words of the scriptures as a kind of cover around themselves, keeping away everything, every interpretation or explanation that a great one ever gave. Very often, therefore, the great seers of the world had to take the scriptures in their hand, the scripture perhaps taken by thousands as their holy scripture. They had to take it as an excuse of the truth; they had to give to humanity while leading the life. (living scripture)

If then the difficulties arose and owing to the differences of the scripture[5], so many divisions of religions arose; and the human race has been divided into so many different religions owing to the differences of the book. If a wise man reads the same book, when man's eyes are open, when his heart begins to see, he sees nothing but the sacred scripture, the whole life is a sacred scripture. He can read then the so-called scriptures of all different sects and religions with a full knowledge because he is the one who knows the right meaning of the scriptures.

And what has happened is that those who kept their authority on the multitude, kept them under their influence by the power and the right over a particle of scripture; have kept humanity unaware of the living scripture which is before them.

They have tried that mankind should sleep and may never read the scripture which is before him, and kept his way only fixed to the few pages they have given. So it is all over the world, in the East, in the West, everywhere, even till now, until man has become so dead he is trying (to find) in occult books, in magic books, some mystery somewhere, he is thirsting for knowledge. If man was given the key to open the truths of life around him, to open the pages of nature's holy books and read from them, he would not have had this (difficulty he has attained?)

For it is not an ordinary mind which can write a scripture. The scriptures which have been given in ancient times have been given by those whose whole lives have been tuned to that high pitch where they could see and read the life; it gives their interpretation. When man is deprived of its meaning today and cannot find (it) in ordinary? writing, he becomes boastful. He has nowhere to see and read the truth for truth. For truth is hidden in the life which is before us and it can be read by rising to that stage, by being tuned to that pitch where the eyes of the heart are open[6] and when he begins to read it, he sees the scriptures and begins to understand its right meaning.

And now coming to the ideal teacher. What generally has happened is that one has remained the ideal. He has called himself the Alpha and Omega, (man has) limited him to a certain time and not recognized him, that he lived even before, that he will live after. In point of fact there is a factor in every individual which one calls mind, a factor where every experience one makes, everything one lives is collected, is preserved, and yet it is not a machine.

It is a creative factor which creates. Imagination, thought, music, poetry, invention, all come from this. A factor which is not only not a machine but which is a creative factor, an intelligent factor, a factor which

5. Tp.: Sk. added a plural "s"
6. Sk.ann: a semi-colon after "open"

wisdom will understand. And it is this which is the principal factor which may be called personality in the body.

As there is in every individual that factor, there is a collective factor also. Therefore the definition of Buddha, from which word the word Boddhisatva came, it is the name of that collective factor. In other words that Universal mind, the mind which has grasped the knowledge from the dawn of creation. Not only the knowledge that every mind collects, but the knowledge which comes from the plants, from the trees, from animal, from bird, from all aspects of life are collected in that collective factor. It is that factor which is called by the Buddhists "Boddhisatva" and by the masters, the moon or the light, or the spirit of guidance. And it is this which Christ mentioned as the Alpha and Omega, and with which he identified himself, being at-one-ment, reflecting that perfect mind, that divine mind.

People have argued and discussed over it. Some have made out of man divine, some have made divine man. In point of fact man is divine, and in this "divine man." All the arguments come from the lack of understanding, and what is it caused by? It is caused by words. Those who learn from (inner learning?) they do not differ. Those who learn by words differ, because it is impossible for every person to make the same by each word he knows.

Each one has his own meaning and when it comes to subtle ideals and philosophy, words do not seem to be able to accommodate, to explain them properly.

Very often we call the wise man clever and the clever one wise. Very often we confuse between the words mind and spirit. Very often we confuse intelligence and intellect. We call intelligent "intellectual" and intellect "intelligence." To give a proper meaning to the word, every one must have his own dictionary. But in the first place he must know himself the meaning of different words, and that, life alone can teach.

If anybody were to say that Brahma the great god of the Hindus was the same as Abraham, the great patriarch of the Beni Israel, people will not believe. And each one has his ideal and that ideal becomes so dear to him and he exhibits that ideal, and he takes that ideal with his imagination and makes it so that no other ideal can ever be produced upon the earth equal to that.

That is why it has always been so difficult for the prophets and seers to ..... They came as the crescent and those thinking of a full moon said "This is not the man we have seen him before." Those thinking (of) a full moon have said: "This is not the man. We have seen him full." If they only knew the nature of the moon was to begin as a crescent. In spite of all the prophets that existed in the Bible and in spite of the prophets that existed in the Hindu Purana's all the great ones had the greatest difficulty because those who were waiting for them, instead of preparing for them denied them, and clung to the traditions of the past.

And now coming to the idea, which is the principal idea which makes religion, (which) is the God ideal. Today there are so many various thoughts upon which people differ. Some think they sympathise with Monism, others say they believe in Pantheism, others call something Hinduism. But whether it is one God or there are many gods, it is the God ideal. Call it Monism, call it Pantheism, that is where man differs. In the right God ideal there cannot be a difference. Those who speak about ~~have called~~ many gods, they ~~are meant~~ mean ~~as many gods~~ one God; they ~~are meant~~ say gods, they ~~are meant~~ mean ~~one~~ God. It is lack of understanding. As I have said, it is the words that make people fight and founder over One God and many gods. But there has never been a religion of many gods (that) it did not make people believe only in various aspects, of one being, one ideal.

Gods in the plural were taught in order to bring all the aspects which are to be seen in the finite into the infinite. Of course there is very often great difference[7] but as Hafiz has said "If you say there is one God, you are right, but if you say there are two Gods, you are right, and if you say there are three Gods, you are right." For the nature of life is such. What does it mean? It means if you see three aspects it is three aspects, if you see one aspect, it is one aspect, there in the Trinity. It was the misunderstanding on the part of those who did not understand the meaning of trinity. In point of fact, trinity was the (means) for man to understand unity. And when one does not understand the truth, it is not the fault of truth, it is the fault of understanding. There are three different aspects. The one who sees, (the seeing, and the seen).

These three aspects make one life and it is this variety of three aspects which makes life intelligible to us, and is summed up in Unity, in oneness that all these three aspects are making it intelligible to us. But in point of fact these three are one. There has been great dispute among people by calling God separate from His manifestation. We have considered God as all. But it is the way it is explained to people. When they are told by a seer that all this which is before us is an illusion, if there is anything that exists, it is that which is not intelligible to us, which is beyond our comprehension, and that is God. The one who said it has said right. But the one who has listened has divided God from his manifestation. In the same way as one would divide man from his body. It is true that man is not his body and at the same time it is man's body, it is man just the same.

The reason we have read the knowledge of Advaita which means the oneness, the opposite of duality, they are ready to point that they dispute and question the personality of God and some even come to such a point in

7. Ibid.: a comma after "difference"

life that they are not ready to believe in such a God who has a personality. But at the same time, if you ask them if you are a thing or a being, he will certainly say "I am a being." He will not admit for one moment he is a thing. If a bubble can say, "I am a being" has that bubble the right to say the ocean is a thing? No doubt the personality of the bubble is nowhere to be compared with the personality of the ocean. There is no comparison, but at the same time, the bubble which is a particle of ocean, if that bubble can claim personality, then would it be unjust to let the ocean claim personality? In point of fact, the personality[8] is the real personality when compared with the bubble which in a moment will dissolve. And very often people, when they advance in philosophy, they hesitate to bow to their friends; they must not bow to anybody, not even greet their friends. Is there anyone who can say "I am independent of this perfect life which is around me, upon which every moment of life depends"? He depends upon the air to breathe, he depends upon the water to make him live, upon every grain for sustenance, upon the earth to have a body.

When life is such, how can one say "I cannot bow." But the question is "Who deserves every bow." It is the One who is All in All. It is He Who is perfect, Who is the perfection of all, the One Who is the perfection of all love, the perfection of all Beauty. Who is the source and the goal of all things, from Whom we all come and to Whom we all return. It is to Him there should be the bow of every soul. Poor or rich, wise or foolish, whatever be the rank or position of the person, to Him the bow of every person is due. When a person refuses to give his bow, he is lost.

---

8. Ibid.: "ocean" instead of "personality"

A typescript of a lecture handed down by Mrs. Prebble (a pupil of Murshida Martin's) to Martha Burk, and inherited from the latter by Miss Hayat Stadlinger, an American mureed, initiated in Suresnes in 1926, who passed it on to the Biographical Department in Suresnes.

1

Farid-ud-din Attar.

Beloved ones of God:[2]

[3]I am to speak today on the subject of Attar, and of his work.[3] Farid-ud-din Attar is one of the most ancient poets of Persia, and it is no exaggeration to say that the work of Attar has been the inspiration of Rumi and of many spiritual souls and many poets of Persia. He has pointed out the way to the ultimate aim of life, by making [4]a sort of[4] picture in a poetic form, and almost all the great teachers of the world, if ever they have been able to show the right way to seeking souls, always have had to adopt a symbolical form of expression, in the form of the story or legend, that might give the key to one who is to know, and might interest the one who is not yet ready, and therefore both may rejoice, the sleeping one, and the one awakened.

And this example has been followed by the poets of Persia and India, and especially the Hindustani poets, and they have made their story in such form that it would be acceptable, not only to the seekers after truth, but also to those in all different stages of evolution.

Documents: No original MS has been received by the archives to date.

Tp.: (a typescript received from Miss Hayat Stadlinger in 1983).
Hq.st.: (a copy of the "tp." with a few alterations, made at Headquarters, Geneva, where the lecture was made into a Social Gatheka).
Hq.t.: (a typewritten copy of the "Hq.st.", nearly identical to the "Hq.st.").
Tp.c.: (a typewritten copy of the "Hq.st." with several differences).

A Dutch translation of the lecture has been published in the magazine *De Soefi Gedachte* of 1952, nrs. 1 and 2.

The lecture was published in *The Sufi Message of Hazrat Inayat Khan*, Volume X (1964), Sufi Poetry, chapter IV.

It is the last lecture in a series of six lectures on "Sufi Poets," given by Pir-o-Murshid Inayat Khan on May 8th, 1923, in the Paul Elder Gallery, San Francisco, U.S.A. (For the program issued by Paul Elder, see Appendix A.)

Notes:

1. Hq.st., hq.t., tp.c.: added "Social Gatheka Number 30" and the invocation: "Toward the One, ..."
2. Ibid.: omitted "Beloved ones of God:"
3. Ibid.: the first sentence was omitted.
4. Tp.c.: "a short" instead of "a sort of"

Attar's best known work is called "The Bird of the Sky,"[5] from which we have taken the idea of the "Blue Bird," and very few have understood the idea of the Blue Bird, or the "Bird of the Sky." It is a very ancient teaching, through the use of the Persian word "sky." This points out that every soul has a capacity which may be called the sky, and this capacity can accommodate the world or the Heaven, whatever it would partake of and hold in itself.

When one walks in the crowd, what does one see? One sees numerous faces. I call them various attitudes. All that you see in individuals, all that stands before you, has expression, has atmosphere, has form. If you call it by one name, it is the attitude; the attitude they have towards life, right or wrong, good or bad, whatever attitude they have, they are themselves that attitude. Does it not show how appropriate is the sky, which means whatever you call it, whatever you may think it? Plainly speaking, whatever one makes of oneself, one becomes that. A source of happiness, or unhappiness, all is in man himself. When he is unaware of this, then he is not able to arrange his life, and as he becomes more acquainted with this secret, he gains a mastery, and it is the process with which this mastery is attained, which is the only fulfilment of this life. It is that process which is explained by Attar in his work of "The Seven Valleys" through which this "Bird of the Sky" had passed.

The first valley is that of the quest. How true it is that every child is born with the tendency to search, to know. What we call inquisitiveness or curiosity, it is born in them, and it represents that inner feeling of quest. This shows us that man is born with this, and he cannot be satisfied unless he has arrived at that satisfaction which means searching for that[6] knowledge which he wishes to have.

No doubt, what prevents man from gaining that knowledge which his soul is really searching for, is himself. It is his small self always standing against him, keeping him from the search of the only thing which is the seeking of every soul. And therefore it may be safe to say that there is no one in this world who is a worse enemy of man, than himself.

In this search one thinks that one must perhaps find out from science, or from art, something which is behind it, and whether through material quest or spiritual, in the end one will arrive, and one must arrive, to that goal, which is the goal of everyone. The scientists and engineers, people who are absorbed in making a search of material things and never think of spiritual things, even they, after making a great deal of search,

5. In *The Sufi Message of Hazrat Inayat Khan* (see above), "The Bird of the Sky" has been replaced with "Mantiq-ut-Tayr, or the Colloquy of the Birds".
6. Tp.c.: "the" instead of "that"

they arrive very near to the same knowledge which is the ultimate knowledge, and therefore whatever a man may seem to us, materialist, atheist or agnostic, we cannot call him so, because in the end his goal is the same, his attainment is the same, if he really reaches the depth of knowledge, if he goes far enough. Whatever his search he will come to the same goal.

And when one has searched enough and found something satisfactory, still he cannot enjoy that satisfaction unless there is one faculty open, and that is the faculty of love and devotion. Do we not see in our everyday life, that people of great intellect and wide interests, very often seem to miss something? When it happens to be a couple where one is very intellectual, the other may feel there is something lacking to make their lives complete, may feel that intellect alone is not enough. What is it? It is the heart which balances life, and the absence of which keeps life dry. It is just like the positive and negative forces. Knowledge and heart. It is these two things which make life balanced. If heart quality is very strong and intellect lacking, then also life lacks balance. Knowledge and heart quality must be developed in balance.

And therefore, according to Attar, that faculty of devotion or quality of heart, is the Second Valley; and the Third Valley is that knowledge which illuminates, which comes by the help of the love element and the intellect. It is that knowledge which is called spiritual knowledge.

Without the love quality developed, is man incapable of having that knowledge? I will answer, yes. There are fine lights and shades in one's life which cannot be perceived and understood fully without having touched the deeper side of life, which is the devotional side. The person who has not in his life been wholly grateful, he cannot know what it is. He who has not experienced in life, humbleness, he does not know its beauty. The one who has not known gentleness, modesty, he cannot appreciate its beauty or recognize it.

No doubt, a person of fine qualities is often ridiculed, if he happens to be in a place where it is not understood, where it is a foreign language. This shows there is a fineness in life for which intellect alone is not sufficient. The heart quality must become open.

A very intellectual man went to Jami and asked him to take him as his pupil and give him initiation. Jami looked at him and said, "Have you loved anybody?" This man said, "No, I have not loved." Then Jami said, "Go, and love first, then come to me and I will show you the way."

Love has its time in every stage of life. As a child, as a youth, as a grown-up person, and whatever stage of life one has reached, love is always asked for and love has always its part to perform; whatever situation you are placed in, among friends or foes, among those who understand you, and those who do not, in ease and in difficulty, in all places, at all times, it has its part to perform. And when one thinks, "I must not let the principle of love have its way, I must close myself against it," he imprisons his soul.

There is only one thing in the world, and that is pure unselfish love, which shows the sign of Heaven, which shows the divine sign, which gives the proof of God. For all the noble qualities which are hidden in the soul, will spring forth and come to bloom when love helps them and nurtures them. Man may have a great good in him and he may be very intelligent, but as long as his heart is closed, he cannot show that nobleness, that goodness, which is hidden in his heart, and the psychology of the heart is such that once one[7] begins to know the heart, life is a continual phenomenon; every moment of life becomes a miracle; it throws a searchlight upon human nature and all things become so clear to him that he does not ask for any greater phenomenon or miracle; it is a miracle in itself. What they call telepathy, thought-reading or clairvoyance, all these things come by themselves, where the heart is open.

If anyone is cold and stiff, he feels within himself as if he were in a grave; he is not living; he cannot enjoy this life for he cannot express himself; he cannot see the light and life outside; he is in his grave. And what keeps man back from[8] development of heart quality? His exacting attitude. He wants to make a business of love. He says, "If you will love me I will love you." As soon as man exacts and measures and weighs his favors, his services and all that he does for one whom he loves, he does not know love.

Love sees the Beloved and nothing else. As Rumi says, "Whether you love a human being or you love God, there will come a day when all lovers, either of man or of God, will be brought before the throne of Love and the presence of that only Beloved will reign there." What does this show? In loving our friend, in loving our neighbor, even in the love that one shows to one's enemy, one only loves God. And the one who says, "I love God, but I cannot love man," he does not love God; he cannot. It is like saying, "I love you very much, but I do not like to look at your face."

And after this Third Valley, where the knowledge of human nature and of the fine feelings which are called virtues, is attained, the next step is what is called in the English language "annihilation." But what we call destruction or annihilation is nothing but change. Neither substance nor form nor spirit, nothing, is absolutely destroyed; it is only changed. But man does not like sometimes[9] to change. He does not know that he cannot

7. Hq.st.: "one" omitted;
Hq.t.: "man" instead of "one"
8. Hq.st., tp.c.: "for" instead of "from"
9. Tp.c.: "something" instead of "sometimes"

live without change. He does not like it, but he cannot live without it. There is not one single moment of our life that change does not come; whether we[10] accept it or not, the change is there. Destruction or annihilation or death might seem a very different change, and yet there are a thousand deaths that we die. Every disappointment; the moment when our heart breaks, it is worse than death. Often our experiences through life are worse than death, yet we go through them. At the moment they seem unbearable; we think we cannot stand it, and yet we live. If after dying a thousand deaths, we still live, there is nothing in the world to be afraid of. It is man's delusion; his own imagination; he makes it dreadful to himself. Can anyone kill life? If there is any death, it is for death; life will not die. To a Sufi some one went with a question; he said, "I have been puzzling for many, many years and reading in books and have not been able to find a definite answer, tell me, what happens after death?" The Sufi said, "Please ask that question of someone who is going to die. I am going to live."

The principle is that there is one sky, which is your own being. It is like the sky. In other words, you call it accommodation. And who has taken possession of this accommodation? A deluded ego which says, "I." It is deluded by this body and mind and has called itself "individual." When a man has a ragged[11] coat he says, "I am poor." In realty his coat is poor, not he. What this capacity contains, that becomes his knowledge, his realization; and that limits him; forms that limitation which is the tragedy of every soul.

Now, this capacity either may be filled with self or may be filled with God. There is only place for one. Either we live with our limitation, or let God reign there in His unlimited being. In other words, we take away the home which always belonged to someone else and fill it with delusion and call it our own, and not only call it our own but call it ourself. That is man's delusion, and all religious[12] and philosophical teachings are given to rid man of this delusion, which deprives him of his spiritual wealth. Spiritual wealth is the greatest wealth, spiritual happiness the only happiness; there is no other happiness.

Once a person is able to disillusion himself, he arrives at the stage described in the Fourth Valley, the Valley of Non-Attachment, and he is afraid. He thinks, "How can I give my home to someone else, even if it is God?" "This is my body, my mind, my home, my individuality. How can I give it away, even to God?"

But in reality, it is not something he can rely upon. It is delusion from top to toe, and subject to destruction. Does anything stand above destruction? Nothing. Then why fear to think for the moment that it is nothing. That natural fear of man comes because he is unaccustomed to face reality.

10. Hq.st., hq.t., tp.c.: "you" instead of "we"
11. Tp.c.: "tagged" instead of "ragged"
12. Ibid.: "religions"

He is so used to dreams, that he is afraid of reality. There is a fear in the minds of people of losing themselves, but they do not know that it is not losing one's self. It is losing illusion. [13]And really, they will find themselves when they lose this illusion.[13] In this illusion, one has lost one's soul, and the process is to come out of it, to rise above it.

When the Fifth Valley, the Valley of Unity, is reached, by that time one has disillusioned one's self, and it is that act which is called in the Bible "Rebirth," when the soul has become disillusioned. It is the birth of the soul. There is the birth of the body and the birth of the soul. And how does this birth of the soul express itself? What does one feel? It first expresses itself in a kind of bewilderment with great joy. His interest in life is increased, all that he sees, he enjoys. He concerns himself little, but wonders at all things. The bewilderment is such that it is a wonderful amusement to look at life. The whole world becomes to him a kind of stage, full of players. He then begins to amuse himself with the people of this world, as one might play with children and yet not be concerned with what they do, for he expects no better. If children do something different from the parents, they[14] are not much concerned; they know it is the stage of the child's life and one cannot expect any better of them. So with this man. Likes and dislikes, favor and disfavor, they interest him, but do not concern him.

And there is another stage. This bewilderment brings him to see the someone reflected who has taken possession of his heart. To see his Beloved in everyone, even in his enemy.

The Beloved is seen in all things. The bowl of poison given by the Beloved is not so bitter. Those who have sacrificed themselves and suffered for humanity, such as Christ, they have given to the world an example showing a soul that has reached the stage where even the enemy appears before the eyes of the God-conscious, as friend, as his Beloved. And it is not an unattainable stage, because the soul is made of love, it is going towards the perfection of love. All the virtues man has learned, love has taught him. Therefore this world of good and bad; thorns and flowers; becomes[15] nothing but a place of splendor.

The Sixth Valley, the Valley of Amazement, is the valley where he recognizes and understands what is behind things; the reason of all reasons, the cause of all causes. For all intuition and power develop in man with the unfoldment.

13. Ibid.: omitted the sentence "And really ... this illusion."
14. Ibid.: "the parents" instead of "they". This same change was made by Miss Stadlinger in the "tp.".
15. Hq.st., hq.t., tp.c.: "become". In the "hq.t." Sk. added an "s" to "become".

And the Seventh Valley, the Valley of Realization of God, is that peace which every soul is looking for. Whether the spiritual or the material, seeking from morning until[16] night for something which will give him peace. To some souls, that peace comes when asleep. But for the God-conscious, that peace becomes his home. No sooner [17]has he[17] closed his eyes, no sooner [17]has he[17] relaxed his body and stilled his mind, and lost from his consciousness the limited, (than)[18] he begins to float in the unlimited spheres.

---

16. Tp.c.: "till" instead of "until"
17. Hq.st., hq.t., tp.c.: "he has"
18. Ibid.: "(than)" omitted

From one of Pir-o-Murshid Inayat Khan's notebooks.

When my prayers arose as burning incense and entered into the sky,
In the heavens they all went in ecstasy, the angels were moved to cry.
The good God woke up from His deep slumber, and said:
I will grant all you ask.
Touching my head most humbly did I say: easy m. . . .

My prayers arose as burning incense, and entered into the sky.
In the heavens they all had an ecstasy, the angels were moved to cry.
The Lord awoke from His deep slumber and said: I will grant all you ask.
Humbly touching my head to the ground, I said: God, make easy my task.

Written in Pir-o-Murshid's handwriting, Spring 1923, California, on a photograph, where he is standing under a triumphal arch:

My prayers arose as burning incense,
and entered into the sky.
In heaven they all had great extacy[1],
the angels were moved to cry.
The Lord awoke from His deep slumber,
and said: "I will grant all you ask."
Humbly touching my head to the ground,
I said: "God make easy my task."

Note:

1. An obsolete form of "ecstasy"

With hearty blessings
Inayat Khan

A record of a press interview in America, as written down by Pir-o-Murshid Inayat Khan in one of his notebooks.[1]

Representatives of the press.

Q. Is Sufism akin to Islam, which was spread with sword?

A. Nothing till now has been taught without a sword. While enemy's sword taught you to be on your guard, Islam's sword has cautioned for hereafter.

Q. Do you believe in Christ~~ian~~'s principle to give other side of the face if on one side you are slapped, or you prefer Mohomad's principle, strike for a strike?

A. We use both wisely: we would give other side of the face if that could ~~improve our~~ be beneficial for both, otherwise we would strike for a strike in case the strike be beneficial ~~for~~.

Q. To which religion or philosophy the Sufism is closer?

A. Sufism being the extract of all, it is ~~not particularly closer to one and~~ one in the essence of all religions and philosophies.

Q. Do you feel the sceptical and critical views of your audience when on the platform?

A. I feel, but do not let them work on myself.

Notes:

1. The language of the questions as well as of the answers is Pir-o-Murshid Inayat Khan's of early 1923, which gives the date "Spring 1923", when he was travelling in the United States. Some of the responses show that Pir-o-Murshid had been in America for some time already.

Q. Do you believe in ghosts and such other superstitions?

A. There is nothing that I do not believe, and nothing that I believe not understanding it.

Q. How ~~do you like~~ our Western country looks to you in comparison of yours?

A. ~~When~~ Yours looks like a simple moving picture, ~~and~~ while ours looks to me like the cinema.[2]

Q. How do you like your visit to our country?

A. I like it very much. To an appreciative ~~visitor~~ view everywhere beauty manifests to admire, while to the critical ~~visitor~~ view [3] spots in everything show that he may criticise.

Q. Have you a good response from our people?

A. I should say so, it is quite natural, as both East and West have attraction of each other.

Q. What do you think about our modern civilization?

A. Everything is for the good, but I must say that it is not yet well balanced.

Q. What is the condition of India at present?

A. A ~~material~~ practical awakening.

Q. What its result will be?

A. All for the betterment.

Q. Don't you ~~want~~ wish that India should be freed?

A. I have resigned my wishes to the will of Allah.

2. "a simple moving picture" may indicate a small device (kinetoscope) for individual viewing, whereas "cinema" would indicate a projected picture.
3. one illegible word in Pir-o-Murshid's handwriting, crossed out by him.

Q. Don't you feel homesick?

A. Everywhere ~~is my home~~ I feel at home.

Q. Why you have taken this trip?

A. To see (the world) and to show (through music the path of God).

Q. When will you go back?

A. When satisfied.

Q. ~~To work as an artist~~ It is not becoming for a pastor of your position to work as an artist.

A. My art is itself my religion, and my ~~posit~~ reputation lies in being regardless of (~~playing performing~~ playing in the Palace or a cafe, all places are equally ~~suitable~~ good for ~~my music~~ me as long as I am playing for my own self and ~~not for others~~ for none other.) the higher or lower places ~~that I may be playing~~, as long as I perform before the Must High.

Q. ~~Do you eat vegetable?~~ Are you a vegetarian?

A. I take food which may be necessary for the time. Sometimes liquid, sometimes vegetable food, sometimes meat, and sometimes I fast.

Q. Why our people are backward in esoteric lines?

A. Because they lack in faith and renunciation.

Q. Why your people are backward in the modern civilization?

A. Because of their negligence and dependence.

Introduction to Gita Dhyana

The five series of ten papers each known as Gita Dhyana have a complex and uncertain history which requires considerable explanation. Unfortunately, there remain a number of unanswered questions which must await the uncovering of more evidence before a convincing account can be given. Much of what follows is of necessity conjectural.

When Pir-o-Murshid Inayat Khan was in San Francisco in the spring of 1923, he gave many public lectures, of which the surviving texts are given in this volume. But, of course, he also gave private classes for the mureeds initiated on his behalf by Murshida Martin, who had so anxiously awaited his return after an absence of twelve years. Some of these classes, probably those for the more advanced mureeds, are the apparent origin of Gita Dhyana. Someone, perhaps Murshida Martin herself, perhaps Samuel Lewis, who belonged to that circle, must have taken down what Pir-o-Murshid said on these occasions (it is not known whether anyone there knew shorthand), and from these notes new sets of papers were created.

These were modelled on the series of "lessons," later called "githas," worked out in London by Sharifa Goodenough in 1917-1920. In these series, the teaching on a particular subject is normally divided into ten short papers, designed to be read aloud to mureeds at the classes.

The Gita Dhyana, in the state in which it has come down to us, reflects different degrees of editing. Some of the papers remain very close to what Pir-o-Murshid might have said; others add words, phrases and even whole paragraphs exhibiting a mode of speech or line of thought quite different from the Pir-o-Murshid's. It may be that in some cases the material from the classes did not suffice to make up a series of ten papers, so other materials may have been added to fill out those series.

This collection has become known in Europe mainly through the agency of Sirdar van Tuyll, who received it from the legacy of Murshida Martin. Sirdar's wife, Saida, wrote in 1966:

> Although Sirdar at one time considered these series of GITHA DHYANA as not authentic, later on, after Sirdar had passed away, many questions asked by other mureeds who owned parts of them (in German) caused Saida to read those she had in English once more. She gave them also to Sakina to read again, whereupon both came to the conclusion that these series GITHA DHYANA must be for the greater part Pir-o-Murshid Inayat Khan's own words, only taken down by

> Murshida Martin, who worked them out and rendered them in places in her own words. The underlined parts (words, phrases and sentences) in these three series contain expressions we never heard Pir-o-Murshid Inayat Khan use ....

After a very careful study of the papers, the present compiler concluded that in a few cases underlined words were in fact most likely to have been used by Pir-o-Murshid Inayat Khan himself, whereas quite a few passages not underlined actually represent additions to what was said by him. Therefore, instead of here reproducing the underlinings of the old copies, all words now considered not to have been spoken by Pir-o-Murshid are put in italics, whether substitutions (of words or phrases) or additions (of sentences or paragraphs or more). These changes would appear to have been made by Murshida Martin, or, in many cases, by her pupil Samuel Lewis. The italicized material has not been indexed, and is included here for the sake of completeness of the Gitas as they exist in the archives. Editing and stylistic adjustment must, quite clearly, also be assumed for the "authentic" passages.

Certain peculiarities of the texts have been retained here, such as the extensive but inconsistent capitalization and the indication of certain important words by leaving spaces between the letters. Those familiar with the teachings of Pir-o-Murshid Inayat Khan will perhaps be surprised to find the name "Allah" used so often for God, or the word "talib" for the mureed, and a much greater than average frequency of other Arabic words. Murshida Martin was Pir-o-Murshid Inayat Khan's first initiate in the West, and the teaching he gave her in 1911, not long after he had left India, made much use of traditional Sufi terminology, which of course continued in use in her centre. It may be that returning after twelve years, Pir-o-Murshid Inayat Khan was prompted by the established usage in that centre to take up this earlier terminology, even though he by that time had gradually been giving up the use of non-Western terms in his lectures in Europe.

A particularly vexing problem arises with respect to the numbering of the papers. In the case of both Series I and Series II, we have not one set of Gita Dhyana, but two. These papers in most cases are not, however, two versions of the same talk, but distinct treatments of related subject matter. In most cases, both sets appear to contain substantially the words of Pir-o-Murshid Inayat Khan himself. There is no satisfactory explanation for the existence of these parallel sets. It might be that the second set in each case was drawn up from answers to questions asked at the end of the talks represented in the first set, as it was Pir-o-Murshid's habit to entertain questions, and no other record of his possible answers has come down to us. This would explain the closeness of subject matter, but does not really explain why the papers should have been presented as though they were separate lectures.

In order to keep these parallel sets distinguishable, the compiler has added a bracketed A after the Arabic numeral identifying each paper of the second set. Thus we have:

Series I, Number 1 and Series 1, Number 1 [A]
and so on to the end of Series 1, and

Series II, Number 1 and Series II, Number 1 [A]
and so on to the end of Series II.

Series I, Numbers 1-10

These papers are in the archives in the form of carefully prepared copies made under Sakina Furnée's supervision, typed by her secretary, Mrs. E. von Derschau, and checked by Sirdar's secretary, Miss An Spirlet. They were made from originals in Sirdar's collection which cannot presently be located. All of this applies as well to Series II, Numbers 1-10 and Series III, Numbers 1-10.

Series 1, 1 [A] - 10 [A]

In the archives of the Biographical Department, these papers exist in the form of a photocopy of an old typescript (o.t.) in a small type. Nothing is known about the location of the original from which this photocopy was made.

Series II, 1-10

These papers are again known in the typewritten copy prepared under Sakina's supervision (see Series I, 1-10), of which the originals have yet to be found.

Series II, 1 [A] - 10 [A]

These papers are known in two copies, one in photocopy from files of papers used by Samuel Lewis in San Francisco (S.L.), the other a photocopy of a stencilled set in Sirdar's files in The Hague (o.t.). There also exists a German translation of this set, apparently made quite early. Mrs. Laura Hoeber, an American mureed belonging to the San Francisco centre, went to the Summer School in Suresnes in 1923, and stayed in Europe to work for the Sufi Message (cf. *Biography of Pir-o-Murshid Inayat Khan*, London: East-West, 1979, p. 514). In 1924, Pir-o-Murshid gave her charge over the centre in Munich, Germany, and she may have wished to use Gita Dhyana in her work there, sent for a copy to Murshida Martin, and translated the papers. (Mrs. Hoeber may have been of German origin.) This is one possibility to explain the connection between these classes given in America and this early, literal German translation. Both the "o.t." and this German translation are designated as "Series III"; however, "S.L." is designated as "Series II," and the closeness in subject matter to the other known set of Series II makes it clear that that is correct. The German translation appears to be closer to "S.L." than to "o.t.," and for this and other reasons we have taken "S.L." as the basic text here.

Series III, Numbers 1-10

This series exists in only one set, the carefully typed copy supervised by Sakina Furnée, (see Series I, 1-10) made from a copy originally in Sirdar's collection in The Hague which can no longer be located.

A copy made under Sakina's supervision of an old typescript in the form of a Gita, from the legacy of Murshida Martin.

Series I. GITHA Number 1.

Toward the One, the Perfection of Love, Harmony and Beauty, the Only Being, united with all the Illuminated Souls who form the embodiment of the Master, the Spirit of Guidance.

DHYANA MEDITATION

Meditation is the name given to the process of the stilling of mind which is most important in spiritual development. Without this stilling of mind, the Divine Spirit does not manifest in the personality, *for otherwise one is held in the sway of the ego.* Both quieting of mind and body and the soothing of the emotions are necessary if one desires to become a master-mind, which is to say, if one wishes to avoid the jarring disturbances of life which disturb most people.

In order to meditate attention is first given to the body, to see that it is relaxed, yet comfortable. Sitting in too soft a chair may make one too drowsy while too hard a chair may make one uneasy. A moderate degree of composure is desirable whether one is seated or in posture. The room should be neither too hot nor too cold, and it is generally best if one is not too hungry, although meditation after a full meal is not so easy nor always so advantageous.

One should learn to breathe rhythmically and to refine the breath by the process called SAFA. In this respect the Sufi meditation differs from that of the Buddhists for the Sufis use the names of God, which is to say the ninety-nine names or attributes offered in Qur'an, or repeat some sacred phrase or Darood which helps to refine the breath. The refinement of breath is a balm to the body and also a chain upon the nufs which seeks refuge in the mind as the body is brought into control.

The doors of the senses should be held closed; shutting the eyes partly or entirely is beneficial. The room should not be too brightly lit nor too dark, but it is by self-control that one must shut out other disturbances. Nevertheless, especially for the beginning a quiet place is desirable *and sound-proof rooms may be used.*

Rhythmic breath holds the mind in place also. Keeping the thought of God before one refines the breath. Sufis practise esotericism mostly,

Document: O.t. See introduction to Gita Dhyana, p. 219

which has the same general effect as silent meditation, but when they meet in groups or when strangers are present such methods are undesirable. However if one can maintain a calm, rhythmical, refined breath, after a time he will not even have to keep the thought of God before him. Thus he becomes an empty cup, only in meditation one keeps the cup empty, one empties the mind of everything.

Meditation is verily the fasting of the mind.

An old typescript in the form of a Gita, of unknown origin.

Series 1 GITHA Number 1.[A]

Towards the One, the Perfection of Love, Harmony and Beauty, the Only Being, united with all the Illuminated Souls, who form the Embodiment of the Master, the Spirit of Guidance.

The first thing that is necessary in meditation is to realise it is an act of attunement, an attunement with God. Therefore while it is necessary to relax, while it is important to control the emotions and the functions of mind and body, it is also important to raise, so to speak, the pitch of the heart, so that this attunement can be accomplished.

It is first necessary to relax the body, to be comfortable, but not to sit in too soft a chair or to lie down, for while the body is resting in meditation it is not in the same condition as in sleep. The reason is that the body is also in meditation, the body also breathes; it breathes through the pores of the skin, and it is necessary to keep the whole body in meditation. This is impossible while lying in a covered bed or among soft cushions. As mystical training is to make the body the temple of God, the body must not be neglected.

Neither must the mind be neglected. It is not enough to subdue thought, it is to raise the pitch, and although it may be said that to overcome one's thoughts, to become master of one's mind, is most difficult, one must face that battle. If one passes into sleep or into a dream or musing state, the mind is relaxed, but it is not properly relaxed. This is running away from the battle, thinking one has won it. One may think one has won the battle, but what has one won? The answer is easily seen when one looks at the great tasks which have been accomplished after meditations, which show that meditation is a positive action, not merely a relaxation.

This is what is meant when it is said that the Sufi is negative to God and positive to man, that he takes all that is given him, and gives all that he has. The Fakir may resemble, so to speak, a strainer or colander, through which much passes, and which retains nothing. He is also a cup which must empty itself to be filled. And of what does the cup of the Sufi empty itself? First, it empties itself of itself.

Document: O.t. See introduction to Gita Dhyana, p. 219

When this is understood, such legends as those of the cup of Jamshyd and the miraculous pitcher of Baucos and Philamon become clear. The pitcher will hold milk no matter how often it is emptied, and the crystal cup of Jamshyd is always full of wine, the Divine Love. The same is seen in the stories of Christ dividing loaves and fishes. What were the loaves? They were Christ's body. And what is Christ's body? It is Divine Wisdom, Sufism.

A copy made under Sakina's supervision of an old typescript in the form of a Gita, from the legacy of Murshida Martin.

Series I. GITHA Number 2.

Toward the One, the Perfection of Love, Harmony and Beauty, the Only Being, united with all the Illuminated Souls who form the embodiment of the Master, the Spirit of Guidance.

DHYANA MEDITATION

In meditation the control over mind *is exerted* through breath and mind. The breath is kept rhythmical and refined and it becomes ever more refined as the consciousness is turned upon it and the light of man's inner being manifests thereon. If the breath is not kept in rhythm, thoughts will enter and this battle against thought, especially against *ego-thought*, is the battle that every saint and sage has to combat continually. For this also will-power is needed. So in Sufism the talib is given a *symbolical concentration* in order to strengthen the will-power, so that not only will this power manifest, but that it can be used to control one's lower nature.

When the breath is kept in rhythm and is refined, the magnetism which is ordinarily consumed in the activities of mind and body is preserved. In whatever we do and in all our thinking and imagining we *consume* energy. This *consumption of energy* brings on old age and weakness. Contrariwise it may be that meditation of itself may cure man's evils, whatsoever they be. For all arise out of nufs, and meditation is the best means to crush nufs.

When one does that, the magnetism which is ordinarily wasted or *consumed, is absorbed into one's personal atmosphere*. This makes of him a battery of life. It is this battery which is used by teachers and healers and all mystics. It is the same energy which is mentioned in Nayaz, that it comes to man through the rays of the sun and the waves of the air and the all-pervading power of space. Through breathing the energy which is conveyed on the air enters the personality through the breath; by silence and by stilling the mind one draws upon the endless resources of space. This absorption is a veritable alchemy and the knowledge of it is the secret of the adept.

There is some benefit when meditation is performed constantly in one place, whether one *has devotions* in a room alone, or in a hall or *chamber* where many gather together. Such a place offers the right accommodation for the highest and finest vibrations and establishes an atmosphere of stillness. This makes it easier for others who come to such a place. The saints are often called upon to preserve the stillness of holy places.

Document: O.t. See introduction to Gita Dhyana, p. 219

The teacher can, by his presence, make the accommodation for still finer vibrations. *So there is at least one advantage to have a teacher who is more than a leader, who can elevate the feeling of a room.* Yet the faith of people, their prayers and their attitudes also help to strengthen the atmosphere of a chapel, a hall or a temple. All things that lead away from self, lead to God.

An old typescript in the form of a Gita, of unknown origin.

Series 1 GITHA Number 2[A]

Dhyana

Toward the One, the Perfection of Love, Harmony and Beauty, the Only Being, united with All the Illuminated Souls, who form the Embodiment of the Master, the Spirit of Guidance.

Beloved ones of God:

In meditation the control of the mind and body is exercised through the breath, and not only in meditation but in all acts and aspects of life, the control of the mind and body is through the breath and this can be discovered when the sight is keen. There are two aspects of this.

First is the creation of one's own atmosphere, and this also has two aspects. There is the regulation of one's breath, the adjustment to the proper rhythm, together with the control of the body and mind. One constantly changing breath can neither meditate nor perform any other function. Therefore breathing exercises and practices are given. These affect the aura about one, and develop the personality. This is the gradual change which takes place during spiritual development unperceived, perhaps, yet very definite.

Besides building this atmosphere about oneself, one affects one's environment. One is able to radiate a magnetism which may be healing, and not only in the sense of helping sick people, but of helping everybody. For who is not sick? It is not only those who have diseases of the body, but everybody who is in need in some way, and the spiritual person can help.

But the best atmosphere is that created in a place where one stays often. That is why it is so important to have a room, a room in which one meditates. The highest vibrations one is able to build up will always remain there, and when one builds still higher vibrations, they raise the pitch of that room. Therefore, when one meditates in such a room, they can heal themselves and send out healing and helping thoughts to another.

Document: O.t. See introduction to Gita Dhyana, p. 219

This helps us to understand the second aspect of building an atmosphere in meditation, that is the use of a chapel or room or temple where spiritual students can congregate. By combining their efforts, they collectively build such an atmosphere, an area of calm and quiet, the centre of fine vibrations, which becomes a healing center. People often imagine about healing pilgrimages and some do not believe in the miraculous cures, but this is a mistake. The faith of the people, their prayers, build up this atmosphere, and the healthy ones who go there actually heal the sick, and the sick, in the area of these purified atoms become well. Therefore the Sufi who understands, will never speak against this type of cure or healing; it may truly be said to be spiritual.

Finally, as one builds up an atmosphere in one's room, so the spiritual teacher builds up the atmosphere in the meditation hall, bringing in his purified personal atmosphere, and raising the pitch so that all who can attune themselves will rise nearer and nearer to that consciousness which is the goal of all who travel on the Path of God.

A copy made under Sakina's supervision of an old typescript in the form of a Gita, from the legacy of Murshida Martin.

Series I. GITHA Number 3.

Toward the One, the Perfection of Love, Harmony and Beauty, the Only Being, united with all the Illuminated Souls, who form the embodiment of the Master, the Spirit of Guidance.

DHYANA MEDITATION

While one does not perform meditation for selfish purposes, nevertheless there is a great gain in personal magnetism and if one needs magnetism or desires it, there is no better manner of obtaining it than through meditation. For then it is that the battery is recharged which has been giving out so much energy in thought, speech and action. All of these things consume vital magnetism and the silence of the sages is to conserve the power that it might be transmuted or used only to benefit the world.

Such things as holding one hand in the other, or folding hands or crossing the legs under the body or even kneeling tend to keep the magnetism from scattering. *The body is a bio-electric vehicle as the scientists are now learning. Breathing in the silence draws energy into it.* The healing practices help even more. But besides this, when one restrains the ego in speech, thought and action, and when one refrains from these things, already the power begins to return to the vehicles of the soul.

Magnetism leaves the body through the nostrils, fingers, eyes, ears, tongue, lips, feet and all over. The controlling of these centres and organs makes of the body a human temple of God. Rhythmic breathing, *rhythmical schedules* and all practices of rhythm are also beneficial. Otherwise the gain that might come in meditation may be frittered away and lost.

To make sure of one's gain it is best to meditate regularly at a certain hour, every day if possible, or less often if this is not possible. This adds to the music of life also. For the gain of one person in magnetism can be the gain of all. The teacher or leader in meditation helps the others because of his increased capacity and also because of his ability to draw the cosmic energy.

It has not been meant that we should be subject to pain, suffering and disease. It is even possible to live a long time in the body without feeling the *ravages of years.* Moses stayed one hundred and twenty years and departed in the full vigor of his energies *because he knew how to tap what*

Document: O.t. See Introduction to Gita Dhyana, p. 219

some have called the cosmic reservoir. Yes, no doubt the reservoir is there and it is not wrong to tap it. Sufism is wisdom and wisdom does not mean to refrain from everything that will bring personal satisfaction or happiness. One does not have to put these things first. One may lead a perfectly balanced life and obtain all the blessings thereof without any danger to oneself or hindrance of spiritual evolution.

The greatest gain, however, is peace, which is paramount even to magnetism. This is obtained in the silence by complete restraint especially against the ever constant activity of mind.

An old typescript in the form of a Gita, of unknown origin.

Series 1 GITHA Number 3[A]

Dhyana

Toward the One, the Perfection of Love, Harmony and Beauty, the Only Being, united with All the Illuminated Souls, who form the Embodiment of the Master, the Spirit of Guidance.

Beloved ones of God:

Something has already been said of the posture in meditation and also of the need of poise. The purpose of posture is to control the magnetism, to control the currents which are generated. If one went into a room where the vibrations are very poor and held out the hands, and separated the feet, the magnetism would be scattered. This might be good for the room, but would not help one very much.

The spirit enters through the breath, but the magnetism of that spirit is transferred to the nerves and blood and carried to the extremities. The magnetism that leaves the body is not through the nostrils, but chiefly through the fingers, the toes and the head area, and in the head area through the eyes, ears, and a little through the crown, chin, nostrils and through speaking. By controlling these *avenues of egress* one retains the strength from Prana, and in that way builds up his own powers. This develops not only the power of the breath, but the power of healing, the power of the word, all powers come through this breath.

The purpose of poise or position is to keep the body in equilibrium, so that one will not sway nor have to exert a force to retain this position, to keep steady. For this reason some mureeds are trained in certain postures and others otherwise, and each exercise or prescription given by Murshid may vary, for the purpose is to help the mureed according to his need.

Rhythm is also necessary, and this rhythm is of two kinds; rhythm in breathing and rhythm in daily life. In meditation the rhythm must be steady, as one learns in the study of Fikar. This is more important than to fix a rate, slow or fast, or to have a light or deep breath, although all of these are important in their effect on body and mind.

Document: O.t. See Introduction to Gita Dhyana, p. 219

But as the whole body, mind and soul unite in meditation, it is important, to have a fixed hour or fixed periods for meditation, to arrange one's time so there are hours for work, play and eating, studying and meditation, and to keep these hours as much as possible. When one is travelling a change may be necessary, but otherwise this should be kept foremost. Fifteen minutes a day regularly will help one much more spiritually than two hours a day at one's convenience. Why? Because these fifteen minutes are devoted to God, and those two hours for the self, and this is not true meditation, which seeks for nothing but the realisation of God.

A copy made under Sakina's supervision of an old typescript in the form of a Gita, from the legacy of Murshida Martin.

Series I. GITHA Number 4.

Toward the One, the Perfection of Love, Harmony and Beauty, the Only Being, united with all the Illuminated Souls, who form the embodiment of the Master, the Spirit of Guidance.

DHYANA MEDITATION

The atmosphere is itself most helpful to those in meditation. Of course there are monks and ascetics who meditate alone in different parts of the world, but even they build up their own atmospheres. There is a great deal of strength gained by a person who can retire to his own atmosphere, and the more sensitive he is the more will he feel it.

Meditation helps one to become more receptive. However if by this term is meant the receiving of knowledge or of wealth or of anything in particular it is not so. Yes, there have been in ancient times and there are today and there may be in later times also those who seek to use spiritual *devices* to obtain material or selfish ends for themselves. But ultimately they must pay for these things and they do not rise thereby above [1]the real, of *karmic interplay*[1].

The receptive person draws the energy of the sphere into himself. For instance it is by such means that SHIFAYAT, the healer, makes of himself an instrument whereby divine energy can find a channel through which it goes in order to reach ultimately the mind and body of a sick person. This shows that the energy can be directed, but in meditation one does not even think about energy. That would be a concentration and would draw forces in a particular direction. In meditation one tries to strip himself of every kind of thought and of every type of motive.

No doubt the one who practises meditation gains in sympathy and in insight. This ability to sympathize is most important for it helps to further break down the differences and distinctions which divide men. *In the negative state one may feel the suffering, pathos and pain of another; if he remains*

Document: O.t. See Introduction to Gita Dhyana, p. 219

Note:

1. "the real of karmic interplay". Even though this does not make sense, it reads so in the "o.t.".

there he cannot be helpful. For this reason Sufis practise Darood or repeat an Invocation before meditation, so that they can better be united with the whole stream of life, which manifests through the chain of illuminated souls, who form the Spirit of Guidance.

The development of insight leads ultimately to expression. One does not primarily practise meditation for the sake of gaining an answer to his problems or questions, yet if one is overburdened he can bring one question with him into meditation, sit quietly, remove all thoughts, watch the breath at every instant and find himself receive a knowledge or instruction as if the universe itself were speaking to him. Then and thus will he recognise the Voice of Wisdom. For in the Silence God Himself becomes the Teacher, the Teacher of all.

An old typescript in the form of a Gita, of unknown origin.

Series 1 | GITHA | Number 4[A]

Dhyana

Toward the One, the Perfection of Love, Harmony and Beauty, the Only Being, united with All the Illuminated Souls, who form the Embodiment of the Master, the Spirit of Guidance.

Beloved ones of God:

The Quality of atmosphere enables one to become more quickly receptive. Receptive to what? To the One, the Perfection of Love, Harmony and Beauty, the Only Being.

Some people believe that meditation brings a relaxation and then one should receive everything. This shows lack of discrimination for there are impressions and thoughts and suggestions that are of no value. What is attunement? It is altering the pitch of the personal will to the Will of God. Whatever one holds before oneself, to that will he become attuned, but if everything is allowed to pass before one's mind, it can become affixed on nothing. It is the same as one first viewing a great city or marvellous scenery; they do not fix their gaze on anything. The Sufi, knowing this, fixes his gaze on God.

In healing, if one does this, he gradually draws the magnetism of the universe and dedicates his body for a healing work. But if he thinks that negativity means attuning to the sick patient, he draws on the condition of the patient instead of the Divine Help, and may take on the illness without helping the sick person much. This comes from a wrong view of sympathy.

Sympathy means an attunement, a feeling with, but there is a negative way and a positive way of sympathizing. In the negative way one feels the suffering, the *pathos*, the pain, and unites in grief but does not bring much help. In the positive way, one raises the other from sorrow, one is able to give them their better condition without taking on the lower condition. This is true healing. That is the reason why one must repeat "Towards the One" so much during the healing service, and gradually attune oneself to the Divine rays which are health-giving.

Document: O.t. See Introduction to Gita Dhyana, p. 219

But this is not only so in healing, but in all forms of inspiration, in poetry, music, art, invention, and all aspects of the creative process. The more one meditates the more one rises to the essence of things, becoming a vehicle for divine expression. There every aspect of life becomes an art and a science.

One going to his meditation feeling, "God is my Teacher, I have something to learn from Him, I will listen attentively", will be rewarded with the greatest blessing, receiving in the Silence and Meditation that which he is capable of understanding, and by this gradually his purpose of life will be unfolded.

A copy made under Sakina's supervision of an old typescript in the form of a Gita, from the legacy of Murshida Martin.

Series I. GITHA Number 5.

Toward the One, the Perfection of Love, Harmony and Beauty, the Only Being, united with all the Illuminated Souls, who form the embodiment of the Master, the Spirit of Guidance.

DHYANA MEDITATION

Nothing is more valuable in the spiritual life than meditation. If he only knew it is more valuable than food, sleep or any of those activities which seem so necessary to him. And this need is known even to the animals. For instance one often sees cats rest with their paws under them. They try to produce a state of calmness in which there is neither thought nor emotion. Many other animals make use of the silence although birds also indulge in praise to God aloud.

Even the machines that man makes break down and need reconditioning and overhauling. There being no perpetuality[1] and there being action and reaction, man has to learn how to recharge his vehicles. Instead he usually argues that he "has not the time" for meditation. Yet meditation is the very thing that will give him the time, and most of all for his own self, for his own welfare.

Meditation is not only the way to healing, it is the key to all things. If all studies were stopped and if there was only esotericism and meditation nothing of Sufism or of spiritual philosophy would be lost. One can dispense with study papers and literature. The real truth is to be found within one's own being. But if there is constant activity and if there is all attention to the world outside, how can man ever come face to face with himself? Instead he grows older with the years and displays loss of vitality so very often. For not only when body is fatigued or mind tired does this loss manifest, but in every display of emotion also.

Meditation is thus far more important than any and all intellectual study. Through the intellect one can only receive what has come to the intellect of others and as they are limited, so he is limited. Besides, he does not get their real knowledge thereby, he only obtains a reflection of it. It is only when one relaxes body and mind that he begins to learn the Cosmic

Document: O.t. See Introduction to Gita Dhyana, p. 219

Note:

1. "perpetuality" is an obsolete form of "perpetuity"

Language. This language is universal and omnipresent, and is understood by the awakened heart.

There should be a balance between meditation and activity. If this is continued one will find his meditation even in his everyday life. So it does not mean retiring to the closet for long periods, expecting some reward therefrom. It is only as the ego is restrained, one increases the capacity within himself for the Divine Light and comes to a realization of his true being.

An old typescript in the form of a Gita, of unknown origin.

Series 1 GITHA Number 5.[A]

Dhyana

Toward the One, the Perfection of Love, Harmony and Beauty, the Only Being, united with All the Illuminated Souls, who form the Embodiment of the Master, the Spirit of Guidance.

Beloved ones of God:

[1]*Actually nothing is needed more in life than meditation. It is more important than even food and sleep and all the activities of life. Those who are only a little observant will notice that cats often lie with the paws under their body, in a posture of meditation, and this is so, they are meditating. They meditate in Silence. Birds, on the contrary, practise Zikar, praise to God, but throughout creation, from rocks and trees to man, everything is in meditation sometimes.*

Even the machinery which man makes will break down if it is not given rest and overhauling, but to man's own vehicles, his body and mind, this is not considered so important or necessary. Many people constantly put off taking up spiritual studies because they "have not the time." They do not see that a little spiritual training will not only give them more time for what they must do, but will enable them to know with their whole heart and soul what they must do. This will make it possible to eliminate all unnecessary acts in life, to devote one's energy to what is vital. Even pleasure and pain become the greatest of mysteries and problems to those not on the spiritual path.

Meditation is not only the key to healing, it is the key to all things. If all the studies were dropped and only the spiritual practices, the invocation and the prayers were retained, nothing of Sufism would be lost. The soul would remain and could build up new bodies. It would be like throwing away one's clothes and thinking the body is lost, but it might be the gainer by such an act.

Meditation is not only far more important than study, it is true study. When one completely relaxes the body and mind, and becomes receptive to

Document: O.t. See Introduction to Gita Dhyana, p. 219

Note:

1. The first four paragraphs of this paper appear to be a working out in her own words by Murshida Martin of the same material which appears in Gita Dhyana Series I no. 5.

God, then the Voice of God will speak to him in the language of the soul. This is true Sufism which can never be explained, yet can clearly be understood.[1]

One can never meditate too much. This does not mean going into one's closet, but it means keeping the heart fixed on God, to keep the mind fixed on the invocation, every moment day and night, so the very breath will keep on calling, "Towards the One." Then the hour will arrive some time when the Talib will realise his true being. And what is that true being? It is God, the Only Being.

A copy made under Sakina's supervision of an old typescript in the form of a Gita, from the legacy of Murshida Martin.

Series I. GITHA Number 6.

Toward the One, the Perfection of Love, Harmony and Beauty, the Only Being, united with all the Illuminated Souls, who form the embodiment of the Master, the Spirit of Guidance.

DHYANA MEDITATION

Harmony is a most important essential in life. Although there have been multitudes who have proclaimed their belief in the brotherhood of man, the accomplishment of it seems to be far away. If one investigates he will discover that harmony between person and person is missing. This brings up a question, is there any way by which harmony can be produced? Yes, persons who mingle often in the same atmosphere may grow closer together, there will be a common bond.

There is one of the reasons why people meditate in group, with or without a teacher or leader. The teacher or leader serves to draw them closer together, to harmonize them, like the conductor of the orchestra harmonises the musicians and their instruments. In the orchestra it is not only the instruments which are brought into attunement to each other but the players themselves. And in the meditation hall the atmosphere serves to tune the hearts of the devotees, to bring them, so to speak, into consonant pitch.

The Healing Service of the Sufis depends upon internal harmony. Therefore the number of participants has been wisely limited. The more persons who join the circle, the more difficult is it to create and preserve a lasting living harmony. Besides, negative persons in it would be attracting the energy to themselves and limiting the healing power. Sometimes even a single undeveloped person can destroy the efficacy of such a Service; sometimes a single undeveloped person may create a disturbance at a meditation group. To protect the group as well as themselves many teachers restrict the number and are careful to examine newcomers.

When a person who lacks understanding enters the meditation group he brings in his lower atmosphere as well as his undesirable thoughts. These interfere with the atmosphere already created and draw energy from it. To use the terms of electricity they discharge it. And sometimes it takes months to create a sacred atmosphere which can be so destroyed in a moment.

Document: O.t. See Introduction to Gita Dhyana, p. 219

Therefore less developed persons are instructed in meditation alone, or they are given opportunities for silence at the Universal Worship and at other meetings which they can sustain. But for the undeveloped, the silence held too long can be harmful. *People who have been over-strained in public corrective institutions have been known to go mad.*

One should therefore begin with quite short silences and increase them as one is able to restrain the mind. The quality of the meditation itself may be quite as important as the length of time used in maintaining silence.

An old typescript in the form of a Gita, of unknown origin.

Series 1 GITHA Number 6[A]

Dhyana

Toward the One, the Perfection of Love, Harmony and Beauty, the Only Being, united with All the Illuminated Souls, who form the Embodiment of the Master, the Spirit of Guidance.

Beloved ones of God:

Harmony is most necessary when two or more mureeds unite for spiritual purposes. In the study of lessons, unless they have a cordial feeling, both will miss the purpose, which is as much to attune their personalities one to the other, as to gain intellectual development from the manuscript. One might even say that that was the real lesson. And when more than two come together, the same adjustment is needed, but when there are several persons, sometimes one or two serve to harmonise others who may not understand each other's nature.

In the Healing Service the presence of a sick, or an unharmonious or an undeveloped person, or one who is not suited for this work, has the tendency either to draw the magnetism to that person or to disperse it, so it will not be of much value. For that reason, it is best to select properly fitted persons for this line of work, and groups should be limited to about seven people. Discrimination of the workers, however, is most important, and if there are less it does not matter, and if there are more, it is better to divide the work and have two groups.

The presence of an undeveloped person has the tendency to break the tension and to discharge the atmosphere. Under such conditions a true positive meditation is impossible. Among the oracles in ancient Greece, it was not only necessary to have the oracle and the seer lead a very pure life, but all those who assisted by forming a magnetic circle had to be pure.

When a person lacking understanding enters a meditation room, it makes it difficult for those who form the embodiment of the Master, the Spirit of Guidance, to direct the true spiritual work. They will not convey lessons or impressions or messages, or else they will require a silence on the part of the one who is learning from them. Sometimes it is important that such people be dismissed from the room. It is also important to arrange classes of people of the same degree of evolution, for they assist one another instead of hindering.

Document: O.t. See Introduction to Gita Dhyana, p. 219

Of course, group silences, in the presence of a teacher, or in a room especially adopted for this work, have always been part of the Sufi training. In this congregation, the earlier Talibs are greatly benefitted, and the more advanced are not held back for they have learned to attune themselves to the atmosphere. By preserving the silence in the room, by closing the doors to the outside world, a condition is brought about so that in time the place becomes holy, and those who feel it will become more and more reverent, and this in turn will increase the sanctity of the atmosphere, that even those who are not on the spiritual path will feel in awe, and be constrained to silence and meditation.

A copy made under Sakina's supervision of an old typescript in the form of a Gita, from the legacy of Murshida Martin.

Series I. GITHA Number 7.

Toward the One, the Perfection of Love, Harmony and Beauty, the Only Being, united with all the Illuminated Souls, who form the embodiment of the Master, the Spirit of Guidance.

DHYANA MEDITATION

The laws of the unseen world are not different from those of the seen world although no doubt they concern more vital forces *and atomic formations* than we see in the objective manifestation. The same word "magnetism" is used to apply to various types of *ultra-physical* phenomena and the same principles hold except that the magnetism of the scientists is closely associated with iron and steel and some other metals; while the vital magnetism makes use of the elements and of the atoms and vibrations of all planes.

In the Healing Service the silence is used to increase the current between several persons; while in one's own practices it is employed to revivify one's own self. But when several persons join in the Service, those who do not give out absorb and by their absorption, they weaken the value of the service. But if all present have practised meditation by themselves they can increase the vital electricity which is sent by thought-power to the sick person.

The undeveloped person acts like an insulator to the mureeds, and can discharge the electricity. This is why Christ said he felt a force leaving him when a woman touched the hem of his garment.[1] To protect against this condition one should have his own room for private meditation, even if it be a cell. He should have his *devotions* there and not use it for any low purpose. Even smoking is inadvisable in such a place. Thus he will create his own atmosphere, add power and magnetism to it and make of it a centre for vital forces and electricity.

The same is true of the meditation hall. The less conversation of all kind that goes on there the better. Ordinary conversation should be restricted. But more subtle is the conversation that goes on within every person. For as soon as there is silence the thoughts begin to move about and to agitate. To overcome that one is urged to repeat a spiritual phrase or to

Document: O.t. See Introduction to Gita Dhyana, p. 219

Note:

1. See the Bible, New Testament: S. Luke 8:46.

watch the breath. In the presence of a teacher, however, all may concentrate upon the breath of the teacher or the heart of the teacher.

The teacher himself seeks to overcome the less developed breath of the pupils and thus increases their capacity. If the pupil has any difficulty in catching the rhythm of the teacher's breath--and this is by no means always easy--then he can concentrate a little upon the teacher's heart, doing this mostly by feeling, and gradually relax all his thoughts first, and then his feelings afterwards. Thus he enters the state that "I am not" which is most beneficial for all students on the path.

An old typescript in the form of a Gita, of unknown origin.

Series 1 GITHA Number 7[A]

Dhyana

Toward the One, the Perfection of Love, Harmony and Beauty, the Only Being, united with All the Illuminated Souls, who form the Embodiment of the Master, the Spirit of Guidance.

Beloved ones of God:

The same laws hold in spiritual development as in the physical world. This can be observed most easily in the study of electricity and magnetism. For instance, when a battery is made up of several cells united, the efficiency is determined by the condition of the poorest cell among them. If one cell is weak, the battery will be weakened, and if one cell is dead, the battery will not function.

In the same way, in the healing circle, if there is one who cannot contribute to the magnetic force, the whole circle is of no value; even if all the others are highly charged with spiritual power, they cannot function as a group with a negative person among them. Likewise, there is such difference between the meditation in the Universal Worship, and that for mureeds only. Therefore, the Murshid, who is a very positive power, does not lead the meditations in the Universal Worship, which are given to Cherags who do not read the sermon. At the same time, the most developed one should give the blessing, for the blessing is given in the center, where the personality serves as the instrument of all the illuminated souls, who form the Embodiment of the Master, the Spirit of Guidance.

In electricity there are conductors which carry the energy, and insulators which do not, but the term is relative, as there are good conductors and poor conductors, and even the best insulator conducts electricity a little, although perhaps immeasurable. So, all persons are on the spiritual path, although most may not know it. But if they did not so function they would be dead in the truest sense, they would be entirely dissolved.

The undeveloped person is like an insulator among mureeds, and can discharge an atmosphere, exactly like the discharging in electricity. On the other hand, the Murshid constantly charges the atmosphere. The

Document: O.t. See Introduction to Gita Dhyana, p. 219

Murshid is like a dynamo which draws power from its Source and by means of which many electric lights may illuminate humanity. Without the dynamo the lights are nothing, and without the Source of Power the dynamo is nothing. In the same way, without the Murshid the mureed is nothing and without God the Murshid is nothing.

An electrical body may be charged to the limit which is called capacity, and a Talib may receive to a limit which is also called capacity. But the capacity of a body may be increased through certain means and the capacity of a Talib may also be increased. And after a body is charged and functions, the power of its function is called potential, which depends upon its own capacity and the capacity of the receiver of that electricity. Likewise the power of the mureed depends both on his energy and the ability of the person whom he is aiding. As an insulator will not receive electricity, but causes a discharge, so must the spiritual person have discrimination, otherwise it will be, as Christ said, casting pearls before swine and that which is holy to the dogs. Verily, in all departments of nature can one find God, if one truly seeks and looks.

A copy made under Sakina's supervision of an old typescript in the form of a Gita, from the legacy of Murshida Martin.

Series I. GITHA Number 8.

Toward the One, the Perfection of Love, Harmony and Beauty, the Only Being, united with all the Illuminated Souls, who form the embodiment of the Master, the Spirit of Guidance.

DHYANA MEDITATION

Many people claim that they desire enlightenment, that they seek self-purification and perfection and are looking for the highest wisdom. Yet when it comes to a question of the acceptance of someone as teacher, they refuse to look to any human being for guidance. They say that God has no favorites, that God is before all and that all are equal to God.

Yes, they are right, and besides God is the only teacher, we all learn from Him. But when they go to school to learn arithmetic or spelling or geography or music, do they learn from God? Then at least they accept the teacher in human form. They may have a little knowledge and they accept the teacher to learn more. When it comes to the esoteric sciences which are much harder to learn and far more subtle in form, then they want nobody, and this very attitude shows the lack of one of the greatest elements in spiritual unfoldment, self-surrender.

What is teaching but the manifestation of divine power through the human heart. It is not the personality of Sheikh or Khalif or Murshid which is the guide. It is that such people have reached a state wherein their own hearts have opened to the degree of making a suitable accommodation for the Spirit of Guidance. Then the light and wisdom may be communicated to pupils through speech or through silence.

The presence of the teacher at meditation acts like a condenser in electricity. It draws the atoms together quickly and charges them with living energy. This is like offering spiritual sustenance to pupils. Pupils rise when the teacher enters, not so much out of respect to the personality as to help in that attunement which may be of so much benefit to themselves. This inner harmony of itself can be a great help to anyone who is on the path to God.

Restraint of speech and thought is most helpful whether a person meditates alone or with others, in the presence of the teacher or not. After a while he comes to be at one with the atmosphere. Thus the first stage of

Document: O.t. See Introduction to Gita Dhyana, p. 219

development is accomplished. After that he begins to grow through that atmosphere and he also helps that atmosphere to grow. This is the second stage. The first stage is closely associated with fana, self-effacement; the second with baka, realization. Those are the two aspects of spiritual development.

When the atmosphere of a meditation hall seems low or depleted, it can be restored through Zikar. Zikar helps elevate the material atoms and vibrations so that they also can become accommodation for baraka, spiritual blessings.

An old typescript in the form of a Gita, of unknown origin.

Series 1 | GITHA | Number 8[A]

Dhyana

Toward the One, the Perfection of Love, Harmony and Beauty, the Only Being, united with All the Illuminated Souls, who form the Embodiment of the Master, the Spirit of Guidance.

Beloved ones of God:

Many people seek enlightenment without a teacher. This shows they have no idea about it, for in enlightenment and with enlightenment there can be no separation, there is no "I" nor "thou." What is the teacher? Is it the personality who is the guide? No, it is not that personality although we call such a one Sheikh or Khalif or Murshid or by other terms.

What is teaching is the Power which is manifesting through that personality, and the love which is in their hearts. It is the power and love which teach, not the personality. When that same personality is not reflecting power and love they are not teaching. The true guide will understand first his own processes, whether he is really reflecting power and love, and then he will understand the mureeds.

The presence of the teacher forms what corresponds to a condenser in electricity. Such a one draws the atoms together quickly and charges them; without a teacher the mureeds could no doubt attain the same condition after a time, but the Murshid does this immediately because he carries his atmosphere with him. When a Murshid enters the Meditation Hall, the atoms at once take the proper arrangement, they become charged, they stand up before Murshid. Therefore when the mureeds rise also, it is not only because of respect, but by that act they attune themselves with the very atoms, otherwise one could say the atoms have more spirituality than those persons. This is true in all cases, even in the Universal Worship, but to a less extent.

In the presence of the teacher, therefore, the positive meditation begins immediately upon his entering the room. The preparatory work should be completed. And how is it completed? By refraining entirely from speech and as much as possible from thought before the Murshid comes. Five, or even three minutes is sufficient for this, but fifteen minutes in the meditation room with the mind wandering, and especially with speech, is

Document: O.t. See Introduction to Gita Dhyana, p. 219

harmful. Those who must enter the Chapel for preparation should refrain from speech for at least fifteen minutes before the meditation time; half-an-hour would be better, but more than this is not necessary. Zikar chant must not be considered as speech, for it has the effect of arranging the atoms, in the same manner as the influence of the Murshid.

A copy made under Sakina's supervision of an old typescript in the form of a Gita, from the legacy of Murshida Martin.

Series I. GITHA Number 9.

Toward the One, the Perfection of Love, Harmony and Beauty, the Only Being, united with all the Illuminated Souls, who form the embodiment of the Master, the Spirit of Guidance.

DHYANA MEDITATION

Meditation may be regarded as consisting of two *portions*, the preparation and the performance. In preparing for meditation one should try to guard against all undesirable thoughts, speech and acts until the hour of the meditation. One should also sit in silence a little before the teacher arrives, watching the breath and keeping the mind as free as possible from thoughts of all sorts. Even idealistic thoughts are out of place in meditation.

Of course the preparation can continue until it includes the entire daily life. Then one can go on from that and identify meditation and the everyday life. This is its perfection. To accomplish this Sufis repeat Darood which is most helpful. It tends at all times to restrain nufs and uses the mind as the body is used. That is to say, just as there are certain hours for eating and others for abstinence from food, so there can be periods in which the mind is used for thought and other periods when it is not used.

The ultimate aim, of course, is to elevate the mind to its buddhic condition. The instructions on the cultivation of insight are also most important. The difference is that in developing insight one may do it consciously, one may be watching the heart and its impressions and thereby become responsive to the All-Pervading Spirit of Wisdom. In meditation one does not try to receive anything, but the purification of mind thereby often opens up the door to inspiration. At least it makes it much easier to receive impressions and hear the Voice which cometh constantly from within.

The teacher can, by his presence, raise the pitch of the soul. The mureed does not surrender before the teacher in order to give special reverence to the teacher as a personality. It is for his own sake that the disciple lays aside his desires and his thoughts. He lays them before the teacher when he practises fana-fi-Sheikh, while in meditation he lays them before God at all times, that is to say, whether the teacher be present or not.

Document: O.t. See Introduction to Gita Dhyana, p. 219

By meditation one relaxes the mind so that it becomes recharged with magnetism. After a little practice one feels it a little; after continual practice one feels it more. Therefore one gradually lengthens the time in the meditation. He either meditates for the sake of resting and restoring the mind, or in order to receive impressions, that is, to develop his intuitive faculty.

An old typescript in the form of a Gita, of unknown origin.

Series 1 | GITHA | Number 9[A]

Toward the One, the Perfection of Love, Harmony and Beauty, the Only Being, united with All the Illuminated Souls, who form the Embodiment of the Master, the Spirit of Guidance.

Beloved ones of God:

Meditation should be considered as consisting of two parts, the preparation and the performance. The preparation consists, first, in refraining from all *wrong* thoughts, speech and acts until the hour of meditation, and in maintaining a short silence before the Murshid enters. If this is done, then one will be ready for the second part of meditation.

The teacher first charges the atmosphere and by this the true Silence is established. This Silence is of great help to spiritual knowledge; it is Saute Surmad or Abstract Sound, which cannot properly be called either Sound or Silence. By attunement with it, one becomes attuned to all in Nature.

But the teacher does more than magnetize the atmosphere. The teacher is the conductor, so to speak, of an orchestra. The instruments must be attuned, and there must be some key note, and it is the Murshid who supplies that key note. What is meant by Fana-fi-Sheikh or Fana-fi-Murshid is that first the Talibs must become attuned to their teacher. After that or during that process they become attuned to each other without the least effort; even those who have very different dispositions become attuned one to another.

This lesson is taught in "The Mysticism of Sound." Unless it is practised, the study of that book is of little value. And when can it be practised? It is practised in every spiritual study and in every meditation. It is not necessary that one should pretend to be friendly or harmonious with a person whose keynote is discordant to his; the way of the Sufi is to introduce other notes to produce a symphony.

The teacher by his presence, raises the pitch of the soul higher and higher, the atmosphere becomes more and more peaceful. After a while the Talib begins to understand the function of meditation, that it is not only a period for rest and relaxation, and revitalisation, but that it is a period of communion with God, for inspiration, for Divine Guidance. If this were not

Document: O.t. See Introduction to Gita Dhyana, p. 219

so, the Spirit of Guidance would not be the Spirit of Guidance, but when it is understood, one knows beyond doubt what is the Spirit of Guidance which leads one to the Goal.

A copy made under Sakina's supervision of an old typescript in the form of a Gita, from the legacy of Murshida Martin.

Series I. GITHA Number 10.

Toward the One, the Perfection of Love, Harmony and Beauty, the Only Being, united with all the Illuminated Souls, who form the embodiment of the Master, the Spirit of Guidance.

DHYANA MEDITATION

The breath of the teacher is, so to speak, a ladder by means of which the mureed climbs on his way to God. The breath of the teacher helps to establish rhythm in meditation and also to refine the atmosphere. The finer the vibrations that are received into the atmosphere, the more beneficial is it to those who participate in the silence. If the pupil is able to adjust his breath to that of the teacher it is most helpful. At the same time the teacher does what he can to reach the heart of every pupil in his presence.

The more the mureed sits in silence before the teacher, the easier is it to adjust the breath of teacher and pupil. It is by this means that the pupil receives the blessing from the teacher. This may be no special knowledge. However it does mean that the heart becomes more sensitive and through its sensitivity it can grow in wisdom, insight, compassion and love.

The Silence itself is a great healer and it is a mistake to depend upon the teacher too much. That is to say, the thought of the teacher can become a hindrance. Teacher should not be regarded so much as a personality before one as a gate to God. There is a fundamental purpose of life and this is uncovered as we remove the *vestiges of self* one by one. There are many ways by which different people can become sensitive to the silence. Whatever way is successfully followed brings something to the talib.

This is an increase of feeling for life itself. The body and mind become purer vehicles of soul. The radiance of the personality and the charm of manner often follow. Thus meditation provides a psychological and moral training.

It is also possible to take a problem into the silence and lay it before God. This means to bring the problem and hold it before one as if in concentration, in order to keep other thoughts away. Then to *drop* this thought, so to speak, *into the lap of God*. This is done by keeping silence of mind and repose and often it happens that then one receives the guidance. Fikar, of course, can by used to help in this.

Document: O.t. See Introduction to Gita Dhyana, p. 219

The more the pupil can receive an answer to his requirements from the silence, the surer will he be in his footsteps forward and the closer every day of his life will he be drawing the Spirit of God toward himself.

An old typescript in the form of a Gita, of unknown origin.

Series 1 GITHA Number 10[A]

Dhyana

Toward the One, the Perfection of Love, Harmony and Beauty, the Only Being, united with All the Illuminated Souls, who form the Embodiment of the Master, the Spirit of Guidance.

Beloved ones of God:

The breath of the teacher is, so to speak, a ladder by which the mureed climbs on his way to God. It is the breath of the teacher which establishes a rhythm in the meditation; just as his personality and atmosphere create the harmony. Both harmony and rhythm are necessary, also pitch.

In the attunement of a violin string, one must turn the peg slowly or the string will break; the same process is in spiritual development which is a gradual change in pitch, but very definite. The vibrations gather around the teacher and flow from the teacher's being. All who are in the room benefit but even the atmosphere about, the building, the grounds, and the vicinity benefit.

After a time, the mureed will adjust his breath to the teacher. This cannot be done consciously by outward observation so much as by silent resignation. In resignation one uses his positive faculties to keep the thought and emotions quieted, but the negative faculties are surrendered to God. In the tuning of an instrument it is only necessary to adjust one string or one note to the key note, and then to adjust the other strings or notes to that one note. This is done not only in the orchestra but in the tuning of pianos and organs. The Talib therefore, should not endeavour to attune all parts of his personality to the teacher, but to gain the key note by resignation of his will.

The next step is to attune the rest of his personality to that Will which has become harmonised and attuned. Then he creates the harmony in himself, for the motto of the Sufi is Unity, not uniformity. At the same time, especially when one finds difficulty in this, one may adopt any customs or habits of the teacher. It is like the violin player who has difficulty in attuning his A string, but may adjust his E or G string with ease, and then fix his A string properly. Therefore, attunement with the teacher is most important, obedience and surrender of the will being most essential, but even

Document: O.t. See Introduction to Gita Dhyana, p. 219

imitation, personal devotion, strict attention to the words, to the study, to daily duties, all these help. This is explained also in the Bhagavad Gita that there is a best road, and at the same time there are many roads, and by whichever road one comes to God, for that person that is the best road.

A copy made under Sakina's supervision of an old typescript in the form of a Gita, from the legacy of Murshida Martin.

Series II. GITHA Number 1

Toward the One, the Perfection of Love, Harmony and Beauty, the Only Being, united with All the Illuminated Souls Who form the Embodiment of the Master, the Spirit of Guidance.

DHYANA MEDITATION

Some people try to meditate in order that they may receive a personal benefit. Others mean by personal benefit a particular gain such as health, wealth, youth or happiness or the attainment of some possession, fame or power. Yes, no doubt these things can be gained by use of inner power, but in the end a price will have to be paid for them.

[1]*When Boddhidharma, the great Buddhist Patriarch, came to China, the Emperor told him of all the fine things he had done and wanted to know what merit he had gained. He was told, "no merit." For meditation is not a practice of the self as conceived and does not bring anything to self. It has nothing to do with gain or loss, good or evil. The continual practice of restraint of thought, however, does cultivate peace of mind. When the mind is properly cleared from thought it becomes like a palace of shining mirrors, which reflect easily the impressions gained from the life within or without.*

The ability to receive these impressions and to respond to them correctly results in the development of the intuitive faculty. Besides that one may gain in ability to control emotions and speech, and so rise in the moral scale of evolution. This is sure to be so when one does not waste any effort thinking of oneself.[1]

No doubt there are times when one should meditate on his own problems. Thinking quietly, one may obtain the answer after a while. *This does not mean to hold the problem so much as to use it to drive away other thoughts, then let it slide away "as the dewdrop into the shiny sea."* The effort itself may often bring the answer without any long indulgence in silence. This shows prajna, kashf, or intuition, the living light from within.

Document: O.t. See Introduction to Gita Dhyana, p. 219

Notes:

1. The second and third paragraphs seem to be Samuel Lewis's additions to this Gita.

By this means also one becomes able to help others, for that same light which brings wisdom to the mind concerning oneself can also bring wisdom concerning another. To help in this one should watch the surface of the heart; after a while one can feel the waves rise and fall. Then one can control those waves or rise and fall with them as one chooses. As those waves are of finer vibrations they take the consciousness beyond the sphere of mind.

Thus while in meditation there is a stilling of mind, there is not a stilling of life. Meditation is far removed from death or sleep. Rather does it increase one's capacity for life and light although if one thinks about these things it is not so. The gain comes when one does not think. Then one may be said to be within the domain of Divine Grace *(Inayat)*[2].

For circulation among the Members of the A.S.C. ONLY.

---

2. "(Inayat)" probably added by those who copied these series, in order to mention the word for "Divine Grace" in Sufi terminology.

An old typescript in the form of a Gita, from a collection of Sufi papers used by Samuel Lewis.

Series II GITHA No. 1[A] DHYANA

(Meditation)

[1]TOWARD THE ONE, THE PERFECTION OF LOVE, HARMONY AND BEAUTY, THE ONLY BEING, UNITED WITH ALL THE ILLUMINATED SOULS WHO FORM THE EMBODIMENT OF THE MASTER, THE SPIRIT OF GUIDANCE.[1]

No one need ask: "What shall I gain by Meditation? In what ways shall I benefit?" If one only knew, it is by means of Meditation that all is gained, not only things are gained, not only attributes and qualities are gained, but even God is so[2] gained.

It is God Who would reveal Himself to us, but so long as we keep our minds on anything else but God, He may be speaking but we do not hear. When we hear His Voice, all knowledge, all direction, all guidance will be ours, [3]everything that we need will be ours[3]. With this understanding one can breast the waves of life; to turn back the tide and to[4] surmount obstacles will become possible.

Speaking of Intuition is of itself of little value. The mystic does not speak, he uses[5] the inner faculties in everyday life and so Insight becomes a means of sustaining and understanding realities. To every question there is an answer and the key to the answer is in the question. One of the best means of finding the answer is to enter into Meditation. Then the question may arise: "Should I meditate on this problem?" It is not wrong to meditate on any problem but it is always wise to seek Divine Guidance. Meditating in a prayerful attitude, knowing that God will help, relieves one from further concern, and there is nothing in life more valuable.

Documents:

S.L.: See Introduction to Gita Dhyana, p. 219
O.t.: See Introduction to Gita Dhyana, p. 219

Notes:

1. O.t.: the Invocation has been omitted.
2. Ibid.: "so" omitted
3. Ibid.: omitted, "everything that we need will be ours"
4. Ibid.: "to" omitted
5. Ibid.: "sees" instead of "uses", which change may have occurred mistakenly when the text was copied

Sometimes the answer will come as a simple direction, easiiy understood. Sometimes a feeling will come which may not seem so clear or direct, but when one follows the guidance which comes from the heart, often one will find the obstacle in life disappear like a dissolving mist. Care and worry prevent a proper solution, while surrender of self always helps to clear the path from the perplexities of life, bringing calm and peace. The Sufi who does this knows that God is All-seeing, All-knowing.

For that reason, over and over again the Invocation is repeated, repeated at different times and bringing each time one closer to the Reality which it expresses. All problems may be as tests in life. In the ancient Egyptian mysteries, the Hierophant is reported to have said to the neophyte: "You have nothing to fear but yourself." It was Jesus Christ who said: "My yoke is easy my burden is light," meaning, give up your problems, take them before Allah in loving surrender and they will be solved and you will be healed.

(For circulation among members of the A.S.C. only.)

A copy made under Sakina's supervision of an old typescript in the form of a Gita, from the legacy of Murshida Martin.

Series II. GITHA Number 2.

Toward the One, the Perfection of Love, Harmony and Beauty, the Only Being, united with All the Illuminated Souls Who form the Embodiment of the Master, the Spirit of Guidance.

DHYANA MEDITATION

The great obstacle to be overcome in meditation is the false ego, or nufs. When the body is restrained it seeks refuge in the mind. People who are nervous, who have digestive troubles, or are suffering physically should not meditate in group. It is not for them to receive the finer vibrations. Yet meditation is the best medicine for them, if they can keep quiet only a few moments. Those who are indisposed should meditate often and for only short periods.

In preparing for meditation one should have regard for his stomach and body generally. That is why attention is first given to the physical vehicle by the Sufis. Those who might otherwise find it hard to keep silence may be instructed on the path of sound and develop through music and Zikar. While this training has the tendency to produce ecstasy, it also develops a capacity for receptivity of finer vibrations, and although in a different way from meditation, it is beneficial. The Meditation Hall itself can be elevated through the use of holy music and repetition of Zikar at certain times.

The repetition of the Invocation is the first step toward mental control. A concentration--if one wishes to call it that--on the Invocation may be used to soothe the *ego-thoughts* which are otherwise so disturbing. Whether reason or memory or imagination agitates, one should repeat the Invocation or perfect[1] a Darood and keep on with his repetition in order to avoid any personal thoughts. For no one has room in his heart for God and self both, it is one or the other.

The tendency of nufs is to turn us from the One to the many, *enticing* us with the intoxication of the endless things of the manifest world. Thus man becomes attached to the stream of nothingness. Then he loses sight of his true being. This it is which brings him all his troubles. At first he turns to meditation so that his troubles will not bother him so much. Then he learns

Document: O.t. See Introduction to Gita Dhyana, p. 219

Note:

1. "perfect" may have been copied mistakenly as "perform".

to control those affairs that have been troubling him. Finally he develops calmness and that calmness he can carry with him when he leaves the meditation hall. The stronger that calmness the surer he will find his footsteps in life.

Nevertheless one has to be sure of himself first and the wise have maintained their silence for long periods. Besides this helps those who take up concentration and thus indirectly helps man in every line of progress.

An old typescript in the form of a Gita, from a collection of Sufi papers used by Samuel Lewis.

Series II | GITHA No. 2[A] | DHYANA

(Meditation)

[1]TOWARD THE ONE. . .[1]

The great obstacle to be overcome in Meditation is the false ego or Nufs. What is it that prevents us from concentrating our thoughts and feelings on God? It is the nufs. In the Hebrew religion there is the Shema or cry, "Hear, O Israel, the Lord our Lord[2], the Lord is One." And there is the answer to the Cry, "And thou shalt love the Lord thy God with all thy Heart and with all thy Soul and with all thy Mind." And these directions should be considered as a unity, for the light of the soul shines in the heart and is reflected in the mind.

Plato wrote that we lived in a shadow world, where we confused the shadow of ourselves with reality. This is the nufs, the false ego, which stands in the light before God, causing, so to speak, a spiritual eclipse. In Meditation, one does not have to hold such a thought for this false self is overcome through meditating upon the true Self, which in reality is God. The modern devotee may repeat the Invocation, "Towards[3] the One, etc. instead of the shema and it will produce the same effect. There is no difference between them in the language of heart and soul; the forms in words may be different, but the acts, thoughts, feelings and results are the same.

Whenever the nufs seems to hold us in its sway, it is through meditation we may find freedom. To the Sufi, pure meditation includes more than going into one's room only; any act of life which is done with dependence upon Allah or which makes us aware of Him, whether in reading or studying or working or contemplation or prayer or meditation or any duty of everyday life, all may become part of a universal meditation which marks every breath and every heartbeat in life. Then as we observe more plainly the true purpose

Documents:

S.L.: See Introduction to Gita Dhyana, p. 219
O.t.: See Introduction to Gita Dhyana, p. 219

This whole Gita seems to be Samuel Lewis's version, made in order to complete this series. He may have made it from annotations of a lecture by Pir-o-Murshid.

Notes:

1. O.t.: the Invocation appears above the Gita.
2. Ibid.: "God" instead of "Lord"
3. Ibid.: "Toward"

of life, the momentary obstacle[4] which may have appeared like a great cliff, becomes as a tiny step through our growth and understanding, and by taking this step, what was once a hindrance becomes an aid to our development.

The nufs turns us from the One to the many, enticing us with the things of the[5] world. Then man attaches himself to one thing after another which brings at best momentary satisfaction; through his spiritual practices the Sufi learns to chain the nufs, to perceive it is only a shadow of reality, and finding the sun of truth within[6] his being, looking upon it, one is no longer aware of the shadow.

Then the nufs is not destroyed but harnessed. The whole of man's being is attuned to God and everything within him serves God. This is the work of all on the path of illumination, of whatever school they may be. There is no other obstacle than this false self and there is no better means of controlling it than by meditation and by practising the Presence of Allah.

(For circulation among members of the A.S.C. only.)

---

4. Ibid.: "obstacles"
5. Ibid.: "this"
6. Ibid.: "with"

A copy made under Sakina's supervision of an old typescript in the form of a Gita, from the legacy of Murshida Martin.

Series II. GITHA Number 3.

Toward the One, the Perfection of Love, Harmony and Beauty, the Only Being, united with All the Illuminated Souls Who form the Embodiment of the Master, the Spirit of Guidance.

DHYANA MEDITATION

Meditation is the one general practice which is open to all mureeds and to the generality as well. It is introduced as a silence in the Universal Worship and in the meetings of the social and educational department of the Sufi Movement, known as the Brotherhood.

[1]*Meditation is the most universal means of the spreading the message, which in a certain sense is no message, only the call of humanity to praise God and to show consideration one for the other.*[1]

[2]*As meditation is new to the West there may be practical aids which help in the first stages. For instance the talib, after his Bayat, may be given a sacred phrase to repeat, which will be generally known as a Wazifa. The Wazifa is based upon a sacred phrase which holds as thought some attribute of God. It has a positive and negative use. The negative use is for purification and the positive use is to build up the characteristic within the personality which is needed for success and attainment in life.*[2]

Wazifas are generally repeated audibly, a certain number of times as esoteric exercises. But they may be repeated mentally and silently and thus used as Darood. This helps in keeping out all unwelcome incoming thoughts, by which is meant any thought that interferes with the goal in view. In meditation all thoughts, of any nature whatever, are *wayfarers* and should be removed. Unwelcome thoughts have no more place in the meditation hall than have unwelcome persons, only it is that we can easily prevent the unwelcome persons from entering, while a constant warfare is required to restrain the unwelcome thoughts.

Document: O.t. See Introduction to Gita Dhyana, p. 219

Notes:

1. This sentence may have been added by Murshida Martin.
2. This paragraph appears to have been added by Samuel Lewis.

Sufism is not a code of rules. The purpose of instruction is to help the pupil to help himself. Through peace of mind one not only helps himself, he can more easily help others. Peace of mind removes the obstacles which stand between personality and personality. If there is any loss which comes in not having peace of mind it is a loss which everyone can feel and know. Although in the spiritual life one need not seek happiness directly, the struggle for peace of mind removes most of those things which stand in the way of our experience of happiness.

Therefore as one is successful in maintaining meditation a short while, he is encouraged to keep up longer meditations. Those who find it hard to do this in the everyday life are welcomed to the practice of Khilvat by which they, at stated times, can withdraw from worldly activity and be guarded and protected in their hours of silence, meditation and devotion.

An old typescript in the form of a Gita, from a collection of Sufi papers used by Samuel Lewis.

Series II GITHA No. 3[A] DHYANA

(Meditation)

[1]TOWARD THE ONE, THE PERFECTION OF LOVE, HARMONY AND BEAUTY, THE ONLY BEING, UNITED WITH ALL THE ILLUMINATED SOULS WHO FORM THE EMBODIMENT OF THE MASTER, THE SPIRIT OF GUIDANCE.[1]

Besides meditation, each talib is given special instructions[2] suited to his need, while journeying the path toward Unity. One such form of instruction is the WAZIFA, or repetition of sacred phrases for various purposes.

If it be asked what is the purpose, it may be answered that as the purpose of all rain is to return to the ocean, so the purpose of every soul is to return to God. Some drops unite in little streams, to flow down the river which ultimately loses itself in the ocean. So the practice of each Wazifa may be for some particular purpose, yet all these purposes unite just as the streams unite, and finally come to their destination.

Wazifa is both positive and negative, to build up faculties which are necessary and to remove undesirable qualities. So Sufis use Wazifas in purification, but the Sufi always recognizes God as the Perfection of Love, Harmony and Beauty, as the Perfection of all qualities and as the Perfection of Perfections. If strength is needed, strength comes from God; if love is required, God is love; if one must perform Justice, God is Judge and Forgiver.

Wazifas may be repeated audibly or silently in the performance of any act or duty in life. By this means the devotee draws from God the help he needs, attuning himself to the qualities of God at that moment. So besides the regular practice of Wazifa a specified number of times as assigned to the talib by his teacher, so one may meditate upon the Wazifa at all times and use it even when it is no longer part of one's spiritual exercises.

Documents:

S.L. See Introduction to Gita Dhyana, p. 219
O.t. See Introduction to Gita Dhyana, p. 219

Notes:

1. O.t.: the Invocation appears above the Gita.
2. Ibid.: "instruction"

Sufism is not a code of rules; the purpose of Sufism is to bring souls to God realization. Allah is beyond all Attributes and Qualities, being All Essence. Understanding this every breath can become a meditation wherein one puts full dependence upon Allah and there will be no moment which will not be a meditation, no moment of separateness from God.

(For circulation among members of the A.S.C. only.)

A copy made under Sakina's supervision of an old typescript in the form of a Gita, from the legacy of Murshida Martin.

Series II. GITHA Number 4.

Toward the One, the Perfection of Love, Harmony and Beauty, the Only Being, united with All the Illuminated Souls Who form the Embodiment of the Master, the Spirit of Guidance.

DHYANA MEDITATION

There is always a question of how much one can develop through silence and how much through sound. In answer it should be stated that ultimately all development leads to the Universal Sound which has been called the "Voice of the Silence" and which is silence with respect to the noises and clashings of manifestation but which is not nothing-ness or death.

Zikar practice is of tremendous advantage to the young in that it helps elevate their vital forces and even to experience ecstasy. Thus they are drawn away from passion and materiality. The music has a certain influence of itself, and along with the sacred phrases that form the words +)[1] there is a most elevating effect. This elevating effect can be felt within the personality as one practises Zikar more and more so that after a while he will be able to witness his own progress. It also has an effect upon meditation, that sometimes after Zikar meditation is much easier.

In the orient, especially in the Buddhist countries, gongs and other instruments summon the worshippers. After a gong is sounded one often finds it easier to meditate. No doubt it causes a certain stirring up of the air of the room and when this air vibrates it affects all the physical processes in the room. This effect is communicated inwardly through the channels of breath, and often results in the removal of the thought that has been present. Most forms of music in this respect tend to cleanse the mind of the thoughts it has been holding and may take it into a revery.

Revery itself is not meditation. Revery helps to control thought but does not stop the memory or imagination. For this reason the mureed is instructed how to watch the breath and keep it flowing rhythmically. Every thought produces some change in the breathing. If the breath is held constant

+): Here probably meant: the sacred phrases that the words form.

Document: O.t. See Introduction to Gita Dhyana, p. 219

Note:

1. It is not known who added this note.

by will-power, it chokes off the incoming thoughts; then they find no rootsoil in the mind. But this is not enough. In addition one tries to purify the mind constantly. This is done through the use of sacred phrases although Zikar is also helpful in that. Then, after a while one may be able to control the elements of the breath, to keep the ether dominating, or to add to the light.

By such means the calm and peace of the soul come to the fore, and penetrate the outer personality. All exercises which aid in this accomplishment are to be considered as parts of the inner life. The theory of this is not involved and requires no knowledge of metaphysics.

An old typescript in the form of a Gita, from a collection of Sufi papers used by Samuel Lewis.

Series II GITHA No. 4[A] DHYANA

(Meditation)

[1]TOWARD THE ONE, THE PERFECTION OF LOVE, HARMONY AND BEAUTY, THE ONLY BEING, UNITED WITH ALL THE ILLUMINATED SOULS WHO FORM THE EMBODIMENT OF THE MASTER, THE SPIRIT OF GUIDANCE.[1]

There is a question, if meditation is required to develop in the Silence, why is Zikar sometimes chanted and why are some practices said aloud? The answer is, that there are certain purposes in each practice, and that the ordinary distinction between sound and silence does not hold true from the Divine point of view.

For instance, in Zikar one may become able to arrange the atoms in order and rhythm and harmony. When mureeds chant in groups, they often magnify the power of the atoms. Often this brings the same effect as the presence of the teacher, but generally Zikar awakens the soul so as to produce alertness or even ecstasy.

In Zikar the thought is kept on all the syllables and sounds, making it difficult to think of anything else. If the Zikar becomes automatic and is recited without proper thought and feeling, it still is of value because of the intrinsic power of the atoms responding to sound. Besides that, it harmonizes one with the atmosphere and attunes one with all Zikar atmosphere, so one cannot continue the practice without developing out of it the necessary thought and feeling which will then carry one along.

When this is accomplished, one becomes attuned to the spiritual souls higher in evolution and becomes awakened to impressions, and may even arise to that state when the separateness between mind[2] and heart disappears in the realization of Zikar. So Zikar may be called the finest thought expressed in the finest material form with the highest spiritual purpose. It becomes the perfection of the sounds uttered by the tongue.

Documents:

S.L. See Introduction to Gita Dhyana, p. 219
O.t. See Introduction to Gita Dhyana, p. 219

The whole Gita seems to be Samuel Lewis's version, made in order to complete this series. He may have made it from annotations of a lecture given by Pir-o-Murshid.

Notes:

1. O.t.: The first three words of the Invocation appear above the Gita.
2. Ibid.: "heart" instead of "mind"

Zikar is best understood through its performance. In singing and chanting one purifies one's being, even one's mind. Then one develops into a Zakir, who is the embodiment of Zikar and the vehicle of the Message of God. The Zakir is the mureed perfected in Zikar.

The moral of Zikar is humility and in its performance the nufs is absorbed like the shadow when light is turned on it. Zikar is important for those needing power and inspiration, while meditation is for those desiring calm and peace. Each are necessary for those who seek God in all forms, and each is only of value when practised; then each fulfils its purpose better than any explanation can give it.

(For circulation among members of the A.S.C. only.)

A copy made under Sakina's supervision of an old typescript in the form of a Gita, from the legacy of Murshida Martin.

Series II. GITHA Number 5.

Toward the One, the Perfection of Love, Harmony and Beauty, the Only Being, united with All the Illuminated Souls Who form the Embodiment of the Master, the Spirit of Guidance.

DHYANA MEDITATION

Fikar is a practice which is *indulged in* by most Sufis by which they keep before themselves the nothingness of ego and the Allness of God, to learn and feel until they know that God is the Only Being. One may say that the disciple in Fikar can be called Fakir, the poor one, the unattached person. For the fulfillment of Fikar is that there is nothing in the world, in heaven or upon earth, which can cling to the personality who is determined to complete his journey back to God.

[1]*Therefore Fikar aids much in the purification of mind. It forces the thoughts away, it may be called the vacuum cleaner of the mind. It helps to preserve mental magnetism and to restore it when lost. It is valuable in strengthening any mental faculty, and in restoring those which are lost. So in a certain sense Fikar accomplishes the same results as meditation.*

Meditation consists of preparation, performance and application, which means action. Then when one holds the spirit of unity at all times the whole of life becomes a meditation. In this meditation differs from Fikar which has to be performed in a certain way and which cannot very well be done in the presence of others or when there is any possibility of a disturbance. The performance of meditation can reach the goal, however, when one can maintain full inner rapport without there being any impediment to outward activity.

Meditation aids greatly in the development of insight which can become the deepest faculty of the mind. There is no limit to the length of time one may indulge in it either. Akbar, the great Sufi Mogul Emperor of India, was able to get along with practically no sleep, often meditating for hours at night instead.

Document: O.t. See Introduction to Gita Dhyana, p. 219

Note:

1. These five paragraphs are probably Murshida Martin's version, made from her annotations of Pir-o-Murshid's lecture.

Meditation may be performed at any time although there is a certain advantage if the same hours can be used every day. The length of it does not matter so much although it often requires several minutes to accomplish that stillness which is the real meditation. Some persons cannot do it in less than thirty minutes; therefore a gradual lengthening of the period of meditation to that time is advantageous. But after one is able to control thought, it does not matter so much, one can obtain the stillness ultimately even with a single breath.

Nevertheless from time to time a meditation of two hours is valuable, or in its place, a silence over a longer period in which there is full restraint of speech and as much as possible of thought and action.[1]

An old typescript in the form of a Gita, from a collection of Sufi papers used by Samuel Lewis.

Series II | GITHA No. 5[A] | DHYANA

(Meditation)

[1]TOWARD THE ONE, THE PERFECTION OF LOVE, HARMONY AND BEAUTY, THE ONLY BEING, UNITED WITH ALL THE ILLUMINATED SOULS WHO FORM THE EMBODIMENT OF THE MASTER, THE SPIRIT OF GUIDANCE.[1]

Fikar is the perpetual possession of the Sufi, and the devotee has often been called Fakir, the poor one. But what is this poverty? It is the poverty of non-attachment[2], of those who are poor in spirit but blessed by Allah. The Sufi may be outwardly poor, yet inwardly he may not[3] be called rich for he may be said to possess everything and nothing. His satisfaction is in God and he may be master of wealth, while those who own wealth among the generality are better termed servants of wealth.

Every meditation is a Fikar when rightfully performed. In meditation heart and mind are centered upon God, and this is true in Fikar also. Only in Fikar one is given special syllables or a special form, which is absent in general meditation. Yet Fikar can be called an intensification of the highest[4] meditation, keeping the heart fixed on God.

Meditation consists of preparation, performance and application, which means action. So the true meditation is not separate from the rest of life. This is especially true when one gains power and magnetism through meditation to be applied in healing or other spiritual work.

In meditation there are two general results: the development of the faculty of insight and the growth of the personal atmosphere. Once this atmosphere is built, Fikar becomes a natural performance, and as it is said in Salat, at every moment of our lives we draw closer to God. Through this surrender of self, through keeping the gaze and concentration steadfast on God, all becomes natural, and it is the most natural thing in life to be ever aware and responsive to God.

Documents:

S.L. See Introduction to Gita Dhyana, p. 219
O.t. See Introduction to Gita Dhyana, p. 219

Notes:

1. O.t.: The first three words of the Invocation appear above the Gita.
2. Ibid.: "non-attainment" instead of "non-attachment"
3. Ibid.: "not" crossed out afterwards
4. Ibid.: "higher" in place of "highest"

The goal to be attained is that the spiritual condition be continuous through all of life. As the great Sufi saint Abu Sa'id ibn Abi-l-Khair has said, the Sufi may eat and drink, work and play, sleep, and trade in the market, yet he does not forget God for one single instant. That is the life of the true Fakir and that is the Fikar, which unites the inner and outer lives in the completeness of God realization.

A copy made under Sakina's supervision of an old typescript in the form of a Gita, from the legacy of Murshida Martin.

Series II. GITHA Number 6.

Toward the One, the Perfection of Love, Harmony and Beauty, the Only Being, united with All the Illuminated Souls, Who form the Embodiment of the Master, the Spirit of Guidance.

DHYANA MEDITATION

The watching over the breath is important both in meditation and out of it. By guarding the breath one learns to control the ego, and from a practical view one develops in efficiency in action. For this purpose there are many esoteric exercises which are given the disciple by the teacher at various stages of his development, also according to his particular need.

In meditation one should observe the rhythm of the breath until one is able to get the mind quiet. If the mind cannot be quieted, one may just watch the rhythm of the breath continually. Yet one may also purify the breath, as by Darood. After a while there may be a tendency for the breath to become more and more refined. Then one will find that it is difficult to watch and indeed there is no need to observe breath when one enters the real silence.

[1]*As one enters the real silence he begins to receive the energy of space which is the energy of life. Nevertheless the talib should pay no attention to it. Sometimes he will become sensitive to light and after a while this light may increase more and more until his whole inner being may become radiant with light. Nevertheless he should pay no attention to it. The heart may pound, the heart may beat, the heart may consume all the fires of consciousness until there is no more thought. Nevertheless the talib should pay no attention to it.*

There may be visions, or there may be light or there may be colours or there may be nothing. The talib should pay no attention. For those may be called the delights of heaven. If one is able to control all thought and emotion and then enters into a sphere or a state of unworldly phenomena, that only means that he has passed a certain place, it does not indicate his place of arrival. Anything which attracts or detracts keeps the seeker away from the goal.

Document: O.t. See Introduction to Gita Dhyana, p. 219

Note:

1. Paragraphs three, four and five may be Murshida Martin's version, made from her annotations of Pir-o-Murshid's lecture.

Of course there may come a time when one is drawn into the light or drawn into the heart-sphere, when one feels that line of demarcation between person and person depart, when one is conscious of space being within oneself and not without, and when one has no longer any time-conception but feels as if living in eternity. Such a one may be said to be in meditation, such a one may be said to be at the gates of Samadhi.[1]

An old typescript in the form of a Gita, from a collection of Sufi papers used by Samuel Lewis.

Series II GITHA No. 6[A] DHYANA

(Meditation)

[1]TOWARD THE ONE, THE PERFECTION OF LOVE, HARMONY AND BEAUTY, THE ONLY BEING, UNITED WITH ALL THE ILLUMINATED SOULS WHO FORM THE EMBODIMENT OF THE MASTER, THE SPIRIT OF GUIDANCE.[1]

It is often difficult to keep the mind in condition during some breathing exercise. In the Purification Breath it is not enough to keep the mind on the syllables YA SHAFEE, YA KAFEE. At first the thought will bring strength and purity but the advancing talib should ever bear in mind that this practice and all practices are means of uniting the souls[2] to God. God is the Healer and the practice is His medicine which is used to heal and purify His vehicle, so he may occupy and use it.

In the same way, the practice of Kasab can become more potent when faculties are unified. Concentration on the practice helps, but if difficulty occurs it is not wrong to do some self-examining. All conditions are reflected in the breath, and if any obstacles persist, one should consult the spiritual teacher. At the same time, proper meditation also helps, for any thought whatever has a harmful effect on a breathing practice.

Activity of the mind greatly alters the rhythms[3]. Therefore Kasab is more related to concentration than to meditation, only it should be natural. So before all practices a meditation is of benefit, during which time by the supression of thought, the breath takes on a natural rhythm, invigorating the body and healing the mind, which makes the practice of Kasab easier.

The goal of all meditation is balance, and in balance the goal itself is to be found. In the progress toward that goal rhythm may appear to be more important than balance yet nothing should be done to force the breath in its depth, in its power, in its otherwise natural movements. Disease and

Documents:

S.L. See Introduction to Gita Dhyana, p. 219
O.t. See Introduction to Gita Dhyana, p. 219

Notes:

1. O.t.: The first three words of the Invocation appear above the Gita.
2. Ibid.: "soul"
3. Ibid.: "rhythm"

crime are often the result of irregularities of the breath, so of all things, this order and balance should be preserved and it is best preserved through meditation.

Therefore it is not necessary to consciously strive to alter the breath rhythms, but the steady repetition of those spiritual exercises which have been given to one by the teacher helps more than anything else on the path toward God.

A copy made under Sakina's supervision of an old typescript in the form of a Gita, from the legacy of Murshida Martin.

Series II. GITHA Number 7.

Toward the One, the Perfection of Love, Harmony and Beauty, the Only Being, united with All the Illuminated Souls, Who form the Embodiment of the Master, the Spirit of Guidance.

DHYANA MEDITATION

The inner life is not separate from the outer life, being only a larger life, *which takes into consideration far more than appears on the surface manifestation*. Although when we speak of "inner life" we include esoteric practices, meditations, dreams, visions and various experiences and efforts, it does not exclude the everyday life. Instead of adding any burdens to an over-troubled world, meditation shows how to avoid difficulties and overcome burdens.

One need not try any special posture in meditation other than than which is common to the country where he finds himself. Lying down, however, is not satisfactory for then the heart-currents change in direction and besides, it is easier to fall asleep, which would destroy the purpose of the meditation. Of course when one is alone one may use any position or posture which one finds convenient and beneficial. The object is always to get into the silence; the method is not so important.

Meditation, *being universal in application and scope*, need not be regarded as a substitute for prayer. In some countries people meditate, in other places pray, elsewhere they have different sacred customs. All of these *basically* may be accepted by the Sufi. *He prays when he is in need and he prays when he praises God; praise of God is his chief prayer, like it is that of the angels. Yet there is always need to enter into the silence above sound, and find the peace which is above even joy. Therefore meditation is an ultimate practice which stands alone and in this respect is above all other methods.*

As man enters the silence, so does the silence enter into him. As he unites with the universe, so does the universe manifest in him. This is true, no matter what be his path or his training. Ultimately he arrives at this destination. But this is the silence of all-life, which without containing anything may be said to contain all-things. *Therefore one is said to enter the world-egg or world-womb. This accounts for the teaching of the Mother of the World, the Divine Mother, the Bodhisatva Avalokitesvara or Kwan-yin. It*

Document: O.t. See Introduction to Gita Dhyana, p. 219

represents the stage of realization of union with the silence, and as all may so unite, all are said to have a common mother. The silence of the womb and the silence of Universal Sound are each used to symbolize the other.

An old typescript in the form of a Gita, from a collection of Sufi papers used by Samuel Lewis.

Series II GITHA No. 7[A] DHYANA

(Meditation)

[1]TOWARD THE ONE, THE PERFECTION OF LOVE, HARMONY AND BEAUTY, THE ONLY BEING, UNITED WITH ALL THE ILLUMINATED SOULS WHO FORM THE EMBODIMENT OF THE MASTER, THE SPIRIT OF GUIDANCE.[1]

The inner life is not separate from the outer life, but is a fuller and larger life. What is necessary is to put first things first. The mystic does more than quote scriptures; he not only says "Seek ye first the Kingdom of God," his whole life is absorbed in that[2] seeking. Therefore some people have thought that through meditation everything can be gained and all their desires be[3] fulfilled. From a certain point of view this is true, but it does not take into account what is one's desire.

The outer life is full of change and in all circumstances the desires are different. When a desire is granted often it is no longer a desire, and more often it does not have the effect sought. In many cases it is discovered that the thing or event brings a quite different and even contrary result than the one expected.

The Sufi looks to God for all things, praying to the God of Health for vigor and to the God of Wealth for his sustenance, keeping steadily before him the idea and ideal that there is one God, from Whom all blessings flow. He does not consider it wrong to seek guidance [4]from God[4] concerning his daily affairs. *Yet as the heart strengthens and insight increases all becomes more and more clear, and at the same time life continually presents its puzzles. So most necessary in life are seeking the will of God and performing it. These things are more important[5] than anything else.*

Documents:

S.L. See Introduction to Gita Dhyana, p. 219
O.t. See Introduction to Gita Dhyana, p. 219

Notes:

1. O.t.: The first three words of the Invocation appear above the Gita.
2. Ibid.: "that" omitted
3. Ibid.: "be" omitted
4. Ibid.: "from God" omitted
5. Ibid.: "important" omitted

So the talib makes God his continued need and often his daily problems become clear to him. Then one learns also to understand the difficulties of others, to sympathise with them and to help them. The difference between the ordinary person and the spiritual seeker is that the ordinary person is quick to praise and blame, enjoys being praised and seldom wants to be corrected; the seeker reserves his praise for God, is willing to take blame, striving to understand the[6] critic and feeling sorry for his ignorance, which in the end only does the other one harm.

Sufism has been called the path of blame (malamat), of blame from and by the world. But Sufism is also the path of satisfaction, of satisfaction in and with God. In meditation one rises above praise and blame, above good and evil, above wickedness and virtue, and attains Wisdom. One sees the hand of God in all things and at all times and praises Him every moment of his life. This is the true spiritual way of living and is not connected with asceticism or needless discipline; it is a natural life, the most natural way of living.

(For circulation among members of the A.S.C. only.)

---

6. Ibid.: "his" instead of "the"

A copy made under Sakina's supervision of an old typescript in the form of a Gita, from the legacy of Murshida Martin.

Series II. GITHA Number 8.

Toward the One, the Perfection of Love, Harmony and Beauty, the Only Being, united with All the Illuminated Souls, who form the Embodiment of the Master, the Spirit of Guidance.

DHYANA MEDITATION

[1]*One speaks of entering into the Silence in meditation and one may wonder whether there is an entrance into the Silence which is different from the union with God. Christians speak of God as the Word and so associate God with life and movement. Buddhists accept the doctrine of the silence and ignore the existence of any God, and assume thereby that there may be no Universal God Who is All in All. Thus the different religions, based upon the same realization, have given out doctrines which are radically different. This is because no two mind-views or mind-moulds of supermental life may be the same.*

The object in meditation is to enter the supermental life. One calls it entering the silence because one finds that silent life which is fundamental to all things, which is described in the opening section of "The Mysticism of Sound." That, however, is the first step. For if one remained there he would enter the stage of no-being, instead of the stage of all-being.

According to the Buddhist teachings man first identifies himself, in thought at least, with the objective world; then with the subjective world; then with the union of the subjective and objective. But between the union with the subjective and the ultimate state there is one of nothingness, which has been called the Void. All have to pass through that and some mystics have called that stage, "The Dark Night of the Soul." Then one seems to be alone and speaks of "The Flight of the Alone to the Alone." But this is not the ultimate stage.

One does first have to contend with external noises in meditation. Then one has to struggle with one's thoughts and this is such a battle that sometimes all of life is not enough. Yet there are periods when one can rise above the mind, when the mind grows fatigued, and falls below the will-

Document: O.t. See Introduction to Gita Dhyana, p. 219

Note:

1. This whole Gita seems to be Samuel Lewis's version, made from his annotations of Pir-o-Murshid's lecture.

power. Then one enters the silence. Often one abides there thinking this is the ultimate state. The Arhats of Southern Buddhism still think so with the result that their realization does not bring them into union with all things. They deny the existence of God, and it is no wonder, for their realization is not the Divine Union. They get into the Void, the nothingness and remain there.

But there is a higher stage and for this love is needed which comes through self-sacrifice on the one hand and heart-awakening on the other. Even in meditation, when the heart is alive, one may find that union. It often comes through union with the teacher first (fana-fi-Sheikh); it ultimately leads to union with God (fana-fi-lillah). The realization it brings, baka, proves to one that the false self is not the real self and the life which appears in us, which we refer to as ourself is not different from the universal life.[1]

An old typescript in the form of a Gita, from a collection of Sufi papers used by Samuel Lewis.

Series II | GITHA No. 8[A] | DHYANA

(Meditation)

[1]TOWARD THE ONE, THE PERFECTION OF LOVE, HARMONY AND BEAUTY, THE ONLY BEING, UNITED WITH ALL THE ILLUMINATED SOULS, WHO FORM THE EMBODIMENT OF THE MASTER, THE SPIRIT OF GUIDANCE.[1]

One can always take his questions[2] to God. Of course one often has his spiritual teacher, his Murshid or Sheikh near at hand, who may and often must be consulted when doubt arises. The spiritual teacher can best help the mureed when the mureed looks upon the teacher as a link on the chain which connects him to God.

The saints and sages who have been gifted with insight often commune with God and through their inner heart development have been able to achieve God's purpose in this world. In meditation one is consulting with God, feeling God. This does not mean that one has a special meditation for every little problem. Keeping fixed periods for communion with God, establishing rhythms and devoting the whole heart to God at those times helps more than anything else.

Especially early morning meditations are valuable for consulting with God, and receiving help. Gradually this spiritual communion will become such a power, such a reality, that it will continue day and night. The heart will awaken and the intuitions tell one how to act, when to move, to travel, to marry, to make any important change in life, or even to meditate or perform extra spiritual deeds. In this condition gradually all of life takes on a grand unity.

The Sufi always meditates before taking any important steps in life. When the mind is clear and passive and the heart awake, God will speak. The Sufi does not enter meditation for something special, for his desire may not be God's desire. The true lover, the devotee, seeks union rather than reward and the union is the greatest of all rewards. Yet meditation is the

Documents:

S.L. See introduction to Gita Dhyana, p. 219
O.t. See Introduction to Gita Dhyana, p. 219

Notes:

1. O.t.: The first three words of the Invocation appear above the Gita.
2. Ibid.: "question"

method by which Allah Himself works and all great murshids meditated when they had great duties to perform, for they realized that not they but Allah was the real Actor and Performer.

There are many blessings in meditation, there are many blessings in preparing for meditation, there are many blessings resulting from meditation, but meditation itself is the greatest of blessings.

(For circulation among members of the A.S.C. only.)

A copy made under Sakina's supervision of an old typescript in the form of a Gita, from the legacy of Murshida Martin.

Series II. GITHA Number 9.[1]

Toward the One, the Perfection of Love, Harmony and Beauty, the Only Being, united with All the Illuminated Souls, Who form the Embodiment of the Master, the Spirit of Guidance.

DHYANA MEDITATION

Students of Oriental art have observed that the methods and techniques used in the West are different from those in the East. The Occidentals seem to spend more time in execution, the Orientals in planning. Yes, this may be so, only when we study the fundamentals of Oriental art deeply we find that the real preparation of the artist is himself. If he can get himself into the right mood, if he has established the right rapport with his subject matter, the work is not so different from the playing of a piece of music in the West. Even though it is a creative[2], it seems to follow a silent pattern, an invisible form which is there to be copied, and the executive[2] of which brings inspiration.

Now this shows that the Silent life is not the void and instead brings all the seeds of life. Those who are only able to go so far in meditation do not reach the place where they can partake of the tree of life. Sometimes they keep the self-conception before them. Often they do not surrender fully. And this may be because of a lack of response to beauty. The esthetic sense, which is not always far from the spiritual feeling, may be undeveloped in them.

In meditation one's energies are turned Godward. That is to say, not only into the silence, but into the life which is the soul of the silence. Sufis call that, "The perfection of Love, Harmony and Beauty." Often the single words "love," "harmony" and "beauty" fail to impress one fully. There is an expectancy of them from others. The true mystic instead seeks to uncover them from within himself. And the difference between the Sufi and the ordinary man is that in the former it is as if God Himself were speaking and acting.

Many know about the simile of the empty cup; few there be that find the attainment of it. It is as one voids oneself of one's self, and then is filled with light. Man's duty is to action, that is, the emptying of ego; to God go the

Document: O.t. See Introduction to Gita Dhyana, p. 219

Notes:

1. This whole Gita seems to be Samuel Lewis's version, made from annotations of a lecture given by Pir-o-Murshid.
2. Even though "creative" and "executive" do not seem to make sense here, it is written so in the "o.t.".

fruits of the action, which come to man as the filling of light, which we call inspiration. Therefore Mohammed used to consider himself only as the pen of God. He refused to be classed along with authors and poets. He said that Qur'an was more than man's poetry for it echoed the Divine Wisdom. He challenged his opponents to produce such a book, and they could not.

All the great artistic achievements of the Orient as well as Qur'an have come from the emptying of self, which is followed by the pouring in of the Silent life into one's being. That Life represents all wisdom and beauty, in other words, God. Thus the artist who practises his meditations not only finds God, but makes use of his knowledge in his everyday life.

An old typescript in the form of a Gita, from a collection of Sufi papers used by Samuel Lewis.

Series II GITHA No. 9[A] DHYANA

(Meditation)

[1]TOWARD THE ONE, THE PERFECTION OF LOVE, HARMONY AND BEAUTY, THE ONLY BEING, UNITED WITH ALL THE ILLUMINATED SOULS WHO FORM THE EMBODIMENT OF THE MASTER, THE SPIRIT OF GUIDANCE.[1]

It is often wondered how artists and musicians in the Orient could advance in their development far beyond those of the West. The reason is that they spend so much time in meditation. Sometimes the whole life of an artist is absorbed in a single task, and many beautiful things have been made in this manner.

In truth it is God Who is the Master Mind. The great Sufi poets who have been among the most[2] famous on earth spent much time in meditation. Their whole life was like a meditation and their poetry was the result of meditation and it consisted of praise of God, rejoicing in the Beloved, and songs to the Source and Goal of humanity.

Even today we find some mystical poets and artists in the East. They meditate many hours before taking up their tasks. Without a definite purpose, a work has not much use or value and the efforts are often wasted. Real Beauty should not be considered as something different from Wisdom nor Wisdom as apart from Beauty.

In Meditation all one's energy is turned Godward and so becomes strengthened manifold. This explains why it has been possible for mystics to write great works without becoming fatigued. There is no fatigue when one works as an instrument for Heaven. The difference between the Sufi and the ordinary man is that the Sufi realizes that it is God Who performs all actions. When the average man writes a letter, his arm becomes tired, yet the pen is not tired. But when God writes and man is His instrument, man is like that pen, he can work for a long period without becoming tired.

Documents:

S.L. See Introduction to Gita Dhyana, p. 219
O.t. See Introduction to Gita Dhyana, p. 219

Notes:

1. O.t.: the first three words of the Invocation appear above the Gita.
2. Ibid.: "most" omitted

Mohammed used to consider himself only as the pen of God. He refused to be classed as an author. He said the Qur'an was more than man's poetry for it echoed the purest Wisdom of God. So he challenged his opponents to produce a Qur'an and one proof of his Prophethood is[3] that he alone was able to produce such a book.

Sufis and mystics have inspired much of the great spiritual architecture of the world, whether of India or the other parts of Asia and the Indies. The tomb of Akbar, the Taj Mahal, the temples of Angkor and Borabodur, all point to marvellous spiritual inspiration. The men and women who labored in such places probably found great inner joy; they had to spend much time in meditation and their outward performance was the reflection of their inner lives.

The Sufi realizing God as the perfection of Beauty, is the lover of Beauty. He appreciates all true beauty and endeavors to make his life beautiful in all its aspects. There is nothing in life which cannot be brought to perfection.

(For circulation among members of the A.S.C. only.)

---

3. Ibid.: "was" instead of "is"

A copy made under Sakina's supervision of an old typescript in the form of a Gita, from the legacy of Murshida Martin.

Series II. GITHA Number 10.

Toward the One, the Perfection of Love, Harmony and Beauty, the Only Being, united with All the Illuminated Souls, Who form the Embodiment of the Master, the Spirit of Guidance.

DHYANA MEDITATION

It may be asked if there is perfection in meditation, and the answer to this depends largely by what one means. Yes, there is a state called "Samadhi" wherein one continues to live, when one lives and moves and has his being in God, or at least one has a realization which is not limited by the ego outlook. The attunement to God which comes through meditation and heart-awakening is such that openly and consciously as well as conscientiously one finds himself beyond the distinctions and differences which divide men.

[1]*The term "Baka" is used by Sufis to denote realization. It is then that one finds the Divine Life in the Silent Life. One can call it Silent Life which is the void, which comes when one is freed from attachment to subject and object, when one is attracted neither by the pleasures of this world nor the joys of the next. But if one continued in such a state there would be a tendency to retirement, to asceticism, to the crushing of the life-force in oneself, as if only by the destruction of life could sorrow and inharmony be terminated.*

The Buddhists and Hindus have used the term Nirvana to indicate the state when one rises above distinctions and differences. This seems to have a negative emphasis to followers of other religions who emphasize rather the Kingdom of God. This Kingdom of God rightly speaking is beyond heaven. Heaven is really the kingdom of man, the state in which all of man's desires are fulfilled. It is not the Kingdom of God. In Malakut no doubt all of man's desires are accomplished, which makes Malakut the sphere in which Kadar, the human will "holds sway," just as on earth, Jadar, the necessity of nature "holds sway." But there is beyond these another state.

Lahut is the name given to the plane of oneness beyond all differences and distinctions, in which one experiences the life as a whole and from

Document: O.t. See Introduction to Gita Dhyana, p. 219

Note:

1. Paragraphs two, three, four and five seem to be Samuel Lewis's version, made from annotations of a lecture given by Pir-o-Murshid.

which one receives all energies and functions and power, serving God there from. But Hahut, which has been called a plane, represents that in which God alone is, in which God is all in all, and there is none else.

The perfection of meditation is therefore that which produces the perfection of consciousness. It begins as a clearing of man's mind, in removing the false ego. It terminates not only in the attainment of divine consciousness by man, but the reverberation of that consciousness through man as if in reality and in all realization only God exists. Sufis call this state Risalat, which is the perfection of humanity.

This paper should be followed by at least 30 min. meditation.[1]

For circulation among the Members of the A.S.C. ONLY.

An old typescript in the form of a Gita, from a collection of Sufi papers used by Samuel Lewis.

Series II | GITHA No. 10[A] | DHYANA

(Meditation)

[1]TOWARD THE ONE, THE PERFECTION OF LOVE, HARMONY AND BEAUTY, THE ONLY BEING, UNITED WITH ALL THE ILLUMINATED SOULS WHO FORM THE EMBODIMENT OF THE MASTER, THE SPIRIT OF GUIDANCE.[1]

It may be asked whether there is a perfection in meditation, and the answer may be "yes" or "no" or both "yes" and "no" and still neither "yes" nor "no." For the perfection in meditation is the perfection[2] of all perfections.

Through right meditation one becomes attuned to God and so to all creation including humanity. There are many grades and steps in spiritual devotion, wherein one becomes attuned to his teacher, to the world teacher, to the prophets of God, and to Allah himself. Even after one reaches the last stages it is only a beginning, for then man ceases to be and God [3]lives truly[3] in and through one. This is called "baka" by the Sufis. Of this condition Christ has said: "Many are called but few are chosen," and Krishna taught that very few realized his being and of these only a few sustained that realization.

The true work of the Sufi is not only to attain to God-consciousness but to make this realization absorb more and more of life. In that condition one never loses sight of Allah for an instant, day or night, asleep or awake. This may truly be called the purpose of life, the fulfilment of the inner life.

But progress does not cease there. In that state called "fana-fi-lillah," when the soul is absorbed in God, one loses the false sense of being and finds the true reality. Then one finally experiences what is termed "baka-fi-fana," where the false ego is annihilated and merged into the true personality which is really God expressing Himself in some wondrous ways[4]. This is the same also as Nirvana where the true reality of life is experienced and expressed. This means that the true life is in God, the Only Being, and through God-realization man finds his true self.

Documents:

S.L. See Introduction to Gita Dhyana, p. 219
O.t. See Introduction to Gita Dhyana, p. 219

Notes:

1. O.t.: the first three words of the Invocation appear above the Gita.
2. Ibid.: "perfecting" instead of "perfection"
3. Ibid.: "truly lives"
4. Ibid.: "way"

Initiation is the beginning and perfection is the end, the making complete. But where is the beginning and where is the end? They are both in Silence, in God. In the Silence we were born and to it we return.

Therefore the perfection of meditation is meditation. It is the perfected souls who continue ever in meditation, being absorbed in[5] meditation, creating from their meditation and living in that meditation. The spiritual life is the drawing of sustenance through the breath from God. It is a life of praise, yet of sobriety and balance, a life of fulness and emptiness both, being empty of self and filled with God. This is the true purpose of initiation and spiritual training from the moment the mureed takes Bayat until the Eternity of Eternities, Time without Ending.

6

[7](For members of the A.S.C. only.)[7]

---

5. Ibid.: "that" added
6. Ibid.: "(This paper to be followed by a long meditation of 20-30 minutes.)"
7. Ibid.: this sentence was omitted.

A copy made under Sakina's supervision of an old typescript in the form of a Gita, from the legacy of Murshida Martin.

Series III. GITHA Number 1.

Toward the One, the Perfection of Love, Harmony and Beauty, the Only Being, united with All the Illuminated Souls, who form the Embodiment of the Master, the Spirit of Guidance.

DHYANA MEDITATION

Meditation is the task of escaping from the control of the lower mind and living in the heart. It is only when the consciousness is in the heart that the soul can be free. By "heart" is meant not only physical heart but all that is physical that is connected with the heart, and at the same time it includes all the higher emotions, purer thoughts and deep intuitions. All these belong to the heart.

Heart differs from the mind and body in that body cannot heal itself and mind cannot heal itself. Mind can heal body, but this healing will not be permanent unless the mind is also purified. Heart not only heals mind and body, heart heals itself. Through the bloodstream heart heals the body, and to a certain extent helps the mind, but through breath, will and the inner light, heart can completely purge the mind of all its pain.

All birth, growth and decay, as *the blessed* Buddha taught, are accompanied by pain. In disease and injury this pain is more acute, but the average man is continually in pain. As pain at ordinary times is less than during suffering, it is not noticed. Souls released from the body or enjoying the ecstasy or spiritual release while in the body, discover the great distance between what man has set up for himself and what God has ordained for him.

Pain arises from thought. If there were no thought there would be no pain. This is observed to some extent when nerves are removed. Even if thought were a chemical activity as some materialists claim, it would only mean that the pain took on a chemical form. It is not so difficult to understand that outer change requires adjustment and so brings some suffering, and the same is true with inner change--it is often accompanied with suffering.

When mental activity is inspired from within and though it is still associated with the senses without being dependent upon them, then the intellectual functions may continue without this pain and suffering. This is

Document: O.t. See Introduction to Gita Dhyana, p. 219

the true Nirvana, wherein faculties are continued *unimpaired*, without being joined to the nufs, the ego. Then the light of the soul, pouring from the heart, illuminates the mind. *This is the buddhic or intuitional condition.*

One of the main purposes of meditation is the control of thought so that the mind will be illuminated by this life and light from within. Spiritual practices which purify the breath make it possible for the breath also to be used as a vehicle of the soul. Breath is the greatest help yet can be the greatest hindrance. In meditation[1], especially according to the Sufi methods, no direct attention is paid to the breath, yet the more it is purified, the easier it is for the heart to illuminate the mind.

One physical aspect of this is that the whole being is in rhythm in meditation. The body is at rest, the flow of the breath and blood is rhythmical, the mind vibrations become quiet, and gradually through long practice, all the functions of the mind such as thought, reason, memory, I-ness, become dormant. Sitting at ease or in posture, holding a divine thought, the heart gradually controls the mind and the inner light becomes visible, so to speak, before the naked eye.

Another aspect is the activity of the blood itself. The bloodstream touches every part of the body and brain, so heart touches every aspect of life. It is this life in the heart which is the destiny of the soul to experience either upon earth or in Malakut, and one need not wait for it until he returns to the sphere of the heart itself. By meditation one not only brings heaven to earth, but reaches the heaven of heavens while here.

For circulation among the Members of the A.S.C. ONLY.

Note:

1. In the old typescript the word "some" and a plural "s" had been added ("In (some) meditation(s)"), but were put in parentheses by Sk. with a note reading as follows: "in parentheses, because added by those who copied these series."

A copy made under Sakina's supervision of an old typescript in the form of a Gita, from the legacy of Murshida Martin.

Series III. GITHA Number 2.

Toward the One, the Perfection of Love, Harmony and Beauty, the Only Being, united with All the Illuminated Souls, who form the Embodiment of the Master, the Spirit of Guidance.

DHYANA MEDITATION

Every manner of concentration draws blood to a center. In thought blood is drawn into the brain area. If all the blood were withdrawn the life would be withdrawn, and the nerves would become dormant. Alcoholics and dope fiends interfere with this rhythm and so destroy the connections between the physical body and more subtle vehicles of the soul. This may eliminate pain but it does so by destroying life. Strictly speaking, every drunkard and partaker of drugs is to a certain extent dead.

Whenever an injury occurs and whenever there is any damage done to the body from within, inflammation follows. That is, blood rushes to that part and if there is any break in the normal rhythm, pain follows. Keeping thought on the pain serves to increase it by drawing still more blood and giving more life to it besides increasing the irregularity of rhythm. On the other hand, suggestion sometimes turns the life force in other directions and relieves the physical and psychological strain.

Meditation has a great advantage over suggestion for it not only keeps the heart in rhythm, it places the center of life-force there. When the mind assumes a burden from the body, the body may benefit, but the mind bears the burden. But when the heart takes the load from mind and body, it heals itself. The heart is its own medicine. Therefore meditation can cure every ill of body, mind or heart.

All these are the negative value of meditation, the purgative processes by which body, mind and heart are purified. Yet life is more than negation or purgation. Life is something real, something positive, something magnetic. So continued meditation draws all strength to the center of one's being, to the heart, and from there it radiates to all parts of body and mind.

Just as the body has its breaths with inhalations and exhalations, so mind has its periods for observation and inner concentration, and so heart

Document: O.t. See Introduction to Gita Dhyana, p. 219

has its periods of contraction and expansion. It is the contraction and expansion of the heart which draws the blood to it and circulates it through the body. The purified blood not only carries physical energy and prana, it is the vehicle for all spiritual energy in the body.

Just as the animals in the ocean draw their sustenance from the sea water, so the body of man really draws all sustenance from the blood. It is the blood which assimilates the food from the intestines and distributes it everywhere, and it is the blood which removes waste particles and poisons. So the blood and heart nourish, purify and energize this physical vehicle.

Likewise the heart and blood purify the mind and this is accomplished in meditation. People who do not read or think overmuch are not so susceptible to pain. Savage warriors often fall without a murmur. This is partly due to their daily life which does not focus all consciousness in the brain and partly due to their use of music and song which make them insensible to pain while under its influence. This magnetic anaesthetic influence often lasts for hours or days.

It is our artificial and highly specialized intellectual life with unnecessary concern and worries which destroys the rhythm of the heart-beat and makes it difficult to place the center of gravity of the personality where it belongs. Sleep at best gives only partial relief. Meditation and the practice of the Divine Presence remove self-consciousness, the greatest obstacle to calm and peace. Pure meditation itself is the desirable condition and brings all desirable results.

A copy made under Sakina's supervision of an old typescript in the form of a Gita, from the legacy of Murshida Martin.

Series III. GITHA Number 3.

Toward the One, the Perfection of Love, Harmony and Beauty, the Only Being, united with All the Illuminated Souls, who form the Embodiment of the Master, the Spirit of Guidance.

DHYANA MEDITATION

Pure meditation aids one to reach into the inner recesses of the heart. Concentration is principally concerned with mind, whereas meditation, while not entirely disconcerned with mind, centers the soul where it belongs: in the heart. Anyone can be called eccentric who has not found the center of his being, and spiritual balance is impossible until this is accomplished.

Spiritual life is one of unity, not of separation. Whoso believes that life in the heart means withdrawal from the body does not know the meaning of life. Blood plays a more important part in physical existence than anything else. Thus Sura 96 begins: "Read in the name of your Lord Who created, He created man from a clot."

Now this has great significance for it is blood which distinguishes animal from vegetable more than anything else, and in the evolution of higher forms it is the organization of heart and veins and arteries which becomes most complex. They serve not only the physical body but make feeling possible. So increase of function in all worlds corresponds to the importance of the heartlife in those worlds.

And what is heart? Heart is the seat of life. So Allah has been called the Beneficent and Merciful. The whole life becomes clearer when these processes are understood. It may even be said, there is more of divine energy in those animals where heart is most important, and there is still more divine energy when the consciousness is centered in the heart and bloodstream.

Now peace comes when self is in harmony with the rhythm of the heart. This is accomplished in two ways. In silent meditation all vibrations are stopped and one enters into the life-stream in the heart; in music, the rhythm and harmony are directed to and through the heart so that it takes up the proper pulsation.

Document: O.t. See Introduction to Gita Dhyana, p. 219

Everyone knows that all music affects the heart, but such effects may or may not be beneficial. So for many it is not required to exercise this control over the heart and mastery comes through love and surrender. So if there is any form of concentration to be used in meditation, it consists in first getting into the rhythm of the heart, even though it be by watching the heartbeats, feeling them and harmonizing with them.

Then one centers all feeling in the physical heart and out of feeling selects love, and out of love, Divine Love. So meditation may be said to begin with a great sweep at the outside of a circle, getting further and further within that circle until one reaches the center of the circle, and at the same time that very centralizing of attention draws to one all that God has, for to him that gives all to God, Allah bestows whatever is his[1] need.

For circulation among the Members of the A.S.C. ONLY.

Note:

1. In the old typescript the word "his" had been replaced by "man's", but "man's" was put in parentheses by Sakina. See Series III, nr. 1, note 1.

A copy made under Sakina's supervision of an old typescript in the form of a Gita, from the legacy of Murshida Martin.

Series III. GITHA Number 4.

Toward the One, the Perfection of Love, Harmony and Beauty, the Only Being, united with All the Illuminated Souls, who form the Embodiment of the Master, the Spirit of Guidance.

DHYANA MEDITATION

The Sufi does not wait until the hereafter to attain his spiritual independence. He does all he can here and now, realizing that the Presence of God does not depend upon the fact that he is inhabiting a gross or subtle body. Qur'an teaches that man is the Khalif of God, meaning that he can seek and serve God here and now.

Life in the heart is not dependent upon the soul being in Nasut, Malakut or Djabrut. Life in the heart comes when consciousness is centered in feeling. The first object of feeling is to attune feeling, thought and action within oneself. Among the Hindus Bhakti, Jnana and Karma Yoga are often considered as different, but in the Sufi system they are united. No attempt is made to consider any part of life as fundamentally separate from the rest of life or to consider each as intricate parts of a whole.

The mystic conceives life as a whole and does not separate it into divisions. The first unity to be attained is the unity of the self, the real self, and not only what thought can grasp of being. This self is higher than thought and thought is its faculty. In the common life instead of thought being a faculty of self, selfhood has become a faculty of the mind and this causes endless confusion.

This confusion comes to an end when God is perceived. By meditation one finds it is possible to exist without thought and that cessation of thought does not mean cessation of knowledge. Instead it often means the beginning of knowledge. When one escapes from the thought of self and self-consciousness, real knowledge becomes possible, which is called Ilm by the Sufis.

Of the faculties of mind, none are of greater importance to the soul than the collection of knowledge, yet knowledge is the means, not the end.

Document: O.t. See Introduction to Gita Dhyana, p. 219

When by centering consciousness in the heart one can[1] perceive freely into the mind, the knowledge of both this world and that world[1] *are one's possessions*.

Meditation therefore leads to unity of one's being by linking body, mind and heart to God. Cessation of movement, thought and feeling, instead of bringing death, bring life. All that was shut out when one depended upon his feeble insight, his limited intellect and his untrained feeling become the possessions of the heart, where the light of Allah is burning upon one's inner shrine.

For circulation among Members of the A.S.C. ONLY.

Note:

1. It is difficult to suggest a grammatical reconstruction of this sentence. Possibly instead of "perceive" "receive" was said.

A copy made under Sakina's supervision of an old typescript in the form of a Gita, from the legacy of Murshida Martin.

Series III. GITHA Number 5.

Toward the One, the Perfection of Love, Harmony and Beauty, the Only Being, united with All the Illuminated Souls, who form the Embodiment of the Master, the Spirit of Guidance.

DHYANA MEDITATION

Those who are always longing for peace with others, who want to lead others, to teach others, to bring others to God or to some earthly goal and who have not found peace or God or that earthly goal, what can they accomplish? Only those who have joined mind to heart can link the mind of another to heart. Man's control over his body often makes it possible for him to move it or stop it at will, but for every thousand men who can stop their legs, perhaps one can control his mind, and for every thousand who can put brain to work or rest at will perhaps not even one has power over his heart to control all feelings.

Now the purpose of Meditation can be called a purpose of man or the requirement of God. Man needs Meditation to attain voluntary control over his being and to unify each part of his being with the whole. God also needs Meditation for in the beginning He existed without action or thought and when He completed the Universe, He again entered into His primordial state of stillness.

All conditions of God: rest, action, thought, concentration, meditation, love, ecstasy, song and silence are co-existing. God enjoys His Nirvana in His highest state and in His lowest state. Man, because of his faculty of analytical conception, considering rest and activity separate, finds it difficult to attain Nirvana here and now.

Man, *engulfed* in this world of activity, loses sight of his inner being, forgets how to rest and is a stranger to peace at heart. The great sages therefore have come to remind him of the treasures he carries with him and to attain them he has to enter into rest and silence. At the same time it cannot be said that one has attained to the highest condition of meditation until one is able to meditate even in the midst of action and struggle. If unity is once attained there, it is not so difficult to bring others to the *doors of salvation*.

Document: O.t. See Introduction to Gita Dhyana, p. 219

Control of breath and mind are not so difficult when one knows the uses of Wazifa and Darood. To keep the heart at rest and peace, Fikar is important. If Fikar is continued at all times, day and night, asleep or awake, then it is God Who dwells there and this is the highest state man can achieve of himself. Anything of a marvelous nature that seems to come after that comes not of his effort but through the beneficent Grace of Allah.

Leader will he be who leads himself, ruler will he be who rules himself and benefactor will he be who has supreme control over his heart; who is not driven hither and thither by all the turbulent waves of life, who can control even passion and sentiment in his heart and who can keep his glance upon Allah whether he walk on a path of primroses or face the greatest difficulties and opposition in the turmoil of his life.

A copy made under Sakina's supervision of an old typescript in the form of a Gita, from the legacy of Murshida Martin.

Series III. GITHA Number 6.

Toward the One, the Perfection of Love, Harmony and Beauty, the Only Being, united with All the Illuminated Souls, who form the Embodiment of the Master, the Spirit of Guidance.

DHYANA MEDITATION

Meditation contains the cure for all troubles, the remedy for every difficulty, the balm for every pain. What may be called Cosmic Consciousness may be considered in two aspects: A growth of sympathy and feeling, or the expansion of the heart until it is filled with nothing but the light, thought and feeling of God.

In the first condition while one may not be in the highest h a l , yet one is a true h a k i m, a physician and a wise man who can heal himself and others. When the heart overflows with love, the body and mind are *surcharged* with magnetism and so great is the power of this magnetism that it can benefit others thousands of miles away. Yes, it is possible to concentrate on loved ones and through Meditation, when one is bathed in the Ocean of Divine Love, such factors as distance and time do not matter.

Thus religion teaches to pray for the dead. How can we benefit the dead? We can, if the prayers come from sympathy and benignity, but if they are painful duties we do little good to ourselves or others. Better than prayer is the communion of saints which becomes possible when Meditation is maintained in the heart; then the sympathetic vibrations pass from plane to plane and one on earth can help one in heaven and one in heaven can assist many upon earth.

The brotherhood of Sufis is not determined by time or space. Unity is beyond all limitations. The words of Khatum, recorded as prayer, are really assertions of metaphysical realities: God is the Perfection of Love, Harmony and Beauty, Who is the Lord of Heaven and earth. He opens our hearts[1] and then we hear His Voice which is constantly coming from

Document: O.t. See Introduction to Gita Dhyana, p. 219

Notes:

1. O.t.: "(in Meditation)" had been added by those who copied these series. See Series III nr. 1, note 1.

within[2]. He gives us His great Goodness and He teaches us His loving forgiveness[3]. [4]He raises us above the distinctions and differences which divide men, sends us the Peace of His Divine Spirit, and unites us all in His Perfect Being.

This is the state of God and becomes the m a k ā m of the sage. By placing himself in God's position, and maintaining that attitude he attains to the first kind of Cosmic Consciousness, one of universal love and feeling. All growth of heart makes this more and more possible.

In Meditation, therefore, listen to Allah speak, and record your impressions. Feel His Love and Presence, perceive His Glory and Light. All are there within the heart of man, the a r a s h of God. And by constantly maintaining this state, all of life becomes a meditation and a blessing.

For circulation among the Members of the A.S.C. only.

---

2. Ibid.: "(in impression, intuition and inspiration)" had been added by those who copied these series. See Series III nr. 1, note 1.
3. Ibid.: "(if we would only perceive)" had been added by those who copied these series. See Series III nr. 1, note 1.
4. Ibid.: "(By His Grace)" had been added by those who copied these series. See Series III nr. 1, note 1.

A copy made under Sakina's supervision of an old typescript in the form of a Gita, from the legacy of Murshida Martin.

Series III. GITHA Number 7.

Toward the One, the Perfection of Love, Harmony and Beauty, the Only Being, united with All the Illuminated Souls, who form the Embodiment of the Master, the Spirit of Guidance.

DHYANA MEDITATION

When man speaks God is silent and when man is silent God may speak. It is foolish to talk and discuss Cosmic Consciousness. It is, perhaps, even less unworthy to speculate upon what to do when dead. It is easier to fly an airplane under earth, or for a camel to walk through the eye of a needle than for one to consider Cosmic Consciousness. When Jesus used this last phrase about the rich man not being able to attain to the Kingdom of God, he meant that one who cared for the things of creation left no accommodation for the Creator, and as man cannot serve both God and Mammon, either the heart is attached to those things which are smaller than itself--whether with the riches of earth or heaven--or it is filled with the Divine Light which is even greater than the heart. Yet the heart can become larger than all the Universe when filled with this light.

In the state of Unity there can be no variety. Bathed in the light of the Divine Sun, selfhood seems lost but only seemingly so. What is the soul? R u h is the ray of the Divine Sun. As ray has no existence apart from sun, so soul is nothing but God. In the existence of soul beyond the heart sphere there are not souls strictly speaking. *This has been called the o v e r s o u l*; by mystics it is sometimes known as N u r i M o h a m m e d, where man escapes manhood with its limitations and only God exists. And what is the condition of God there? It is there that Allah is clothed in all His Attributes, in His Glory and Majesty, upon His Great Throne.

Man does not approach God in His Throne except in the state of Godhood[1]. This is told in the Masnavi in the story of the man who approached the highest heaven first as the servant and then as the slave of God, but was rejected. When he came the third time as the very self of God, he entered

Document: O.t. See Introduction to Gita Dhyana, p. 219

Note:

1. O.t.: "(fana-fi-lillah)" had been added by those who copied these series. See Series III nr. 1, note 1.

into the Glory of God. This same allegory is also the basis of the Mantiq-ut-Tair of Attar, with its tales of the Simurgh.

The purpose of Meditation is to enter upon a state of unity, - thought of unity, feeling of unity, life of unity.- When we study the Nature of Allah we find in His Higher State, when He had not yet touched the condition of Nuri Mohammed, He was in a condition of Unity. This state is called W a h d a t; it is the condition of the Unity of God, where He is conscious of Himself and recognizes His Unity. In this state God was in Meditation, yet was conscious of Himself.

Now from this condition of Meditation He projected His being outwardly into the condition called W a h d a n i a t, and there all the merits of God appear: His Being, and Goodness and Love and all merits. They came in this projected condition which He projected out from the Heart of His Being when He was in Meditation in the state of Unity.

Sufism says: follow God. So first it is to attain to this condition of unity, which comes through Meditation in the heart. Then when one discovers the reality in the heart is nothing but God, and life is nothing but God, the next step is to attain to the Divine Grace, H a r i a t, as was *projected into* the condition called Wahdaniat as a condition of God, but Nuri Mohammed as the goal of the whole humanity, where every blessing is attained and the soul drinks of the waters of everlasting life.

A copy made under Sakina's supervision of an old typescript in the form of a Gita, from the legacy of Murshida Martin.

Series III. GITHA Number 8.

Toward the One, the Perfection of Love, Harmony and Beauty, the Only Being, united with All the Illuminated Souls, who form the Embodiment of the Master, the Spirit of Guidance.

DHYANA MEDITATION

The life of God is an art. Without the practice of Meditation the spiritual man is a theoretical being. *Meditation being an act based on the behavior of Allah,* it is the means by which all divine attributes are attracted to man.

The spiritual man is not necessarily the same as the moral man from the worldly point of view. He is the master of morals, knowing that the true moral is Love. Through love for God and by Union with God he attains the state of Cosmic Unity where the life of God, b a k a, becomes the reality. In fact when one reaches this stage of God-realization, he can no longer be judged. His actions are determined by Wisdom, not by judgement.

Bodhisattva was one who through Meditation had thrown off the shackles of the limited self and so experienced and expressed reality while on earth. The ideal of the Sufi is the same and the Sufi makes all life as one, so that his spiritual deliverance need not lead him to disobey the accepted rules or customs of life about him, and also, that by being an example to those around, he may lead other persons Godward without any interference in their general routine or manner of life.

One who has reached spiritual attainment through Meditation looks upon all aspects of life both as God and as man. As man he may or may not express personal preferences and exhibit distinguished habits; as the Khalif of God he does not place great value in anything except those acts which enable the soul to attain and retain union with God, such as Meditation, Prayer, Breath Control, Safa and Concentration.

The manner of the sage is important not as an end in itself, but as a means for helping others. Those who pattern their outer lives after a saint gain something through the harmony effected, but those who take for an ideal standard the inner life of the saint have definitely placed themselves on the ladder which leads upward to God.

Document: O.t. See Introduction to Gita Dhyana, p. 219

Difficult as it is to attain Cosmic Consciousness, ten thousand times more difficult is it to retain that condition. So soon as one feels toward another, "Thou art different," then it is lost. So soon as one sees another as other than Allah, then it is gone. Even kindness toward another without feeling of union, without deepest sympathy, turns one from unity to duality. Goodness, kindness, piety are not enough; any feeling except of unity debars one from unity and so from God. Consequently every breath may have to be watched, to maintain at every moment of our lives extreme care and watchfulness.

As Iblis, the angel of light, was rejected from Heaven because he would not bow down to man, so one who has attained the highest mystical states, who has entered into supreme union in Allah, Who has sat on the Arsh-throne higher than Djabrut, and to whom all the angels have given obeisance, even as Iblis, King of the angels, will he be expelled from Eden the instant he fails to bow down to the humblest man, and show every respect and consideration to the least of God's creatures. For unity with God is only completed when God is seen as Love, Lover and Beloved, and when all in existence partakes not only of the Nature but of the very Essence of Allah.

A copy made under Sakina's supervision of an old typescript in the form of a Gita, from the legacy of Murshida Martin.

Series III. GITHA Number 9.

Toward the One, the Perfection of Love, Harmony and Beauty, the Only Being, united with All the Illuminated Souls, who form the Embodiment of the Master, the Spirit of Guidance.

DHYANA MEDITATION

Meditation is the method for the attainment of all things, all states, all conditions. It is both a means and an end[1]. It is the life of God in man and of man in God. The supreme achievement of Meditation is the constant condition of harmony with God, with oneself and with the world. This is called Samadhi by the Hindus.

In this state comes the end of desire and the satisfaction of the desire. Desire comes to an end because it is seen that all those things which attracted the limited self have no permanent value, and at the same time the love of Allah, which is the supreme desire, has its fulfilment in the peace and unification which comes to the heart. And again, if there is perseverance in Meditation, the state will give rise to indifference so that there can be no desire.

Heart is the source and fountain-head of life. Even physical life will be lengthened when people perceive the value of the heart's functions, how even the most vital centers and organs of the body are dependent on it. Here is also the fulfilment of dreams, for when the light of the inner spheres falls upon the surface of the mind and is reflected in the eye, then the faculty of Insight is gained which makes life easier and enables one to see into the future.

Future is determined partly by the past and partly by the energy which is poured from the physical sun in this world and from its counterparts in the higher worlds. Even insofar as it arises from the past, this can only be perceived through the faculty of Insight, for until one is capable of rising above the intellect, one is bound by time, space and *conditioned existence*.

All disease and pain, all illness and affliction end when life is centered in the heart. Then through sympathy and harmony one controls the

Document: O.t. See Introduction to Gita Dhyana, p. 219

Note:

1. O.t.: "(that is, objective)" had been added by those who copied these series. See Series III nr. 1, note 1.

vibrations in others which have already been mastered in oneself. Sympathy and attunement make it possible to circulate one's atmosphere of peace after it is once attained. This achievement of peace with oneself which comes mostly through Meditation, is the supreme achievement of man.

All the higher stages, all the higher grades, all the places in the Spiritual Hierarchy become filled only by those who have attained this inner peace. By that they have been able to touch the source of pain everywhere and anywhere and so bring healing to suffering humanity. This faculty of healing, this power of helping, this ability to teach need not be sought. Those who have trodden the path to God and acquired self-control through Meditation will discover that these possessions are theirs, only because their hearts have been set on God, they have not always been aware of the many gifts and treasures He has bestowed upon them.

Verily to him who hath surrendered to God, there is no end of power for wonder-working, but greatest of all wonder-working is the manifestation of Divine Love in and through and around one's being.

A copy made under Sakina's supervision of an old typescript in the form of a Gita, from the legacy of Murshida Martin.

Series III. GITHA Number 10.

Toward the One, the Perfection of Love, Harmony and Beauty, the Only Being, united with All the Illuminated Souls, who form the Embodiment of the Master, the Spirit of Guidance.

DHYANA MEDITATION

In the Silent Life all this confusion that appears on the outside subsides into a gentle hum, a hum which can be called the music of the spheres. These vibrations fill all space within and without one's being and can be heard by a keen ear. They may be called the vibrations of life itself which fill the Ocean of Life. All things live and move and have their being in them.

In Meditation as one approaches unity, one begins to perceive more of this inner silent life, and as it is expressed through one, one feels more of the Divine Purpose of being. All thought, action and speech then affect the heart favorably or unfavorably. This is much higher than conscience, for while conscience gives one the best in oneself, the illuminated heart can receive even the best that is in God.

Meditation is the suppression of all conscious personal thought and feeling. It is not the prevention of consciousness, feeling and thought. The conditions of Allah are these: That He became aware of Himself (Wahdat); that He gave rise to Love and all feelings because of this awareness (Wahdaniat); that He brought this consciousness to the surface through thought and so projected the created worlds.

Man, through habit, perceives the outer world and then carries that experience inward to his mind and then carries the thought deep into his heart. This can be regarded as the opposite of the Divine activity, but really it is the reciprocal. From the condition called Wahdaniat come all activities of Sifat, which manifest in all forms. It is only the power of spirit which makes this possible. While spirit condenses, so to speak, in matter, matter also etherializes into spirit. When man transforms action into thought, he does it, and when he transmutes action or thought into feeling, he does it still more.

From the cosmic view it can be seen that all this work of man transmuting action into thought and action or thought into feeling is

Document: O.t. See Introduction to Gita Dhyana, p. 219

nothing but the reciprocal method Allah has used to bring spirit back to spirit, after it has entered the dense condition of matter. In other words, all this comes from the Divine Inhalation and Exhalation by which vibrations become coarse when passing from the One to the many and become fine again in passing from the many toward the One.

Even animal bodies are too coarse to complete this refinement. Only in man, the hu-man, is it possible, and only then when man has perceived this special union with God, which was true all the time, only the truth had not *embedded* itself in his consciousness. In his spiritual awakening he realizes this and so serves as the means by which the spirit can return to God Who gave it, as the Bible and Qur'an teach.

So while Meditation may be considered as the means by which man returns to God, as the means by which matter is retransformed into spirit, as the means by which the cosmic balance and reciprocal activities and mechanics are maintained, in its final aspect it is the means by which God returns to God, by which Sifat is permanently united to the Zat and the ultimate and absolute Unity of the Cosmos eternally maintained.

For circulation among the Members of the A.S.C. ONLY.

From a newspaper, the *American* of Philadelphia, no date.

Philadelphia, May[1]

The philosophies of the orient and the occident which have as their basic principles the rendition of service to man and the spreading of the gospel of love and understanding, while necessarily similar in essence, are expressed in widely different ways, *he said*.

"In America we find this philosophy finding expression chiefly in big business and thru such organizations as your Rotary clubs. In other words, it is expressed in action. In India our great philosophers are poets and mystics. They mix little with the world of business."

"Each of these schools could learn much from the other. Perhaps you in America have got a little too far away from the more ascetic side of the philosophy, while we in India have, perhaps, lost touch with the material. A welding of the two schools into one thru an interassociation of ideas and methods of expression would result greatly to the benefit of both and would hasten the coming of world-wide understanding and co-operation."

Note:

1. This article seems to be based on a personal interview on 30 or 31 May, the two days Pir-o-Murshid Inayat Khan is known to have been in Philadelphia.

From a newspaper, name unknown, Philadelphia, 2 June 1923.

Philadelphia, May 31[1]

Commercialism is ruling the art of America and the progress of music, art and literature, including the stage, follow the desire of the masses rather than setting a standard for the masses to live up to, *according to Pir-o-Murshid Inayat Khan ....*

He holds the individual as the panacea for the evils of the future. *He...explains that* the ultimate salvation of the world lies in the inherent good of individual humanity.

He sees America as a pleasure-seeking Nation, childish and playful. "I find among the people here a gayety of life and a desire to do good. The nation is filled with people of open minds. This spirit of pleasure seeking means a prosperous country."

"It is the individuals of the country that count. They are ultimately responsible for the action of the Nation as a political entity. We can trust to the goodness of the human soul and we can reach far."

"I have visited your playhouses and find that though art is good here, there is a bowing to these things that the masses will like, and therefore will succeed financially. That is a fault which gives too much of a tendency to commercialism, but which will be corrected as the Nation ages."

"The United States is an example of how the humans can live in accord without the national strife and interracial feeling that is seen in Europe. It is an example for the world, and when the power of the individual rises to its height in Europe it will live in a like peaceful manner."

Note:

1. From an interview.

A photocopy of an old typescript.

New York, June 1st, 1923[1]

The Path of Initiation.

There is very much written and very much said about the Path of Initiation, and people who have touched different schools of occultism have understood it differently, and have different ideas as to initiation. But when one considers the word initiation, it only means a step forward, which can be taken with hope and with courage. For without courage and without hope it would be most difficult to take a step forward.

If I were asked to explain the meaning of initiation in plain words, I should say, it is like when a person who has never known how to swim, for the first time takes a step into the river or into the sea, and does not know whether he will swim or whether he will be swept off. Every person has an initiation in the worldly sense in some form or other. The business man when he begins a new enterprise, something which he has never done before, and there is something new he wants to bring into it, and there is nothing else to support him, except that at this moment he thinks, "no matter whether it is loss or gain, I will take a step forward, I will go into this enterprise, and I do not know what will happen afterwards." He has gone into a worldly initiation. And a person who wants to learn to ride, and he has never before been on horseback, he has never controlled a horse and does not know where the horse will take him, he has never had the practice, and therefore his first attempt of riding on the horse is an initiation.

But initiation in the real sense of the word, of the word as it is used in the spiritual path, that initiation is, when a person in spite of having a religion and belief, an idea, an opinion about spiritual things, in spite of all this, he thinks that he can take a step in a direction which he does not know, so when he takes the first step, that is an initiation. Gazzali, a great

Document:

"O.t." (a photocopy of an old typescript from the United States, where the lecture was given and from which it passed on to International Headquarters in Geneva.

The lecture has been published in *The Sufi Message of Hazrat Inayat Khan*, Volume X (1964), with many omissions, additions and changes.

Notes:

1. At the bottom of the "o.t." appears the following note: "Given at the Sufi Center in New York, June 1st, 1923. Written down by Khushi Marya Cushing".
After having been initiated by Pir-o-Murshid Inayat Khan at Suresnes in 1922 during the Summer School, Mrs. Marya Cushing (Khushi) helped to organize Pir-o-Murshid's tour through the United States in 1923, and she had formed a group of interested students in New York.

Sufi writer of Persia, has said that entering the spiritual path is just like aiming an arrow at a point which one does not see, so that one does not know what it is going to hit. One only knows his own action, and does not see the point aimed at. Therefore the path of initiation is difficult for a worldly man. Human nature is such that a man born in this world, and who has become acquainted with the life of names and forms, he wants to know everything by name and form, he wants to touch something in order to know that it exists; it must make an appeal to some of his physical senses before he thinks that something exists; without that he does not think anything can exist. Therefore for him to take an initiation on a path which does not touch any senses is difficult. He does not know where he is going. And besides this, man has been taught from his childhood a certain faith and a certain belief and he feels himself so bound to that particular faith or religion that he trembles at every step that he may have to take, which may seem perhaps for a moment different or in a contrary direction to what he has been taught. Therefore to take the first step in the path of initiation for a thoughtful person is difficult. Of course a person who is driven by curiosity may jump into anything, but to him, whether he has initiation or not, both are the same. To one who goes seriously into initiation, the first step is the most difficult.

Initiations, according to the mystics, are twelve, divided into four stages; just like the twelve semi-tones in the octave, or the twelve drums in the ear. The first three initiations are the first three steps, taken with the help of a guide on the earth, whom one calls in the Sufi terms a Murshid, a teacher. In Vedantic terms he is called a Guru, a teacher. It is someone who is walking on the earth, someone who is a human being and who is placed in the same situation as everyone else, in the midst of the active life and subject to all tests and troubles and difficulties as everybody else; and therefore the help of a friend who is a human being is the first and most important step on these first three stages of the path.

In the East you will rarely find a person taking the spiritual path without the guidance of a teacher, for it is to them an accepted fact that it is most necessary that these first three steps at least be taken by the help of someone living on the earth a human life. And when we trace in the traditions we find that all the great prophets and masters and saints and sages, however great, they had an initiator. In the life of Jesus Christ one reads that he was baptized by John the Baptist, and in the lives of all great prophets and seers there is always someone, however humble or modest or human, and very often not at all to be compared with the greatness of those prophets, but at the same time, there was someone who first took these three steps with them. The mother is really the first initiator of all the prophets and teachers in the world; no prophet or teacher, however great, no saint, has been born who has walked alone without the help of the mother, she had to show him how to walk. Therefore it is only a wise thing to take the help of a Guru on the path of Truth.

Then there comes the question of how to find the real Guru. Very often people are in doubt, they do not know whether the Guru they see is a true Guru or a false Guru. Very often a person comes into contact with a false Guru in this world where there is so much falsehood. But at the same time I am sure that a real seeker, who is not false to himself, will always meet with the truth, with the real, because it is his own real, sincere faith, his own real sincerity in earnestly seeking that will become his torch. The real teacher is within, that lover of reality is one's own sincere self, and if one is really seeking Truth, one will certainly find, sooner or later, a true teacher. And suppose if one came into contact with a false teacher, what then? Then the real One will turn the false teacher also into a real teacher, because reality is greater than falsehood.

There is a story, told about a dervish, a simple man, who was initiated by a teacher, and that teacher passed away, and that man came into contact with some clairvoyant, who asked him if he had guidance on his path. The man replied, "yes, my Master, who passed from this earth. I had for some time his guidance when he was living, and now what I want is just a blessing of someone like you." But the clairvoyant said: "I see by my clairvoyant power that the teacher that has passed away was not a true teacher." When this simple man heard that, he would not allow himself to be angry with him, but he gently said: "this teacher of mine may by false, but my faith is not false, and that is sufficient." As there is water in the bottom of the earth so there is truth at the bottom of all things, false or true. In some places you have to dig deep, in some places only a little, that is the only difference, but there is no place where there is no water. You may have to dig very, very deep in order to get it, but in the depths of the earth there is water, and in the depth of all this falsehood which is on the surface, there is truth, and if we were seeking for the truth we shall always find it some time or another.

When one wants to protect oneself from being misguided he shows a tendency, a kind of weakness that he thinks in himself there is no right guidance. If he realizes that in himself there is right guidance he will always be rightly guided, and his power will become so great that if his guide is going wrong, the power of the pupil will help him to go right, because the real Teacher is in the heart of man. The outward teacher is a sign. The Persian poet has said that the one who is a lost soul, even if he be with a Savior he will be just the same, because his own clouds are surrounding him. It is not a question of a guide or teacher; the obscurity which his own mind creates surrounds him and keeps him blind. What can a teacher do?

There is a story of the Prophet Mohammed, that living next to his house there was a man who was very much opposed to the Prophet and talked against him, but he saw that the people to whom he spoke had belief in the Prophet, and nobody had in him. Then years passed, and many believed and many gave their life for the Message of the Prophet. And it so happened that there came a time when there were hundreds and thousands of people coming from hundreds of miles, thousands and thousands, from different countries to pay a visit to the Prophet, and that man still lived in the neighbourhood, but he had never discarded his opinion once formed. And one day someone asked the Prophet, "What is the reason when this man has seen a day when nobody listened, when nobody adhered, and he has seen the time when thousands of people have been benefitted, and those who come here are filled with bliss and joy and blessing, and that this man next door always criticises, always opposes." And the Prophet said, "His heart has become a fountain of obscurity; he produces from his own self the clouds which surround him; he cannot see." And he was sorry for him. The idea is that that perception of the light shows the thinning of the veil that covers the heart, and the more the veil becomes thin, the greater becomes the power of the light within to illuminate.

The next step, the second step in initiation, is to go through the tests that the teacher gives. In this initiation there is a great deal that is amusing, if one thinks about it. It is like looping the loop; sometimes the teacher gives such tests to the pupil that the pupil does not know where he is; whether this is true, or this is false. For example, I will tell you, there was a great Sufi teacher in India, a Chishti and he had a thousand adherents who were most devoted pupils, and one day he said to them: "I have changed my mind." And the words "changed my mind" made them so surprised, - they thought then[2] our teacher has changed his mind, what is the matter?" And they asked him, "what is the matter, how have you changed your mind?" He said, "Now I am beginning to feel that I must go and bow before the Goddess Kali." And these people, among whom there were doctors and professors, well qualified people, could not understand this whim, that their great teacher in whom they had such faith, wished to go into the temple of the Goddess Kali and bow before the Goddess of the hideous face, - a God-realized man, in whom they had such confidence! And the thousand disciples went away at once, thinking: "What is this? - it is against the religion of the Formless God, against the position of this great Sufi, that he wants to worship the Goddess Kali." And there remained only one pupil, a youth who was very devoted to his teacher. He followed his teacher when he went to the temple of Kali. The teacher was very glad to get rid of these thousand pupils, who were full of knowledge, full of their learning, and who did not really know him, it was just as well that they should go. And as they were going towards the temple of Kali, he had spoken to this young man three times, saying: "Why do you not go? Look at these thousand people, who had such faith and such admiration, and now I have said just one word, and they have left me. Why do you not go with them? The majority is right." But this pupil would not go, but followed him. And the teacher had such a revelation and inspiration in all this, to see how strange human nature is, how soon they are attracted and how soon they can fly away, it was such an interesting phenomenon for him to see the play of human nature, that he was full of feeling, and when they arrived at the temple of Kali he had such an

2. It is not clear if the word "then" refers to "thought" or to "our teacher has changed...".

ecstasy that he fell down and bowed his head low. And the young man who followed him did the same. And when he got up he asked this young man: "Why do you not leave when you have seen a thousand people go away, why do you follow me?" The young man answered: "There is nothing in what you have done that is against my realisation, because the first lesson you taught me was that 'Nothing exists, save God'. If that is true, then that is not Kali, that is God also. What does it matter whether you bow to the east or to the west or to the earth or to heaven, when nothing exists except God, then there is nobody else except God to whom to bow, even in bowing to Kali. It was your first lesson to me." All these learned men were given the same lesson, they were students and very clever in these things, but they could not conceive of that main thought, which was the center of all the teaching. It was this same young man who became then the greatest teacher in India, Moinuddin Chishti. To his tomb at Ajmer every year thousands of people of all religions make pilgrimages, Hindus, Mohammedans, Jews and Christians. For the Sufi all religions are one.

There are tests of many kinds that the teacher may give to his pupil, to test his faith, his sincerity, his patience. The reason is that before the ship starts to go out into the sea the superintendent first goes and sees whether every screw is right before starting the voyage, and that is the duty of the teacher. Of course it is a very interesting duty. Besides that the path of the mystic is a very complex path. What he says perhaps has two meanings: the outer meaning is one and the inner meaning is another. What he does has perhaps two meanings, an outer and an inner meaning, and a person who only sees things outwardly cannot perceive the inner meaning. He cannot understand his action, his thought, his speech, his movement, what he means by it, because he only sees the outer. And in this way the pupil is tested.

There is another example that is given in the mystic books of the East, the example of Moses. One day Moses was walking with his teacher and guide, and there they saw a mother sitting on the bank of the river, and a child that was playing there suddenly fell into the water and got caught by the waves and was being drowned. And Moses called out to his teacher to extend his arm of might to save this child, and exclaimed "This child is being drowned." The teacher did not say one word. He did not make one move. Moses thought, "How unkind, what kind of a person is my teacher; are we learning wisdom from him, - he is not even moved by this accident, he is walking there calmly and not even answering." They went a little further, and there was a boat with some people in it, and there was something broken in the boat and the water was coming into it and the people were being drowned. And Moses said, "O do something to save the people in this boat." But the teacher did not even answer. Moses could not understand that this was a mystical lesson. And when Moses spoke about it, the teacher said: "I told you the first lesson was to be quiet." Moses said: "how could I be quiet when a child was drowning?" The teacher said: "Are you learning mysticism?

I gave you your first lesson to be quiet." After some time the teacher gave him the explanation, when the time came, why he did not save the child, and showed him the reason behind it, and how just was the scheme of Nature behind all this, and where there was a greater power there was a greater insight; with the power there was insight. As the teacher had the power, he could have saved, but at the same time he had a greater insight into what was meant by it. And therefore very often to the pupil the teacher may appear to be very unreasonable, very odd, often very meaningless, very often unkind and cold and unjust. And during these tests if the faith and the trust of the pupil do not endure from the second initiation he will step backward, but if he endures through all this, then there comes the third step, the third initiation.

The third initiation contains three stages: Receiving the knowledge attentively, contemplating upon all one has received patiently; assimilating all the outcome of it intelligently. Thereby the mission of the teacher in this world is finished. Gratitude still remains, but his principal work is finished.

The fourth initiation which the seeker gets is from his ideal. And if you ask me who is this ideal, who can give that, the answer is that no living creature on earth, however great, can prove to be the ideal of anyone else. Yes, for a time he may be, but not for always. The great ones like Buddha, Zoroaster, Christ and Krishna who have been the ideal of humanity for thousands of years, when did they become the ideal? During their lifetime? No. Yes, during their lifetime they gave a sense of being the ideal, they left impressions that afterwards proved them to be ideals, but in their lifetime they could not prove to be the ideal. And what is the reason? The reason is that even perfect man is limited in that imperfect garb of humanity. The human limitation covers perfection. However great, however deep, however spiritual a person is, with all his goodness, with all his inspiration and power he is limited. His thought, speech, word, his action, everything is limited. A man cannot make himself as the imagination of his pupil. Imagination goes further than the progress of man; the imagination of every person is his own, and therefore one can only make one's ideal oneself. No one has the power to make the ideal of another person, and therefore the great Saviours of humanity, it is their impression, it is their goodness, it is what little seed of an ideal they left behind them that became just like a little grain, and that grain put into the soil of a devotee's heart developed into a plant and bore fruits and flowers as it was reared. Therefore in this fourth initiation there is that ideal of man's imagination. He may call it Christ or Buddha, he may call it Mohammed or Moses or Zoroaster; it is his ideal; it is he who has made it; it is his Saviour, and certainly it will save him if he considers him his Saviour. But he has to make it; if he does not make it, the Saviour will not save him. He must make it his Saviour. When once he has made his Saviour then he is face to face with that perfection which his heart has created, that impression of Christ or Buddha which he has taken in himself has now flowered and grown into the form of a tree, and bears the flowers and fruits which he has desired. No doubt this initiation is a phenomenon in itself. If once this initiation is received man begins to radiate, to radiate his Initiator Who is within him in this ideal.

And there is the second step which is the fifth initiation. In the fifth initiation man does not imagine his ideal, but man finds his ideal a living entity within himself, a friend who is always close to him, within him; he can just bow his head and see his friend, - he is there. To the real devotees of Christ, Christ is near, as near as they are to themselves, their own self. In their time of trouble, in their difficulty, always he is there.

The third stage, which is the sixth initiation, is the one where Christ then speaks, where Christ then acts; their acts become the actions of Christ, their speech becomes the speech of Christ. And when one arrived at that initiation one need not declare before humanity how greatly he loves his Lord, or Saviour, or Master, he becomes a proof himself, his life is the proof, his word, his action, his feeling, his attitude, his outlook. And, friends, life is such that no falsehood, no pretence, can endure, nothing false can go far; it will only go a step and tumble down; it is only the real which will go on, and the[3] real, the less it expresses itself. It is the lack of reality that makes a person express "I am so and so," "I have such great love for God," and "I am so spiritual" or "pious" or "so clairvoyant" or "I have such psychic power" or "I say that [4] that." When one sees one does not need to say that he sees, everybody sees that he has the sight. If one's eyes are closed then such a one tries to say "I see," although the eyes are closed. But when the eyes are open one need not say one sees. How difficult it is today, when so many people ask "are you clairvoyant, can you see?" And what do they see? They have perhaps seen some colour or some light here and there, or something peculiar, which means nothing. Perhaps it is their imagination. And then there are others who encourage them [4] make them more [5]. In this way the man of the spiritual path is being spoiled; people feed their pride by telling how much they see. When one begins to see one cannot say it; it is something which cannot be said. How can you say it? When you see with the eyes of Christ you can only see, you cannot say; when you hear with the ears of Christ you can only hear; there is nothing to be said.

The further initiation, which is the seventh, is the initiation in God. There is an account in the story of Rabia, a great Sufi. She once saw in her vision the Prophet, and the Prophet asked her, "Rabia, to whom have you given your devotion?" And Rabia said: "To God." And the Prophet said: "Not to me?" Rabia said: "Yes, Prophet, you include God, but it is God." There

3. One illegible word before "real", which may be "more"
4. One word illegible at the end of a line of the photocopy, which could be "and"
5. One word unclear, probably "mad"

comes a stage where a person rises above even the ideal he has [6]. He rises to that perfect Ideal Who is beyond the human personality, Who is a perfect Being, because every human personality has a limitation. And therefore in this initiation one rises to the spheres where one sees no other than God.

And in the second stage to it, which is the eighth initiation, is when one communicates with God, so that God becomes to him a living entity; God is no longer an ideal or an imagination; God is no longer one whom he has made, but the one Whom he has once made has now become alive, a living God. Before that there was a belief in God, there was a worship for Him; perhaps He was made in the imagination, but in that stage God becomes living. And what phenomenon this shows! This faith and this stage is a miracle in itself. The God-realized person need not speak or discuss the name of God; the godly person's presence will inspire God in every being, a godly person's presence will charge the atmosphere with the sense of God. Every person that comes spiritual or moral or religious, or the one who has no religion, he will feel God in some form or other. The prophets and the holy ones who have come from time to time to give to the world some religion, some ideal, they have not brought any new ideas, they have not brought a new belief in God, because belief in God has always existed in some form or other. What they brought was a living God. When there only remained God's name in the scripture or in the people's imagination, or on the lips of the followers of a certain religion, and when that name began to become a profane name, a vain repetition, then such souls have been born on the earth and they have brought with them a living God; if they gave to humanity anything else besides, law and ethics and morals, they were secondary. The principal thing that they gave to the world was a living God.

And the ninth initiation is what in the Sufi terms is called Akhlak Allah, which means the manner of God. A person who touches that plane or that realization expresses in his manner the manner of God; his outlook in life is God's outlook, his action, his thought, his word is God's action, thought and word. Therefore the prophets who came at different times said that this is Kalam-Ulla which means "the word of God," just like the word "Bhagavad Gita" means "The Song Celestial." Why? Because at that stage God himself speaks. Those persons turned into that Perfect Spirit, and moved by that Perfect Spirit they acted, for their action is no longer their own action, - it is the action of God. Their word is no longer a human word, it is the word of God.

And the last three initiations, of course very few arrive in their lifetime to touch them, because after these nine initiations then begins what are called the phase of Self-Realisation. Those who have not yet arrived at that, when they begin to declare such affirmations as "I am God," and "We are Gods," they are nothing but vain repetitions, they spoil the God-Ideal. They do not know what they are saying. If we only knew that to say every

6. One word unclear, probably "made"

such word we ought to be authorized, we ought to be entitled to say it, - if we only knew, we would be very careful what we say. But it is that stage, after having gone through all these different stages of consciousness, when one arrives at that stage one can speak very little, because it is the Self-expression. It is beyond the stage of religion and even God-action, it is the stage of Self-expression. But that stage of Self-expression comes when a person has thoroughly dug himself out deeply, so that nothing of himself has remained but that divine substance, then alone he is authorized to express himself. And therefore the ninth initiation is the awakening of the real Self, the real Ego. Therefore this comes by meditation, the meditation which makes one forget one's false self, one's limited self, one's small self. The more one is able to forget it, the more that Self awakens. And in the next stage a sense of splendour comes. In the Persian language it is called Hyra ....[7] It is the same stage as when a child is born and he begins to see everything so new, - this old world, which one has gone through, - and he now begins a new world again. As soon as the point of view is changed by the help of meditation, all this world which is before everybody and which everybody is seeing, one sees it quite differently. One begins to see reason behind reason, one begins to see cause behind cause, and one's point of view also changes for the religion. It changes because for the same thing, for one action for which the average man would accuse, would want to punish a person, would want to blame a person, the soul who has risen to that, neither can he judge nor can he blame, he only sees, but he sees the cause behind the cause. Now whom shall he accuse, whom shall he blame? How can he keep from forgiving, whatever be the fault, because he sees what is behind the fault, he sees the reason there, - perhaps a greater reason than the person sees who has committed the fault. Therefore, naturally, all that manner, the manner of continually sacrificing, the manner of spontaneous love and sympathy, the manner of respect for the wise and for the foolish, and for the deserving and the undeserving, this all comes and expresses as divine life, and it is at that stage that the human soul touches perfection and becomes divine and does fulfil its real purpose in life.

---

7. The word "Hyra" and the sentence appears to be unfinished. Possibly "Hayrat" is meant, meaning bewilderment (see Glossary).

A typescript of unknown origin (Tp.c.)

New York, Sufi Centre.
Between June 1st and 7th, 1923

Self-Realization.

Many people claim that self-realization is the ultimate attainment of Truth, or the attainment of God; but I think it is not by selfrealization that God is attained; it is by God-realization that the real self is attained. Although it is only a twist of words, in point of fact both ideals mean the same.

Many think that self-realization may be learned, but really speaking every person in this world, in whatever he is doing, whether right or wrong, or good or bad, he is treading the same path, which may be called selfrealization. If a person is doing good, he is realizing the self, if he is doing wrong he is realizing the self too. He is seeing in this life what horrible effects his life produces, what results his actions, his attitude produce. Therefore both realize self just the same. Self-realization is nothing but projecting the self before one, and looking at it. That is self-realization which everybody does. An artist realizes self by putting his heart and soul into his art; he produces it before him, and so he sees the colour and the beauty and the genius that was hidden in him reproduced before him, and it gives him a satisfaction. A singer realizes his self when he sings, and when he hears his voice and it pleases him and inspires him, in that he realizes the fulfilment of his being born on earth. A person who has the desire to do good, he realizes himself in his good actions. Every little good he does, that

Documents:

D.tp. (a draught, rather poorly typed, of the tp.c.).
Tp.c. (a typescript of unknown origin).
Km.t. (a typewritten copy made by Km. from the tp.c. with some errors corrected).

Between June 1st and 7th, 1923, a series of lectures was given at the Sufi Centre in New York on the subject of "Self-realization," which may have been taken down in sh. by Khushi Marya Cushing. She took down another lecture, given at the same place on June 1st, 1923 (The Path of Initiation).

The typescripts in the archives present the teachings on "Self-realization" as one long lecture; however, since Pir-o-Murshid seldom gave lectures of such length, and since the date written above is "between June 1st and 7th," the typescripts must combine lectures on the same topic given over several different days. The breaks between the lectures seem to come at the following points:

par. 7: "All fear and confusion...",
par. 11: "All these different religions...",
par. 14: "What is wanted to-day...".

brings to him a new joy and a new happiness, it produces in him that satisfaction which his soul is looking for, and that comes out of self-realization. When a person goes wrong and he does wrong in this life, by that wrong he realizes the self; he sees where he was wrong, and what was its effect. By his own dissatisfaction and by the outcome of that wrong he has realized the self. He begins to know, if he has some sense, that: Myself does not choose that effect, although the action I have done, by its results it is not desirable. Therefore the next time he chooses a better way and a different way. If he does not trouble about it then he goes on the wrong path until that experience comes, when he says: No, myself has not sought that path, myself always sought a path which not only in the beginning was pleasant, but which is pleasant as well in its results. That is the self-realization. Self-realization is to allow that beauty, that harmony, that love, that kindness which is hidden in us to manifest and when it has manifested through the form of art, or science, or one's action in life, or one's manner, or one's attitude, or everything one does, one sees oneself produced before him and that is what causes his satisfaction.

And again, you will see people depressed and in despair, people sorry and worried about nothing, and if you ask them, they will give you a thousand reasons for their distress. And yet they do not know what is the real reason for their distress. There is only one reason behind it all, although outwardly there seem to be many different reasons, and that one reason is that either the condition of life, or some situation in life, or something has hindered the path of their self-realization. All that is there in the realm of beauty, or goodness, or manner, or the tendency to love or to be loved, or the desire to do something, to express something, has been choked. There are a thousand forms in which that self-realization might take place, and yet it may not happen. And the person may begin to feel uncomfortable, because the soul has come upon the earth for that reason, -- its one desire is to realize itself. Whether it be a material person or a spiritual person, or whatever be the character of a man's evolution, his innermost ideal, his continual craving, his greatest longing and desire is to realize self. He does not say it in those words, but it is so just the same.

A person will realize the self in the form of vanity, in the desire that he must have such a position, and when he has come to that position, there comes a satisfaction to him, and he thinks: "I have arrived at this position where I wanted to be." That is again a form of selfrealization. A person thinks: "I must learn so much." After having acquired that knowledge he thinks he has realized the self also. Another person thinks he must be so rich, or must have such an environment, position or rank in life, or do something good or bad in life, -- whatever be his conception. But at the same time, the ideal behind it all is the same, -- the self-realization; and it is in something that man has left after coming into this world, -- it is the nature of the soul, it is the innate nature of God.

And again, with all the desire of realizing the self, and with every effect[1] that man makes in accomplishing that idea, there always remains something missing in his life. And what is it that is missing? It is the true self-realization. Although man realizes self in the different expressions of his mind and heart, the soul is not realized fully, because the manner of realizing the self is different. As man begins to realize the self outwardly, so man goes further and further away from the self. When a person says, (and naturally every person thinks in that way) for instance, when a person is in a palace, in beautiful surroundings, all that is there is inspiring him with the idea of riches and grandeur. He naturally begins to think: "I am rich." He does not know that he is not rich, but it is the environment that is rich, yet he begins to think at once that he is rich. It is so intoxicating, that he does not stop to think that it is not so. As soon as one is brought into a richer, better surrounding, he feels the riches and grandeur. It seems that everything that is there impresses him so much that it intoxicates him entirely, and makes him feel he is a different person altogether. And when a person finds himself in rags he begins to think he is poor. In reality his rags are poor, not he. If he knew what he is! And as the poor rags make him feel poor, and as the palaces make him feel rich, that shows how man lives day after day far removed from self-realization, -- always living in the circumstances before him, what is around him, always impressed by what he is looking at, what he is conscious of, and always unconscious of what he himself is. No doubt, it is not his fault; it is the nature of life, the illusive nature of life which is called by the Hindus "the amazing[2] Maya." It is such that if once we stop to think about it, we shall find that there is not one single moment that this illusive life, full of falsehood, allows a person to rest and think of himself. It is constantly there to make him unaware of himself, that man may always remain far apart from his own self, ignorant of his true self. And therefore, all doubts and confusions and all worries, all ignorance, every kind of despair and distress, and the lack of power and of inspiration, all is caused by the lack of that true self-realization.

There is a very interesting story often told in the East. Once a lion was roaming in the wilderness, and came upon a flock of sheep, and to his very great surprise in this flock there was a young lion running about. It happened that this young lion had been taken in its infancy and brought up among the sheep. What amazed the lion the most was that this little lion became frightened too and began to run away. Then the lion forgot all about the sheep and just went after the little lion and all the sheep ran away, and this little lion was caught by the big one, and stood there frightened and trembling. And the big lion said: "What are you, my son, why are you so afraid of me?" The young lion tremblingly said: "Oh, I am frightened; I am a sheep, I am afraid of you. I have never seen you before." The lion

---

Notes:

1. D.tp., Km.t.: "effort"
2. Km.t.: "mazing"

said: "Certainly you are not a sheep, you are a lion." "Oh," the young one said, "no, no, I am a sheep, let me go among the other sheep; I am afraid of you." The lion said: "I will not let you go unless you see for yourself that you are a lion. Come with me." So that young lion, trembling for his life had to walk with that big lion, until they came to a pool of water. And the big lion said: "Now you look into the water, and then look at me, and then look at yourself; if the likeness is the same, then you are a lion also, you are not a sheep." And the more the young lion looked into the water, the more he saw that yes, he was not a sheep, he was a lion, although a small one, but yet he was a lion. And all his fear then disappeared and the young lion went happily away.

All fear and confusion is the outcome of ignorance of the self, and all the wisdom and happiness and every kind of bliss is in the realization of self. But when a person opens his eyes and looks out and does not see what he is, then, as the nature of his being is like a mirror, according to the Persian mystics, therefore in this mirror becomes reflected all that is exposed to it. And therefore the[3] mirror-like soul begins to say that, "I am that which is exposed before me or what I reflect." It does not know that "if I reflect something it must not necessarily be myself." If the mirror reflects somebody's face, it does not mean that the mirror is that person; the mirror is the mirror; the person is the person; but for that moment the mirror is reflecting it. It is a very great point that sometimes intellectual people interested in the study of metaphysics or philosophy, become so interested in the metaphysical side of it and want to find out the reason of everything, that they find everything but themselves. All the events of the past life and all the conditions of the future life, and all the names of different planes, colours and spirits and everything, and all the names of elementals, and if there is anything remaining it is the self, -- all else is found. And they are so contented and pleased with the knowledge that they think that is all the knowledge there is and there is nothing more to be learned. But at the same time there is a continual craving to learn and know and understand something, -- they cannot find where it is or what it is; and if they are digging they are digging in the same direction in which they have been digging. They have found something, which appeals to their reason, and they wonder if they could find something more. They think it is an added knowledge. If one only knew that self-realization cannot be an added knowledge; it is the original knowledge. It is not a knowledge which is acquired; it is knowledge which is there already. One has to find it; it is something to discover; it is not something to attain. If a person will go on attaining for thousands of years he will not attain to it, because it is something to be discovered. It is, really speaking, the uncovering of the self-knowledge that is the discovering of the Divine Knowledge.

And now the question comes: How can one attain to it? What is the way of attainment to that self-knowledge? It must be attained by a contrary process, -- by the process, not of learning, but by the process of unlearning.

3. D.tp., Km.t.: "this"

There are some who are born with that attitude; they are born mystics. Their soul has that attitude from the beginning. And there are others who have to find it, who have to attain to it. But at the same time the longing is in every heart.

There is an interesting story told of a Master, a well-known Sufi, in the Punjab. He was a born mystic. And when he was a very young child, he was sent to school. The first lesson they teach is the lesson of the figures. And the first character given is the straight line, which makes o n e, and which is called in the Eastern language "~~Aleph~~" "Alif"[4], the first letter. And this child, the same as all the children, had this letter given to him. All the other children learned five or six letters at the same time, but that child continued with the first letter. And when the teacher asked, "Have you finished with that, shall I give you another?" he said, "No, I have not yet finished. So the teacher did not give him any other lesson that day. And the next day the child again replied that he had not yet finished with that figure. And so it went on for a whole week, and the teacher could not understand it, and he said to the parents: "I do not think this child will learn anything, please take him home." And at home the parents began to be annoyed with him also, thinking that he did not learn what he ought to learn. And as the child grew, the dissatisfaction of the parents and the conditions at home made him go away from home. But he did not forget the lesson the teacher had given him. And he lived in the solitude of the forests in different places. After many years when he had grown up, he had developed a wonderful personality. Then he went back to his village, and his great desire was to visit the old school and the old teacher, who happened to be still there. And he went and saluted the teacher very humbly, but the teacher did not recognize him, so he said, "I am that same pupil of yours who could not learn anything more." The teacher was amused, but very glad to see him. Then he asked the teacher if there was anything else to learn, because now he was beginning to understand the first lesson. The teacher was impressed by this developed personality saying such a thing, because now this person was a power in himself. He said, "If you wish, I shall write the lesson on the wall." And he made a sign on the wall and the wall divided in two, making one line of the figure he had written. The teacher seeing the miracle, bowed before him. He said, "Do not bow, you are my teacher, you have taught me the first lesson. But after that first lesson I have not found that there is any second lesson to learn. That is the first lesson and the last lesson."

If the sacred scriptures, the Vedas, have taught anything, it is that there are not two, but only one, the Only Being. If any prophet or any seer or any religion, if Jesus Christ has taught anything, it was Unity. And so it was, time after time, when religion was presented in different forms, when man's ideal seemed to have disappeared. Since it is the natural tendency of man to realize the self in the outer life, so he has forgotten that oneness,

4. D.tp., tp.c.: "Aleph", afterwards changed by Sk. to "Alif"; Km.t.: "Aleph"

and becomes[5] interested in the duality of life, and his search for something that his soul is craving, continues in a direction in which he will never find it, and that is the direction of duality. And there is a reason. The reason is that the direction of duality has for some time a great interest for a person. But although duality is very pleasing, duality is not satisfaction. Satisfaction is found in unity. In duality there is pleasure, and as long as man has not distinguished between pleasure and satisfaction he will not enjoy the truth that unity gives.

All these different religions that we have to-day in the world and again in every religion so many different sects and churches, each thinking that the other is wrong, and everyone thinking that their own particular idea is right, -- in this way the world is going on, and humanity is going on, everyone thinking that they are pious and they have a religion and they have a belief, -- if we only knew that the religion, or belief, or church, or community, or sect, that these things cover the soul and prevent it from finding the ultimate Truth, -- the Truth which alone is the Saviour, the Truth which alone is God, the Truth which alone is all the satisfaction there is, and all the treasure that man has to attain. And all the power and inspiration and all that man requires, it is there in the Truth. And still man wonders, and people dispute over their religious beliefs and faiths, and their sects and communities. Think of how many battles have been fought in all different civilizations over the religious ideas and differences of their churches. They have fought because the God of that particular people was different from the God of the others; because their Saviour or Lord was different from the others.

Is it not time someone could see from this point of view, from the point of view of unity, upon which the foundations of all religions have been built? And no Messenger, no Lord or Saviour, prophet or seer ever came and preached and taught humanity and elevated humanity without having been inspired by that spirit of unity, of oneness. And yet the followers of each of them have taken the words as the truth, and not what is behind the words. They have taken a particular scripture, changed perhaps a thousand times in the history of the world. That scripture was something, but not the living inspiration. They have fought those living souls who sympathized with them and gave their lives to lift them, and who sacrificed everything to go and teach them, and who have risked their lives and suffered all the tortures that could be put upon them. They have crucified and flayed them. And yet, in spite of all they have named religion or belief, and all they have called virtue, and even knowledge, -- now it seems that humanity does not awaken to understand what is beyond all sects and religions, what is behind all those different beliefs and faiths which are all different forms in which the truth is expressed, -- the one and the same truth, the realization of the one life which is beneath and beyond all beings and all things.

5. Km.t.: "become"

And if you ask me, what benefit has one, what does one gain by that realization, the answer is: That if there is any gain, it is in the realization of truth, and all the loss belongs to ignorance. If there is any phenomenon, if there is any miracle, if there is any happiness, if there is any inspiration, if there is any harmony or peace, if there is any beauty, or any great attainment to be made, it is all in the realization of truth. And imagine how man wanders away from that main thing, interested in everything else but that most important thing in life. There are many who are seeking for some power, power in order to attain some little worldly advantage. Whenever man realizes what power the thought of unity has, what power the realization of that oneness gives, he will not seek for limited powers, because there is the unlimited power there at hand. Or people seek for some little inspiration here and there. One can study little things, but at the same time that study cannot give that living inspiration, and in the realization of unity there is a living inspiration. As soon as one has touched it, one has touched the universal treasury. Every knowledge, the knowledge of every person, and the knowledge of all that has vanished and gone, all belongs to that soul, because that soul then touches that perfect goal in the realization of that oneness. That all the different communications that people seek for, what communication is there that is not there? Are we not in oneness? If we seem to be many, it is only the illusion of our eyes. In reality we are not many, we are the one and the only life there is. It is the realization of that oneness that will put us in connection, in contact, with all the souls there are, those who are living here and those who have passed away. The communication then is not difficult, because once you contact with the One, then you contact with all. But when a person will contact with a little drop, it does not mean that he is in contact with the ocean, he is limited and in this way we limit ourselves by our smallness of view, by our childish fancies, by our pleasure in seeing a limited horizon in life.

What is wanted to-day is to elevate one's self and the life around and about one to the higher spheres, the greater realization. What a pity it is that at this time when there is a world-awakening of people, so that there is a world-awakening in spiritual matters also, at such a time when we begin to work in the spiritual life, the first great difficulty that comes before the spiritual worker and which he has to combat, is the satisfying of these childish fancies and imaginations. And if the spiritual worker wants to make a success in his work, he cannot but feel tempted and inclined to satisfy those childish fancies, and by that I mean, to keep them asleep, to keep them interested in their childish fancies. It is just like giving the child a toy; whereas I would have given the toy and the lesson at the same time, that by that toy the child would have learned something else, instead of giving the child the toy and saying: "just play, and do not learn; it does not matter, it is your pleasure, so just play." It is true, let them play, but at the same time give them something so that by that play they may be able to realize the truth, that their play may be inspiring to them and may elevate them. If that play interests them so, that they do not want to see anything else, it is really speaking, dragging them along on a road which is not the road their soul is seeking, which is not the attainment that is for them. Therefore what is wanted to be learned is not only for those who are seeking after truth, but for those also who are working in the spiritual field, -- the lesson is for us also, because we are doing what little spiritual work we can. We are all responsible for working at this time of spiritual awakening each in our own way, doing what little we can.

The one thing we can do is to keep man away from substitutions, not to give him more substitutions, but to keep him away from them; to keep man away from dabbling in things which are not so very important, which are only amusement for him, which are like moving pictures for him; to elevate him to the higher consciousness that he may come closer and closer to the ideal he is constantly seeking for. The best means that can be adopted is the only means that has always been considered to be the best, and that means is God. To awaken man to seek God, to promote that ideal which Jesus Christ has taught when he says: "Seek ye first the Kingdom of God and all else will be added unto you." To promote that ideal let man seek first, above everything else, the God-ideal. By that I do not mean, let man believe in God. If man only believed in God he might just as well believe a thousand years in Him, he will not progress any further. No, the belief in God is not sufficient; it is only the preparatory step. It is that man must be taught the making of God. The first essential of the process is to make our God, make Him in the thoughts, make Him with your imagination, make Him with your ideal, make Him with your devotion, make Him with your service and worship; make Him with your surrender in humbleness, make Him by kneeling down before His perfect Being and humbling yourself, which is limited. And once God is made, when He is made to sit on a throne and He is crowned with God-hood, then one part of the journey is perfected. Now then another part begins. The other part is to know what relation God is to man, and how close man can be to God. Then one sees that the relation between God and man is a line; one end of the line is God, the other end of the line is man himself. The line is one; the ends are two; one end is perfect, the other end is imperfect. And when one will raise the consciousness from this imperfection and will desire to attract and come closer to that perfect Being, one will be drawn towards perfection, because the law of gravitation draws its own element. Man is made of the earth and the part of our being which belongs to the earth will be drawn by the earth. The part of our being which belongs to the soul will be drawn by that part of man's being which is his true being, which is not his coat, like the body, which is his true self, which is God Himself. And if man will raise himself and make the attempt to arise, and if he will make the inclination to go toward that perfection, he will be drawn by that perfection, because he belongs to that Perfect Being, he is the very self of that Perfect Being, and that is why God was made and worshipped. That is why, in this ideal, the purpose of life becomes fulfilled.

UNA: INTRODUCTION

The play *Una* was begun by Pir-o-Murshid Inayat Khan in June, 1923, while on board the S.S. "Olympic", returning to Europe after a tour of five months in the United States. The last two weeks in New York had been hectic, and the time on board ship was no doubt a welcome respite. Pir-o-Murshid Inayat Khan was accompanied by Mr. Fatha Engle, an American mureed who was going to Suresnes at the Pir-o-Murshid's request, and Mrs. Eggink-van Stolk, who was given the name Bhakti during this trip. The play was originally called "The Artist," and the main character called "Bhakti," certainly with Mrs. Eggink in mind, as Pir-o-Murshid also selected her to play the role in the first performance. The manuscript still exists, and contains much of the first act of the play and some of the material for the third act. Because Pir-o-Murshid made so many revisions later, it was decided to present this manuscript in a typed reproduction, so the reader would be able to see the play in this formative stage (the manuscript itself is very hard to read); this appears first following this Introduction.

When Pir-o-Murshid was back at his home in Suresnes, he dictated the play to Murshida Sophia Saintsbury Green, no doubt using the sketch he had made on shipboard. We also have this manuscript, which forms the basis for our text of Acts 1 and the earlier version of Act IV. Many revisions are evidenced in this manuscript, including the changing of the name of the main character to "Una" from "Bhakti," which was apparently considered too exotic a name for an American. Pir-o-Murshid assigned parts to various mureeds, and left it in their hands to produce the play. This was accomplished, after many rehearsals, in August of 1923, with Pir-o-Murshid Inayat Khan in attendance, and it seems to have been a great success.

Act II of the play appears suddenly in a later typescript (of which no date or provenance are known), but the language makes it clear that it was written by Pir-o-Murshid.

Act III was not yet finished in the version in Murshida Green's handwriting, and therefore we have taken a later text, which is complete, as the text for this act (though the differences from Green's manuscript are noted).

For Act IV, Green's manuscript is the basis of the first text we give; however, later, on a copy of a typescript made by Murshida Goodenough, Kismet Stam indicated the moving around of some speeches or parts of speeches, with a note "Changes dictated by Murshid" on the top, and this rearrangement has formed the basis of all subsequent texts. Because these shifts would prove impossible to follow if only shown in footnotes, it was decided to present a second version of Act IV, which, however, differs from the first version only in the order in which the lines are said.

Not long after the first performance, a discussion of the play with Pir-o-Murshid Inayat Khan took place, which Sakina Furnée took down in shorthand. For the text of this discussion, see *Complete Works of Pir-o-Murshid Hazrat Inayat Khan,* 1923 II, July-December, East-West: London and The Hague, under August 31.

[A typed reproduction of the manuscript in the hand of Pir-o-Murshid Inayat Khan, written on board ship on the way back from America in June, 1923]

UNA

Toward the one the perfection of
love harmony and beauty — The Artist
united with all the ilumminated
souls who form the embodiment
of the Master the spirit of guidance

(Bhakti-Comming to her studio)
after a long absence.

It is a breath of joy indeed to be in my studio again,
away from all the turmoil of life. It is a joy
which is beyond words, a happiness which can
-not be found else whare.
My studio has been neglected for such a long time.
I have been occupaied with no end of things, bussy
answering life's unseassing demands, but when
ever I find time any one and the only thought
is to come to the studio and be my self again.
Niether home has joy for me nor do I find happi
-ness else where. No one at home understands me
and those out side home are absorbed in thair own
lives. Every step I take I am drawn back and
from every thing I try to withdraw I am thrown
into it's very depths. While walking I find pits
on the way and by standing my legs become stag.......
The rop there is to hold breaks it is withered the
rock I find to sit upon crumbles, it is of sand
Everything I purchase costs me more than it is worth
and all that I sale I sale for nothing-
my enthusiasm is pinched at every move I make,
and my hope breaks under every blow that falls
upon it. By the pinprics I have every day in life
my heart has becom ful of wholes. I continually
experience the tragedy caussed by life's limmitations
Life, life, what a puzzle you are to me the
only distraction in life I have is my art.

(Taking the instruments in her hand)

Now my instruments you be my companians

(looking above)

The sun is glorious spreading its rays to
lift my heart to cheerfulness.

2

(a knock upon the door)

Hear! Some one is already calling even before
I started to work.

(opens the door Maya a girl)
enters-

Maya-

Hallow Bhakti dear I have been looking for you
all over the place, where have you been all this time.
Were you hidding your self from friends? But
dont we find you in the end? you cant very well
hide from us can you! Well Bhakti
darling tell me how are you getting on with your
work? (Looking at the half done statue)
Is this something that you are working with?
Dear me, what a dull occupation Cant you find
any thing else to do? (Bhakti perplexed but speech)
-less
Bhakti dear you spend hours with this
useless kind of work in this solitary studio
I cant understand how you can do it.

(Bhakti after a moments pause)

My dear girl When have I any time to work?
all day long I am bussy doing some thing at
home at night for hours I lay awake thinking
about making the ends meet. As you well know
that my parents now ancing to the age are no
longer responcible, it is I upon whom the care
of home rests.

When ever I find a spare momment I come here
to my studio and try to forget life's doing this work,
cares
the only work I live for.

Maya-My simple girl is this the work you live
for? I would not give that much for a work that
brings nothing in return. It is simply a wast of time.

~~I would~~ Bhakti A real art will never bring the

appropriate ~~rewards~~ and to exact returns ~~from~~
returns
for the art would be like bringing beauty a to
the market ~~place.~~ Maya__
I cannot understand how you can lock your self
up in this solitary studio. If I had no one arround
me to talk to life would become so monotonous
that I would not khnow what to do with it.
Bhakti-Maya my dear girl I am only happy when
I am left to be by my self. I dont need anyone
to talk ~~t~~-with, & sillence is never too long for me.
Maya-you peculiar girl you sertainly are a riddle to
solve.

3

read
Now tell me dear, did you ~~this~~ the morning gossip?

Bhakti-you know that I dont read pepers I have
much to do at home besides I am not particularly
interested in the senssational storys of the papers
announcing
~~talking about~~- some ladys death in the morning and
of the same person still living in the Evening news.
Maya-But do you know the rate of money exchange how
much our money has gone up Bhakti-It does not
make much defferance in our life we who live
hand to mouth from day to day and more over
the iedia of profitting once self by the loss of another
has ~~never appealed to me~~- more or less been foraign
to my nature. Maya-I am sure Bhakti you

do not even know the name of the mair who is very recently
ellected in our town do you? No I dont know Maya
quite another than that of your's
My dear girl I ~~do not~~- live in ~~your world~~ ^ Maya-
You sertainly are behind time. ^Last night I was invited
at the Society banquet given at Mrs. Wilkinson's every one
in the town who is some body was invited there we had
music and dance jaz playing all night long, ~~and~~ we
had lots of fun there.
We have a fancy dress ball comming next week X
the local
it will be a grand affair indeed all ^ papers are
~~mucin~~talking a lot about it.
~~speaking about it, but I am getting tired of these~~--
however
afternoon teas I can manage to go to four or five
receptions a day but I ~~indeed~~ can~~not go to all.~~
attend any more.

---

written sideways along edge

---

all comming thair will guise them selves as what thay were in thair past life

wont it be a fun?
(Bhakti smiles)
Maya-~~continues~~
You must
come to this
fun event for it
~~you will disapp~~
it will be a great
disappointment
to us all and
Bhakti dear I
know well that
you ~~do not~~ always
avoid giving
pain to any
body if you
can
possibly
avoid. ~~Good~~
you must come
now do you
promise? Yes
I know you do.

Bhakti-This kind of life is
~~It is all~~ for you big people ^ not for me. Maya-I really
wish Bhakti you were not living such a retired life
it is such a pity to be like this it is living like not
do
living, of what use is the life, if you ~~did~~ not live it.
Bhakti-I am not at all interested in the society life
it is for the fashionable people I am quite contented
Maya must
with my life as an humble artist. now I ^ leave
Bhakti dear I am sorry to have taken much of your time
from your work.
(thay kiss each other good buy)
But be sure and come: orava- and Bhakti closses the door

Bhakti (to her self) -~~Thay~~ ~~never have~~ I dont know why
me
people dont leave ~~you~~-alone, thay have thair life, I have
my own life to live I cant understand people urging
way of living others
thair own ~~life~~ upon ~~you~~. Well, I suppose that is the
way of the world.
join in ~~Society~~
Thay tell me I dont y ~~accompany~~ them ~~to~~ thair ~~balls~~
entertainments
and thearters, to me the very world is a stage, life is
unseassinly
a continual play running on ^ with its meriad
it is
varietys, old as old can be and yet ^ ever new.

4

Fancy dress ball takes place people enter Maya recieving
them in the decorated ball room. First commer
enters
Maya-who are you? I am pitter the great of Russia
Maya Welcome your majesty-the commer-and
this is the Zarina ~~and this is the cown prince~~........
Some of them anothen enters The Maharaja dhiraja
~~All~~ And who is this-I am Veer Shamsher rane
Jang Bahadoor of ~~Nepaul~~ ~~in~~ India and this
is the Maharani ~~Lilawati dhe Kitatake~~
great ....
~~dhuma Kita taka dha Maya Maj-how do you~~
Welcome Raja and Rani
~~call he? Maharaja her original title is Kidana~~
~~Kita take gathy gina dha-(Maya wh~~irls her eyes
~~and finger arround her head & says~~ Salam
to you ~~both come in~~. Another enters-All-who are
All
you I am the qeen of Sheeba- Come in come in.
of shibavery Another one enters.
queen we are glad to see you. ~~All~~-- All-
and who are you-I am the King Hwangti of China
this is wel beloved we welcome
and ~~this is~~ my queen- All-~~we bow~~ to your Majesty
All- Kind Luisse the 6th
Another enters and who is this-I am ~~the Nepolian Bonapart~~

another enters All-
~~the world conquerer~~ - and who is this ~~with you this~~
~~I am~~ she-I am the Mary Antonet-another
enters ~~??? she says~~ what is your name mari antonet
all is one already there
all ~~Woman enters~~ but she Meri I am the real Mary antonet
~~of the~~ All how can the / mari antonetenkarnet
and maybe
as two persons- ~~she is~~ rong in her memmory of
a
the past I am right-the 1st one no I am right ~~in~~
both
~~my conception you are sertainly rong~~. Thay ~~begin to~~ fight.
dear parant (?) told me that I am the Mary Antonet
All ask the Nepolian to tell who was the real
Mariantonet but Nepolian ~~him self~~ says I my
self am not quite clear in my mind about this
question then thay both fight with Nepolian untill
he runs away and all seperate them.
says
(Another enters) I am the Khesraw the great Sha of Percia
Some
Welcome your majesty welcome another I am
some one Rissen
King That the Pharoh (~~rissen from the grave~~
the night (?)
from ~~the~~ grave that was recently dug up ~~by the~~
~~his~~ up
I am under the guide of my spirit guide who was an
American Indian & had died on the battle feald he
~~is~~ always with me he never leaves me alone even
keeps ~~ever~~
~~when any~~
for a single moment. And tells me ~~every~~
~~should~~ what
~~thing I do wether I must do it or not~~ I must do &
what I must not do. if he tells me to hald ~~while ?~~ I halt
when every he tells me to obey I obey.
Maya-~~announcing ?~~
(announces) the Maharaja will sing an Indian
Song.
(He sings)
Maya (announces) The Shah will sing a percian Song.
(He sings.)
then (thay all dance.) (Thay move about ~~and~~
talking ~~and~~ another)
with one

Maya-(on one side) And when did you come
taking We did not see you comming.
Dhobi-I just came in.

Maya-what were you in your pest ~~in~~ life?

Dhobi-I dont know anything about the pest life
I only know ~~of this life~~ what I was in this life
before I entered the society- Maya-and what were
Maya-Well dont fight you are both Mary
~~ma~~ Atonets born at different times.

---

sideways

---

you will you tell me-Dhobi I was a londriman.
Have you always been a londriman Dhobi not atall before
Do
that I was a barber Maya you mean to say you began
~~to~~ your life as barber no in the beginnang ~~I was a~~
amazed life as a
chimnisweep- Maya(~~Laughed~~ much in her self) how
amusing, but how you happened to enter the Society
Dhobi-it ~~is~~ was that
during the war ~~time~~ I made ammunitions & became
rich since then every where I am ~~being~~ invited & received
in the society-but to tell you the truth I do not like
this sort of life-I feel lonesome do you know what I
would like? I would like to mary a ~~nicely~~ nice looking
young
girl , do you know what I mean I would like to mary
a real good good girl-tell me if you know of any.
already
Maya-Did you not mary before-Dhobi The Past has passed
now that
the pressent is pressant It is the future ~~to which~~ we look forward
to. Maya-Do you mean to say that you never married
before ~~I~~ Dhobi-I married twenty times before but
have
what is about it just now. Whare ~~are~~ all your wife's
gone, thay did not all die. Dhobi. I always passed
them over before thay ever did die. I can assure you
that I did not kill one but devorced them all.

---

sideways (other direction)

Marya every evening
Some-~~O what a~~ wonderful ~~open~~(?) do you go to any spit scllences yes I do
~~ever~~
how ~~you mine~~
~~welcome at~~ the home of
a trumpet medium

---

sideways

---

a most splendid medium and she gives most wonderful
magnatic treatments in one momment she can make
the pain run from head to heart. ~~and in~~ same--what
a wonderful power. Are you ~~a medium too~~ have you
pcichic
any Clarevoyant power Marya-no I have not yet
~~arrieved attained to that~~ arrieved to ~~that som~~ such
worderful attainment I am an simple ~~woman~~
ordinary person
an humble artist.

Ballroom

Maya standing at the

Entrance to recieve people as

they come.

1st	(enters)	Maya	(announces)	Pitter the great of the ĉazr of Russia.
~~2nd~~	"	"	"	~~Queen Elizabeth of England.~~
~~3rd~~	"	"	"	~~King Luisse the 6th of France.~~
4^{2}th	"	"	"	King Hawangti of China
5^{3}th	"	"	"	Khasraw the Shah of Percia
6^{4}th	"	"	"	Jung Behedonmeharaje of Nepaul
7^{5}th	"	"	"	Mary Antonet of France
8^{6}th	"	"	"	King That the Farrow of Egipt
	Some-just arose from his grave that was dug up.)			
9^{7}th	"	"	"	Mary Antonet of France

MS. Murshida Green

UNA[1]

[2]List of Characters[2]

	Character	Actor
	Una	Mrs. Eggink
	Statue	Sirdar[3]
	Helen	Mme. Lafitte
	Father[4]	Mrs. van Hoens[3]
	Ouvrier[5]	Mr. Bauer
	Aunt[6]	Mme. van Hogendorp
	King Tut	Mushraff Khan
	Queens 1 & 2[7]	Lakme[3] & Judy Sheaf
	Shah of Persia	Maheboob Khan
	Sultana	Shadi[3]
	King Akbar[8]	Ali Khan
	Queen of Sheba	G. I. L.[3]
	Snake Charmer	Saida[3]
	Greek Philosopher	Miss Hoeber[3]
	Dante	Mrs. Shemetsky
	Beatrice	Mrs. Sheaf
	American Indian	Mr. Engel
~~Hassan~~	Yusuf & Zuleika	Mr.[9] van Engen[3] & Miss van Braam

Documents:

- Ms.I.K. (a manuscript in the hand of Pir-o-Murshid Inayat Khan, incomplete, reproduced in typescript above).
- Ms.Gr. (dictated by Pir-o-Murshid to Murshida Sophia Green and Kefayat Gladys LLoyd;).
- Tp.1. (an old typescript showing some corrections, used by the person playing Helen in an early performance).
- Gd.t.1 (a typescript corrected by Gd.).
- Gd.t.2 (another copy of the last act from Gd.t.1, with changes written in medium blue ink by Kismet Stam, and a note in the upper right hand corner of the first page, "Changes dictated by Murshid").
- Tp.2 (carbon copy of a typescript without corrections).
- Tp.3 (Acts II and IV only, with corrections in ink and pencil).
- Bk. (*Three Plays*, Deventer, Netherlands, 1939).

Notes:

1. Tp.1, Gd.t.1: add, "A Play in Three Acts"; Tp.1 further adds "by Hazrat Inayat Khan". As the use of the title "Hazrat" during the lifetime of Pir-o-Murshid Inayat Khan is not attested, the cover sheet may have been added later.
2. Tp.1., Gd.t.1: "Characters";
   Tp.2: "Persons";
   Bk.: "Characters of the Play"
3. "Sirdar" refers to Baron van Tuyll; the name "van Hoens" is properly spelled "van Goens"; "Lakme" refers to the daughter of Mr. and Mrs. van Hogendorp; "Shadi" refers to the wife of Maheboob Khan; "G.I.L." refers to Kefayat Gladys I. LLoyd; "Saida" refers to Baroness van Tuyll; "Miss Hoeber" was actually Mrs. Hoeber; the name "van Engen" should be spelled "van Ingen"; "Engel" should be "Engle". For information on these and others in the list, see *Biography*.

ACT I[10]

[11](In studio)[11]

~~B~~[12] UNA [13](Coming into studio after a long absence)[13]

It is a breath of joy indeed to be once again in my studio, away from all the turmoil of life. It is a joy which is beyond words. It is a happiness which cannot be found elsewhere. My studio has been neglected for such a long while. I have been occupied with no end of things, busy answering life's unceasing demands. But whenever I find time, my one and only thought is to come [14]to the studio[14] and be myself again. Home has no joy for me, nor do I find happiness anywhere else. No-one understands me and all those whom I know are absorbed in their own lives. Every step I take I am drawn back, and all that I try to[15] withdraw from is forced upon me. The rope I try to[15] hold breaks, for it is rotten; the rock I seek to rest upon crumbles, for it is made of sand. In the world's fair, everything I purchase costs more than it is worth, and if I have anything to sell, I get nothing for it. By the continual pinpricks that I feel through life, my heart [16]becomes ~~like~~ perforated[16]. ~~Ah,---Life!---you---are---in-~~
~~puzzle~~
~~deed-a-problem-and--if-it-were-not--for-my-Art-I-could-not--en-dure-you!~~ Oh! life you are indeed a puzzle! the only solace I have is[17] my Art.

4. All other documents: "Una's Father"; Tp.2 and bk. also add "Una's Mother"
5. In Tp.1 and all subsequent documents, this character is called "Workman"; only in Ms.Gr. is he called "Ouvrier", French for "worker". Bk. reads "A Workman (M. Jules Ferrier)".
6. All other documents: "Helen's Aunt"
7. All other documents: "First Queen" and "Second Queen"
8. All other documents: "Emperor" instead of "King"
9. Bk.: adds "Butler" and "Guests"; following the list of characters, all other documents add: "The scene is laid in the United States./ Time: the Present." Tp.1 and Gd.1 further add: "Act I: Una's Studio./ Act II: Ballroom./ Act III: Una's Studio."
10. For Act I, Ms. Gr., the oldest "complete" (except for Act II, added later on) manuscript, dictated by Pir-o-Murshid to Murshida Green (and, in a few places, to Kefayat LLoyd) is used as the basic text. This copy was used by a prompter in an early (the first?) performance, and in several places is marked "Prompter" and "cue"; these incidental markings have been ignored in the text. A standard format has been adopted (name of character speaking in upper case letters in margin, stage directions in parentheses, etc.), and the very haphazard punctuation of this handwritten ms. has been minimally normalized.
11. All other documents: "Una's studio"
12. For the first six pages of Ms.Gr., everywhere "B" is written, then crossed out and "Una" written instead. Apparently Pir-o-Murshid Inayat Khan decided to change the name of the character from Bhakti to Una while dictating this ms. From its page 7 on, the ms. has only "Una", except for a single instance in the last act (see footnote 146).
13. Tp.1, Gd.t.1: "Enter Una (after a long absence)";
Tp.2: "Enter Una, who has long been absent from her studio";
Bk.: "Enter Una, who has long been absent."
14. Bk.: "here"
15. Tp.2, Bk.: this phrase omitted, probably a copying error (from the repetition of the words "try to")
16. Bk.: "is riddled"
17. Tp.1, Gd.t.1, Bk.: "in" added

(Takes ~~chis~~ one of her tools in her hand)

My tools! you are the companions of my solitude.

(Looks up at the glass roof)

The sun! The glorious sun is sending its rays to lift my heart to cheerfulness.

(Begins to work at the incomplete[18] statue)

My statue! for[19] how long have I[19] not touched you!

(A knock at the door [20]is heard[20])

Here is some-one already calling before I even[21] begin work!

(Opens the door; HELEN enters)

HELEN: My dear B Una, I have been looking everywhere for you! Where have you been all this long time? Were you hiding yourself[22] from your friends? If so, be sure we shall find you in the end. You cannot[29] run away and hide from us!

B UNA: I did not mean to hide. After a long time I just had a moment to come to my studio. I have not even begun to work yet.

HELEN: (Looking at the half-done[23] statue)

Is this something that you are working at? Dear me, what a dull occupation. Can't you find anything else to do?

(B UNA perplexed and speechless)

Una dear, you spend[24] hours with[25] this useless work in this solitary studio. I can't understand how you can do it.

18. Tp.1: "incomplete" changed to "unfinished", followed by all other documents
19. Tp.1: "for" omitted;
Gd.t.1, Tp.2, Bk.: "How long is it since I have"
20. All other documents: "is heard" moved to between "knock" and "at the door"
21. Tp.1: "even" omitted
22. Bk.: "yourself" omitted
23. Tp.2, Bk.: "finished" in place of "done"
24. Tp.1: "your" added
25. All other documents: "at"

~~B~~ UNA: (After a moment's pause)

My dear girl, when have I any time to work? All day I am busy at home. At night I lie awake for hours thinking how to make both ends meet. You know that my parents are no longer able to be responsible for the household; they have both aged very much, and it is upon me alone that the care of the household[26a] depends. Yet, whenever I have a moment, I come here [26b]to the studio[26b] and try to find forgetfulness[27] in doing this work, the only thing I really care for.

HELEN: You simple girl! Is this the work you live for? I would not give that much[28] for work that brings nothing better; it is simply[28] waste of time. Excuse me for telling you so!

UNA: Art seldom brings any material returns. Besides, to expect any would be to me like offering beauty in the market-place.

HELEN: I cannot[29] understand how you can shut yourself up in this solitary studio[30]. If I had no-one round me to talk to life would become so monotonous that I should not know what to do with it.

UNA: Well, I am happy only when I am by myself; I don't want anyone to talk to; silence is never long enough for me.

HELEN: Well, you certainly are a riddle! Now tell me the truth, Una, did you read the "Morning[31] Gossip" this morning?

UNA: You know quite well that I don't read the papers; I have too much to do. And besides, I am not particularly interested in the sensational stories in the newspapers; they generally an-~~say-one--thing-in-the-morning--and-contradict-it-in--the evening-~~
nounce[32] one thing in the morning and quite its[33a] opposite in the evening.

HELEN: Do you know the rate of the[33b] exchange today?

26a. Bk.: "house" in place of "household"
26b. Bk.: "to the studio" omitted
27. All other documents: "oblivion" in place of "forgetfulness";
Gd.t.1: first "forgetfulness" was typed, then erased and "oblivion" typed instead
28. Tp.1: "(snapping her fingers)" added, followed by all other documents; also, all other documents insert "a" before "waste of time"
29. Bk.: "can't"
30. Ibid.: "place"
31. Ibid.: "Daily"
32. Ibid.: "say"
33a. All other documents: "the"
33b. Ibid.: "the" omitted

UNA: Whether[33c] money goes up or down does not make much difference ~~to me. In~~ in our lives when we live from hand to mouth [34]from day to day[34]. Moreover, the idea of profiting by the loss of another has always been foreign to my nature.

HELEN: Do you know the name of the new mayor who has just been elected?

UNA: No, indeed I do not[35]! My dear girl, I live in quite another world from yours.

HELEN: You certainly are behind the times[36]. Last night I was at a ball given by Mrs. Wilkens. Everyone[37a] in the town who is somebody[37b] was present. There was music and dancing all night and great fun. There is a Founder's Ball coming off next week and Auntie is on the committee. She has asked me to help her. Everyone has been asked to come disguised as someone they thought[38] they were in their past lives. Won't that be amusing?

(UNA smiles)

You will come, Una dear, won't you? Though I know that you always avoid social functions. But all the local papers are talking about this. Do come, please.

UNA: Society life is for people like you, Helen, not for me.

HELEN: Una! I really wish you were not living such a retired life. What is the good of life if you don't live it?

UNA: I am not at all interested in society life[39]. I prefer the life of a humble artist.

HELEN: It seems that no-one can change your ideas, Una. I must be going now. I am sorry to have kept you so long from your work. Now be sure and come to the ball. Au revoir.

(They kiss [40]one another[40]. Exit Helen)

33c. Tp.1: "the" added
34. Bk.: "day by day"
35. Ibid.: "don't"
36. Tp.2: "time"
37a. Tp.1, Gd.t.1, Bk.: "everybody" in place of "Everyone"
37b. Bk.: "anybody" in place of "somebody"
38. All other documents: "think"
39. Bk.: "life" omitted
40. Tp.1, Tp.2, Gd.t.1: "each other";
Bk.: omitted

UNA: (soliloquises[41])

I don't know why people can't leave me alone! They live their own lives, why can't they let me live mine! (Sighs) Well, I suppose that is the way of the world.

(A knock at the door. UNA opens it[42])

Father! Is that you? Yes, I'm here. I had a spare moment so I thought I would come and try to finish some work I was doing here.

([43]UNA brings[43] FATHER in, holding his arm, and seats him in an armchair)

Well, Father, what have you come to tell me?

FATHER: My dear child, you are wanted at home, as your mother is not well. When you are out, everything goes wrong.
~~brought you up~~
Besides, I have never/liked the idea of your being an artist.
[44]~~as you know very well we have had no Artists~~[44]
In our family / and there has never been any wish for any of the family to become artists. Our people look upon it quite differently [45]to the way in which you do[45]; as for myself, I never could have imagined you an artist.

UNA: Dear Father, these[46] are the old ideas! Now science and art are the great qualifications of the age. And you know, dear Father, I do not do this as a profession; it is my love for art which occupies me with it.

FATHER: Una, my child, though we have been for some time in poor circumstances, still[47] we have always considered our dignity; your mother is depressed and very often feels sad to see you so unlike the other girls in our family who go into Society.

UNA: Father, my society consists of the little works of art which are round me in this studio. I feel at home here, and every moment while I am working here I am happy.

41. All other documents: "soliloquises" omitted
42. Ibid.: "the door"
43. Ibid.: "Leads her" in place of "Una brings"
44. Tp.1, Gd.t.1: "as you know very well, we have never had any artists"; Tp.2, Bk.: the same, except "artist" instead of "artists"
45. All other documents: "from you"
46. Ibid.: "those"
47. Ibid.: "yet"

FATHER: My dear child, there are many things in the world besides art which are to be sought in order that one may be really happy. If you never see anyone, no-one will ever know you.
~~which will amuse you~~
There are many other things in life / if you will seek for them. Art is all very well / to amuse oneself with, but it is not
~~as a thing~~
everything that one needs in life.

UNA: (Is[48] silent; after a moment)

All I need, Father, is to make you and Mother happy in every way I can; that is the only thing that interests me in life, and
~~only~~
if I have any personal interest, it is / in my art.

~~for~~
FATHER: My child, I must go home and / [49a]take care of[49a] your mother. She is not at all well. Come as soon as you can.

UNA: Yes, [49b]dear Father[49b], I will.

(They kiss [50]each other[50] and he[51] goes out)

(Soliloquises[52])

Never a moment have I to concentrate my mind on my work. How true it is that the world of every soul is different, for the life of one is not the life of another. I wish I could be here to[53] continue my work, but life in the world has so many obligations[54] that one cannot ignore them and at the same time live happily. Well, I must hurry or I shall keep poor Father waiting! My work! When shall I be free to come to you again? Especially now that I have to make preparations for this ball.

48. Ibid.: "remains"
49a. Tp.2, Bk.: "look after"
49b. All other documents: "Father dear"
50. Bk.: "each other" omitted
51. All other documents: "the father"
52. Ibid.: "soliloquises" omitted
53. Ibid.: "and"
54. Bk.: "duties"

(UNA puts away her tools and leaves [55]the studio[55] for her home)

[56]End of Act I[56]

---

55. Ibid.: "the studio" omitted
56. Tp.2, Bk.: "Curtain."

ACT II[57]

Scene: Mother's bedroom; Mother ill in bed.

Una enters, embraces her mother.

UNA. Dear Mother, I was sorry to hear that you [58]did not[58] feel well. No sooner had father left the studio than I hurried[59a] to see, Mother dear, how you were. As[59b] much as I love my art, I do not wish to be away from home, Mother dear, when you are not well.

MOTHER. Dear girl, with us, old people, there is always something[60]; one moment we feel well, the other[61] moment we [58]do not[58] feel well. What worries my mind, is to see you given to one direction. The art to which you are so much devoted, [62]to us is[62] a foreign word. For you know, however poor we may be in our family, there is [63]not such a thing[63] known among us as an artist.

UNA: Dear Mother, it is not that I love art in order to become an artist; I want to become nothing; it is beauty that I love.

MOTHER. My simple child, beauty is to be seen in nature, you need not [64]go for[64] art in order to see beauty. Besides as they say: the country is made by God, the[65a] town is made by man.

UNA: Dear Mother, I have always felt that what is not completed in nature, is finished in art by the Master[65b] of all things. The hand of the artist is guided by the eyes unseen.

MOTHER. But what do you gain by devoting all your time to something in which you [58]do not[58] wish to make your career? You must think of the future, my dear girl!

57. This act appears for the first time in Tp.2, which therefore is the basic text used here.
58. Bk.: "don't"
59a. Tp.3: "home" added
59b. Ibid.: "As" omitted
60. Bk.: "wrong" added
61. Ibid.: "next" in place of "other"
62. Ibid.: reordered to "is to us"
63. Ibid.: "no such thing"
64. Tp.3: "go in for";
Bk.: "go to"
65a. Tp.3: "the" omitted
65b. Ibid.: "Maker" in place of "Master"

UNA: Mother dear, we all make our future with whatever we do. But it is the future that will tell what we made. Life to me is the making of something; it only depends[66a] what we make. [66b]We each make something[66b], even[67] it is we who make our highest ideal.

MOTHER. What do you mean by ideal, my dear child? There is no such a[68] thing, my darling girl. Ideal is not to be found in this world. You are yet too young, my darling, to know this. When we were young, we thought also of ideal, but alas, in the end we found that it was only a word.

UNA: [69]Right you are[69], Mother, there is never an ideal to be found under the sun if we did[70] not make it. It is we who, out of our own selves, give all that the ideal wants for it to become an ideal. What we make remains, what we are is destroyed. Rumi says in his *Masnavi*: "[71]Beloved is all in all, the lover only veils Him; [71]Beloved is all that lives, the lover a dead thing." One creates a heart out of a rock, another turns a heart into a rock.

MOTHER. Say simple things, my dear girl. This is all confusing to me; what your mother wants is your welfare, your happiness, this is all we wish for you, I and your father both.

FATHER: (Enters.)[72] Are you here, Una? Prepare[73] to go to the ball. [74a]Did you forget[74a] you were invited to go to Mrs. Wilkins' house?

UNA: I had quite forgotten, Father. Thank you for reminding me. I'll just go and get[74b] ready. (She embraces her mother and departs.)

CURTAIN

66a. Ibid.: "upon" added
66b. Ibid.: "Each makes something"
67. Bk.: "even" omitted
68. Tp.3: "a" crossed out with typed slash; Bk.: "a" omitted
69. Bk.: reordered to "You are right"
70. Tp.3, Bk.: "do"
71. Tp.3: "The" added
72. Bk.: "(Enter Father)"
73. Ibid.: "Get ready"
74a. Ibid.: "Have you forgotten"; Tp.3: "that" added
74b. Bk.: "be" in place of "get"

An old, typed document (Tp.1)

ACT III[75]

[76]Scene: Ballroom in Aunt's house.

Aunt, aided[77] by Helen, receives the guests, who are announced by the names of the characters they have assumed: Shah of Persia, Sultana[78], King Tut, [79]Queen of Sheba[79], Emperor Akbar, Greek philosopher[80], Dante and Beatrice, Yusuf and Zuleikha arrive and are announced and received by Aunt and Helen.

[81]First Queen of Egypt enters.[81]

BUTLER. The Queen of Egypt, Consort of King Tut.

[82]Second Queen of Egypt enters.[82]

BUTLER. The Queen of Egypt, Consort of King Tut.

FIRST QUEEN. (To Second Queen). You were[83] not the consort of King Tut, I was[84] his consort.

SECOND QUEEN. Not at all, it is I who was his consort.

FIRST QUEEN. Nonsense! You don't know what you are saying.

HELEN. Let us ask him which was his Queen. He has just risen from his grave. (She is seen [85]to ask[85] King Tut.)

75. For Act III, originally known as Act II, Tp.1 has been taken as the basic text, since Ms.Gr. lacks the whole first part of the act and has no text for Una's recitation later in the act. All differences between Ms.Gr.--the earlier text--and Tp.1 have of course been noted.
76. For this whole section, Ms.Gr. has only:
"Queens arrive & quarrel
~~Mushraff-Khan~~
Helen "Let us ask him
One
(he has just risen from his grave)
Tutankamen
~~Mushraff-Khan~~--looks at both Queens slowly & carefully then says scornfully ...."
77. Bk.: "assisted"
78. Ibid.: omits "Sultana"
79. Ibid.: "Queen of Saba"
80. Tp.2: "philosophers"
81. Bk.: "(Enter First Queen ..."
82. Ibid.: "(Enter Second Queen ..."
83. Gd.t.1: first "are" was typed, then crossed out, and "were" typed instead.
84. Ibid.: similarly, first "am" was typed, then crossed out and "was" typed above.
85. Bk.: "asking"

KING TUT. (Looks slowly and carefully at both Queens. Scornfully:)[76]

I don't think that either of them has ever been my Queen.

(Turns away.)

[86](American Indian arrives[86], Helen greets him.)

HELEN. Were you an American Indian in your past life?[87]

AMERICAN INDIAN. No, I don't know what I was in the past, but for the last twenty years I have had an American Indian guide.

HELEN. Do you mean a living guide?

AMERICAN INDIAN[88]. No[89a], a spirit.

HELEN. How did you find a spirit guide[89b]?

AMERICAN INDIAN. I began by hearing taps at the door for a year before this guide appeared to me, and since then he is always with me.

HELEN. How wonderful! And what does he look like?

AMERICAN INDIAN. [90](With importance.)[90] Just like me!

([91]Walks about[92] and is welcomed by all.)

(To [93]First Guest[93].) Are you a medium?

FIRST GUEST.[94] No.

AMERICAN INDIAN. (To [95]Second Guest[95].) Are you a[96] psychic?

SECOND GUEST.[94] Not yet.

AMERICAN INDIAN: (To Aunt[97]) Are you clairvoyante?

AUNT[94]: I don't even know what you mean by clairvoyante.

86. Ibid.: "(Enter American Indian ..."
87. Ms.Gr.: "Mr. Engel's Part"
88. Ibid.: this part is designated "Mr. Engel" instead of "American Indian".
89a. Ibid.: "No! No!"
89b. Ibid.: "guide" crossed out
90. Ibid.: "importantly"
91. Bk.: "He" added
92. Ms.Gr.: "round"
93. Ibid.: "~~one person~~ Mrs. van Goens"
94. Ibid.: "Answer"
95. Ibid.: "~~another~~"
96. Gd.t.1, Tp.2, Bk.: "a" omitted
97. Ms.Gr.: "~~to a third~~ To Mme v Hogendorp"

AMERICAN INDIAN: If you want to know you must go to a séance and hear the Trumpet Medium.

[98](Continues conversation.)[98]

BUTLER: Monsieur Jules Ferrier.[99]

FERRIER (WORKMAN): (Enters,[100] looking nervous.)

(Aunt[101] greets him and passes him on to Helen.)

HELEN: How extraordinary! Among all these[102] kings and queens you come as a plain workman! Were you that in your past life?

WORKMAN: I don't know anything about my past life, and I only know what I was in this one before [103]I joined[103] the Four Hundred.

HELEN: And what was that?

WORKMAN: I was a workman[104].

HELEN: But have you always been a workman[104]?

WORKMAN: No, before that I was a barber in England.

HELEN: And before that?

WORKMAN: Oh, well, before that I was a chimneysweep.

HELEN: You amusing man! But how did you get into Society?

WORKMAN: Oh, I made a lot of money in the war, and now I am invited and received everywhere. But, to tell you the truth, I [105]do not[105] like the life. I feel out of place; I feel lonely too, and I would[106] like to marry. Do you know of any nice girl to introduce me to?

HELEN: Have you[107] been married before?

98. Ibid.: "Pretends to go on talking etc."
99. Ibid.: "At the door they announce M. Jules Ferrier"
100. Ms.Gr.: "F. enters";
Bk.: "(Enter Ferrier, a workman, ..."
101. Ms.Gr.: "Lady Austruther" in place of "Aunt"
102. Bk.: "the"
103. Ms.Gr.: "joining"
104. Ibid.: "Workman" everywhere called "Ouvrier", French for worker.
105. Bk.: "don't"
106. Ibid.: "should"
107. Ms.Gr.: "not"

WORKMAN: (Nodding his head and looking mysterious) The past is past, the present is present; it is the future that we look forward to!

HELEN: I asked you if you had been married before.

WORKMAN: (Impatiently) Suppose I had been married twenty times before, what about it just now?

(At this moment UNA is announced. While HELEN greets her, the WORKMAN looks at her with interest.)

HELEN: What a pleasant surprise to see you at last! Are you really here? I can't believe my eyes! But why aren't you dressed [108]as anything[108]? What are you supposed to be?

UNA: Myself.

HELEN: But what were you in your past life?

UNA: Myself.

HELEN: Yourself! What do you mean by that?

UNA: Self means always self; it cannot be any other.

HELEN: You have the queerest ideas, my dear girl!

(Aside) What fun it would be to introduce that odd man and this simple girl to each other. I will presently.

(Snake dance)[109]

HELEN: (To WORKMAN) There is a young lady over there whom you would like. I am going to introduce you to her.

WORKMAN: (Eagerly) Right you are! I am sure I should like her! For among all these kings and queens [110]she and I are[110] the only two who are dressed simply.

108. Bk.: "as anything" omitted
109. Ms.Gr.: the following, later crossed out: "looks at her with interest, after some long interval Helen introduces him to her--after Snake dance"
110. Bk.: "we're"

(HELEN introduces them [111]to each other[111]. The [112]WORKMAN holds[112] out his hand, but UNA [113]draws back slightly[113], then [114]puts out her hand[114], but [115]without looking[115] at him.)

WORKMAN: I'm glad to meet you, Miss.

UNA: ([116]Silent, [117]eyes cast down.)

HELEN: Now you two must excuse me, I have other things to do.

(She leaves them; they sit down.)

WORKMAN: I wonder, Miss, how it happens that among all these[118] who are here only you and I are so simply dressed. I suppose you don't know your past incarnations any more than I do mine[119]? I am so glad to have found you among all these smart people.

UNA: (Still silent, looking down.)

WORKMAN: Can you dance, Miss? Everyone can but me, it seems. I would not mind trying if you would be my partner, for I am sure we should make a good pair.

UNA: (As if waking from a dream) Dance? I never dance.

[120]WORKMAN: But I am sure you would like it.

UNA: I do not mind looking on while other people dance.[120]

(Aside) I feel my soul dance when my body is still.

WORKMAN: (To himself) She seems to be in the clouds. I'll try my luck.

(Enter HELEN)

HELEN: (To UNA) Please come and sing or dance.

111. Ms.Gr.: no "to each other"
112. Ibid.: "Ouvrier puts"
113. Ibid.: "slightly draws back"
114. Ibid.: "gives it"
115. Ibid.: "does not look"
116. Ibid.: "still";
Bk.: "remains"
117. Gd.t.1, Tp.2, Bk.: "her"
118. Bk.: "those"
119. Ms.Gr.: no "mine"
120. Bk.: this exchange omitted (probably a typographical error stemming from the repetition of the word "dance")

UNA: [105]Do not[105] ask me to take part [121a]in it[121a], I am enjoying looking on[121b].

HELEN: [122]But do take part[122].

UNA: The spectators alone know [123]the real[123].

HELEN: Come and do something.

UNA: What shall I do?

HELEN: If you cannot[124] sing, recite something.

UNA: Very well.

[125] ([126]Recites:)

I have loved in life and I have been loved.
I have drunk the bowl of poison from the hands of love as nectar, and have been raised above life's joy and sorrow.
My heart aflame in love set afire every heart that came in touch with it.
My heart has been rent and joined again,
My heart has been broken and again[127] made whole,
My heart has been wounded and healed again,
A thousand deaths my heart hath died, and thanks be to love, it liveth yet.

I went through Hell and saw there love's raging fire, and I entered Heaven illumined with the light of love.
I wept in love and made all weep with me,
I mourned in love and pierced the hearts of men,
And when my fiery glance fell on the rocks, the rocks burst forth as volcanoes.
The whole world sank in the flood caused by my one tear,
With my deep sigh the earth trembled, and when I cried aloud the name of my beloved I shook the throne of God in Heaven.

121a. Ms.Gr.: no "in it"
121b. Ibid.: "at it"
122. Ibid.: "take part in it"
123. Bk.: "reality"
124. Ibid.: "can't"
125. Ms.Gr.: has only "Recitation from Love & [sic] Human & Divine", a book prepared by Murshida Goodenough in 1919, based on Pir-o-Murshid's teaching, entitled "Love: Human and Divine," where the passage appears as the "Conclusion," p. 78.
126. Bk.: "She..."
127. Ibid.: moved to after "whole"

I bowed my head low in humility, and on my knees I begged of Love,
"Disclose to me, I pray thee, O love, thy secret."
She took me gently by my arms and lifted me above the earth, and spoke softly in my ear,
"My dear one, thou thyself art love, art lover, and thyself art the beloved whom thou hast adored."[125]

WORKMAN: [128]How nice, Miss! I enjoyed your poetry so much. I could not understand what it was all about. What interested me was one word. You know what that was, don't you?

UNA: No, which?

WORKMAN: "Love," that is all there is to think about. All these people are all interested in that one thing: love.

UNA: I do not know it yet. To me it seems a blasphemy to hear it on the lips of ordinary people. I [105]do not[105] know a being living on earth[129] an example of this word.

WORKMAN: Miss[130], you are talking of big things. I don't mean that at all. What I know about love is to be cheerful and gay. See how happy the other people are. Why should not you and I be the same?

UNA: Gaiety is not my way of being happy. What are these pleasures to me?

WORKMAN: Miss[130], you are too serious for me. What's the use of being so melancholy?

UNA: If I do not join in the gaiety, it does not mean that I am melancholy. I seek happiness in myself.

WORKMAN: [131]But I want you to seek it in me. For you know how I feel when I look at you. But[132] you are trying to hold me off by talking so beautifully, but you look so beautiful when you are sad that I feel like kneeling at your feet. [133]You know that the thing I want most in the world is to see you laughing.[131]

128. Ms.Gr.: this passage in hwr. Kf.
129. Tp.2, Bk.: "who is" added
130. Bk.: "Miss" omitted
131. Ms.Gr.: the words "longish speech" with a mark + after, then on the back of the page, following a +, the rest of the speech in hwr. Kf.
132. All other documents: "but" lacking, but reinserted in hwr. Gd. in Gd.t.1
133. Ms.Gr.: "But"

UNA: You can see many people here laughing. You must enjoy it with them.[134] Poor man, [135]look for your[135] gaiety somewhere else.

([136]Turns away and leaves him. Walks [137]across the stage[137]. Stands still.)

UNA: O human nature! It's a continual study to see the different directions that the mind takes.[138] Yet how few there are whom you can really call human beings. Alone at home, alone in the society of others, I suppose to be alone is my lot. And it never wearies me. [139]Life in the world is most interesting to me, but solitude away from the world is the longing of my soul.[140]

(Minuet)

[141]CURTAIN[128]

---

134. Bk.: adds "(to herself)"
135. Ibid.: "Why does he not look for his..."
136. Ms.Gr.: "she"
137. Ibid.: "down stage";
Tp.1, Gd.t.1, Bk.: "across stage"
138. Ms.Gr.: "Any" [sic]
139. Ibid.: "Repeats from Gayan"
140. See Gayan, Gamaka 20.
141. Ms.Gr.: "Then"

Ms. Murshida Green

ACT IV (Version 1)[142]

UNA. [143]Beloved image! the ideal of my soul ~~you have~~ thou hast been conceived in my heart[144], and I have nursed ~~you~~ thee so long with my tears until ~~you~~ thou hast manifested to my vision. Did I make sacrifices for ~~you~~ thee? No! ~~You~~ Thou art the outcome of my love. How long! How long shall I wait to hear a word from ~~you~~ thee? Whether in the studio or elsewhere I have worked for ~~you~~ thee and thought of ~~you~~ thee alone! Dear, dear image, ~~you~~ thou art the ideal of my heart. Oh! Speak to me. I have yearned to hear thy voice if it were but once.

[145]~~Bhakti~~[146] UNA: Thy whisper to the ears of my heart moveth my soul to ecstasy. The waves of joy which rise out of my heart form a net in which thy living word may swing. My heart patiently awaiteth thy word. Deaf to all that cometh from without, O thou who art enshrined in my heart, speak ~~again~~ to me; [147]thy voice exalteth my spirit[147]. When thou art before me, my beloved, I rise upon wings and my burden becometh light, but when my little self riseth before my[148] eyes, I drop to earth and all its weight falleth upon me.[145]

STATUE: Yes, I speak, but I speak only when thou art silent. Thou hast found thy happiness in working in the studio which is my world. Thou [149]first imagined my distance[149] as I lived in thy imagination. Now thy imagination has become ~~truth~~ a reality and my existence has become truth. So thou madest me to be the masterpiece of thine art. Now I am the result of thine art ~~with~~ and in finishing me thou fulfillest the purpose of thy life.

142. For the first version of Act IV, known earlier as Act III, Ms.Gr. has been used as the basic text and compared with Tp.1 and Gd.t.1. For the second version, see footnote number 156.
143. Tp.1: "(addressing statue)" added;
Gd.t.1: originally "Alone" was typed, then erased
144. Tp.1: "soul" in place of "heart";
Gd.t.1: "soul", later crossed out and "heart" added in hwr. Gd.
145. Ms.Gr.: this passage in hwr. Kf.
146. Ibid.: this is the sole recurrence of the name Bhakti in the play after the "B"s of the first few pages.
147. Tp.1, Gd.t.1: omitted
148. Ibid.: "mine"
149. Ibid.: "didst first imagine my existence"

[150]UNA: I would willingly die a thousand deaths if by dying I could ~~attain~~ gain thy ~~most lofty~~- beloved presence. If it were a cup of poison thy beloved hand offered, I would prefer that poison to the bowl of nectar. I value the dust under thy feet, my precious one, most of all the treasures the earth holds. If my head could touch the earth of thy dwelling place, I would proudly refuse Khusrou's crown. I would gladly[151] sacrifice all the pleasures the earth can offer me if I could only retain the pain I have in my feeling heart.[150]

STATUE: Dost thou love me? Then first learn what love means. Love means sacrifice, one continual sacrifice from the beginning to the end. I come to life only when thou [152]becomest dead[152].

([153a]Cue for[153a] bowl)

I offer thee this cup of poison; take it if thou wilt.

(UNA [153b]takes cup[153b])

STATUE: Awake! Awake! Thou hast gone through death but hast not died. The sacrifice thou madest did not after all rob thee of thy life, it has only raised thee above death. Now thou art living with my life. ~~Now~~ it is thy love which has given thee the life after death, a life to live forever.

[154]UNA: Thy light hath illumined[155] the dark chambers of my mind. Thy love is rooted in the depth of my heart. Thine own eyes are the light of my soul. Thy power worketh behind my actions. Thy peace alone is my life's repose. Thy will is behind my every impulse. Thy voice is audible in the words I speak. Thine own image is my countenance. My body is but a cover over thy soul. My life is thy very breath, my beloved, and my self is thine own being.

CURTAIN[154]

---

150. Ms.Gr.: this passage in hwr. Kf.
151. Tp.1, Gd.t.1: "gladly" omitted
152. Tp.1: "comest to death"
153a. Tp.1, Gd.t.1: "Holds out a"
153b. Ibid.: "takes the cup, falls down as though dead"
154. Ms.Gr.: this passage in hwr. Kf.
155. Tp.1: "illuminated"

Murshida Goodenough's type, with emendations by Pir-o-Murshid Inayat Khan.

ACT IV (Second Version)[156]

Scene: Una's studio

UNA. (Addressing[157] STATUE) Beloved image, the ideal of my soul, thou hast been conceived in my soul and I have nursed thee [158]so long[158] with my tears, until thou hast manifested to my vision. [159]When thou art before me, my Beloved, I rise upon wings and my burden becometh light, but when my little self riseth[160] before mine eyes I drop to earth and all its weight falleth[161] upon me.[159] Did I make sacrifices for thee? No. Thou art the outcome of my love. How long, how long shall I wait to hear a word from thee? Whether [162]in the studio[162] or elsewhere I have worked for thee and thought of thee alone. Dear, dear Image, thou art the ideal of my heart. O speak to me! My heart patiently awaiteth[163] thy word, deaf to all that cometh[164] from without. O thou who art enshrined in my heart, speak to me. I have yearned to hear thy voice if it were but once.

STATUE: Yes, I speak, but I speak only when thou art silent.

UNA: Thy whisper to the ears of my heart moveth[165] my soul to ecstasy. The waves of joy which rise out of my heart form a net in which thy living word may swing.

156. For the second version of Act IV, the basic text (Gd.t.2) is a (carbon?) copy of Gd.t.1 for this act, on which corrections have been put in a medium blue ink by Kismet Stam, with a note in the upper righthand corner, "Changes dictated by Murshid". Because these changes almost all involve shifting a speech or part of a speech to another position, the changes are very difficult to follow if only put in footnotes; because this represents the author's final revision of the act, we give it in a separate text, compared with the later Tp.2, Tp.3 and the Bk.
157. Bk.: "the" added
158. Tp.2, Bk.: "so long" omitted
159. Tp.3: this sentence later crossed out by hand
160. Bk.: "rises"
161. Ibid.: "falls"
162. Ibid.: "here"
163. Ibid.: "awaits"
164. Ibid.: "comes"
165. Ibid.: "moves"

STATUE: Thou hast found thy happiness in working in [166]the studio[166] which is my world. Thou didst first imagine my existence as I lived in thy imagination; now thy imagination has become a reality and my existence has become truth. So thou madest me to be the masterpiece of thine art. Now I am the result of thine art, and in finishing me thou fulfillest the purpose of thy life.

[167a](Holds out a bowl)[167a]

Dost thou love me? Then first learn what love means. Love means sacrifice, one continual sacrifice from[167b] beginning to[167b] end. I come to life only when thou [168]becomest dead[168].

UNA: I would willingly die a thousand deaths if by dying I could gain thy beloved presence. If it were a cup of poison thy beloved hand offered, I would prefer that poison to the bowl of nectar. I value the dust under thy feet, my precious one, most of all the[169] treasures the earth holds. If my head could touch the earth of thy dwelling place, I would gladly[170] refuse Khusrou's[171] crown. I would sacrifice all the pleasures the earth can offer me if I could only retain the pain I have in my feeling heart.

STATUE: (Holds out a bowl)[172] I offer thee this cup of poison. Take it if thou wilt.

(UNA takes the cup, falls down as though dead)

STATUE: (Raises her in his arms, embraces her, and kisses her and brings her to life again) Awake! Awake! (She opens her eyes) Thou hast gone through death but hast not died. The sacrifice thou madest did not after all rob thee of thy life. It has only raised thee above death. Now thou art living with my life. It is thy love which hath given thee the life after death, a life to live forever.

166. Ibid.: "this place"
167a. Tp.2, Tp.3, Bk.: omitted
167b. Ibid.: "the" added
168. Tp.3: marked out and changed to "comest to death"
169. Bk.: "the" omitted
170. Ibid.: "proudly" in place of "gladly"
171. Ibid.: spelled "Khusru's"
172. Gd.t.2: the intention may have been to move this instruction. (See note 167a.)

UNA: Thy light hath illumined[173] the dark chambers of my mind. Thy love is rooted in the depth of my heart. Thine own eyes are the light of my soul. Thy power worketh behind my actions[174]. Thy peace alone is my life's repose. Thy will is behind my every impulse. Thy voice is audible in the words I speak. Thine own image is my countenance. My body is but a cover over thy[175] soul. My life is thy very breath, my Beloved, and my self is thine own being.

CURTAIN

---

173. Tp.2, Bk.: "illuminated"
174. Tp.2, Tp.3, Bk.: "action"
175. Tp.2, Bk.: "the" instead of "thy"

APPENDIX A

EVENTS
SPRING
SERIES
and
San Francisco
engagement of
INAYAT KHAN
Pilgrim of
MUSIC
LITERATURE · PHILOSOPHY
Direction of
Paul Elder
239 POST STREET
SAN FRANCISCO.

A Pilgrim of Music, Literature and Philosophy

Paul Elder Announces a Notable Season
The San Francisco Engagement of

Pir-o-Murshid Inayat Khan

A Series of six Wednesday morning lectures on Music, March 28th to May 2nd, at 10:30 o'clock; a Series of six Tuesday afternoon lectures on Sufi Poets, April 3rd to May 8th, at 2:30 o'clock; a Series of six Thursday evening lectures on Spiritual Philosophy, March 29th to May 3rd, at 8:15 o'clock. A Special Easter Discourse, Sunday evening, April 1st, at 8:15 o'clock.

In the Paul Elder Gallery, 239 Post Street, San Francisco

(Air conditioned and vitalized by electro-ozone equipment.)

PIR-O-MURSHID INAYAT KHAN, Sufi Mystic, Philosopher, Poet and Musician, was born in 1882 at Baroda, India, and is descended from sixteen generations of spiritual teachers and five generations of distinguished musicians. His life has been devoted to the study of philosophy and music, the two studies linked and interwoven, the mysticism of sound and the mysticism of life being one and indivisible.

Music and mysticism were his heritage from both his paternal and maternal ancestors, among whom were numbered Moula Bux, the Beethoven of India (whose portrait is in the Victoria and Albert Museum at South Kensington, England), and St. Jummashah, the great seer of Punjab, who was canonized and is revered as a saint to this day by the people of India.

The Pir-o-Murshid (Great Master) came from India to the United States in 1910, and, after spending something less than a year in this country lecturing at universities and other centers, went to Europe, where he has been ever since, lecturing, writing and teaching. He is devoting his life to spreading the Sufi message of the fundamental unity of humanity, and to restating the inner wisdom common to all mankind, in terms of the religious philosophy of Love, Harmony and Beauty.

Through his lectures and his books he is well known in London, Paris, Geneva and other European cities. Following are quotations from a few of his press notices, the earnestness and enthusiasm of which attest the greatness of his genius:

"As a lecturer Inayat Khan is thoughtful and earnest and has a pleasant manner. He is a man of great intellectual abilities, of vast learning and of profound knowledge of human nature."
(From the *Kentish Independent.*)

"This musician is at the same time a poet and philosopher, as were all the great Sufis of bygone days. His great strength lies in a radiating faith in the religion of unity."
(From the *Comedia*, Paris.)

"Inayat Khan is a man of striking personality, possessed of glowing and eloquent eyes, and strangely deliberate and sedate in his bearing. He says: "Sufism takes music as the source of all perfection, since sound was the first source of creation."

(From the *Daily Citizen*, London.)

"Inayat Khan speaks English excellently, and his tall figure in a long robe of apricot colored cloth, with the great Sufi jewel on his breast, is very impressive."

(From the *Evening News*, London.)

During his stay in San Francisco, the address and headquarters of Pir-o-Murshid Inayat Khan will be at The Sufi School of Philosophy, 153 Kearny Street, Studio 308.

His public lectures will be delivered in The Paul Elder Gallery, 239 Post Street.

MUSIC: A series of six Wednesday morning lectures, March 28th to May 2nd, inclusive

It is refreshing in these days when some of the most prominent "realist" composers in Europe seem to be trying to debase the art hitherto called the "divine art," to know that with the Orientals music has always been based on a philosophical and spiritual foundation. As the history of Ancient India is a sealed book, and its time-honored civilization is undoubtedly of a very high standard, so their ancient music is a locked treasure of which the key is lost. The Aryans of India, however, were first and foremost in developing the art very nearly to perfection. Music was correlative with the teaching of Vedas, and singing was an inseparable part of devotion. The Hindus use quarter-tones, making their scale twice as refined as ours. Twenty-four tones are used where we only use twelve. This is a refinement beyond our present dreams. The originator of the Hindu music was Mahadeva, the Lord of the Yogis, and the performer of it was Parvati, his beloved consort. Krishna, the Hindu incarnation of God, was also an expert musician who charmed both worlds by the music of his flute, and inspired the Yogis to dance to its rhythm. This is called Raslila, or Sacred Performance. The whole system of the Hindu religion and philosophy is based on the Science of Vibration. As Sufi Shams Tabraz says in his poem on the origin of Creation, "The whole secret of the Universe is wrapt up in Sound."

Wednesday Morning, March 28th, at 10:30 o'clock
THE SCIENCE AND ART OF HINDU MUSIC.

Wednesday Morning, April 4th, at 10:30 o'clock
THE PSYCHIC INFLUENCE OF MUSIC.

Wednesday Morning, April 11th, at 10:30 o'clock
THE HEALING POWER OF MUSIC.

Wednesday Morning, April 18th, at 10:30 o'clock
SPIRITUAL DEVELOPMENT BY THE AID OF MUSIC.

Wednesday Morning, April 25th, at 10:30 o'clock
THE MYSTERY OF SOUND AND COLOR.

Wednesday Morning, May 2nd, at 10:30 o'clock
THE MUSIC OF THE SPHERES.

Tickets: Single lecture, One Dollar
Season Ticket, six lectures, Five Dollars

SUFI POETS: A series of six Tuesday afternoon lectures, April 3rd to May 8th, inclusive

---

Tuesday Afternoon, April 3rd, at 2:30 o'clock
THE POET AND THE PROPHET.

The various scriptures of the nations are interpreted by the Prophets and Spiritual Poets of every age, not as dogmas, but as appeals to the heart of man. They point the way to our spiritual freedom; with one stroke of the pen they emancipate us as souls, and with the other they have shown us to speak straight from the heart, and with all spontaneity, breaking the barriers of human limitation and spiritual bondages. To interpret Persian religious and philosophic poetry with full understanding of the sense intended by the writer, requires intimate acquaintance with Moslem thought, and in particular with theology and mysticism.

Tuesday Afternoon, April 10th, at 2:30 o'clock
OMAR KHAYYAM.

All authorities, intellectual and spiritual (despite the fallacies of modern interpretations), describe this poet as one who drank deeply of wisdom, and this is revealed through his many famous works on astronomy, mathematics, metaphysics and philosophy. He was a master of the exact sciences.

Tuesday Afternoon, April 17th, at 2:30 o'clock
JALLAL-U-DIN-RUMI.

The Masnavi has all the beauty of the Psalms, the music of the hills, the color and scent of roses; but it has more than that, it expresses in song the yearnings of the soul to be reunited with God.

Tuesday Afternoon, April 24th, at 2:30 o'clock
SHAIKH MUSLIH-UD-DIN SAADI.

The Gulistan (Rose Garden) represents the consummation of a wide knowledge of life and men, and though Saadi's own life was fraught with hardships and trials, he maintained serenity of spirit and a heart attuned to the great problems of humanity. In the simplicity of his heart he says tenderly of his own work:

"We give advice in its proper place,
Spending a lifetime in the task.
If it should not touch any one's ear of desire,
The messenger told his tale;
It is enough."

Tuesday Afternoon, May 1st, at 2:30 o'clock
HAFIZ.

Hafiz breathes originality in all his works; he has defects, but only his own; he has beauties, but only his own. He may be condemned, but cannot be compared. He is considered by some authorities to be the greatest poet of any age or country. The name Hafiz literally means "the man who remembers." He spent his life remembering God and preserved these remembrances in verses which to this day are consulted as oracles.

Tuesday Afternoon, May 8th, at 2:30 o'clock
FARID-DU-DIN ATTAR.

The Mantiqu't Tayr is a description of the Mystical Quest of the Birds (Sufi Pilgrims) for the Simurgh (God).

1st. Valley of Search.
2nd. Valley of Love.
3rd. Valley of Knowledge.
4th. Valley of Non-attachment.
5th. Valley of Unity.
6th. Valley of Amazement.
7th. Valley of Realization of God.

Tickets: Single lecture, One Dollar
Season Ticket, six lectures, Five Dollars

SPIRITUAL PHILOSOPHY. A series of six Thursday evening lectures, March 29th to May 3rd, inclusive

Thursday Evening, March 29th, at 8:15 o'clock
A UNIVERSE IN MAN.

Thursday Evening, April 5th, at 8:15 o'clock
THE SPIRIT OF GUIDANCE.

Thursday Evening, April 12th, at 8:15 o'clock
REVELATION WHEN AWAKE AND WHEN ASLEEP.

Thursday Evening, April 19th, at 8:15 o'clock
THE LOST WORD.

Thursday Evening, April 26th, at 8:15 o'clock
THE SOLUTION TO THE PROBLEMS OF THE DAY.

Thursday Evening, May 3rd, at 8:15 o'clock
THE COMING WORLD RELIGION.

Tickets: Single lecture, One Dollar
Season Ticket, six lectures, Five Dollars

THE MESSAGE OF THE AGES. A Special Easter Discourse

In the East, the wise men of all ages have followed the Star. For many generations the East has given the great teachers for mankind. Again it will sing the song for humanity. The flowering of humanity, God's ideal, still remains the Message of the Ages.

Sunday Evening, April 1st, at 8:15 o'clock

Tickets, One Dollar

BIBLIOGRAPHY

A Sufi Message of Spiritual Liberty, Inayat Khan $1.50
The Confessions of Inayat Khan .... .65
The Message, Inayat Khan .... .35
In an Eastern Rose Garden, Inayat Khan 2.50
The Bowl of Saki, Inayat Khan 1.00
The Inner Life (Lectures), Inayat Khan .... (ready soon)
Notes from the Unstruck Music, the Gayan Manuscript, Inayat Khan .... (ready soon)
The Path to God, S. E. M. Green .... .35
Diwan of Inayat Khan, Jessie Duncan Westbrook 1.50
Sufism, C. H. A. Bjerregaard 1.50
Pearls from the Ocean Unseen, Zohra Mary Williams .... .75
The Phenomenon of the Soul, Sherifa Lucy Goodenough 1.00
Love: Human and Divine, Sherifa Lucy Goodenough 1.50
Akibat: Life after Death, Sherifa Lucy Goodenough 1.00
Selections from the Rubaiyat and Odes of Hafiz, rendered into English verse by a member of the Persia Society of London 4.00
The Way of Illumination, Inayat Khan 1.00
The Alchemy of Happiness, Inayat Khan .... .15
Sufism (a quarterly magazine for seekers after truth) .... .25
The Scroll of Wisdom, Saadi 1.00
The Rose Garden of Saadi 1.00
The Confessions of Al Ghazzali 1.00
The Persian Mystics, Rumi 1.50
The Persian Mystics, Jami 1.50
Bustan ("Garden"), Saadi 1.50
The Rubaiyat of Hafiz, translated by L. C. Byng 1.00
Odes from the Diwan of Hafiz 3.00
The Rubaiyat of Omar Khayyam, translated by Edward Fitzgerald .... $1.25 up to $15.00
The Kasidah, Sir Richard F. Burton 1.25
Masnavi, Rumi. 2 vols 12.00
Mantiqu't Tayr, Attar ....

(These books are on sale at Paul Elder's.)

APPENDIX B

General Note on Classification.

It should be noted that the classifications--"Gatha," "Social Gatheka," "Gita," etc.--under which the teachings of Pir-o-Murshid Inayat Khan have come down to us, are not necessarily original; many were added later according to an intended use for the teaching.

For example, the large category of "esoteric papers" received their classifications gradually according to the needs of the increasingly ordered courses of instruction for initiates. Even though from the very early days in London (1915-16) Pir-o-Murshid gave "lessons", some of which were restricted to members and/or initiates, the systematization of these into series did not begin until considerably later. The first sets assembled became known as "Gitas," though these are not all the same as the Gitas known today. From 1921 to 1923 several new series were made, mostly of teachings given 1920-22, which were eventually called "Gathas." However, the word Gatha does not appear originally on any of the documents (often it was written on later), suggesting a relatively late date for the adoption of this word (perhaps late 1923).

Another use to which many of the lectures were later put was for reading aloud at meetings of one of the activities of the Sufi Movement (after October, 1923). Thus, for example, a series of "Social Gathekas" was made, from already existing texts of lectures, for reading at meetings of the World Brotherhood. "Religious Gathekas" were assembled for reading, in place of a sermon, at the service of the Universal Worship; "Gathekas" were made to read to candidates for initiation in the Sufi Order. "Cherags' Papers" were gathered for the instruction of those ordained to perform the Universal Worship. Many of these papers were later published as parts of books; for instance, many of the Religious Gathekas were incorporated in the book *The Unity of Religious Ideals* (London, 1929).

As this indicates, material for publication could be taken from a category established for a different purpose. The texts of many lectures, particularly later copies, are marked "Public", which generally does not mean that they were given to the public, but that the editor or worker considers them suitable for publication. Those marked "Private", on the other hand, were to be reserved for some special use. Many lectures have had their categories changed over the years. Classes originally given to initiates only, or papers made for restricted classes, have later been published. Recently (1982), the whole set of Gathas has been published as a book; earlier, many of the Gitas had appeared as parts of books.

Taking all this into consideration, it would seem prudent to avoid any assumptions about the original intended use of a particular teaching based on any subsequent classification.

Classification of Lectures Given from January to June 1923.

In the left-hand column are listed the names of the Headquarters' papers and their numbers. In the right-hand column appear the titles and dates of the corresponding lectures in their original form.

		Original texts of the lectures:
Gathas:		
Originally classified as Gatha Tassawuf (without number), then included in the book *The Unity of Religious Ideals*, 1st ed. (1929).	=	"Divine Grace is a loving impulse..." .... 1st week Jan.
Gitas:		
Gita Dhyana - Meditation		These lectures are known only in their already classified form. .... Spring 1923.
Social Gathekas:		
Social Gatheka no. 18 Social Gatheka no. 19	=	"Shaikh Muslih-ud-Din Saadi" .... 24 Apr.
Social Gatheka no. 26 Social Gatheka no. 27	=	"Khwajah Shamsu-d-Din Mahomed Hafiz" .... 1 May
Social Gatheka no. 30	=	"Farid-ud-Din Attar" .... 8 May
Gathekas:		
Gatheka no. 28	=	"Innocence" .... 7? Jan.
Gatheka no. 29	=	"Influence" .... 8 Jan.
Gatheka no. 40	=	"Ideal among nations..." 26 Febr.
Sangathas:		
Sangatha I no. 82	=	"How to Progress in the Spiritual Path in Everyday Life" .....9 Jan.

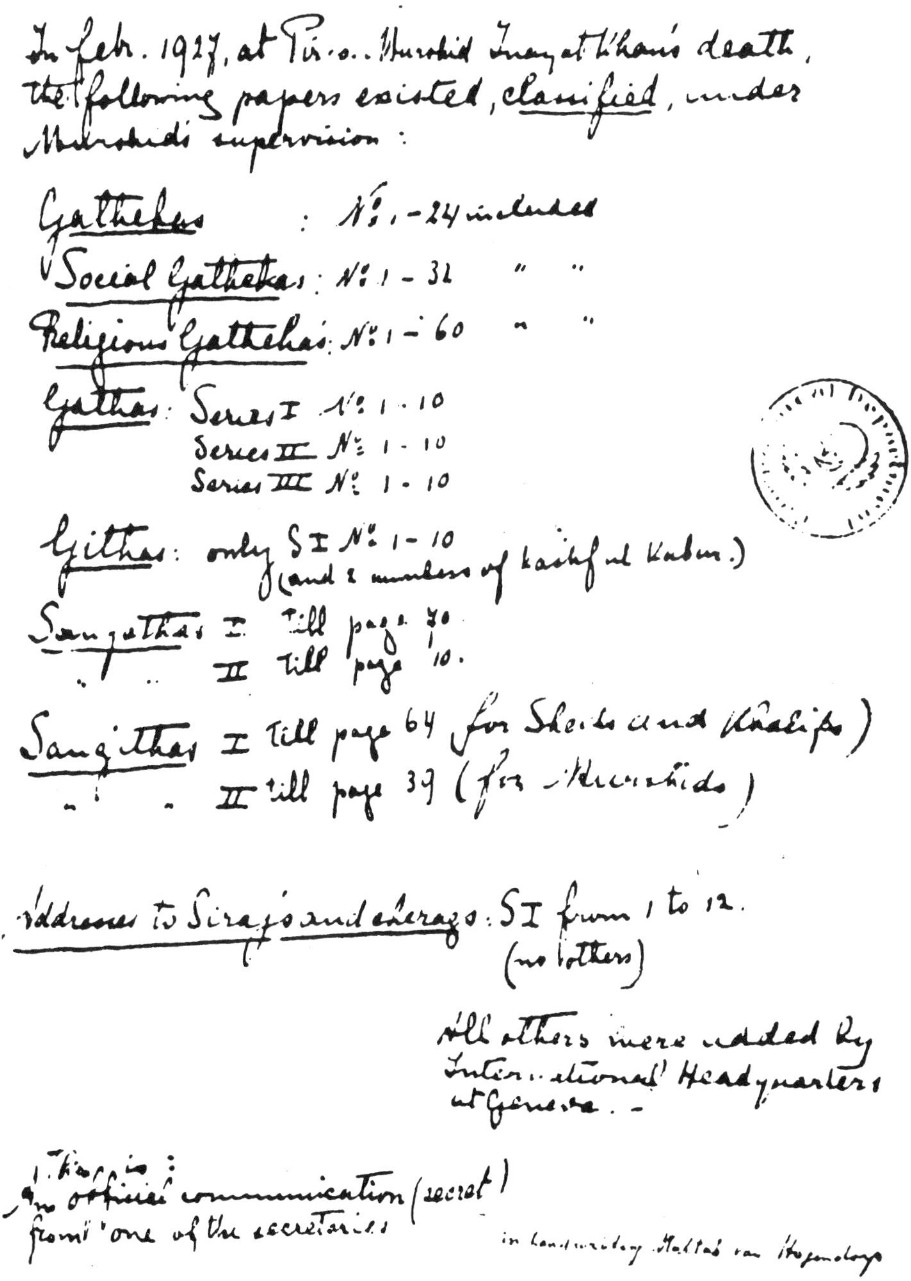
In Febr. 1927, at Pir-o-Murshid Inayat Khan's death, the following papers existed, classified, under Murshid's supervision:

Gathekas : No. 1-24 included
Social Gathekas : No. 1 - 32 " "
Religious Gathekas : No. 1 - 60 " "
Gathas : Series I No. 1 - 10
Series II No. 1 - 10
Series III No. 1 - 10
Githas : only S I No. 1 - 10 (and 2 numbers of Kashf ul Kabur.)
Sangathas I till page 70
" II till page 10.
Sangithas I till page 64 (for Sheikhs and Khalifs)
" II till page 39 (for Murshids)

Addresses to Sirajs and Cherags: S I from 1 to 12. (no others)

All others were added by International Headquarters at Geneva. -

Kopie: An official communication (secret) from one of the secretaries

in handwriting Mahtab van Hogendorp

List of papers issued by I.H.Q. under Murshid's supervision, in handwriting of Mahtab van Hogendorp.

APPENDIX C

LIST OF MISSING LECTURES: January - June 1923

The information on missing lectures from the period January - June 1923 has been found in newspaper articles, in public announcements and in Pir-o-Murshid Inayat Khan's letters to his mureeds. Only if the newspaper articles on missing lectures contain quoted words of the Pir-o-Murshid have these parts of the articles been inserted in this book.

6 January	The Hague (Netherlands) Anna Paulownastraat	*Brotherhood*, from a newspaper article in *De Nieuwe Courant*, The Hague.
18 January	Belgium	*Sight Development*
21 January	London	*Reading the Future*
23 January	England	*Nature's Religion*
25 January	London	*Thought Reading*
26 January	England	*The Coming World Religion*
28 January	London	*Character Reading*
27 February	New York	*World Brotherhood* (see newspaper article 27?February), 8:15 pm in the *League for the Larger Life*. On 28th February Pir-o-Murshid wrote to Fazal Mai (Mrs. Egeling, "Last night I spoke to a crowded and most appreciating audience ..."
28 February	New York	*The Path of Initiation*
Beginning March	New York	*Sufism* (see newspaper article early March)
Beginning March	Boston	subject(s) of the lecture(s) unknown
9 March	Detroit	*International Brotherhood* (see newspaper article 9?March)
10 March	Detroit	*Sufi Philosophy* (see newspaper article 9/10 March)
11 March	Detroit	*Man, the Master of His Destiny*
12 March	Detroit	*A Message over the Radio*
21 March	San Francisco	4 pm: *Mystic Philosophy* 8 pm: *The Awakening of the Soul*
22 March	San Francisco	4 pm: *Mystic Philosophy* 8 pm: *Sound and Color: their Psychic Influence and Healing Power*

23 March	San Francisco	4 pm:	*Mystic Philosophy*
		8 pm:	*Revelation, when awake and when asleep*
24 March	San Francisco	4 pm:	*Mystic Philosophy*
25 March	San Francisco	4 pm:	*Mystic Philosophy* (see newspaper article 25? March)
		8 pm:	The Coming World Religion
26 March	San Francisco	4 pm:	*Women's Influence in the World* (see newspaper article 26? March)
		8 pm:	*Sufi Philosophy* (see newspaper article 26 March)
1 April	San Francisco	First Universal Worship in the Church of All, held in the Native Sons' Hall: *The Message of the Ages* (a special Easter discourse)	
2 April	San Francisco	*Radio talk about the Message.* On 1st April Pir-o-Murshid wrote to Fazal Mai (Mrs. Egeling), "tomorrow I am to deliver the Message to the whole world by radio wireless ..."	
8 April	San Francisco	Service of the Universal Worship in which Mrs. Martin was ordained Siraja and two other mureeds became Cherags. The subject of the *sermon* is not known.	
10 April	San Francisco	2:30 pm at the Paul Elder Gallery: *Omar Khayyam*, the second lecture in the series of six lectures on Sufi Poets announced in the program of the Paul Elder Gallery, the only lecture announced there of which no text has reached the archives. A newspaper article in a San Francisco Sunday's paper refers to Pir-o-Murshid Inayat Khan's words about Omar Khayyam, but this may have been said by him in an interview and does not prove that the lecture was actually given.	

13 April	San Francisco	*Sufism* (see newspaper article 13? April)
15 April	San Francisco	11 am. Universal Worship in the Church of All (in the building Native Sons' Hall). The subject of the *sermon* is not known. On 15th April Pir-o-Murshid wrote to Fazal Mai (Mrs. Egeling), "... At the wireless I spoke twice by now which has reached many thousands hearts, and I am told many letters of appreciation are received by that center ..."
22 April	San Francisco	evening, in the Native Sons' Hall: *Brotherhood* (see newspaper article 22 April). On 23rd April Pir-o-Murshid wrote to Fazal Mai (Mrs. Egeling), "The work here is suddenly floorishing and will spread throughout the States as time passes ..."
9 May	Santa Barbara	in the afternoon a *talk* at a tea, given by Mrs. Bachmann, subject unknown. 8 pm: in the Woman's Club House: *Man, the Master of His Destiny*
10 May	Santa Barbara	in the afternoon a *talk* at an informal tea, given by Mrs. Browns, subject unknown. 8 pm: in the Woman's Club House: *Revelation when awake and when asleep*
11 May	Santa Barbara	8 pm: *The Healing Power of Music* at Woman's Club House
12 May	Santa Barbara	3:30 pm: *Art and Religion* at Woman's Club House

13 May	Los Angeles	2:30 pm:	*The Awakening of the Soul*, at the Ambassador Hotel Theatre.
		8 pm:	*The Message of the Ages* in the Lincoln Hall, Walker Auditorium Building.
14 May	Los Angeles	10:30 am:	*Music and Color: Their Psychic Influence and Healing Power* in the Ambassador (Italian Room).
		8 pm:	*Love, Harmony and Beauty* in the Union League Club Auditorium.
15 May	Los Angeles	10:30 am:	*The Power of the Word* in the Ambassador (Italian Room).
		8 pm:	*Revelation When Awake and When Asleep* in the Union League Club Auditorium.

See the announcement of the lectures on 13th, 14th and 15th May on the following page.

foreword

PIR-O-MURSHID INAYAT KHAN, Sufi Mystic, Philosopher, Poet and Musician, was born in 1882 at Baroda, India, and is descended from sixteen generations of spiritual teachers and five generations of distinguished musicians. His life has been devoted to the study of philosophy and music, the two studies linked and interwoven, the mysticism of sound and the mysticism of life being one and indivisible.

Music and mysticism were his heritage from both his paternal and maternal ancestors, among whom were numbered Moula Bux, the Beethoven of India (whose portrait is in the Victoria and Albert Museum at South Kensington, England), and St. Jummashah, the great seer of Punjab, who was canonized and is revered as a saint to this day by the people of India.

The Pir-o-Murshid first came from India to the United States in 1910, and, after spending something less than a year in this country lecturing at universities and other centers, went to Europe, where he has been ever since, lecturing, writing and teaching. He is devoting his life to spreading the ancient Sufi message of the fundamental unity of humanity, and to restating the inner wisdom, in terms of the religious philosophy of Love, Harmony and Beauty.

Through his lectures and his books he is well known in London, Paris, Geneva and other European cities. Following are quotations from a few of his press notices, the earnestness and enthusiasm of which attest the greatness of his genius:

"As a lecturer Inayat Khan is thoughtful and earnest and has a pleasant manner. He is a man of great intellectual abilities, of vast learning and of profound knowledge of human nature."—(From the *Kentish Independent.*)

"This musician is at the same time a poet and philosopher, as were all the great Sufis of bygone days. His great strength lies in a radiating faith in the religion of unity."—(From the *Comedia*, Paris.)

"Inayat Khan is a man of striking personality, possessed of glowing and eloquent eyes, and strangely deliberate and sedate in his bearing. He says: 'Sufism takes music as the source of all perfection, since sound was the first source of creation.' "—(From the *Daily Citizen*, London.)

"Inayat Khan speaks English excellently, and his tall figure in a long robe of apricot colored cloth, with the great Sufi jewel on his breast, is very impressive."—(From the *Evening News*, London.)

"If faddists have held sway hitherto in matters of the East, Inayat Khan holds sway by his depth of knowledge and sincerity."—(*San Francisco Journal.*)

The Series of Six Lectures

Sunday afternoon, May 13th, at 2:30, The Ambassador Hotel Theatre—*The Awakening of the Soul.*

Sunday evening, May 13th, at 8 o'clock, Lincoln Hall, Walker Auditorium Building, 730 S. Grand Ave.—*The Message of the Ages.*

Monday morning, May 14th, at 10:30, The Ambassador (Italian Room),—*Music and Color; Their Psychic Influence and Healing Power.*

Monday evening, May 14th, at 8 o'clok, The Union League Club Auditorium, Third and Hill Sts. —*Love, Harmony and Beauty.*

Tuesday morning, May 15th, at 10:30, The Ambassador (Italian Room),—*The Power of the Word.*

Tuesday evening, May 15th, at 8 o'clock, The Union League Club Auditorium, Third and Hill Sts. —*Revelation When Awake and When Asleep.*

Tickets, single lecture, One Dollar. The course of six lectures, Five Dollars.

Tickets for sale at the PHILOSOPHICAL LIBRARY, 730 S. Grand Avenue.

During his stay in Los Angeles, the address and headquarters of Pir-o-Murshid Inayat Khan will be at The Philosophical Library, Walker Auditorium Building, 730 S. Grand Avenue. Phone, 62539.

18 May	Chicago	afternoon: *The Power of Silence*
18 May	Chicago	evening: *Life an Opportunity*
20 May	Chicago	*The Power within us*
23 May	Chicago	*The Sufi Movement and its Message*
24 May	Detroit	afternoon: *Music and Color, Their Psychic Influence and Healing Power* evening: *The Solution to the Problems of the Day*
25 May	Detroit	*Revelation, when awake and when asleep*

The lectures on 23rd, 24th and 25th May were announced in a newspaper article in the *Detroit Times* of 20th May 1923.

27 May	New York	*The Message of the Ages*
28 May	New York	8:15 pm: *The Solution of the Problems of the Day*
29 May	New York	*The Expansion of Consciousness* 8:15 pm: *Development of Personality*
30 May	Philadelphia	afternoon: *Different types of Revelation* (see newspaper article 30/31 May) 8 pm: *World Brotherhood*
31 May	Philadelphia	3 pm: *The Freedom of the Soul*
1 June	New York	the first of a course of six lectures, given at the Sufi Center in the evening, subject unknown.
2 June	New York	the second of a course of six lectures, given at the Sufi Center in the evening, subject unknown.
3 June	New York	afternoon: *The Reality of the Unseen*, Sufi Center
4 June	New York	the third of a course of six lectures, *The Power of the Sacred Word*, given at The Forum.
5 June	New York	the fourth of a course of six lectures, *The Spiritual Democracy*, given at The Forum
6 June	New York	the fifth of a course of six lectures, *Reciprocity, Beneficence, Renunciation*, given at The Forum.

7 June New York the last of a course of six lectures, *Self-Realization*, given at The Forum.

See the announcement of the lectures given on 4th, 5th, 6th and 7th June on the bottom of this page.

SPECIAL NOTICE

INAYAT KHAN SUFI LECTURES

For the accommodation of a larger number who may wish to benefit by the instruction and guidance of this great teacher, the last four lectures of the course of Instruction lectures, advertised to be held at the Sufi Center, 129 West 79th St., will be held instead at

THE FORUM

279 MADISON AVENUE NEW YORK

Monday, June 4th—"***The Power of the Sacred Word.***"
Tuesday, June 5th—"***The Spiritual Democracy.***"
Wed. June 6th—"***Reciprocity, Beneficence, Renunciation.***"
Thursday, June 7th—"***Self Realization.***"

EVENINGS AT 8:15 SINGLE LECTURES, $1.00

Those interested may interview the Pir-O-Murshid Inayat Khan, by applying to Mrs. Marya Cushing, Representative, Sufi Center, 129 W. 79th St., Phone, Endicott 6598

APPENDIX D

ILLUSTRATIONS OF DOCUMENTS

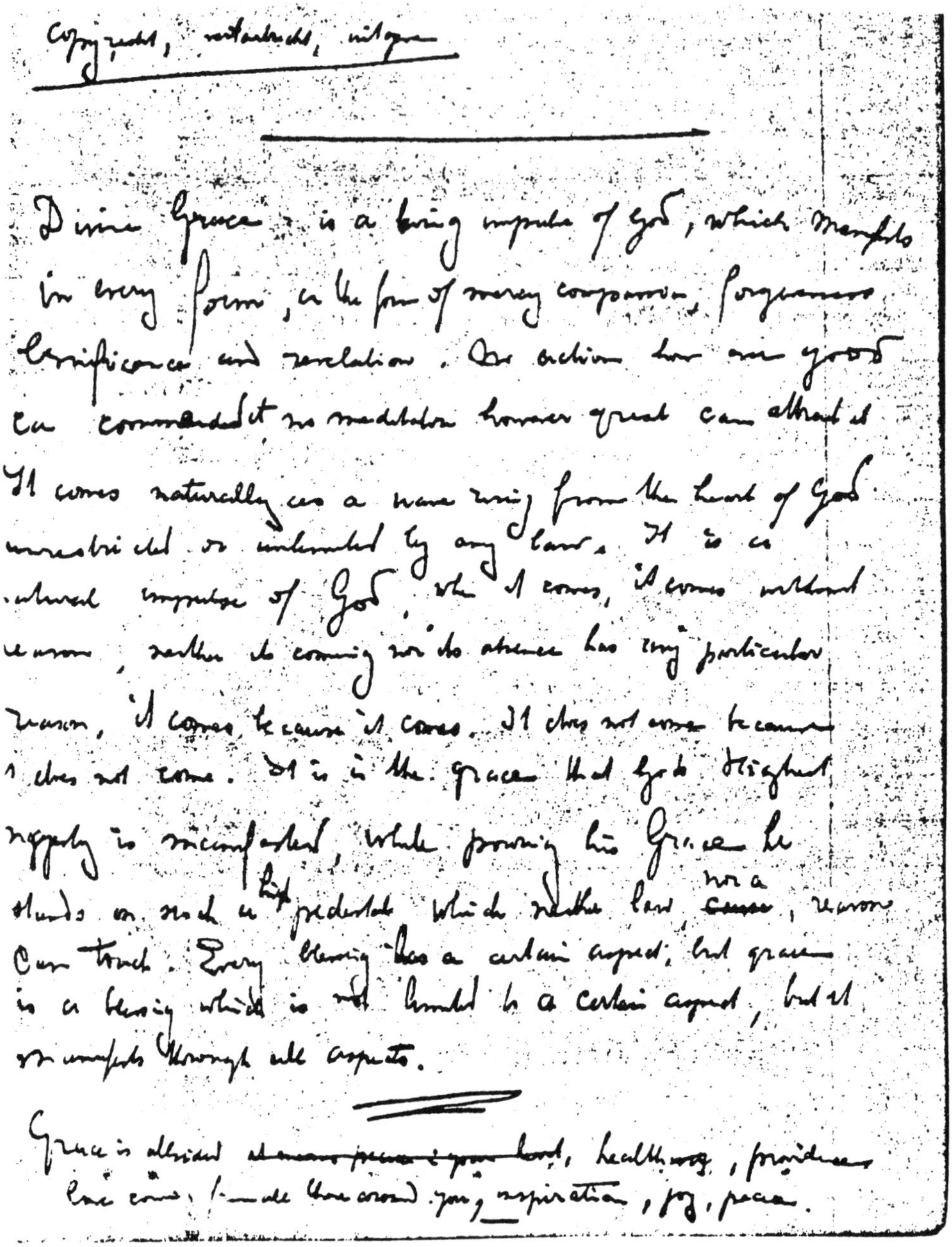

[illegible]

Divine Grace is a living impulse of God, which manifests in every form, in the form of mercy, compassion, forgiveness, beneficence and revelation. No action however good can command it, no meditation however great can attract it. It comes naturally as a wave rising from the heart of God unrestricted or unlimited by any laws. It is a natural impulse of God, when it comes, it comes without reason, neither its coming nor its absence has any particular reason, it comes because it comes. It does not come because it does not come. It is in the grace that God's [illegible] is manifested, while proving his Grace he stands on such a high pedestal which neither law, nor a reason can touch. Every blessing has a certain aspect, but grace is a blessing which is not limited to a certain aspect, but it manifests through all aspects.

Grace is also [illegible], health, wealth, providence, love [illegible], from all three around you, inspiration, joy, peace.

Sirdar's longhand reporting in his copybook of January/February 1923.
Divine Grace, first week January 1923.

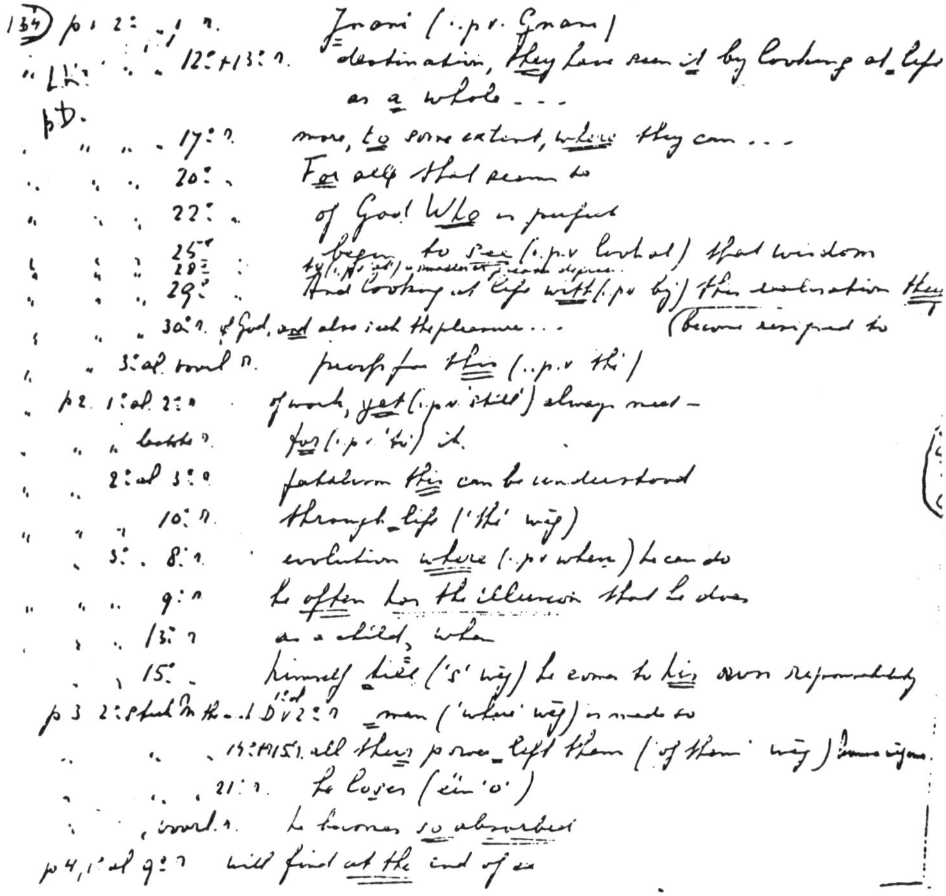
134) p1 2: n. Jnani (i.p.v. Gnani)
12:+13: n. destination, they have seen it by looking at life as a whole...
17: n. more, to some extent, where they can...
20: For all that seems to
22: of God Who is perfect
25: begin to see (i.p.v. look at) that wisdom
29: And looking at life with (i.p.v. by) this evolution they
30: n. of God, and also ... the pleasure... (Become resigned to
3: proof for this (i.p.v. this)
p2 1: of work, yet (i.p.v. 'still') always need –
for (i.p.v. 'to') it.
2: fatalism this can be understood
10: n. through life ('the' weg)
3: 8: n. evolution where (i.p.v. when) he can do
9: n he often has the illusion that he does
13: n as a child, who
15: himself still ('s' weg) he comes to his own responsibility
p3 2: man ('when' weg) is made so
15: all things power left them ('of them' weg) ...
21: n. he loses ('in' 'o')
he becomes so absorbed
p4, 1: will find at the end of ...

Sakina's list with corrections. The double underlining means that so it was written in her shorthand reporting and it should not be changed. **Fate and Free Will**, 13 January 1923.

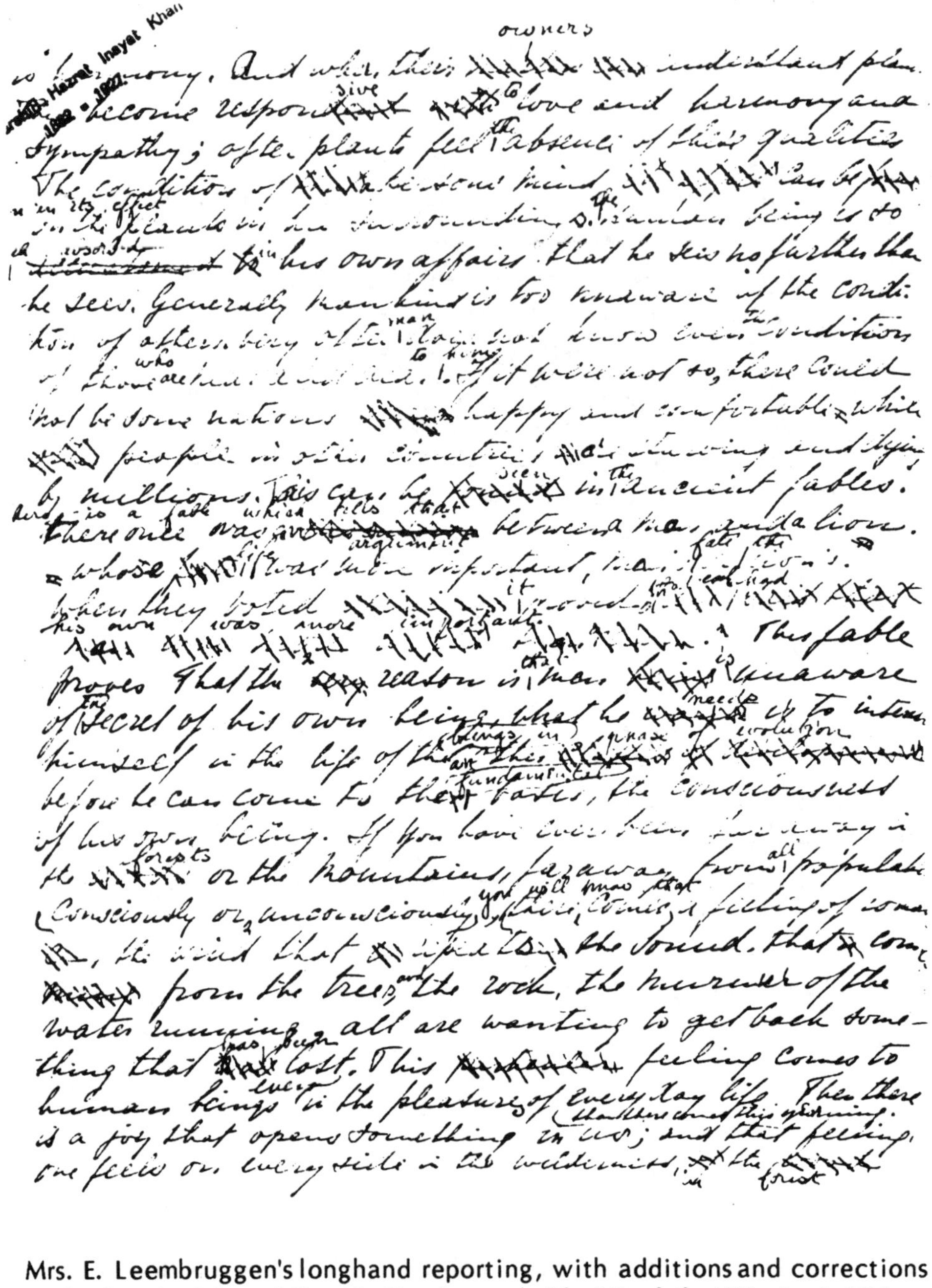

Mrs. E. Leembruggen's longhand reporting, with additions and corrections in the handwriting of Sherifa Goodenough. **The Word that Was Lost**, 15 January 1923.

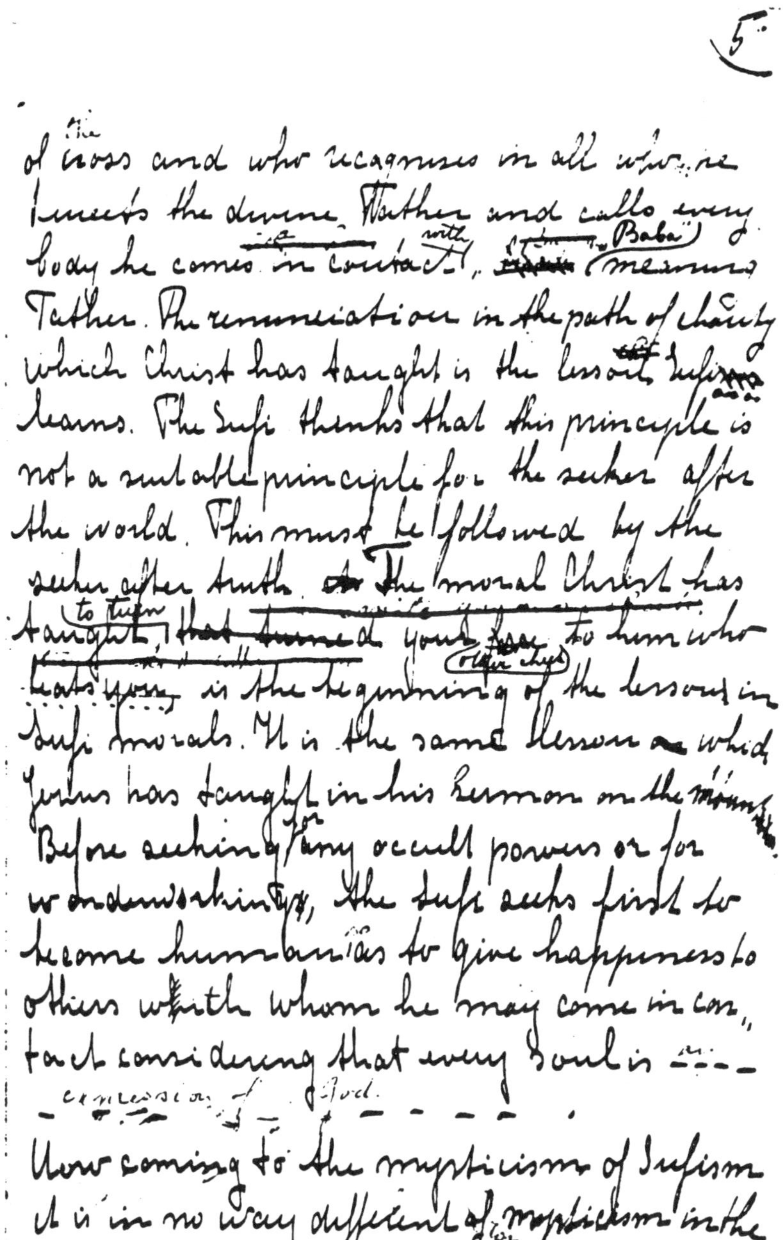

5

of the cross and who recognises in all whom he meets the divine Father and calls every body he comes in contact with "Baba" which means Father. The renunciation in the path of charity which Christ has taught is the lesson Sufism learns. The Sufi thinks that this principle is not a suitable principle for the seeker after the world. This must be followed by the seeker after truth. The moral Christ has taught, to turn your other cheek to him who beats you, is the beginning of the lessons in Sufi morals. It is the same lesson which Jesus has taught in his sermon on the mount. Before seeking any occult powers or for wonderworkings, the Sufi seeks first to become human as to give happiness to others with whom he may come in contact considering that every soul is an expression of God. — — — —

Now coming to the mysticism of Sufism it is in no way different from mysticism in the

Zuleikha van Ingen's handwriting with corrections in Sherifa Goodenough's and Sirdar van Tuyll's handwritings. **Sufism**, 15 or 17 January 1923.

(con of -)

The man, who used to become nervous and excitable when he came home and found no answer to his irritation, he, after being a little uncomfortable became quiet; for there was no stimulus to his agitation. When two or three days had passed, he began to value his wife so much, he thought: „What a great improvement!" He began to see his own faults and began to blame himself, thinking how foolish he was himself and how good was his wife. After a few days the wife had finished the sweets, she went to the healer to thank him and said: „I will give anything if you will only give me a lot of that sweet, it is such a wonderful sweet. It has brought harmony in our home, he is so kind and good to me now, all things are changed because of those sweets, I will give anything for it." The wise man said: „My good lady, it is not the sweets, it is the lesson which was behind it. The secret was in keeping the lips closed."

We have all a thousand troubles. Do we not find in our everyday life, how many different temperaments we have to meet with, those who are worthier than we, others who are less worthy; those who are tolerant, others who are not; those who easily understand and others who cannot and will not understand, the more we talk to them the worse they become. How very often very worthy people tell their friends to be very worthy and talk to them of their belief. But just because of their talking the others cannot accept it, otherwise they would have become

Miss Kerdijk's longhand reporting with corrections in the handwriting of Sherifa Goodenough. **The Power of Silence**, before 18 January 1923.

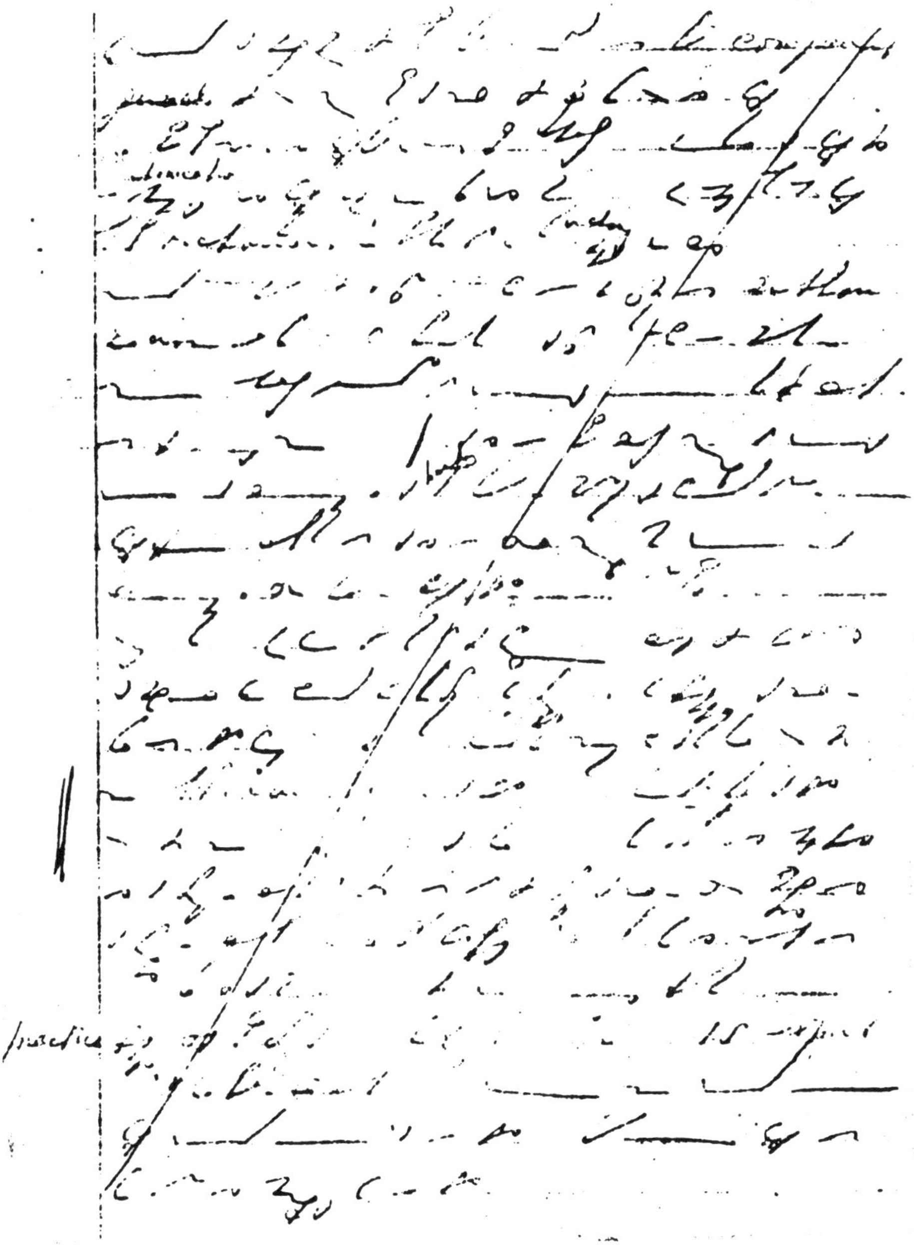

Sakina's shorthand reporting. Although the original shorthand is a little clearer than the photocopy, it shows that at some places the shorthand signs are fading out. The line was drawn through by Sakina to indicate that she had transcribed the lecture. **The Life a Continual Battle**, 5 February 1923.

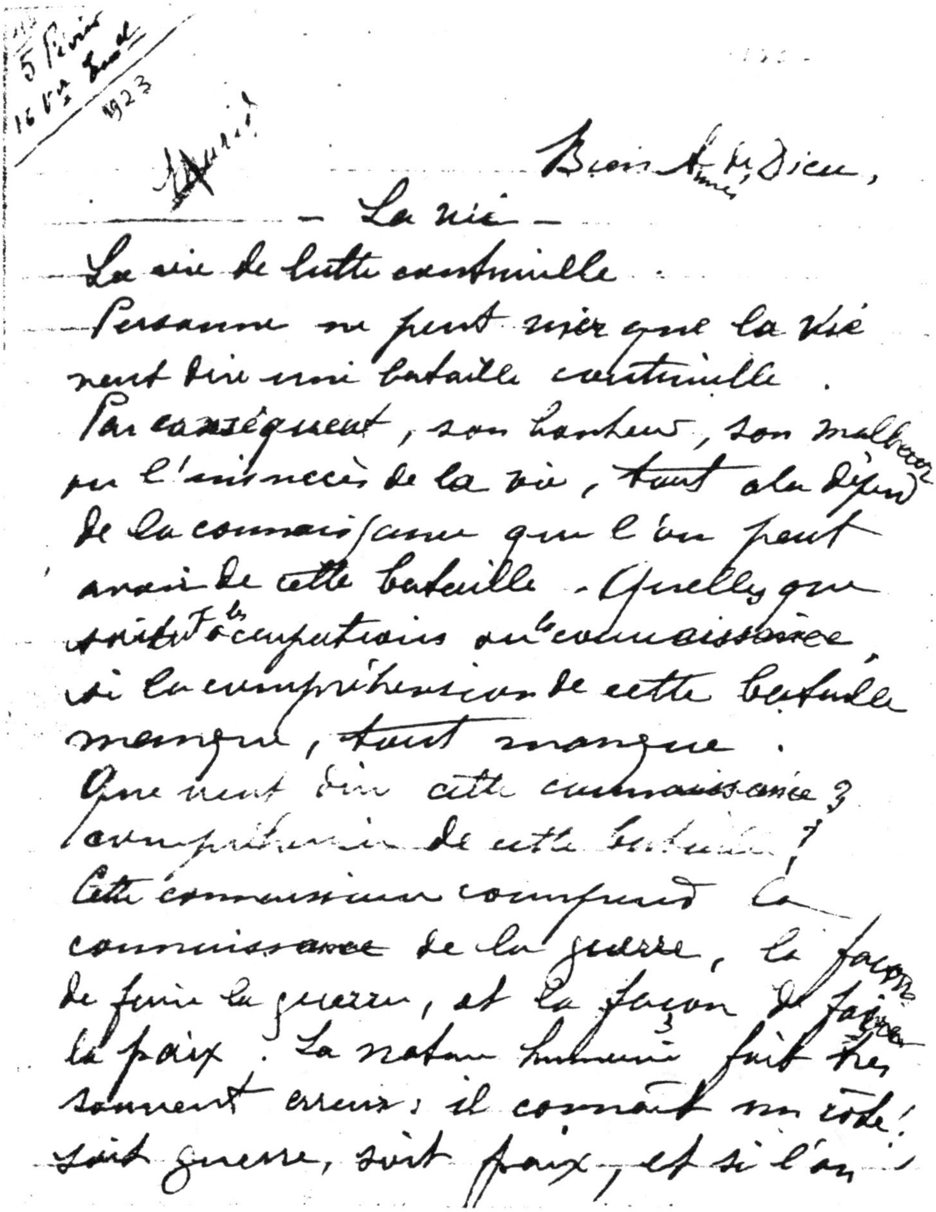

Bien-Aimés de Dieu,

— La vie —

La vie de lutte continuelle.

Personne ne peut nier que la vie veut dire une bataille continuelle. Par conséquent, son bonheur, son malheur ou l'insuccès de la vie, tout cela dépend de la connaissance que l'on peut avoir de cette bataille. Quelles que soient les occupations ou les connaissances si la compréhension de cette bataille manque, tout manque.

Que veut dire cette connaissance? compréhension de cette bataille?

Cette connaissance comprend la connaissance de la guerre, la façon de faire la guerre, et la façon de faire la paix. La nature humaine fait très souvent erreur; il connaît un côté: soit guerre, soit paix, et si l'on

Reporting in the handwriting of Mlle Lefèbvre of a simultaneously given French translation of the lecture **The Life a Continual Battle**, 5 February 1923.

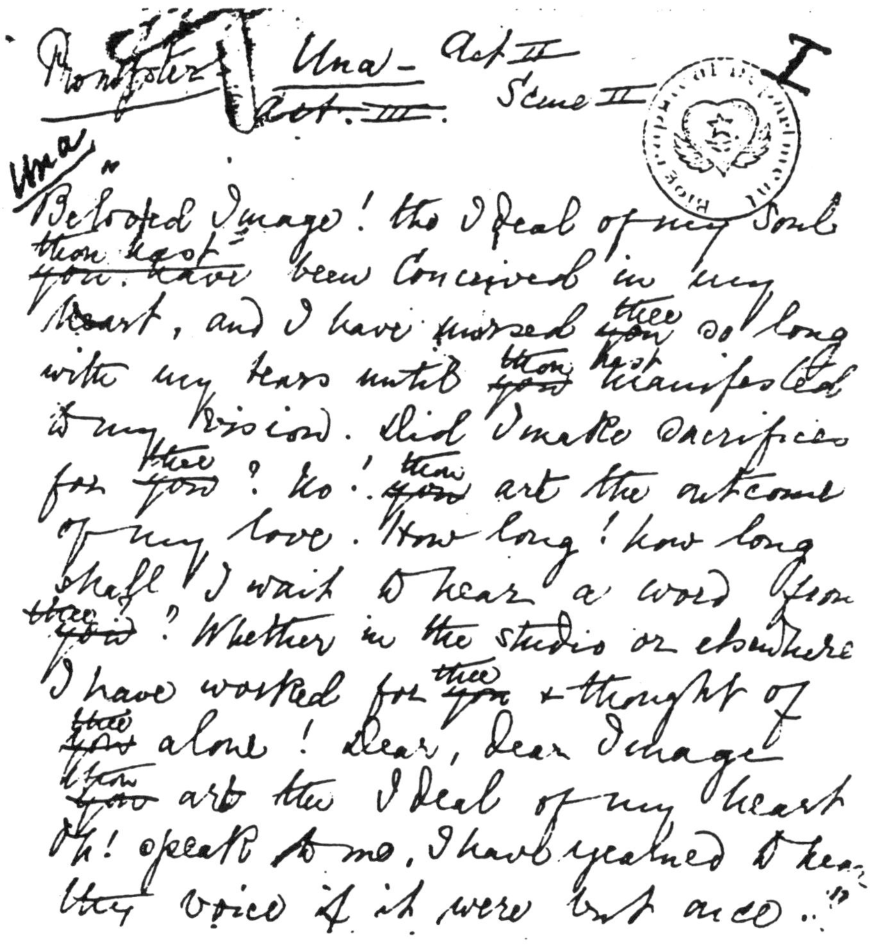

Una – Act II
Scene II

Una: "Beloved Image! the Ideal of my Soul thou hast been conceived in my heart, and I have nursed thee so long with my tears until thou hast manifested to my vision. Did I make sacrifices for thee? No! thou art the outcome of my love. How long! how long shall I wait to hear a word from thee? Whether in the studio or elsewhere I have worked for thee & thought of thee alone! Dear, dear Image thou art the Ideal of my heart Oh! speak to me, I have yearned to hear thy voice if it were but once.."

A page in the handwriting of Sophia Saintsbury Green, to whom Pir-o-Murshid Inayat Khan dictated this text. *Una*, June 1923.

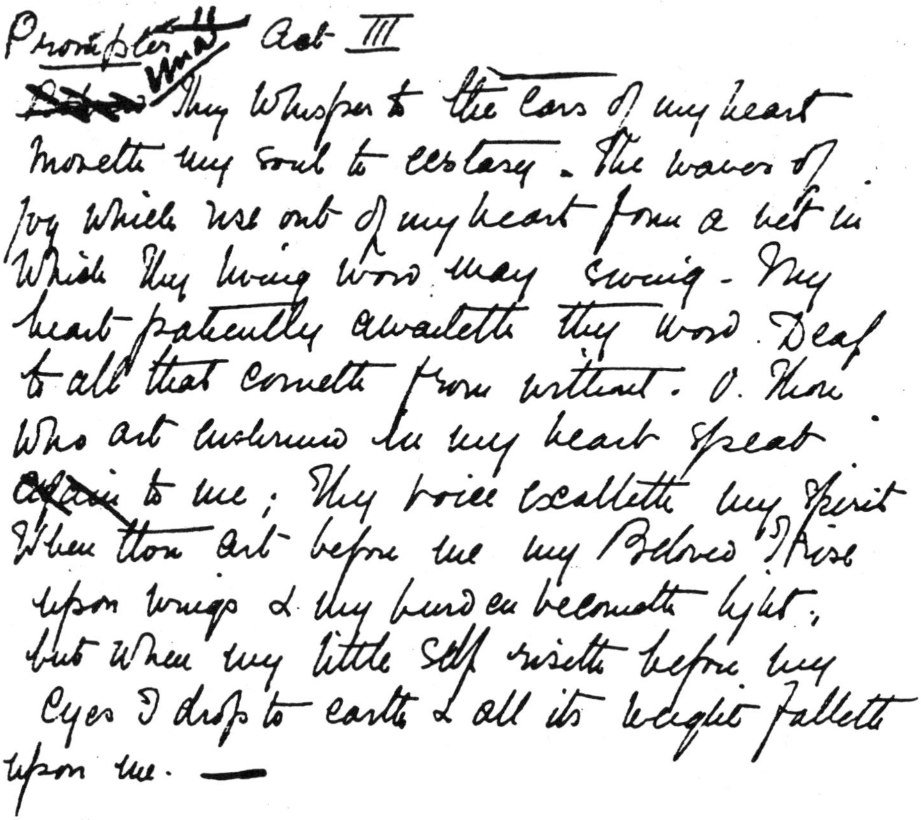

~~Prompter~~ Una Act III
~~[illegible]~~ Thy whisper to the ears of my heart
moveth my soul to ecstasy. The waves of
joy which rise out of my heart form a bed in
which thy loving word may swing. My
heart patiently awaiteth thy word. Deaf
to all that cometh from without. O Thou
who art unknown in my heart speak
~~again~~ to me; thy voice exalteth my spirit
When thou art before me my Beloved I rise
upon wings & my burden becometh light;
but when my little self riseth before my
eyes I drop to earth & all its weight falleth
upon me. —

A page in the handwriting of Keyafat LLoyd, from dictation by Pir-o-Murshid Inayat Khan. *Una*. June 1923.

GLOSSARY OF FOREIGN WORDS

The language to which the word belongs is indicated after the word:

Arabic	=	A
Greek	=	G
Hebrew	=	Hb
Hindustani, Hindi	=	H
Latin	=	L
Persian	=	P
Sanskrit	=	S
Tibetan	=	T
Turkish	=	Tk
Urdu	=	U

The usual meaning of the word, if any, is given first; if the word has a special use or additional interpretation in Sufi terminology, this meaning is given second, indicated by (Suf); the number at the end indicates the page number where the word appears.

Transliterations were made according to the following systems:

for Arabic: *The Encyclopedia of Islam*, (New edition, Leiden, 1960-), except that "ḳ" has been replaced by "q", and "dj" by "j".

for Persian: F. Steingass, *Comprehensive Persian-English Dictionary*, (8th edition, London, 1977).

for Sanskrit: M. Monier-Williams, *Sanskrit-English Dictionary*, (New Delhi, 1976; originally published in 1899), mainly following the Transliteration Committee of the Geneva Oriental Congress, September, 1894).

advaita (S)
- a-dvaita, destitute of duality, unique; non-duality; identity of Brahma, the supreme soul with the human soul; identity of spirit and matter; the ultimate truth, 204

ākāśa (S)
- open space, vacuity; ether; sky, arc of heaven.
- (Suf) - capacity, receptacle, 173

akhlāq (A)
- pl. of khulq: morals; morality; good qualities; manners.
- (Suf) - akhlāq Allāh, the manner of God; the ninth initiation, 332

alif (A)
- the first letter of the Arabic, Persian and Urdu alphabets; also the number one (in the Greek alphabet: alpha), 338

ʽamal (A)
- work; practice; effect; dominion.
- (Suf) - a spiritual practice, 57 note 79

ʽarsh (A)
- roof, canopy; the highest (9th) sphere, the empyrean (where the throne of God is); throne, 313, 317

āsana (S)
- posture; third limb of Patañjali's raja yoga, 57

avatāra (S)
- descent, appearance of a deity upon earth; the incarnation of a deity; the incarnations of Vishṇu.
- (Suf) - Lord of humanity, 17

bābā (T,P,H)
- father; grandfather; child; old, respected man; a sanyāsi, a faqīr; head of the Order of Qalandars, an Islamic Order of faqirs; a leader in the Bektāshi Order of dervishes, 56

baqā (A)
- remaining; duration, permanence; eternity; immortality; life, living.
- (Suf)
  - realization, an aspect of spiritual development, 252
  - one of the last stages of meditation, 301
  - the life of God, 317

bay'at (A,P)
- allegiance; investiture; homage, fealty.
- (Suf) - initiation, 302

bhakti (S)
- devotion, piety, love.
- bhakti yoga, 191, 309

bodhisattva (S)
- essence of reason.
- (Suf)
  - the Spirit of Guidance, 125
  - the Universal Mind, 203

Brahma (S)
- God, the Creator in the Hindu religion, 110
- and Abraham, 203

brāhmaṇa (S)
- a member of the highest Hindu caste of traditional religious leaders and scholars, 110

cherāgh (U), chirāgh (P)
- lamp, light; guide, director; client, dependant.
- (Suf) - a person authorized to officiate in the Universal Worship, 249

czar
- Old Russian: tsésari, in Latin: Caesar; title of the emperor of Russia, 29

dharma (S)
- morality; duty, any given social group's particular caste obligations; law, religion, 57 note 78, 198

dhārṇā (S), dhāraṇā
- sixth accessory to yoga in the *Yoga-sutras* of Patañjali; concentration of mind, contemplation, 57 note 78

dhāt (A), (zāt) (P)
- endowed with; essence, nature; soul, man's self.
- (Suf) - ṣifat and dhāt, 322

dhikr (A), (zikr) (P)
- to remember, to mention; remembering, memory; recital, reading or reciting of the Qur'ān.
- (Suf)
  - praise and glorification of God.
  - a certain spiritual practice (cf. mantra), 44, 57 note 79, 252, 254, 267

dhyāna (S)
- meditation, contemplation; profound and abstract religious meditation; seventh limb of Patañjali's rāja yoga.
- (Suf) - name of a part of Pīr-o-Murshid 'Ināyat Khān's teachings made into gitas

djabarūt
- q.v. jabarūt

djalāl
- q.v. jalāl

djamāl
- q.v. jamāl

durūd (A,P,U)
- benediction, blessing; prayer, praise (esp. of the Prophet Muḥammad).
- (Suf)
  - a spiritual practice, especially for those concentrating on the fanā fī 'r Rasūl, 223, 236, 255, 267, 271, 283, 312
  - words of one such, very general, durūd prayer:
    "O Almighty Lord, shower Thy blessings and benefactions on Muḥammad and his followers as Thou didst on Ibrāhīm and his followers. Praised be Thou and exalted.
    O Almighty Lord, be gracious to Muḥammad and his followers as Thou wert gracious to Ibrāhīm and his followers. Praised be Thou and glorious."

fakīr
- q.v. faqīr

fanā (A)
- to pass away, to perish; mortality, death.
- (Suf)
  - self effacement, 252
  - fanā fī Shaikh, surrender before the teacher for the mureed's own sake, 255
  - fanā fī Murshid, attunement to the teacher, 257
  - fanā fī 'Ilāh, absorption of the soul in God, 301

faqīr (A) - poor, needy; a poor man, a religious mendicant, a darwish.
- (Suf) - negative to God, positive to man, 225

fikr (A), (fikar) - thought, consideration; reflection; idea, imagination.
- (Suf) - one of the courses in Sufism, 57 note 79
  - a spiritual practice, 233, 260, 281, 312
  - fikr and faqīr, 279

gāthā (S) - verse, song, metre; part of the Scripture of the Parsis.
- (Suf) - name of a part of Pīr-o-Murshid ʿInāyat Khān's teachings, *passim*.

gāṭhaka (S), (gāṭheka) - chanter, chanting of a sacred poem.
- (Suf) - name of a part of Pīr-o-Murshid ʿInayat Khān's teachings, *passim* (See also Appendix B.)

guru (S) - teacher, venerable or respectable person; a spiritual preceptor. Cf. Murshid.

ḥakīm (A) - philosopher, sage; physician, 313

ḥāl (A) - condition, state.
- (Suf) - ecstasy, 313

haryat (S) - eager, willing, glad; desired, pleasant, dear, precious.
- (Suf) - divine Grace, a step in attaining to unity, 316

ḥayrat (A) - being astounded; amazement.
- (Suf) - a stage of self-realization in which a sense of splendour comes, as a child when born sees everything new in this old world, 333

hierophant (G) - high priest, official interpreter of sacred mysteries or ceremonies, 266

Hindū (S,P,U) - meaning both Indian and Hindū, 100-5

Iblīs (A) - the Devil, Satan, Lucifer; in the Islamic tradition the angel of light, or perhaps a jinn, punished by God because he disobeyed by refusing to bow down before the first created man; king of the angels, expelled from Eden, 318

ʿilm (A)
- knowledge, science, doctrine.
- (Suf) - real knowledge, after having escaped from the thought of self, 309

ʿināyat (A)
- intending, meaning; preserving, care; favour; gift.
- (Suf) - divine grace, 264

Invocation, the - (Suf) - "Towards the One, the Perfection of Love, Harmony and Beauty, the Only Being, united with all the illuminated souls who form the embodiment of the Master, the Spirit of Guidance", 236, 237, 241, 266, 267

jabarūt (A)
- might, power, omnipotence, dominion; heaven.
- (Suf) - a sphere of the soul, 309, 318

jalāl (A), (jelāl)
- greatness, majesty; power.
- (Suf) - self-discipline, mastery over one's self, 44

jamāl (A), (jemāl)
- beauty, elegance.
- (Suf)
  - beauty; responsiveness, the light of the moon,
  - mercy and compassion, 44

japa (S) - muttering, whispering; repeating passages from scriptures or names of a deity. "Japa is the repetition of any mantra or name of the Lord" (Śivananda, Divine Life Society), 57 note 78

jasna - s.v. yajña

jñāna (S)
- knowledge, the higher knowledge; conscience, intelligence.
- jñāna yoga, the path of knowledge, 25 note 4

kāfī (A) - to be sufficient, sufficiency; entire, perfect.
- (Suf) - the All-Sufficient (a Name of God), yā Kāfī, Oh, All-Sufficient One (in the Purification Breath), 285

kāfir (A) - an ungrateful one, hence, unbeliever, infidel, heathen, 12

kalāmu'llāh (A) - the word of God.
- (Suf) - way of referring to akhlāk Allāh, q.v., 332

Kālī (S) - as a Hindu goddess, a black and destructive, terrifying aspect of the supreme goddess Devi, associated with the goddess Durgā 328-9

karmā (S) - act, work; result, the rhythm of past actions; law of action and the consequences it produces in the present or in a future birth, 84-5, 309

kasb (A) - acquirement, gain; wealth, knowledge.
- (Suf) - a spiritual practice, 57 note 79, 285

kashf (A) - opening, disclosure, revelation; intuition, divine inspiration. Cf. prajña.
- (Suf) - intuition, the living light from within,
- name of subject category of a part of Pīr-o-Murshid ʽInāyat Khān's teachings, 263

khalīf (A) - successor (particularly the successors of the Prophet Muḥammad); the man of God; representative, vice-regent.
- (Suf) - deputy of the head of a Sufi Order, 309, 317

khatm (A), (khatum) - conclusion, end, seal.
- (Suf) - name given by Pīr-o-Murshid ʽInāyat Khān to the final prayer in the Universal Worship, 313-4

khilwat (P), khalwat (A) - solitude; seclusion; a cell (for religious retirement), 279

Khudā (P) - self-revealing, God, 159
compounded from (P) khud (self) and ā (coming) to mean "who comes from his own volition, self-revealing, as a counterpart to Hari (H), "He Who draws all unto Himself".

makām - q.v. maqām

malakūt (A) - Kingdom, Heaven; spirits, angels.
- (Suf) - sphere of thought and imagination, 304, 309

mammon - Armenian word, used in the Bible to personify fortune and profit. The meaning has become that of a power opposite to God, 315

mantra (S), mantram - sacred text, prayer, to be repeated for the purpose of spiritual attainment, 154
- more powerful than a weapon, 44

maqām (A) - place; halt, station; residence, abode; position; basis.
- (Suf) - a stage of spiritual attainment earned by effort, 314

māyā (S) - a substance subject to change, death and destruction; cosmic illusion.
- (Suf) - the illusive nature of life, 336

mleccha (S) - foreigner, barbarian, outcast, 12 note 12

mudrā (S) - a certain class of exercises in hatha yoga; symbols shown in hands during worship, 57 note 78

mukti (S) - liberation, freedom; the realization of the soul's freedom, 120

murīd (A), (mureed) - willing; aspiring; an aspirant, follower, disciple of a murshid, *passim*

murshid (A) - guide, spiritual teacher.
- (Suf) - Pīr-o-Murshid: q.v.

najāt (A) - liberation, salvation; mukti (in Hinduism), nirvāṇa (in Buddhism), 57

nafs (A), (nufs) - breath; essence; self; desire; evil eye.
- (Suf) - ego, false ego, 227, 255, 267, 304

namāz (P), nimāz - prayer, adoration, worship; the prayers, salāt in Islām.
- (Suf) - a course or process of training in Sufism, 57
  - former name of the prayer "Saum" (cf. *Authentic Versions of the Teachings of Pir-o-Murshid Inayat Khan on Sufism*, Sayings Part I, p. 200).

nāsūt (A) - humanity, human nature.
- (Suf) - the physical plane, 309

neophyte (G) - the newly initiated one, 266

nirvāṇa (S) - a Buddhist term: colourless; no difference, no distinction, 57-8
- (Suf) - the realization of the soul's freedom, 120, 301, 304, 311

niyāz (P,U) - poverty, necessity; petition, prayer; wish; present, offering.
- (Suf) - Nayāz, the name of a dawn time purification prayer, 227

nūr (A) - light, brilliance, splendour, illumination; knowledge, truth; a Name of God.
- (Suf) - Intelligence, 25
  - Light of God immanent in the world of names and forms, 39-40
  - Nūr Muḥammad (A), Nūr-e-Muḥammadi (P), Light or Spirit of Guidance, 315-16

Pīr-o-Murshid (P)
- Pīr (P), elder, senior; o (P), wa, ve (A) - "and", "along with" or indicating the joining of two words into a single concept or expression; Murshid (A), director, preceptor, leader.
- title used by `Ināyat Khān during his life in the West.

prajnā (S)
- discernment, intuition; consciousness, awareness; cf. kashf, 263

prāna (S)
- breath, vitality, life.
- (Suf)
  - the central breath, 233
  - life in its physical form as perceived through the physical spheres, 128, 306
  - breath manifested outwardly, 117

prānāyāma (S)
- regulation and restraint of breath; fourth branch of Patañjali's rāja yoga, 57 note 78

rāga
- a particular musical mode in Indian music, 101

rūḥ (A)
- sg. of arwāḥ, soul, spirit, the vital principle, 315

ṣāf (A), ṣafā (A)
- pure, clean; purity.
- (Suf) - purification process, 223, 317

samādhi (S)
- state of superconsciousness when Absoluteness is experienced; identification of the mind with the object of meditation; eighth branch of Patañjali's rāja yoga, 57 note 78, 299, 319

Sarasvatī (S)
- the Hindu goddess of learning, patroness of art, music and literature, the personification of the sacred river, the Sarasvatī, also identified with the goddess of speech, Vac. In later Hinduism she is usually considered the consort of Brahmā, 108-9

ṣaut-e-surmad (A) - continuing sound, eternal sound.
- (Suf) - abstract sound, 257

shāfī (A) - health-giving; healer.
- (Suf) - the Healer (a Name of God),
- yā Shāfī, O Healer (in the Purification Breath), 285

shaghl (A), (shaghal) - work, study;
shughlī shaghīl means an exertion of the truly diligent, an all-absorbing work.
- (Suf) - a spiritual practice, 57 note 79

shifāyat (A,P) (shefāyat) - restoring to convalescence, health-giving, healer, 235
- (Suf) - a rank given in the Sufi healing activity.

ṣifat (A, P) - description; quality, attribute; form, manner.
- (Suf) - manifestation, what is known by the Self, the activities coming from the condition of awareness, 321

sīmurgh (P) - a fabulous bird in Persian legend, symbol of the Divine Ideal in the *Mantiq-ut-tair*, q.v., 316
- in modern Persian can also stand for sī murgh, "thirty birds", hence in the *Mantiq* the only ones, the true mystics, to attain to the sīmurgh and realize their identity with him.

ṣūfī (A,G) - usually derived from ṣūf (A), wool, a piece of wool, or cloth, or thread; woollen (woollen garments were worn by certain groups of ascetics as a mark of penitence and renunciation).
- often related by preference to ṣāf (A), pure, clean.
- with possible influence from the Greek sophos, wise, intelligent.

Sufi, the - in the words of Pīr-o-Murshid 'Ināyat Khān during the first half of 1923: "The Sufi seeks first to become humane, as to give happiness to the others. The Sufi develops friendliness, giving and taking sympathy, sharing one another's burden through life; enjoying all that is beautiful, he seeks divine beauty even in the crowd" (57)

ṭālib (A) - seeker, inquirer; desirous of knowledge; beggar.
- (Suf) - murīd, disciple, 227, 242, 246, 250, 257, 259, 261, 273, 285, 290

tanbūrā (H), tanbūr (P) - a drone instrument of simpler construction than the vīnā, supplying a rich droning accompaniment. The bowl is formed by a gourd in Northern India and is usually of wood in southern India. It has three steel strings and one brass string which are played with the fingers, 103

tapas (S) - austerity, mortification; ascetic self-denial; part of the preliminary side of rāja yoga (Patañjali), 57 note 78

taṣawwuf (A) - verbal noun (infinitive of ṣūf; Sufism, mysticism, contemplation).
- (Suf) - the title of some of Pīr-o-Murshid 'Ināyat Khān's lectures on metaphysics, and the name of a subject category of his teachings in his gathas and gitas, 1 note 1

Vedānta (S) - end (complete knowledge) of the Veda; name of the second and most important part of the third of the three great divisions of Hindu philosophy, called Vedānta either as teaching the ultimate scope of the Veda, or simply as explained in the Upanishads which come at the end of the Veda. Its chief doctrine is that of advaita, non-duality, 57, 69, 171

Vedantic - of Vedānta, used in the Vedas, 25

Vedantist - a student of Vedānta.

vīnā (S), bīn (H) - Indian musical stringed instrument, often used for meditation purposes, played with great mastery by Pīr-o-Murshid 'Ināyat Khān, 118

waḥdānīyat (A,P) - unity, singularity; the belief in the unity of God.
- (Suf) - a condition of God, 316, 321

waḥdat (A,P) - the being single or alone; unity, oneness, solitariness.
- (Suf) - condition of unity of God, 316, 321

waẓīfah (A), waẓ̤īfah (P) - wazafah: to follow; pension, allowance; task, daily performance, daily worship.
- (Suf) - a spiritual practice, 57 note 7, 271, 273, 312

yajña - "jasna" in note 78 of the lecture on Sufism on p. 57 may have been heard instead of yajña, meaning: worship, devotion, prayer, offering, sacrifice.

z̲āt - q.v. dhāt

z̲ikr, z̲ikar - q.v. dhikr

Zoroaster (G) - Greek name for Zarathushtra

LIST OF PERSONS, PLACES AND EVENTS

Abraham, Ibrāhīm, Brahim	Patriarch and prophet, flourished ca. 1750 B.C. Regarded as the ancient founder of their religious tradition by Jews, Christians and Muslims, p. 48, 54, 70, 141, 203
Abū Sa'īd ibn Abī'l Khayr	(967-1049), Persian Sufi teacher and poet, known for his discourses and paradoxical sayings, p. 282
Ajmer(e)	city in Rajasthan, India, famous as location of the shrine of Khwaja Mo'inu'd-Din Chishti (died 1236), the great disseminator of Sufism in India, p. 329
Akbar	Generally regarded as the greatest Mughal emperor of India (1542-1605), who aimed at optimal religious, cultural and social attunement of Hinduism and Islam. He founded the Din-e-ilahi, a ceremonial court cult of religious character, in which different religious rites were included. His palace at Fatepur Sikri and his tomb near Agra are among the finest examples of Mughal architecture, p. 298
'Alī ibn Abī Ṭālib	(ca. 600-661) younger cousin, early adherent and later son-in-law of the Prophet Muhammad, and his fourth successor, reigning from 656-661. Regarded by Shi'ite Muslims as the only true successor, and regarded by many Sufis as the origin of their spiritual pedigree, p. 106
Angkor	architectural site in Kampuchea (Cambodia), capital of Khmer Empire from the 9th to the 15th century, containing the famous temple ruins of Angkor Wat and Angkor Thom, p. 298
'Aṭṭar, Muhammad b. Ibrāhīm Farīd-ud-Dīn	celebrated Persian Sufi poet from Nishapur, traditionally said to have been born in 1119 A.D. and to have been killed by the Mongol invaders in 1230 at the age of 110 (now disputed by some scholars). "Attar" means perfumer. Many of his writings are well-known,

including the Mantiq-ut-tair (Conference of the Birds), Tazkirat-ul-auliya (a prose work on the lives of Sufi saints), the Ilahi Nama (an epic) and others, p. 142.,206-12, 316

Avicenna — Latin rendering of Ibn Sina, q.v.

Baucis and Philamon — in Greek mythology, humble couple who entertained the gods Zeus and Hermes, and thus became priests, and ended their lives by becoming trees together, p. 226

Baum, George — an American mureed, ordained a Cherag and made a Sheikh by Pir-o-Murshid Inayat Khan in America in 1923, p. xii
cf. *Biography of Pir-o-Murshid Inayat Khan*, (London, 1979), pp. 172, 490

Best, Cecil Eric Britten — (1882-1974), met Pir-o-Murshid Inayat Khan in England in 1916. He was ordained a Cherag in 1921, then went to Brasil where for thirty years he represented the Sufi Message. He is the author of several books, p. 108 (Documents)
cf. *Biography of Pir-o-Murshid Inayat Khan*, (London, 1979), pp. 143, 433, 493

Bhagavad Gītā (S) — (The Lord's Song), one of the sacred books of the Hindus. It is part of Book VI of the *Mahabharata* (great epic of the Bharata dynasty), presented as a dialogue between the warrior prince Arjuna and his friend and charioteer, Krishna, who is an avatara (incarnation) of the god Vishnu, p. 262, 332

Bhakti (S) — meaning devotion, love. A Sufi name given by Pir-o-Murshid Inayat Khan to a Dutch mureed, Mrs. G. Eggink-van Stolk, q.v.

Bible — (from the Greek *biblos*, book), the name given to the combined collection of the Hebrew scriptures (known to Christians as the *Old Testament*), and the *New Testament* (Greek Christian scriptures), see Index.

Borobudur great Buddhist architectural monument in central Java (Indonesia), built around 800 A.D. It combines the *stupa* (relic mound) with the *mandala* (ritual diagram). It was neglected from about the year 1000, but was restored by the Dutch, 1907-1911, and again in the early 1970's with the help of UNESCO, p. 298

Buddha (Pāli, S) meaning enlightened one, title of Siddhartha Gautama (ca. 563 - ca. 483 B.C.), founder of Buddhism, the great religious-philosophical system, see Index.

Burbank, Luther American horticulturist. Pir-o-Murshid Inayat Khan visited him in Santa Rosa, California, during his lecture tour in 1923, p. xiii
cf. *Biography of Pir-o-Murshid Inayat Khan*, (London, 1979), pp. 172, 462, 555

Būstān (P), Bostan (T,U) meaning place of fragrance, orchard, garden, a 13th century book of verse on ethical subjects by the Persian poet Sa'di, q.v., p. 164

Chaldeans ancient Semitic-speaking nomad dwellers in the areas at the head of the Persian Gulf between Arabia and the Euphrates delta. Abraham (q.v.) in the *Old Testament* is said to have come from the town of Ur in this area, p. 55

Christ, Jesus (4-6? B.C. - 30? A.D.), Jewish mystical-religious teacher and reformer who became the founder of Christianity, in which he is considered the son of God; in Islam, one of the greatest of the prophets and a "murshid of murshids"; see Index.

Connaughton, E.P.A. born 1887 in Ireland, joined the Sufi Order, (later called the Sufi Movement) in 1918 in the U.S.A. where he became a pupil of Murshida Martin in San Francisco. Pir-o-Murshid Inayat Khan initiated him as a khalif (authorized representative of the Order head) in England in 1919. He was back in San

Francisco for his marriage in 1923 and again met the Pir-o-Murshid on his lecture tour through the U.S.A. that same year, p. xiii
cf. *Biography of Pir-o-Murshid Inayat Khan* (London, 1979) pp. 172, 463, 494

Coomaraswami, Ananda K.

(1877-1947), a leading art historian, who lived and worked in the U.S.A., p. xi
cf. *Biography of Pir-o-Murshid Inayat Khan*, (London, 1979), p. 557f.

Cushing, Mrs. Marya

an American who became a mureed in 1922 during the first Summer School at Suresnes, France. She again met Pir-o-Murshid Inayat Khan at the end of February, 1923 on his arrival in New York, and was able to arrange his disputed entry in the United States with the immigration authorities. She assisted in typesetting the MS of *Notes from the Unstruck Music from the Gayan of Inayat Khan*, published in 1923. A part of the Pir-o-Murshid's lecture tour through the U.S.A. in 1923 was organized by her, especially in New York, and she took down a number of his lectures in shorthand, p. xi, 325 note 1, 334 (Documents)
cf. *Biography of Pir-o-Murshid Inayat Khan* (London, 1979), pp. 169, 173, 208, 464, 495

Daniel (Hb), Daniyāl (A)

Jewish prophetic figure, 2nd century B.C. about whom a book appears in the *Old Testament* (partly in Aramaic) of which the basic theme is the conflict between the religion of the Jews and the paganism of their foreign rulers. In one of the stories of the first six chapters Daniel is thrown into a lions' den but is saved from harm through his prayers, p. 7

Darwin, Charles

(1809-1882), a British scientist, a biologist. As a young man he travelled by ship in the southern hemisphere for five years, collecting the evidence on which he based his later theories. He is famous for his studies and works on the process of natural evolution and formulated a theory (natural selection) to explain its operation, p. 154

David (Hb), Daud, Dawud (A) (ca. 1030? - 962 B.C.), second king of Israel, who established Jerusalem as its capital and enlarged its borders to their greatest extension. He also was a musician and poet, and half of the 150 psalms (see *Old Testament*: book of Psalms) are ascribed to him, p. 48

Debussy, Claude (1862-1918), French composer and pianist who revolutionized the technique and style of music in the early 20th century. He included Oriental musical characteristics in Western music. Pir-o-Murshid Inayat Khan met him in Paris in 1913, p. 119
cf. *Biography of Pir-o-Murshid Inayat Khan*, (London, 1979), pp. 129, 418, 558

Dīwān-i-Ḥāfiẓ (P) collection of lyrical poems (ghazals) in the Sufi tradition by Hafiz (q.v.), celebrating love and the spiritual beauty of nature; there is a remarkable freshness and sincerity in his poetry, which remains popular today, p. 188

Duce, Mrs. Ivy Oneita (1895-1981), an American mureed of Murshida Rabia Martin (q.v.). When Mrs. Martin died in 1947, she named Mrs. Duce as her successor to head the Sufi Order in the United States, which was separate from the European organization. Mrs. Duce had only been studying Sufism for about two years, and felt unprepared for her assignment. Recalling having heard Mrs. Martin refer to Meher Baba of India as a "perfect Master", she went to seek his advice in 1948. Meher Baba, whose followers regard him as the avatar of this age, confirmed her appointment, accepted her as his disciple, and told her to establish a Sufi organization "safe, sane and stable enough to last 700 years". He said as long as she would remain honest, he would help her in her work, and his letters to her show an ongoing encouragement. Earlier in her life she had studied law, served abroad with the American Red Cross, and worked in an international commercial bank in New York and South America. Later she was an editor at Century Magazine. Her marriage to Terry Duce led to her role as an accomplished international hostess in Washington, D.C. After her encounter with Meher Baba, her organization became known as "Sufism Reoriented," and in 1952 some of the mureeds from Murshida Martin's days left. However, from 1960 on, many mostly young people came to seek Murshida Duce's guidance, and her two groups in California and Washington, D.C. numbered about 300. In these groups the teachings of Pir-o-Murshid Inayat Khan, including Gathas and Gitas (v. Glossary), continued to be given. Mrs. Duce wrote to the compiler: "Meher Baba put in our charter that we had to study Inayat Khan, Rumi, Hafiz, and other Sufi Saints". She established successful schools in California and edited and published many of Meher Baba's books. She also wrote four books of her own, in one of which (*How a Master Works*), she describes her relationship with her teacher.

Egeling-Grol, Mrs. Nelly — (1861-1939), a Dutch lady, who became Pir-o-Murshid Inayat Khan's mureed in Switzerland in 1921. She dedicated the rest of her life to the Sufi work and to Pir-o-Murshid Inayat Khan and his family. She placed at his disposal a stately house at Suresnes, Rue de la Tuilerie (France), named "Fazal (Fadl) Manzil", Mansion of Blessings, where she lived with the family from 1922, p. x
cf. *Biography of Pir-o-Murshid Inayat Khan* (London, 1979), pp. 185f, 468, 498f.

Eggink-van Stolk, Mrs. G. — a Dutch mureed, who joined Pir-o-Murshid Inayat Khan for part of his lecture tour through the U.S.A. in 1923, p. xiii, 356
cf. *Biography of Pir-o-Murshid Inayat Khan*, (London, 1979), pp. 173, 200, 479

Egypt — a nation in the northeast of Africa along the Nile river, whose history extends back to the 4th millennium B.C., p. 266

Engle, Earl (1888-1955), an American mureed who studied with Murshida Martin, initiated by Pir-o-Murshid Inayat Khan in March, 1923, and given the name Fatha. He returned to Suresnes with Pir-o-Murshid, and performed several functions in the household, including appointment as secretary and chauffeur. When he returned to the United States, he had a Sufi centre in New York and later in Cleveland (Ohio), p. xii, xiv

Furnée, Miss J.E.D. (1896-1973), joined the Sufi Order in 1921 as one of the first mureeds from Holland, and became Pir-o-Murshid Inayat Khan's secretary. She learned shorthand and took down a great number of the lectures given by Pir-o-Murshid from 1921 to 1926. She had various functions, among them "keeper" of the Biographical Department, created by Pir-o-Murshid in order to safeguard all sorts of documents and objects in connection with the Sufi Message. Pir-o-Murshid gave her the name Sakina, later changed to Nekbakht. In 1950 she created the Nekbakht Foundation, including in it the Biographical Department, p. xvi
cf. *Biography of Pir-o-Murshid Inayat Khan*, (London, 1979), pp. 159, 194, 200, 452, 505f.

Ghazālī, Abū Ḥāmid Muḥammad al (1058-1111), a native of Ghazal, a village near Tus in Khurasan (Persia), Muslim jurist, theologian and mystic, whose work formed the basis of reconciliation between Sufis and the orthodox religious establishment, p. 326

Goodenough, Miss Lucy M. (1876-1937), an English mureed who joined the Sufi Order during World War I and acted as Pir-o-Murshid Inayat Khan's secretary. A gifted linguist and a valuable assistant in the Sufi work, also at the International Headquarters in Geneva, Switzerland; she edited Pir-o-Murshid's lectures for publication in book form or for restricted distribution among the Sufi centres. Pir-o-Murshid

	gave her the name Sharifa, and in August of 1923 initiated her as a Murshida, *passim* (Documents) cf. *Biography of Pir-o-Murshid Inayat Khan* (London, 1979). pp. 141, 154, 166, 180, 202, 427, 506f.
Green, Miss Sophia Saintsbury	q.v. Sainstbury-Green, Miss Sophia
Gulistān (P)	meaning Rose Garden, an important poetical work of Sa'di (q.v.), on ethical subjects like the *Bustan*, but written in prose, interspersed with verse, p. 164, 166
Ḥāfiẓ, Shams-ud-Dīn Muḥammad	(1325?-1389), famous Persian poet, who spent most of his life in Shiraz. He received a classical religious education, and lectured on Qur'anic and other theological subjects and was an adherent of Sufism. His name Hafiz designates one who has learned the Qur'an by heart. He became a poet at the court of several rulers of Shiraz. The principal verse form used by him was the ghazal, a lyric poem of six to fifteen couplets. His poems can be read on different levels of significance, as a picture of the life of medieval Shiraz, as a tribute to his princely patrons, and above all as an expression of the Sufi mystical theology. His best known work is the *Diwan*. (q.v.), p. 113, 186-92, 204
Hogendorp-van Notten, A. Baronesse van	A Dutch mureed living in Vevey, Switzerland with her husband and daughter. She was initiated by Pir-o-Murshid Inayat Khan in 1921. At times she acted as a secretary at the International Headquarters of the Sufi Movement in Geneva, p. 389 cf. *Biography of Pir-o-Murshid Inayat Khan* (London, 1979), p. 154, 194, 202, 449
Ibn Sīnā 'Ali al Husayn	(980-1037), the most famous and influential Arab philosopher-scientist of Islam, whose medical works (*The Canon of Medicine*) were widely known in medieval Europe, where he was known as Avicenna, p. 107

'Ināyat Khān, Pir-o-Murshid Haḍrat — (1882-1927), Indian gentleman-musician and mystic who came to the West in 1910, where he taught Sufism and established the Sufi Order (from October 1923 called the Sufi Movement). Travelling widely, he lived in London during World War I, thereafter in France, where he eventually settled in Suresnes (near Paris) in 1922. In 1912 he married Ora Ray Baker, an American, from then on known as Amina Begum; they had four children. He died, while on his first return tour through India, on February 5th, 1927, *passim*.

Ingen-Jelgersma, J.C. van- — an early Dutch mureed, one of the most brilliant of Pir-o-Murshid Inayat Khan's followers, married to H. Baron van Tuyll van Serooskerken from 1910 to 1920. Her second husband was Jonkheer Yusuf E. van Ingen, by whom she had a son. They led an active Sufi centre in Utrecht, a city in the central part of Holland. Becoming a widow in the early thirties, she continued Sufi work in Holland and elsewhere until she passed away in 1969, p. 53 (Documents)
cf. *Biography of Pir-o-Murshid Inayat Khan*, (London, 1979), pp. 200, 478

Jāmī, Nūr-ud-Dīn 'Abd-ur-Raḥmān — (1414-1492), Persian Sufi poet and scholar, often regarded as the last great mystical poet in Persian. Besides his many poetical works he wrote in prose on the exegesis of the Qur'an, on the prophethood of Muhammad and the lives of the saints. He is the author of: the *Lawā'ih*, a theosophical treatise; several treatises on mysticism and on music; an Arabic grammar; and other writings, p. 208

Jamshīd — figure in Persia's national epic, the *Book of Kings* by Firdausi, as one of the earliest and most glorious kings of the legendary Peshdadi dynasty, owner of the *Jam-i-jahannuma*, the "world-showing cup" through which he could "drink in" all the world's events. One syllable of his name or the other was often used in Persian names and titles, p. 226

Jerusalem, Yerushalayim (Hb) Bayt al-Muqaddas (A) — although usually said to mean "city of peace," it could also be derived from words meaning "the whole city" (on the assumption that it was once divided and then unified). Ancient Palestinian city which under King David was conquered by the Jews and became their capital and central religious shrine (the Temple of Solomon). The city is still regarded as holy, for different reasons, by Jews, Christians and Muslims, p. 176

Jesus, `Isa (A) — v. Christ, Jesus

John the Baptist — (4-6? B.C. - 28? A.D.), Jewish reformer who performed ritual baptism in the Jordan river in Palestine. He baptized Jesus and is regarded by Christians as the forerunner of Jesus Christ, p. 326

Ka`ba — the shrine in Mecca which is the focal point for the direction of prayer and for the Hajj, (the pilgrimage for Muslims), connected in tradition with Ibrahim, p. 55

Kabīr — (1440-1518), Indian mystic and poet, whose ethnic origin is still subject to dispute, but who was adopted by a Muslim weaver. He attempted to unite Hindu and Muslim thought, and was a forerunner of Sikhism, founded by his disciple Nanak. He was greatly influenced by the Muslim mystics, the Sufis. His poetry, in Hindi, was written in a simple language and understood also by the common man. Some of it became part of the sacred book of the Sikhs, the *Adi Granth*, p. 109-10, 200

Karima — a thanksgiving poem by Sa`di (q.v.), p. 162-163

Kerbela (Karbalā') — a place in central Iraq where Husayn, son of `Ali ibn Abi Talib (q.v.) and heir to the Shi'ite leadership after his father's death, was massacred with his family (Battle of Karbala', 680 A.D.), and where his tomb remains an object of pilgrimage, p. 176

Kerdijk, Miss A.
one of the first Dutch mureeds, who translated Pir-o-Murshid Inayat Khan's handwritten texts on Sufism into Dutch and together with another mureed, Mr. van Ginkel, in 1921 brought out two books: *Een Inleiding tot het Soefisme* (An Introduction to Sufism) and *De Soefi Boodschap van Geestelijke Vrijheid* (*The Sufi Message of Spiritual Liberty*), p. 11, 59 (Documents)
cf. *Biography of Pir-o-Murshid Inayat Khan*, (London, 1979), p. 157

K͟hān
v. ʿInayat K͟han.

K͟hayyām, Omar
v. Omar K͟hayyam

Koran
v. Qur'an

Kṛishṇa (S)
said to be the eighth avatara (incarnation) of the god Vishnu, widely taken as an object of devotion in Hinduism; speaker in the *Bhagavad Gita* (q.v.), p. 15, 48, 49, 195

Leembruggen, Mrs. E.
an early Dutch mureed; she was married for a time to A.H. Baron van Hardenbroek, by whom she had a son and a daughter. Pir-o-Murshid Inayat Khan stayed in her house when lecturing in Arnhem, in January 1923. She took down in longhand some of his lectures. In 1923, at the Summer School in Suresnes, she once took over from Sakina Furnée when she for some reason had to interrupt her shorthand reporting of a lecture, p. 35, 46

Lefèbvre, Mlle. H.
an early French mureed from Paris, in whose handwriting many lectures given by Pir-o-Murshid Inayat Khan are preserved. In one of her notebooks Pir-o-Murshid wrote: "Blessed are the innocent who believe and trust simply. Blessed are the unselfish friends whose motto in life is constancy. With blessings, Inayat Khan." Part of these lectures have been written down by her from a simultaneous translation in French while they were being pronounced; another part seems to have been copied, p. 73, 78

Lewis, Samuel L. — (1896-1971), an American, who began his studies on Sufism with Mrs. Martin in San Francisco, having been initiated by the Pir-o-Murshid in San Francisco in 1923. In later years he also was initiated in several other Sufi Orders and in Hindu and Buddhist esoteric schools. He had his own Sufi group in the U.S.A., named *Sufi Islamia Ruhaniat Society*. He is the author of *Toward Spiritual Brotherhood*, in which he attempted to apply the principles of mysticism to science, p. xii
cf. *Biography of Pir-o-Murshid Inayat Khan*, (London, 1979), pp. 172, 569

Lincoln, Abraham — (1809-1865), 16th president of the United States from 1861 to 1865. He preserved the Union through the American Civil War and worked for the emancipation of the slaves. Shortly after his victory he was assassinated, p. 88
cf. *Biography of Pir-o-Murshid Inayat Khan*, (London, 1979), pp. 126, 570

LLoyd, Mrs. Gladys I. — An English follower of Pir-o-Murshid Inayat Khan from London. From 1921 she took an active part in the Sufi work in England and at the Summer Schools at Suresnes, especially as a conductor of prayers and in the Spiritual Healing Branch of the Sufi Order (later called Sufi Movement), p. 356, 373 note 128
cf. *Biography of Pir-o-Murshid Inayat Khan* (London, 1979), p. 485, 518f., 523

Mahābhārata (S) — great epic of the Bharata Dynasty, one of the two major Hindu epics of India along with the *Ramayana*, consisting of almost a hundred thousand couplets describing the struggle for supremacy between two related families, the Pandavas and the Kauravas, based on actual history from ca. 1400-1000 B.C. The *Bhagavad Gita* is part of it. (q.v.), p. 176

Manṭiq-uṭ-ṭair	meaning "colloquy of the birds", an allegorical poem on the mystic's progress toward unity with God. It was written by ʿAttar around 1175 and consists of a hundred thousand verses, p. 206-12, 316
Martin, Mrs. Ada	an American pioneer Sufi worker, Pir-o-Murshid Inayat Khan's first disciple in the United States (1911), made a Murshida and given the name Rabia. She lived in San Francisco with her husband and daughter. In 1923 she received the Pir-o-Murshid in San Francisco during his nearly seven weeks' stay there, and after having visited India, attended the Summer School of 1924 at Suresnes, x, xii, 219 ff cf. *Biography of Pir-o-Murshid Inayat Khan* (London, 1979), p. 359f., 520f., 611
Maṣnawī ye māʿnawī Mathnawi (A), Mesnevi (T)	meaning "The Spiritual Couplets", didactic epic poem in Persian by Jalal ud-Din Rumi (q.v.), consisting of 26,000 rhyming couplets, treating all the mystical thought, theories and images of the Sufism of the 13th century. This work, widely regarded as the greatest work of Persian poetry and very influential in Sufism, has been called "the Persian Qur'an", p. 145-6, 315
Mecca (Makka)	a city on the Arabian peninsula where the Prophet Muhammad was born in 570 A.D.; long before his time Mecca was probably already a station of the "incense route" and continued to be an important intersection of great commercial caravan routes. The Prophet conquered Mecca for Islam in 630. It is mainly known for its shrine, the Kaʿba (q.v.), p. 55
Miller, Mrs. Rebecca C.	initiated in 1912 by Murshida Martin, she met Pir-o-Murshid Inayat Khan in March 1923 in San Francisco, p. xii cf. *Biography of Pir-o-Murshid Inayat Khan*, (London, 1979), pp. 172, 460
Moʿīn-ud-Dīn Chishtī	(1135-1229), became a disciple of Hadrat ʿUsman Haruni and was the eighth in the line of succession from the founder of the

Chishti Order, Abu Ishaq Shami Chishti. His first visit to India took place in 1165 and in 1191 he came for the first time to Ajmer, where he later settled. He is credited with establishing the first important Sufi Order in India, the Chishti Order, which line of Sufi teaching was the main background of Pir-o-Murshid Inayat Khan (q.v.). Even today his shrine at Ajmer (q.v.) is a major object of pilgrimage, p. 328-9

Moses, Musa — Jewish prophet, political leader and law-giver, who may have lived at the time of the Egyptian pharaoh Ramses II (1301-1234 B.C.). He led his people from slavery in Egypt to forty years of wandering in the Sinai desert. On a mountain top he is said to have received the divine law. He died just before his people entered the land they had been promised by God. He is traditionally believed to have been the author of the first five books (*Torah*) of the Hebrew scriptures, see Index.

Muḥammad — (570-632 A.D.), Prophet whose messages from God (Allah) constitute the sacred scripture of Islam (the *Qur'an*). He lived in Mecca (q.v.), but when his Message was not accepted there, he moved to Yathrib (later Medina), from which he conquered Mecca and much of the Arabian peninsula. His followers continued the conquests after his death, eventually establishing a vast empire and extending Islam from Spain to China, see Index.

Napoléon Bonaparte — (1769-1821), French general who became emperor, extending French domination over a large part of Europe. As a political leader, he made many legal and educational reforms, but most of his career centered on military expeditions. In 1815 he was defeated by the British at Waterloo (Belgium) and exiled first to the Isle of Elba in the Mediterranean and then to the South Atlantic island of St. Helena, where he died. His invasion of Egypt and his intended alliance with Tipu Sultan of Mysore were of notable importance for developments in the Middle East and India, p. 29

Omar Khalīf (A) — v. ʿUmar

Omar Khayyām — born near Nishapur (prov. Khurasan, Persia). The year of his birth is taken to be 1025, 1040 or still later. His name Khayyam, meaning tent-maker, shows the profession of his ancestors. He studied at Nishapur and became a well-known scientist (mathematician, astronomer) and poet. His sharp intellect was in conflict with his deep religious feelings. He died at Nishapur in 1123. His collection of hundreds of quatrains, the *Ruba'iyat* (pl. of rubaʿi, quatrain, stanza of four lines) is still famous today and has been translated into almost every languages, p. 392
cf. *Biography of Pir-o-Murshid Inayat Khan* (London, 1979), p. 568.

Panjāb, Punjāb (S,H) — pañc ab, meaning five waters: Indus and its tributaries; an area of the Indian subcontinent, now divided into a northwestern state of India and a northeastern state of Pakistan. The Indian state has a large Sikh population, whereas the Pakistani state is predominantly Muslim. With a combined area of more than 250,000 sq.km., the states are populated by more than 50,000,000 people, p. 338

Paul the Apostle, Saint — (ca. 2? B.C. - ca. 64? A.D.), Jewish Pharisee who underwent a dramatic conversion to Christianity and became a major force in spreading the new faith. He was born in Tarsus (Asia Minor) and was named Saul; later, after his conversion, he was re-named Paul. His writings in the *New Testament* have had a profound influence on Christian thought and practice. He travelled widely and was martyred in Rome, p. 51

Philamon — q.v. Baucis and Philamon

Purāna (S)

meaning old, ancient;
collections in Hindu sacred literature of myth, legend and genealogy (ca. 400-1000 B.C.). The eighteen principal surviving *Puranas* vary greatly in date and subject matter, p. 203

Qur'ān (Koran) (A)

meaning reading, recitation;
the collection of texts revealed to the Prophet Muhammad (q.v.), written down as he had recited them. Considered as the words of God (Allah) Himself, these scriptures are authoritative for Islam, p. 75, 171, 223, 298, 309, 322

Rābi'ah al 'Adawīyya

(713?-802), or Rabiah Basriyy, as she lived in Basra, where she was born into a family of slaves. She devoted herself to the love of God and lived an ascetic life. She became one of the greatest of Sufi saints and recited prayers and mystical poetry, p. 331

Rāma (S)

or Ramacandra, the seventh avatara (incarnation) of Vishnu, the hero of the *Ramayana* (see *Mahabharata*) and considered the embodiment of virtue and chivalry, p. 48, 112

Rūmī, Jalāl-ud-Dīn

(1207-1273), also called Mevlana (T) (our Master), famous Sufi poet in Persian, whose Masnawi (q.v.) has been widely influential. He was born in Balkh (now Afghanistan), but his family fled the approach of the Mongols and eventually settled in Konya (now Turkey), in what was then known as Rum because of its earlier connection with the East-Roman Empire. There he succeeded his father as head of a university and was trained in mysticism. However, his encounter with the derwish Shams-e-Tabriz had a decisive effect on his life and career, and after the latter's mysterious disappearance, he began addressing spontaneous poems to him (Diwan-e-Shams-e-Tabriz). He continued throughout his life to speak poetry while whirling around a column, which was later ritualized into the famous "Turn" of his followers, the Mevlevi derwishes, popularly known as whirling derwishes. His poetry remains immensely popular in all Islamic lands of Persian or Ottoman culture, and has been translated into many languages, p. 113, 141-7, 206

Sa'dī of Shīrāz Muṣliḥ ud-Din
(1184-1291), an important Persian poet and writer who, after his studies, spent many years of his life in travelling. On the mystic path he received instruction from Abdu'l Qadir Jilani, founder of the Qadiri Sufi Order. Sa'di's *Bustan* (q.v.) and *Gulistan* (q.v.) became immensely popular and well-known even in the West, p. 138, 162-8, 181

Saintsbury Green, Miss Sophia E.
(18..? - 1939), one of Pir-o-Murshid Inayat Khan's early mureeds and and pioneer worker in England, and his close collaborator in the Sufi work. She was the first Cheraga of the Universal Worship, and was initiated as a Murshida. She was an outstanding lecturer, the author of several books, and a poet, p. 343, 356
cf *Biography of Pir-o-Murshid Inayat Khan* (London, 1979), p. 149, 152, 443 509f.

Scriabin, Aleksandr, Nikolayevich
(1872-1915), Russian composer of orchestral and piano music. A student of Theosophy, he sought to express in his experimental music certain mystical ideas, and even attempted to fuse music, poetry and dance with colour and scent to create an ecstatic form of worship. His piano works, lyrical and polished, are still admired, p. 119

Shams ud-Dīn Tabrīz, Muḥammad
(13th century A.D.). His name means sun of religion. His parentage is uncertain and little is known about his life. In or about 1244 Rumi (q.v.) met him in the streets of Konya as a wandering derwish, and became his disciple. He disappeared in 1247 and Rumi dedicated his *Diwan* to him, p. 55 note 45, 142-4

Shiva (S)
q.v., Siva

Śiva (S)	meaning the auspicious one; name of the absorbing and reproducing Hindu deity, the third god of Hindu Trimurti, represented as a great Yogi and ascetic. Pir-o-Murshid Inayat Khan considered him as one of the great prophets, p. 48
Solomon, Shlomo (Hb), Suleymān (A)	(flourished 10th century B.C.), third king of Israel, successor to his father David, and builder of the Temple in Jerusalem. During Solomon's forty-year reign (972-932 B.C.), he greatly strengthened the economic and military position of his country, and formed many foreign alliances through marriage. The Ark of the Covenant, which his father had brought to Jerusalem, was housed in a fine structure, later destroyed. The kingdom he had built divided, after his death, into Israel (north) and Judah (south, including Jerusalem). He was famous for his wisdom, and several books in the Jewish scriptures are attributed to him, p. 48, 126, 154, 187
Stadlinger, Miss Hayat	an American mureed, who first met Pir-o-Murshid Inayat Khan when quite young, in 1923, at the lectures given at the Paul Elder Gallery, San Francisco, U.S.A. In 1926, while travelling with her mother, she encountered Pir-o-Murshid in Paris "by accident" and then attended part of the Summer School in Suresnes, where she was initiated by Murshida Saintsbury-Green (q.v.). She lives in Oakland, California, where she has maintained a Sufi Centre and performed the Universal Worship throughout her long life, p. 100 and *passim*
Stam, Miss D.K.	a Dutch mureed, initiated by Pir-o-Murshid Inayat Khan in Switzerland in 1922 and given by him the name Kismet. She learned shorthand and typewriting and became one of Pir-o-Murshid's secretaries from 1923 on, beginning at the Summer School in Suresnes. Her handwriting in this function is found for the first time in one of the MSS of the play *Una*, where Pir-o-Murshid dictated some changes to her, p. 356

cf. *Biography of Pir-o-Murshid Inayat Khan*, (London 1979), pp. 11, 12, 202, 204, 271, 480, 525f.

Tāj Maḥall (A, P)

taj meaning crown, tiara; mahall meaning place, place of alighting, town quarter; architectural monument in Agra (south of Delhi), India, built in 1632-54 by the Mughal emperor Shah Jehan as a mausoleum for his deceased wife, Mumtaz Mahall. Built of white marble inlaid with precious stones, this world-famous building, which overlooks the Jamna river, became the emperor's tomb as well, p. 298

Taneyev, Sergey (Tanieff)

(1856-1915), Russian pianist and composer who studied with Tchaikovsky and succeeded him as director of the Moscow Conservatory, where he taught Scriabin (q.v.). He left a few finely wrought compositions which are rarely performed, but helped to spark an interest in Renaissance music, p. 119

Tuyll van Serooskerken, H.P. Baron van

(1883-1958), an early Dutch mureed of Pir-o-Murshid Inayat Khan, initiated in 1921, and given the name Sirdar. He was a pioneer worker for the Sufi Message, and its National Representative in Holland. From 1910-1920 he was married to Miss J.C. Jelgersma (v. Ingen - Jelgersma, van), and in 1922 he married Miss H. Willebeek Le Mair. He made his house in The Hague into a Sufi Centre and had a congregational hall built onto it for the Universal Worship and other Sufi meetings to be held, p. 53
cf. *Biography of Pir-o-Murshid Inayat Khan*, (London, 1979), pp. 166, 200, 529f.

Tuyll van Serooskerken-Willebeek Le Mair, Mrs. H. van

(1889-1966), met Pir-o-Murshid Inayat Khan in 1921 and became his mureed. In 1922 she married H.P. Baron van Tuyll van Serooskerken and helped him with the work in their Sufi Centre. She was an artist and is well-known for her designs and paintings, and also for her luxury-book illustrations.

She also took interest in dance and music and Eastern languages, p. 53
cf. *Biography of Pir-o-Murshid Inayat Khan*, (London, 1979), pp. 529f., 587f.

ʿUmar ibn al Khaṭṭab — (ca. 586-644), second khalifa (successor) to the Prophet Muhammad, under whom the Arab conquest of Syria (including Jerusalem) and Mesopotamia was carried out. He was an imposing figure noted for his simplicity and sternness, p. 196

Veda (S) — meaning knowledge; the name of certain celebrated works which constitute the basis of the first period of the Hindu religion. The oldest of its hymns is assigned to a period between 4000 and 2500 B.C. (by others to a period between 1400 and 1000 B.C.), when the Aryans had settled down in the Panjab. These scriptures in Sanskrit are in poetical form, comprising a liturgical cycle of hymns and prayers, and are regarded as the most sacred of Hindu writings, p. 102, 128, 338-9

Wilhelm, Kaiser — (1859-1941), German emperor from 1888 to 1918, who presided over his country's defeat in World War I (1914-1918). He became and remained famous in Asian and African lands as the hero who severely threatened and decisively shook the colonial powers, England and France. He lived and died in exile in the Netherlands, p. 29

Wolff, Mr. and Mrs. — American followers of Pir-o-Murshid Inayat Khan from Los Angeles, U.S.A., who in 1923 drove Pir-o-Murshid by car from Los Angeles to San Francisco, p. xii, xiv
cf. *Biography of Pir-o-Murshid Inayat Khan*, (London, 1979), pp. 169, 173.

Zarathushtra (Avestan), Zoroaster (G) — prophet who lived in the northeast of old Iran (Bactria), flourishing probably in the 6th c. B.C. or earlier. He is the founder of the religion which bears his name (also known as Parsiism--meaning of Persian origin--in India, where it mainly survives in the Bombay area), emphasizing the beneficent role of Ahura Mazda (Wise Lord) and promising immortality and bliss in the afterlife to the faithful. This religion had a profound, if now mostly unacknowledged influence on the development of the moral and monotheistic tradition in Judaism, Christianity and Islam. Thus, e.g., the word and conception of Paradise (Firdaus) is of Zoroastrian origin, p. 48-9

INDEX